ITALIAN POETS AND ENGLISH CRITICS, 1755–1859

PATTERNS OF LITERARY CRITICISM

General Editors

ITALIAN POETS AND ENGLISH CRITICS, 1755-1859

A Collection of Critical Essays

Edited and with an Introduction by

BEATRICE CORRIGAN

The University of Chicago Press
Chicago & London

Library of Congress Catalog Card Number: 68-54483

THE UNIVERSITY OF CHICAGO PRESS, CHICAGO 60637
THE UNIVERSITY OF CHICAGO PRESS, LTD., LONDON W.C.1
THE UNIVERSITY OF TORONTO PRESS, TORONTO 5, CANADA

ACKNOWLEDGMENTS

I should like to express my gratitude to the General Editors of the Series: especially to Dean Ernest Sirluck for his interest and encouragement, and to Professor Richard J. Schoeck, the supervising editor of this volume, for the patient care with which he read the manuscript and for his many excellent suggestions. I should also like to thank Miss Francess Halpenny and Miss Barbara Plewman of the University of Toronto Press for their professional advice; and the editorial staff of the University of Chicago Press for the preparation of the manuscript for publication.

Acknowledgments are due as well to J. M. Dent and Sons, Ltd., and to Chapman and Hall, for permission to reprint passages from their editions of Hazlitt and Landor.

CONTENTS

INTRODUCTION

This anthology represents the first century of English critical interest in Dante, Petrarch, and Boccaccio. This interest was long delayed, as is evident from the date of the first essay, 1775, although the Trecentisti had long been familiar to their fellow poets. Chaucer brought back from his travels a knowledge of Italian literature which was to provide the basis for much of his own poetry; yet though he speaks of Dante in the *Canterbury Tales* as a great poet, and of Petrarch as a learned clerk and the poet laureate, he says nothing of their lives and does not name their works. Boccaccio, to whom he owed so much, he mentions not at all.

From the fourteenth century on, English poets visited Italy in steady succession, returning, as their poetry shows, with a constantly renewed familiarity with Italian literature, both old and new. But though the influence of Petrarch and Boccaccio, and to some extent that of Dante, continued to permeate English literature, it was not until the latter half of the eighteenth century that English critics[1] attempted to form some consistent idea of the life, character, and literary achievements of each of the three great Tuscans.

The essays assembled here mark significant moments in this rediscovery of the Middle Ages. They are not concerned, except incidentally, with Italian influence on English literature, or with translations of Italian poets.[2] The authors included are distinguished in fields of literature other than criticism; indeed the majority of them are poets. Their essays illustrate the development and range of the great British and American reviews of the early nineteenth century, for many of them appeared first in periodicals. Two, those of Coleridge and Carlyle, were orginally delivered as lectures, another proof of the widening interests of the new middle class, better educated and eager for literary culture. These attempts to reevaluate the Italian poets are accompanied by a steadily growing interest in the biographical

[1] This term is used throughout the Introduction to include all critics publishing in English, whether they are English, Scots, Americans, or Italians.

[2] For scholarly works in this field see the appended bibliography.

and historical background of literature. They also trace a striking change in literary values.

At the beginning of the eighteenth century the European reputations of Dante, Petrarch, and Boccaccio seemed—to use a suitably medieval metaphor—securely fixed upon the wheel of Fortune. Petrarch was at the summit, the greatest of modern poets. Boccaccio as a prose writer—for his poetical works were almost forgotten—stood a little below him. Dante, poet though he was, occupied the lowliest place of all, condemned to obscurity by his presumed ignorance of the classics. The wheel seemed motionless; yet as Dante, familiar with Fortune's instability, had remarked, "Le sue permutazion non hanno tregue"; and by the middle of the century there were already premonitory tremors.

In England, at the beginning of the period covered by these essays, Petrarch's influence was still strong, and his closest rival, Metastasio, was universally acknowledged his inferior in strength and passion, if not in sweetness. Numerous editions of the *Canzoniere* appeared in Italy in the eighteenth century, but it was comparatively late that the *Rime* were published in London, in 1784 and 1796. In 1777 a translation, by John Mott, of thirty sonnets and three odes appeared, but the translator alleged the difficulties of the task as his reason for proceeding no further.

The *Decameron* was still read and imitated with little waning of popularity, and interest in Boccaccio was always lively, stimulated as it was by recurrent controversies with censors and by the unchallenged preeminence of his work as a model for Italian prose style. Even in the seventeenth century, clerical attack and defense had given it publicity. In 1725 an unexpurgated edition in Italian was printed in London[3] and was reprinted twice in the two years following. English translations—the first had been made in 1620—appeared in 1702 (reprinted in 1712) and 1741. Boccaccio was of course a favorite with the writers of the Enlightenment both in France and England, and his depiction of multiform man, as Landor phrased it, of the human heart through all its foldings, seemed timeless, always apposite whatever the changes in society.

Dante's work, on the contrary, was little known, though in

[3] The first complete edition of the *Decameron* after 1559 (when it was placed on the *Index* by Pope Paul IV) was in 1665.

Italy Alfieri's admiration was bringing him belated and grudging appreciation. To England and France in the eighteenth century the world of the last great figure of the Middle Ages seemed incredibly remote and barbarous. The French school of criticism, prizing as it did elegance, good sense, restraint, and proportion, and rejecting enthusiasm and the singular expression of profound emotion, dismissed the *Comedy* as unworthy of serious consideration. Indeed it was Voltaire's sneering comments on Dante in his *Essay on the Epic Poetry of the European Nations from Homer down to Milton* that prompted the first study in this collection. The *Essay* had appeared in 1727 while Voltaire, still not securely established in his career, was spending a period of exile in London; and at that time it had not excited much attention. But by 1755 Voltaire's fame had blossomed, and his literary decrees were so reverenced that Giuseppe Baretti felt impelled to challenge his unfair estimation of Dante.

Baretti had come to London from Turin in 1751, in search of fresh experiences and greater freedom for his pen than he could enjoy at home. He became a friend of Dr. Johnson and emulated him by producing an Italian-English dictionary which is still a standard authority. His *Dissertation upon the Italian Poetry* is a spirited defence of his native literature, which he felt was neglected and misunderstood in England, and it contains one of the first serious accounts in English of Dante and his work. This Franco-Italian controversy is typical of the pattern of Italian studies in England during the succeeding century, which often take the form of review articles on foreign books,[4] translations, or original works in English.

Despite Baretti's loyalty to his compatriot, it is evident that he did not find Dante congenial as an individual, and he defends him less wholeheartedly against Voltaire's attack than he was to do for Shakespeare twenty years later.[5] It is impossible not to see in his account of the poet's life the instinctive distaste of the man of the Age of Enlightenment for the product of a less polished era. Though himself a satirist and a man of independence, Baretti is shocked by Dante's insolent lack of deference to his patrons and by his fierce party feeling. Yet in *The History of*

[4] The *Foreign Review* and the *Foreign Quarterly Review* contained many articles on European books which were still not translated.

[5] In his *Discours sur Shakespeare et sur monsieur de Voltaire* (1777).

the Italian Tongue, written four years later as a preface for his *Italian Library*, Baretti recognizes the inferiority of Petrarch to Dante in "vehemence of expression, strength of thinking, and variety of invention." Though Petrarch, Baretti finds, surpassed Dante "in propriety, exactness, and elegance . . . he is rather too soft and tender whenever he mentions his joyless love for his chaste friend. I think him effeminate in many places," Baretti adds, "but this is my particular opinion."[6]

Baretti finds Boccaccio as excellent in prose as Dante and Petrarch were in verse, though his style, constantly natural in humorous descriptions and burlesque narrative, strives too much to be eloquent and pompous in serious passages. "But," he adds "that commendation which Boccaccio deserves from the admirers of Italian language and eloquence, is entirely forfeited if we look on his *Decamerone* with the eyes of moralists and Christians."

Despite his earlier strictures against Dante, in his *History* Baretti warns his foreign readers not "to weigh the *Divine Comedy* in the scales of modern criticism, but to make allowances for some strange mixture of pagan and Christian notions, considering that our poet was not only a mortal man like any other, and consequently subject to err; but that he writ before any body dreamt of those rules that have forced subsequent geniuses to confine even their mad flights within the boundaries of method."[7]

Baretti's deference to French standards of criticism, reluctant though it is, and his condemnation of Dante's arrogance and Boccaccio's indecency, were to be echoed through the rest of the eighteenth century.

In 1775 a *Life of Petrarch*, the first to appear in English, was published by Susannah Dobson; it won such popularity that it went through six editions by 1805 and probably inspired John Mott's translations mentioned above. It was reprinted in Philadelphia in 1817 and so is of added importance as contributing to the knowledge of the poet in North America.

Mrs. Dobson merely compiled and translated her *Life* from the famous biography of Petrarch by the Abbé Jacques François

[6] "A History of the Italian Tongue," *Prefazioni e Polemiche* (Bari: Laterza, 1911), p. 126.

[7] *Ibid.*, pp. 122–23.

de Sade (disreputable uncle of a notorious nephew) which had appeared eleven years earlier. She herself, however, wrote a Preface, in which she paid tribute to Petrarch's work in collecting manuscripts and "helping to lay the foundation on which the superstructure of science was built." Her chronology was rather shaky, for she credited Brunetto Latini with aiding Petrarch in this task as well as with inspiring Dante to write "that whimsical poem called the *Commedia.*"

The Abbé's identification of Laura as a married lady of his own family who had borne several children shocked all readers of sensibility. Indeed, a distinguished Scottish jurist, Alexander Tytler, Lord Woodhouslie, spent much of his leisure time for thirty years in composing refutations—based on legal arguments about the validity of evidence—of such a slanderous charge.[8] Mrs. Dobson, however, accepted the identification, and though she was sure the connection between the poet and his lady was innocent, she found it impossible on the grounds of religion and morality to exempt Petrarch and Laura from censure. Yet she is convinced that "to susceptible and feeling minds Petrarch will ever be dear. Such, while they regret his failings, and consider them as warnings to themselves, will love his virtues; and, touched by the glowing piety, and heart-felt contrition, which often impressed his soul, will ardently desire to partake with him in those pathetic and sublime reflections, which are produced in grateful and affectionate hearts, on reviewing their own lives and contemplating the works of God. It is too worthy of our notice here to be omitted," she adds, throwing a curious light on the unfashionable status of religion in eighteenth-century England, "that a man, who was the first genius of the age in which he lived, and whose society was sought and delighted in by persons of the highest rank and learning, thought it no derogation to his talents or politeness, to introduce sacred and moral observations both in his letters and conversation."

Mrs. Dobson's *Life of Petrarch*, compilation though it was and unsatisfactory as many critics found it, was to be cited as an authority for some 75 years. Moreover, in her discussion of the moral problem posed by Petrarch's illicitly placed love, she ini-

[8] Henry Hallam remarked that his standard of conduct was taken "not from Avignon, but from Edinburgh, a much better place, no doubt, and where the moral barometer stands at a very different altitude." *View of the State of Europe During the Middle Ages* (London, 1855), 3: 481.

tiated a controversy which was to concern critics of both Petrarch and Dante until modern times. Boccaccio had identified Dante's Beatrice as Bice Portinari, the circumstances of whose life fitted neatly into the story told in the *Vita Nuova*, and who, like Laura, was a married woman. He had obligingly—and most unusually—identified his own Fiammetta as Maria d'Aquino, the illegitimate daughter of King Robert of Naples, married to a French noble at the Neapolitan court; and he was thought to have described in detail his successful courtship of the lady in his *Elegia di Madonna Fiammetta.*[9] But Beatrice, Laura, and Fiammetta had all been accepted as conventional poetical symbols until the eighteenth century, when a new interest in biography persuaded critics to consider them real women, subject to judgment by moral and social codes which had changed little in four hundred years, and which were particularly important to English readers.

In 1774 Thomas Warton, who had been professor of poetry at Oxford and was later to become Poet Laureate, began to publish a *History of Poetry* which was still uncompleted at his death in 1790. Throughout the work he acknowledges the influence on English poets exercised by both Petrarch and Boccaccio, though he gives no detailed account of either. He was evidently ignorant of almost all Boccaccio's writings except the *Decameron* and the *Teseide*, for he says of him that

> having seen the Platonic sonnets of his master Petrarch, in a fit of despair he committed all his poetry to the flames, except a single poem, of which his own good taste had long taught him to entertain a more favourable opinion. This piece, thus happily rescued from destruction, is at present so scarce, and so little known, even in Italy, as to have left its author but a slender proportion of that eminent degree of poetical reputation, which he might have justly claimed from so extraordinary a performance. It is an heroic poem in twelve books, entitled *Le Teseide*, and written in the octave stanza, called by the Italians *ottava rima*, which Boccaccio adopted from the old French chansons, and here first introduced among his countrymen.[10]

[9] Despite his confession of adultery, Boccaccio's private life remained uncensured. Readers may instinctively have perceived that the story of Fiammetta was, as modern scholarship has shown, only a beautiful fiction.

[10] *History of English Poetry* (London: Thomas Tegg, 1824), 2: 179–80.

Warton adds in a footnote, without giving any authority for his erroneous statement, that two other works by Boccaccio are extant, the *Amazonida* and the *Forze d'Ercole*.

At the end of his section on Thomas Sackville, who had also depicted a descent into Hell, Warton described the *Divine Comedy* at some length. Divided between distaste for Dante's lack of polish and reluctant admiration for the power of his descriptions, he makes no attempt to conceal that he considers not only the poem but its author whimsical. His observations show how alien the Middle Ages seemed to the typical well-educated man of the eighteenth century, convinced by French standards of criticism that no work of a nonclassical period is worth serious consideration. It is strange to find a professor of poetry who is himself a poet showing so little concern for accuracy and so little feeling for his subject. Warton does not even seem to understand the metrical principles of *terza rima*, for he misspells and transposes words so that the rhyme is destroyed. Nor is his knowledge of Italian more than superficial, for his quotations from Dante contain too many errors to be blamed on the printer, and they remain uncorrected in subsequent editions of the *History*.

Susannah Dobson's contention that religious feeling was considered ridiculous in the England of her time is supported by Warton's impatience that anyone should consider the afterworld a suitable subject for a long poem, and by his jeers at the religious fervor of the *Comedy*. For him Dante's theology has lost all relevance, man's destiny is devoid of spiritual significance, and the concept of sin is ridiculous; hell is too grotesque, heaven too tiresome, to form suitable subjects for poetry. What the age which so eagerly devoured Gothic novels most appreciated in Dante were his "fine strokes of the terrible," the "sombrous cast in his imagination"; and it is significant that though Warton devotes nine pages to the *Inferno* and two to the *Purgatorio* he dismisses Paradise in five disdainful lines.

One other work of the eighteenth century that should be mentioned is the *Encyclopaedia Britannica*. The second edition, published between 1777 and 1784, was unique among other English encyclopedias of the day because it contained, to quote its advertisement, "Biographies of the Most Eminent Persons in Every Nation." Most of these biographies—indeed, it is said, some three quarters of the whole work—were compiled by a brilliant but bibulous literary hack, James Tytler (unrelated to Petrarch's champion, Alexander), a familiar figure in the taverns and pawnshops of Edinburgh. When the publishers of the *Britannica* engaged him at 17 shillings a week to work on articles for the second edition, they housed him in Holyrood Palace where he would be safe from arrest and debt, knowing that, as they phrased it, "his conduct had been marred by almost perpetual imprudence." It was almost certainly he who, in that suitably ancient and august abode, composed the biographies of Dante, Boccaccio, and Petrarch, which were published without change in subsequent editions.

Presented in a jaunty tone that masks their wealth of ignorance, the three articles in question contain some curious statements. "John Boccacce," we are told, "one of the most polite and learned writers of his age, made a long stay in Sicily, where he was in high favour with Queen Joan. . . . He wrote several books, some learned and serious, others of gallantry and full of stories. It is by his *Decameron*"—the only work that the encyclopedist mentions by name,—"that he has immortalized himself. Petrarch found so many charms in this composition that he was at the pains to translate it into Latin for his own satisfaction."

This last glaring blunder—for Petrarch had translated only the story of Griselda and had damned the rest of the *Decameron* with very faint praise indeed—may indicate that Tytler was abridging a longer account. He cites no sources, but several of the sentences in his article are quoted verbatim from the English translation of Bayle's *Dictionnaire Historique et Critique*. (Bayle and Warton are acknowledged by Tytler in his article on Dante, which deserves no further mention).

Petrarch's biography he relates with long quotations from Susannah Dobson, but adds a strange unascribed parallel. "A resemblance," he concludes his article by saying, "has been traced in several instances, between this admired poet and our late famous Yorick. Both we know had great wit and genius, and no less imprudence and eccentricity; both were canons or prebendaries, the Italian of Padua, and the Englishman of York; they both 'ran over France, without any business there.' If the bishop of Lombes patronized and corresponded with the one, a prelate of the English church, now deceased, desired in a letter to *shandyize* with the other. In their attachments to Laura and

Eliza, both married women, these two prebendaries were equally warm and equally innocent. And, even after death, a most remarkable circumstance has attended them both; some persons, we are told, stole Petrarch's bones, in order to sell them; and, in like manner, Yorick's body, it is confidently affirmed, was also stolen, and his skull has been exhibited at Oxford."

The final triumphant juxtaposition of two equally mythical anecdotes is indeed remarkable. Equally remarkable is the apparent lack of protest against such uninformed articles in a widely acclaimed reference work. Their reappearance in later editions of the *Britannica* is irrefutable proof of English neglect and ignorance of medieval culture at that era.

With the beginning of the nineteenth century, the tide slowly and uncertainly turned toward more temperate shores. In 1797, sixteen years after Warton had praised Voltaire at Dante's expense, an English clergyman, Henry Cary, received his first charge, a quiet country parish in Staffordshire, and there indulged his boyhood passion for blank-verse translation by beginning a version of the *Purgatorio.* In 1805 he published the *Inferno*, in 1814 the entire *Divine Comedy*; and he succeeded in proving, despite Warton's claim, that there was a better way than Voltaire's to make Dante popular with English readers.[11]

Unfortunately, Cary's translation had been preceded in 1802 by that of Henry Boyd, private chaplain to a viscount. Boyd's translation, or rather paraphrase, in a curiously unsuitable six-line stanza, was the first complete version in English, but it met with both critical condemnation and public apathy,[12] which probably accounted in part for the initial lack of success of Cary's translation. This latter passed unnoticed until 1817, when Coleridge met Cary, conceived a warm admiration for his work, and brought his *Divine Comedy* to public attention in the lec-

[11] William Hayley in his notes to Epistle III of his *Essay on Epic Poetry* (London, 1782) gave a translation of the first three cantos of the *Inferno*, adding that he had been solicited to execute an entire translation; "but the extreme inequality of this Poet would render such a work a very laborious undertaking, and it appears very doubtful how such a version would interest our country."

[12] Boyd's translation of Petrarch's *Triumphs* in 1807 (the first since 1554) was much more successful.

tures he delivered in London in 1818. A second edition of the translation was immediately called for, the reviewers praised it highly, and for many years Cary's *Divine Comedy* was the form in which most English-speaking people were familiar with Dante. The 1805 edition of the *Inferno* was prefaced by an admirably sober account of Dante's life, based on reliable sources, and this Cary revised in subsequent editions as the discoveries of Italian scholarship made it necessary. In the Preface he remarked (and so prophesied the course of Dante studies in the twentieth century) that not only must more editions and manuscripts be consulted but "the line of reading which the poet himself appears to have pursued must be diligently tracked."

At about the same time, two works had been published in Paris which exercised great influence for many years. They were translated into Italian, widely reviewed, and cited by a generation of English critics. These were Pierre Louis Ginguené's *Histoire littéraire d'Italie*, which came out between 1811 and 1816, and Simonde de Sismondi's *De la littérature du Midi de l'Europe*, published in 1813. Ginguené was born in 1748, and his critical standards are still those of the classical eighteenth century. Indeed, much of his material is taken from Girolamo Tiraboschi's *Storia della letteratura italiana*, published between 1772 and 1782. Traditional also, though to a lesser degree, were the criteria of Sismondi, who received a classical education but became familiar with the early phase of Romanticism through his friendship with Madame de Staël. His pioneer work on the Italian Republics won him fame as a historian, and in 1810 he was invited to deliver a series of lectures in Geneva on the literature of Southern Europe, which he later revised for publication.

William Hazlitt reviewed this latter work in the *Edinburgh Review* in 1815 (eight years before it was translated into English by Thomas Roscoe), and his article marks an important development in Italian studies in England. By the time it was written, Sir Walter Scott's series of romantic narrative poems—from *The Lay of the Last Minstrel* in 1805 to *The Lady of the Lake* in 1810—had rescued the ideas of chivalry and ideal love from the ridicule to which Warton had consigned them and had made possible a more sympathetic appreciation of the Middle Ages. And in different ways the Revolution and the Romantic movement had undermined the eighteenth-century ideal of polite literature and had taught readers to value originality and profound feeling as more important than elegance.

Sismondi, though he paid tribute to the three Tuscans, only echoed the conventional opinions of a past generation, for like Ginguené he drew heavily on Tiraboschi. Hazlitt, the first important English critic to read Italian medieval literature with sympathetic perception, rejected indignantly his half-hearted praise as well as his ill-founded objections, with what is unmistakably a new voice in criticism. Whereas Warton seventy years before had found Dante hopelessly antiquated, Hazlitt, as many twentieth-century writers were to do, claims him as a contemporary, to be judged by contemporary standards: a poet who has more deep-working passion and imagination than Milton and whose great power is his combination of subjective emotion with external realism, qualities particularly congenial to Romantic theory and practice. Himself pugnacious and independent, Hazlitt considers Dante's refusal to fawn on patrons and his fierce partisanship in politics virtues rather than failings. Unlike his classically minded predecessors, he does not consider love a comic passion, and his own misadventures of the heart equip him to justify sympathetically Petrarch's exaggerations in the language of love. Calling in as interpreter his own experience, Hazlitt makes Petrarch, like Dante, his own contemporary; and, acknowledging the irrational, obsessive nature of love, he is able to appreciate the poet's skill in recording its every evanescent mood.

But it is Boccaccio who calls forth Hazlitt's most ardent championship. As usual, Sismondi had praised the *Decameron's* style while deploring its license (though oddly enough he also deplored that Petrarch's relation with Laura was platonic); and Hazlitt's defence is spirited and pithy. He himself loved the *Decameron*, as did many of his fellow Romantics, and, also like them, he was particularly fond of the tales about noble love and noble actions which were so often neglected by readers in search of other stimulation. References to the *Decameron* abound in his letters. Of all the stories, he loved most that about Federigo degli Alberighi and his falcon. To reproach critics of Boccaccio with their own gross tastes was a masterstroke in his counterattack.

Although Hazlitt's critical approach is new, his scholarship is outdated. It may be questioned whether he had read the *Decameron* in Italian or in translation: he misspells Federigo's name and surname and speaks of other characters by the names they bear in translations or in Dryden's versions of their stories. It is noticeable too that in talking of Dante he twice writes Genevra instead of Francesca. Hazlitt suspects that the stories in the *Decameron* are not all original, but he does not speculate on their sources. At least he is more open-minded than an anonymous reviewer of William Roscoe's *Italian Novelists* in the *Edinburgh Review* of 1825 who repelled indignantly the suggestion that all Boccaccio's *novelle* were not of his own invention as a slander on the integrity of an estimable author.

Hazlitt's tolerant generosity was not shared by Coleridge, who in his lectures of 1818, which survive only in the form of notes, roundly condemns the *Decameron* for its indecency. Like William Hayley before him, he admires the neglected romances of Boccaccio and seems to echo the regret that

> . . . strange to tell
> On his bold lyre Oblivion's shadow fell;
> His richer Tales engros'd the World's regard,
> And the bright Novelist eclips'd the Bard.[13]

Indeed, one of Coleridge's unaccomplished projects was to translate all the works of Boccaccio with the exception of the *Decameron*. Yet despite all his protests he must have had a certain fondness for that work, for one of his finest later poems is *The Garden of Boccaccio.*

In the Notes for the Lectures nothing appears under Petrarch's name except the dates of his birth and death, and the line, "Petrarch was the final blossom and perfection of the Troubadours." A few notes in a copy of the *Canzoniere* owned by Coleridge show, however, that unlike Hazlitt he found the poet's thoughts ridiculous but his diction, despite the *concetti*, simple and sweet.[14]

The lecture on Dante has survived in a more complete form than the others. Though Coleridge refers to Cary only marginally, he uses Cary's translation for all his quotations from the *Divine Comedy*, and he expands two passages from the prefatory *Life*: the comparison with Milton in the effects of visual realism, and the recommendations for a study of Dante's own reading. Like Hazlitt, Coleridge is impressed by the subjectivity

[13] Hayley, Ep. III. ll. 131–34.

[14] *Coleridge's Miscellaneous Criticism*, ed. Thomas Middleton Raysor (Cambridge: Harvard University Press, 1936), pp. 24–25. Raysor also quotes a manuscript fragment praising Petrarch's "fascinating delicacy in the choice and position of the words and the flow of the metre."

of Dante's style and actually applies the word "romantic" to his reverence for ancient poets. There is a surprising anticipation of Ruskin in Coleridge's praise of medieval commerce and its relations with the arts, as well as in his parallels between art and literature and the contrast between the Parthenon and the Gothic architecture of York Minster; though as a counterpart of the latter he names Shakespeare rather than Dante.

In the same year, 1818, Henry Hallam published his *View of the State of Europe in the Middle Ages*, devoting a chapter to medieval literature as a function of culture. In some ten pages of this study he presented a judicious estimate of Dante and Petrarch but mentioned Boccaccio only as a lecturer on the *Divine Comedy*. Hallam's book was so widely read that he became one of the most frequently quoted authorities on the Italian poets.

In 1812 Boccaccio had received some unusual publicity when a copy of the *Decameron* printed in Venice by Valdarfer in 1471 was sold by auction in London to the Marquis of Blandford for the then unprecedented sum of £2, 260. It had belonged to the Duke of Marlborough, who had paid £226 for it; and it was believed (erroneously) to be the only perfect copy of that edition in existence. The stir caused by this transaction is mentioned by many writers of the day and may have encouraged William Pickering in 1825 to bring out a new edition of the *Decameron* in Italian, with illustrations by William Stothard and a *Discorso storico sul testo* by Ugo Foscolo as an introduction.

Foscolo at that time had been in England for eight years and had established his reputation as a critic with his series of essays on Petrarch. He had, however, never attained financial security, and need to earn money may account for his consent to review his own *Discorso* anonymously for the *London Magazine* in 1826. His interest in the *Decameron* is philological and historical, rather than purely literary, and his is the first account in English of the strange fortunes of the work during and after the Counter-Reformation. In it he exhibits the anticlerical bias which he shared with many Italian liberals and which probably found a ready response in English sympathies. His taste for Greek studies is apparent in his dislike of Boccaccio's heavy Latinized constructions, which had indeed set an unfortunate stamp on Italian prose style. He does not attempt to excuse the *novelle* from the charge of indecency, but he does echo Hazlitt's rebuke to those who see little else in the *Decameron.*

Foscolo's *Essays on Petrarch*[15] have remained a landmark in Petrarch criticism, for Italian and English scholars alike. His perfect knowledge and practice of prosody enabled him to appreciate Petrarch's skill as no one of that era save Leopardi could hope to do. Foscolo's own poems gave new life and meaning to such Petrarchan themes as memory, solitude, tomb meditations, fame, and patriotic melancholy. His own frustrations–exiled as he was, like Petrarch, in a country where his native language was a foreign tongue; separated forever from those he loved in Italy; seeking new loves which proved but pale reflections of the old–gave his *Essays* peculiar insight and poignancy. His *Parallel between Dante and Petrarch* is the first detailed examination of the two schools of poetry, and his essays on the *Love of Petrarch* and on his *Character* draw their wealth of illustrative material from the letters as well as from the poems.

Just as Hazlitt's article had indicated the first serious attempt in England at a critical approach to medieval Italian literature, so Foscolo's work marks the moment when such travesties as the articles in the old *Encyclopaedia Britannica* became impossible. Consequently the *Penny Cyclopaedia*, which came out between 1833 and 1843, has a certain importance as a proof of the greater accuracy considered due the general public in a new era of popular education.

Charles Knight, its publisher and editor, had grown up in an age when not only did Warton jeer at Dante but some of Knight's flippant acquaintances commonly spoke of Shakespeare himself as "Silly Billy."[16] Knight found this levity unseemly and devoted himself to elevating popular taste by providing instructive yet entertaining literature at a low price. The *Penny Cyclopaedia* undertook to impart scholarly knowledge in a popular style, and Knight was particularly proud of its biographical articles. The author he chose to write the articles on Italian history and literature was André Vieusseux, a Neapolitan who left Italy at an early age, fought in a British regiment during the Penin-

[15] First privately printed (16 copies) in 1821, and published commercially by John Murray in 1823.

[16] *Passages of a Working Life During Half a Century* (London: Bradbury & Evans, 1864), 1: 46.

sular War, and after the peace settled in England. In 1824 Knight had published his *Italy and the Italians*, with an appendix on modern Italian literature, and he was a regular contributor to *Knight's Quarterly Magazine*. His articles in the *Cyclopaedia* are based on Foscolo's studies as well as on Italian and French sources. They are sober, well informed, and list correctly the minor works of each author. They are of particular importance because they appeared in a standard reference work which was widely used for many years.

Knight had earlier commissioned Thomas Babington Macaulay, then at the beginning of his career, to write two articles for his *Quarterly Magazine*, and *Criticisms on the Principal Italian Writers* appeared in January and April, 1824. They show all the self-confidence and verbal exuberance of the brilliant young writer: wide-ranging in their allusions and quotations, both classical and modern, they are far above the level of contemporary "popular" writing and are always entertaining and stimulating. Macaulay's chief authority, he admits, is Sismondi, but his own judgments are original and vigorous, his style full of striking images. Cary's criticism of Dante's delineation as being grotesque compared with Milton's sublimity struck Macaulay as it had struck Coleridge; but whereas the latter accepts and enlarges it, the former confutes it, as Ruskin was to do even more conclusively.

The frequency with which Macaulay couples Dante's name with Shakespeare's indicates the rising esteem with which the nineteenth century regarded these nonclassical poets, though they had not yet reached the eminence accorded Petrarch and Cervantes. Macaulay cannot completely share this opinion of Petrarch and is repelled by his affectations. Yet he is stirred by the Roman aspects of his career, which appeal strongly to Macaulay's taste for the classical past. The future historian dominates from time to time the literary critic, as when he recalls the triumphs of Petrarch's coronation on the Campidoglio or reviews the character of love in Greek, Roman, and barbarous ages.

Macaulay followed Hallam's example and did not include Boccaccio in his survey. But this neglect was more than counterbalanced by Walter Savage Landor's laudatory comments on the *Decameron* in his imaginary conversation between Petrarch and Boccaccio, the *Pentameron*, published in 1837. In the *Decameron* (which Boccaccio has ruefully suggested burning) there is, Landor makes Petrarch protest, "more character, more nature, more invention, than either modern or ancient Italy, or than Greece, from whom she derived her whole inheritance, ever claimed or ever knew. Would you consume a beautiful meadow because there are reptiles in it; or because a few grubs hereafter may be generated by the succulence of the grass?"[17]

Even the licentious stories may have an ambiguous usefulness:

> Young men . . . will read them with more pleasure than is commendable or innocent. Yet the very time they occupy with you [Boccaccio], would perhaps be spent in the midst of those excesses or irregularities to which the moralist, in his utmost severity, will argue that your pen directs them. Now there are many who are fond of standing on the brink of precipices, and who nevertheless are as cautious as any of falling in. And there are minds desirous of being warmed by description, which without this warmth, might seek excitement among the things described [p. 153].

Through Petrarch's lips, Landor thanks Boccaccio, as many nineteenth-century travelers were to do, for having made Tuscany the most pleasant and interesting part of Italy:

> Indeed we can scarcely walk in any quarter from the gates of Florence, without the recollection of some witty or affecting story related by you. Every street, every farm, is peopled by your genius; and this population can not change with seasons or with ages, with factions or with incursions. Ghibellines and Guelphs will have been contested for only by the worms, long before the *Decameron* has ceased to be recited on our banks of blue lilies and under our arching vines [p. 251].

Landor's dislike of Dante is characteristic of his eighteenth-century education (he was born in 1775) and his devotion to the classics. It is more serious in tone than Warton's, though he renews some of the latter's charges, notably those of filthiness and malignity. Calling Dante "the great master of the disgusting" (p. 192), he makes Petrarch condemn in the *Divine Comedy* "the loose and shallow foundation of so vast a structure; its unconnectedness; its want of manners, of passion, of action, consistently and uninterruptedly at work toward a distinct and worthy purpose; and lastly (although less importantly as regards

[17] *Complete Works* (London: Chapman & Hall, 1931), 9: 152. Subsequent page references are to this volume.

the poetical character) that splenetic temper, which seems to grudge brightness to the flames of hell, to delight in deepening its gloom, in multiplying its miseries, in accumulating weight upon depression, and building labyrinths about perplexity" (p. 239).

The *Inferno* particularly excites his condemnation, and he makes Petrarch call it "the most immoral and impious book ever written"; "a vast desert," with "its greater and its less oasis; Ugolino and Francesca di Rimini." Nevertheless, Petrarch admits, "Dante's powers of language are prodigious; and, in the solitary places where he exerts his force rightly, the stroke is irresistible. But how greatly to be pitied must he be, who can find nothing in paradise better than sterile theology! and what an object of sadness and of consternation, he who rises up from hell like a giant refreshed!" (p. 168.)

And with many of these strictures Boccaccio agrees, though he does point out some of the beauties of the *Paradiso* and comment on the "glorious tract of splendour" that Dante can conjure up in a single line (p. 214).

If Boccaccio stands first in Landor's esteem and affection, Petrarch is second, but at some distance and with some reservations. In the *Pentameron* he appears as the supreme poet and critic, whose judgment as well as whose place in literature is unchallenged. But six years later, in the long review article included in this collection, Landor is more guarded in his commendation. This may be because he dislikes the book under review, a *Life of Petrarch* published in 1841.

In 1828 Archdeacon William Coxe, the biographer of Correggio and Parmigiano, died leaving an uncompleted manuscript of his contemplated biography of Petrarch. Thomas Campbell (who had shown his interest in Italian literature as early as 1822 by commissioning Foscolo to write a series of articles for the *New Monthly Magazine*) was asked by the publisher Henry Colburn to edit this manuscript. Finding it intolerably confused and, so he said, stupid, Campbell offered instead to write a *Life* himself, tempted to undertake such an unaccustomed and initially distasteful task by the £200 it would bring him. The sale of his works had fallen off, and he was paying out of his own purse to have wood vignettes engraved for the elegant Moxon edition of his poems.

"I had always," he wrote to a friend soon after he had begun his reading for the work, "until of late, something like an aversion to Petrarch, on account of the monotony of his amatory sonnets, and the apparent wildness and half insanity of his passion for Laura. I used to say to myself (indulging, I confess, a rather vulgar spirit of criticism), hang these cater-wauling sonnets! They afflict my compassion."[18] He was convinced that Laura had not reciprocated Petrarch's love, and that the poet was a pitiful fellow who could be in love for twenty years without any of the pleasures of hope. But he read diligently, both Petrarch's poetry and all the earlier biographers, Italian as well as French; and though for a time, in ill health and spirits, he despaired of finishing the two-volume work, in the fall of 1839 he was able to report, "A happy change has taken place in my frame of mind regarding my manufacture of the 'Life of Petrarch.' He was a fine fellow; and (though he loved a married woman twenty years) I admire the grace of his writing."[19] It is this admiration that he expresses in the critical summary with which he closes the *Life*, and which was used as a preface to the first complete translation of Petrarch's poems, published by Bohn in 1859.

The unjustifiably acrimonious tone of Landor's opening remarks in his review of the *Life* indicates a proprietary feeling toward Petrarch which Campbell has offended. His review takes the form of a long biographical narrative, with highly individual comments. But he uses the biography ingeniously as the framework for an extensive account of Petrarch's poems, dealing with their style and metrical form as Campbell had scarcely attempted to do. Landor's own classical learning and interest in prosody are very evident in these passages, and his treatment of the poet may be compared to Foscolo's. Yet like Coleridge he is too eager to condemn the trivial defects of Petrarch's *concetti*, new when the poet had used them but, more easily imitated than his nobler qualities, worn to shreds within two centuries after his death and no longer worthy of comment.

The studies of Macaulay, Campbell, and Landor mark the end of the period of English criticism dominated by Ginguené and Sismondi, who, however, continued to be read, particularly the

[18] *Life and Letters of Thomas Campbell* (London: Moxon, 1849), 3: 249.

[19] *Ibid.*, pp. 278–79.

latter in Roscoe's translation. They mark, as well, the end of the period when Dante could seriously be considered to have any rival in eminence. Both Campbell and Landor speak of Petrarch's fame as belonging to the past, and as having always been higher in Italy than in England. Shelley's admiration for Petrarch and his imitations of the *Trionfi* seem to Landor an aberration. Indeed, love was no longer the dominant theme for poetry in Victorian England, though one distinguished exception, Mrs. Browning's *Sonnets from the Portuguese*, is in the Petrarchan tradition both in form and content. It is true also that Italian poets–notably Foscolo and Leopardi–continued to draw inspiration for themes and technical innovations from Petrarch's poetry; whereas, as Campbell shrewdly points out, the lack of an adequate translation–if any translation of lyric poetry, which depends so much on the juxtaposition of certain sounds and words can indeed be adequate–made Petrarch almost inaccessible to English readers whose knowledge of Italian was not perfected in youth.

The biographical approach to literature, combined with rigid moral standards, also dimmed Petrarch's reputation in England. It had become necessary to admire the man before entertaining an admiration for his work, and Petrarch's love for a married woman, his failure to excite in his readers what Coleridge called "a gush of manly feeling," made him a figure to be regarded rather with pity than with an impulse towards emulation.

Boccaccio too, despite Landor's encomium, sank lower, if not in popular affection, at least in avowed esteem. A novel and advanced attempt to defend the *Decameron* on aesthetic grounds was indeed made in 1841 by Samuel Gray Ward, writing in the periodical of the New England Transcendentalists, *The Dial.* Graduated from Columbia University in 1831, Ward had gone to Europe, studied in France and Germany, and returned to his home in New York in 1835 with an impressive library of foreign books. It was probably during his residence in Paris that he adopted the theory of the nonmorality of art which Victor Cousin had developed in his lectures at the Sorbonne and which had been further expounded and practised by Théophile Gautier.[20] Ward's defense of Boccaccio in the form of an open letter

[20] Van Wyck Brooks in *The Flowering of New England* (New York: Dutton, 1940), p. 383, points out Ward's early use of the phrases "creative criticism" and "significant form" in an article on "Criticism" written in 1849 for Elizabeth Peabody's *Aesthetic Papers.*

to Margaret Fuller, then the editor of *The Dial*, could have found little support among Anglo-Saxons at that period. Though he later became the friend of Longfellow and Charles Eliot Norton, his thesis is not echoed by either English or American writers.

Dante's star, on the contrary, rose steadily. The early Romantics had admired in him particularly his fierce independence—his perception of the importance of the individual within all social and moral frames—for they were confident in the dawn of a new age of freedom and the rights of man. But before the middle of the nineteenth century that illusory dawn had been darkened by the smoking chimneys of industrialism, and thinking men were aware that the prison house of eighteenth-century convention had been exchanged for the gloomier incarceration of materialism. Dante had been fortunate indeed in his translator: Cary's *Divine Comedy*, its style perhaps more uniformly elevated than that of the original, had become as familiar to English readers as Milton's *Paradise Lost*, and two strong currents in the fast-flowing tide of Victorian thought, mysticism and hero-worship, carried Dante to an eminence which would never again be challenged. He is, as Carlyle phrased it, canonized. Both currents were antitheses of eighteenth-century rationalism, and both were natural in an intellectual generation uneasily conscious that material and technical advances had not increased human dignity and happiness or furthered spiritual development. The idealization of the Middle Ages which had commenced with Sir Walter Scott and was to reach its apogee with Ruskin was as complete a misconception as the opposite image held in the eighteenth century. But it was ardently entertained, and Dante lent himself admirably to various interpretations, some almost mythological in nature.

Carlyle, convinced that his age needed heroes to lead it toward a heroic destiny, delivered in 1840, three years after the publication of his *French Revolution*, a series of lectures on Heroes and Hero-Worship. There, in his thunder-toned prose, he claimed for Dante a role not too far removed, perhaps, from the Florentine poet's own conception of his vocation—that of the Poeta-Vates, seeing "a solemn law in the universe, pointing out his destiny with an awful and beautiful certainty," and divinely inspired to interpret to his people the divine mysteries without whose knowledge they will perish.

Like Landor, Carlyle prefers the *Purgatorio* and the *Paradiso* to the *Inferno.* He is the first English critic to point out—as no historian, and particularly no friend of Mazzini could fail to do—Dante's significance to Italian nationalism in those troubled years of the Risorgimento. And by coupling him with Shakespeare as an archetype of the Poet as Hero, Carlyle declared his own conviction—voiced elsewhere in his works—that Dante was one of the few supreme figures in world literature.

Leigh Hunt, however, protested vehemently against this attempt to see in Dante an inspired leader of men and a poet who could do no wrong. Toward the end of his literary career, Hunt, in youth the friend of Shelley, Byron, and Keats, and still a belated Romantic, followed the popularizing fashion initiated by Charles Knight and compiled his delightful *Stories from the Italian Poets.* This work, dedicated to Shelley's son, was published in Paris in 1846. The first section is devoted to Dante, with a long introduction, sometimes very original, sometimes reviving old objections in a new form. All the generous liberalism in politics and religion of Hunt's youth is evident in this preface, given a new immediacy by the repressive policies of the Austrian Empire and by sectarian developments in England, which were causing a growing distrust of Roman Catholicism. The Catholic Emancipation Bill of 1829, though it had not completely ended the disabilities of Catholics, had met with hot opposition. Even more disturbing was the dissension in the Anglican Church itself, first publicly manifested in Keble's sermon of 1833, "On the National Apostasy." Newman's attack on the Thirty-Nine Articles and his secession to Rome in 1842 shocked and distressed loyal members of the Church of England, especially because his popularity attracted so many important converts that his new coreligionists prophesied triumphantly that within a generation England would return to the faith of its fifteenth-century forefathers.

This danger inevitably affected the light in which Englishmen read the Italian poets. Boccaccio's strictures on ecclesiastical corruption had been quoted by Protestant reformers from the days of Olimpia Morata and Thomas Pope Blount and were regularly cited by English apologists for the *Decameron.* Thomas Campbell follows this tradition when he says:

> I would ask if Boccaccio's faults as a writer are not more than atoned for by his love of truth, by his faith to Nature, by his

> joyous benevolence, and by his honest hatred of hypocrisy, fraud and bigotry. I would ask also what it was that stirred up the enmity which first repudiated his *Decamerone*. Was it the love of innocence and virtue? No such thing! It was the anger of imposters, of voluptuous priests, and of exposed sinners of every kind that armed a host of furies against him. He was accused of sacrilegiously rending the veil that had concealed the vices of the church—of therefore being an heretical reformer. And so in truth Boccaccio was, without knowing it himself. I consider him, as well as Dante and Petrarch, to have been, all three of them, great practical reformers, though unconscious patriarchs of the Reformation.[21]

Hunt could accept this for Boccaccio, whom he loved and whose traces in Tuscany he followed with all Landor's affection; but his cheerful, sweet-tempered nature could not tolerate Dante's insistance on grim retribution. Warton had found Dante's theology ridiculous; Leigh Hunt, a gentle humanitarian, could not condone its cruelties and inconsistencies, and he recoiled from the idea that a more enlightened age might fall again into so dark an abyss. Yet no critic perhaps has had a power equal to Leigh Hunt's in describing certain peculiar qualities of Dante's *Inferno*, and the images which the Ugolino canto summons to his mind have a fine wild horror like a fragment from a romance by Mary Shelley. Nor has any writer equaled Hunt's appreciation of Dante's angels—their beauty, their differences, their colors—which come to life on his page like a succession of figures in stained glass.

Hunt's fears that England might be lured back to medieval forms of religion proved unfounded; the nineteenth century was a century of doubt, though it was indeed seeking for some valid ethical code which need not depend on supernatural revelation. Like Carlyle, but with a bolder reinterpretation, Ruskin saw in Dante the supreme interpreter of the laws of Nature, laws from which, he was convinced, man could learn the laws which should govern his own conduct. The laws of Nature, Ruskin considered, were divinely ordained, and the key to their understanding was truth. The ethics of the dust, if carefully studied, would disclose principles for the ethics of man. The highest and noblest periods of art were those in which the artist had been most faithful to Nature, and those periods, as Ruskin explained in *Modern*

[21] *Life of Petrarch*, 2: 46.

Painters, were the classical era, the Middle Ages, and, potentially, the modern age, if the teachings of Turner were grasped and observed.

As Homer epitomizes the classical conception of landscapes, so Dante exemplifies the medieval perception of the transcendental meaning of Nature. Carlyle had seen in the *Divine Comedy* "a magnificent crystallization of Catholicism, more glorious and lasting than its finest Gothic cathedrals." Ruskin goes even further, and attaches a mystic significance to the date of Dante's vision, just as Dante had attached a mystical significance to the recurrence of the number nine in his associations with Beatrice. "I have said," he remarks in *The Stones of Venice*, "that all great European art is rooted in the thirteenth century; and it seems to me that there is a kind of central year about which we may consider the energy of the Middle Ages to be gathered; a kind of focus of time, which, by what is to my mind a most touching and impressive Divine appointment, has been marked by the greatest writer of the Middle Ages in the first words he utters; namely the year 1300, the 'mezzo del camin' of the life of Dante."[22]

The first medievalist among English writers on Dante, Ruskin alone interprets the *Divine Comedy* not only in a historical or biographical framework, as earlier critics had done, but within the whole context of medieval thought. For him as for Dante, physical Nature is an expression of the divine mind, and his illuminating study of the landscapes of the *Comedy* and their spiritual significance is in startling contrast to Macaulay's remark on "how little impression the forms of the external world appear to have made on the mind of Dante."

From earliest youth Ruskin had read Dante with earnest attention; he quotes more frequently from the *Comedy* than from any other work except the Bible; and his occasional commentaries on passages from the poem elucidate allegorical profundities to which other writers had so far been blind. Even the grossness of the demon cantos, which Warton and others had deplored, is shown by Ruskin to have an underlying meaning which makes them essential to Dante's conception of divine justice.

In *Modern Painters* Ruskin uses not only Cary's translation but also that of Charles Bagot Cayley, recently published. Cay-

[22] *Works*, 10: 400.

ley, a pupil of Dante Gabriel Rossetti, had sent Ruskin a copy of his work, an unflattering opinion of which Ruskin expressed in a letter to Rossetti. He evidently found however, a freshness in Cayley's rendering which pleased him, and he borrows from him the expression Evilpits for the *Malebolge* which Cary had not attempted to translate.

One barrier still existed to Dante's complete acceptance by the Victorian public as a figure for veneration: his love for a married woman. Though less distasteful because less prolonged than Petrarch's love for Laura, it still seemed irreconcilable with a divinely inspired prophet. Earlier writers had either, like Warton and Hunt, jested about the situation or had refused to accept the fact of Beatrice's marriage. One had even gone so far as to say that she died a nun. Shelley, however, whose own views on matrimony were unconventional, anticipated later critics when he declared in his *Defence of Poetry* that

> Dante understood the secret things of love even more than Petrarch. His *Vita Nuova* is an inexhaustible fountain of purity of sentiment and language: it is the idealized history of that period, and those intervals of his life which were dedicated to love. His apotheosis of Beatrice in Paradise, and the gradation of his love and her loveliness, by which as by steps he feigns himself to have ascended to the throne of the Supreme Cause, is the most glorious imagination of modern poetry.[23]

The publication in 1839 of the *Vita Nuova* in Pietro Fraticelli's edition of Dante's minor works aroused fresh interest in the book; and Hunt, despite his jocose references to the famous love, is well aware, as is Carlyle, of the importance of Beatrice to the *Divine Comedy*. Four translators began to render the *Vita Nuova* into English, independently of each other, at about the same time. Ralph Waldo Emerson, calling it the Bible of love, almost unique in the history of sentiment, began a translation in 1843 but did not complete it. It was Joseph Garrow, half-Scot, half-Hindu, the father-in-law of Thomas Adolphus Trollope, who in 1846 published the first English translation, *The New Life of Dante Alighieri.* This was printed in Florence and so attracted less attention in England than it deserved. Its introduction gives a good summary of the arguments for and against an

[23] *Prose Works* (London: Reeves & Turner, 1880), 7: 125.

allegorical interpretation of the work—an interpretation which Garrow rejects, as do, he says, all his literary friends in Italy. He himself agrees with the opinion of the French translator, Délécluze, that the *Vita Nuova* is the first modern Romance.

In 1859 a more famous version was published by Charles Eliot Norton in a privately printed edition of 100 copies. Parts of it had already appeared that same year, incorporated in a series of three articles in the *Atlantic Monthly*. The young Norton had read *Modern Painters* and acquired its author's love for Dante before he first met Ruskin in 1855. Their casual acquaintance was renewed in 1856; from then on they remained close friends and correspondents, and Ruskin's influence is plain in Norton's *Atlantic Monthly* articles. In 1857 Norton visited a Pre-Raphaelite exhibition in London and admired a painting by Dante Gabriel Rossetti of the death of Beatrice.[24] Early in that year he had begun his translation of the *Vita Nuova*, unaware that Rossetti also intended to turn the work into English. In 1861 Rossetti's translation, less accurate than Norton's but destined to become a minor classic, appeared at almost the same time as the first commercial edition of Norton's version.

In Rossetti's overripe rendering and in Norton's ecstatic re-evocation of a Florence where Nature and Love were eternally radiant, the poet who had repelled so many by his vindictive cruelty was transfigured into what Matthew Arnold called "the hero of a sentimental but strictly virtuous novel."[25] The discovery in 1840 of Giotto's portrait of Dante in the Bargello undoubtedly played some part in creating the new figure. It depicts a young man, grave, sensitive, visionary, in striking contrast with the grim later portrait, also by Giotto, which Macaulay and Carlyle describe. A line drawing after the portrait appears as the frontispiece to Garrow's translation.[26]

[24] Ruskin purchased from Rossetti a watercolor of "The Meeting of Dante and Beatrice at a Wedding Feast" and sent it to Norton in 1860, saying, "It was really a mere chance his having done that subject. It came in so pat for your *Vita*." *Letters of John Ruskin to Charles Eliot Norton* (Boston: Houghton, Mifflin, 1905), 1: 96–97.

[25] *Essays in Criticism*, 3d ser. (Boston: Ball, 1910), p. 107.

[26] A tracing of the portrait was given to D. G. Rossetti's father by Seymour Kirkup, the Anglo-Florentine chiefly responsible for its discovery. It was evidently the model for the face of Dante in D. G. R.'s series of scenes from the *Vita Nuova* from 1848 on. In 1852 Rossetti executed a watercolor of "Giotto Painting the Portrait of Dante," with Beatrice, passing by in a procession, the object of Dante's rapt gaze.

The cult of purity, and dissatisfaction with marriage as a social institution, endeared this image of Dante, too, to readers of the mid-nineteenth century. In New England the study of Swedenborg, a favorite author of the Transcendentalists, had already made the idea of angelic marriage familiar and beautiful. Swedenborg was read in Britain as well; and the ideal of the perfect union, the "maiden passion for a maid," as the true source of all virtue, was powerfully set forth in Tennyson's *Idylls of the King*, published the same year as Norton's essays on the *Vita Nuova*.

The ultimate refinement of this doctrine sees in a child the only sure embodiment of innocence; and the figure of the lovely little girl who inspires a pure love and dies young appears in both Victorian life and letters. It had been present even earlier in Blake and was part of Dicken's own experience as well as of his work. One of Landor's finest lyrics, "Rose Aylmer," was inspired by the subject, and Landor is moved to a brief moment of sympathy with Dante when he contemplates "the little virgin Beatrice Porticari [*sic*] who breathed all her purity into his boyish heart, and inhaled it back again."[27] In 1858 Ruskin had first met Rose La Touche, then ten years old, and his feeling for her was, in his own eyes at least, this same sublimation of passion. It is possibly no coincidence that two men very close to him, Rossetti and Norton, engaged simultaneously to translate a work in which he must have found special significance. This significance is evident from a letter written in 1867 when, his hopes of marriage to the "glorious little angel" having faded, he is despondently rereading Norton's *Vita Nuova.* "It falls in much," he confesses, "with my own mind—but, when death or life depends on such things, suppose it should be *morte nuova* day by day?"[28]

Ruskin's conception of Dante as the Mystic of Nature had also been shaken. A couple of years after he had written the chapter on medieval landscape in *Modern Painters* he underwent a counterconversion, a loss of faith in the bond between religion and art. The devoutness of the artist was immaterial, and "to be a first-rate painter—you mustn't be pious; but rather a little wicked and a man of the world"; for despite the degree of

[27] *Works*, 9: 245.

[28] *Letters to Norton*, 1: 170.

piety that inspired them, "things done delightfully and rightly were always done by the help and in the spirit of God."[29] Yet despite his change of heart, Ruskin as the preeminent arbiter of taste had effectually preached the cult of an already canonized Dante; a cult which was fervently embraced by the Pre-Raphaelites and carried across the Atlantic by Norton to an ardent group of Harvard disciples among whom Longfellow was already a fellow worshiper. Indeed, in 1867 a new edition of Norton's *New Life* accompanied the first complete edition of Longfellow's *Divine Comedy*. And the triune aspects of Dante as the Poet-Hero, the Scribe of God, and the seraphic lover, coexisted in varying proportions through the remainder of the century.

By 1865 the relative reputations of the three poets of the Trecento were firmly established, and again an encyclopedia may be used to illustrate this phase of critical judgment. The editors of Appleton's *New American Cyclopaedia*, published between 1857 and 1864, commissioned James Russell Lowell to write the article on Dante. This, later remodeled as an essay, was much admired and frequently reprinted. The article on Petrarch was given to an able young man who had just graduated from Yale and was later to become a distinguished Chaucer scholar, Thomas Raynes Lounsbury. He treats his subject with competence and an evident sympathetic understanding of the Middle Ages. Boccaccio was entrusted to Ormond Tiffany, who was then and has remained obscure; he described the *Decameron* as "an inexhaustible repertory of wit, beauty, and eloquence, although unhappily deformed with such licentious thoughts and descriptions as render it in a great degree unfit to be read by anyone of pure mind."[30]

Dante's position beside Shakespeare and Goethe as one of the

[29] *Ibid.*, pp. 67, 70.

[30] If Lowell had written the article, it would have been more temperate. He says of Boccaccio in a letter to Howells in 1864: "I find [his style] very charming, and him clearly the founder of modern prose. A singular sweetness, ease, and grace. . . . And then the just visible unobtrusive play of humour—a kind of heat-lightening round the horizon of his mind without a harmful bolt in the whole of it. And then there is no great mischief in his dirt. When Casti versifies his stories you feel this—for Casti makes them bad." *Letters of James Russell Lowell*, ed. C. E. Norton (New York: Harper & Bros., 1893), 1: 339.

supreme figures of Western European literature was never again to be questioned. Though William Roscoe and John Addington Symonds succeeded in shifting popular interest to some extent from the Middle Ages to the Renaissance, Norton continued to kindle enthusiasm for Dante through successive generations. Bernard Berenson was among his students; Mrs. Jack Gardner attended his public lectures, and Henry James frequented his study.[31] When T. S. Eliot registered at Harvard Norton was still alive and active.[32] Thus Ruskin's original inspiration lived on as an enduring bond between North America and Europe and continued to form Anglo-American taste well into the twentieth century.

Neither Petrarch nor Boccaccio regained the esteem they had enjoyed during the eighteenth and early nineteenth centuries. Petrarch's lyrics were either neglected or excited languid commendation. Even Bohn's publication for the first time, in 1859, of all his Italian poetry (by some thirty translators ranging from Chaucer to J. H. Merivale) could not stimulate a new Petrarchan vogue. Indeed, it was evident that though the older translators had been poets of eminence, the best known among the later names was that of Leigh Hunt. And in 1878 Symonds went so far as to suggest that "his poetry exhausted but a small portion of his intellectual energy," and that his Latin works, letters, and humanistic studies were his true claim to renown.

Boccaccio's fate was more complex. The interest shown in his minor works by Foscolo and Coleridge soon faded and was not to revive until this century. No longer even invoked as the Protestant champion, he was, as the folklorist Joseph Jacobs put it, relegated "to the top shelves, whence he is only supposed to be removed furtively and at moments of weakness."[33] His

[31] Van Wyck Brooks, *New England: Indian Summer 1865–1915* (New York: Dutton, 1940), p. 254 and note. In 1869 James stayed with Norton in London and was introduced by him to Ruskin. James also encountered Samuel Gray Ward at Norton's house. *The Letters of Henry James* (New York: Charles Scribner's, 1920), 1: 16, 20.

[32] In 1932 Eliot was Charles Eliot Norton Professor of Poetry at Harvard and paid tribute to Norton in his opening lecture. Kermit Vanderbilt, *Charles Eliot Norton: Apostle of Culture in a Democracy* (Cambridge: Harvard University Press, 1959), p. 230.

[33] *Boccaccio Done into English* (London: George Allen, 1899), p. ix. Jacobs wrote the introduction to the 1890 edition of Painter's *Palace of Pleasure.*

Decameron, once honored by editions dedicated to the Royal Society of Antiquaries, or adorned with illustrations by Stodhart and an introduction by Foscolo, still circulated in undistinguished translations, sometimes appearing in "limited editions" for the collector of pornography. Yet references in letters and journals show how many visitors to Italy sought out, as Landor's Petrarch had predicted, the scenes of Boccaccio's stories, and delighted in the landscape of Certaldo because it had first been dear to him. And the *Decameron* remained as a living source of inspiration despite its apparent disgrace: both Tennyson and Longfellow retold the story of Federigo and his falcon which Hazlitt had loved so well.

At the beginning of the period represented by this collection, critics judged a work of literature by firmly established standards accepted throughout Western Europe and ultimately based on Aristotelian and Horatian poetics. Differently interpreted though these might have been since the sixteenth century when they first established their supremacy, the classical theorists were still invincible authorities; and none of the controversies between ancients and moderns, no battle of the books however savage, had seriously weakened their prestige. Known as French, though its origin had been Italian, this school of criticism was not concerned with the personality of the author or with his historical or social background. Universal rules are necessarily applicable in all ages and all countries.

With the coming of Romanticism, ancient tyrannies of taste and government collapse together, and the new vogues are as ephemeral and experimental as the new governments. The individual may now form his own judgment, often based on emotional response rather than on considered standards of style and form. Critical writing becomes a source of income for the poet, who estimates his fellow poets by the support they lend to his own predilections and prejudices, literary, social, religious, and political. The new objective French criticism which concerns itself with *l'art pur*—and of which Ward was an unheeded harbinger—does not make itself felt in England until late in the nineteenth century.

With increasing interest in biography and history, the poet is judged as an individual too, and the defects of the man may easily obscure the merits of his poetry, particularly in an age when moral standards are becoming ever more rigid, and when the reading public is rapidly growing in size but not in sophistication. At the same time, because he is considered as an individual, the poet may inspire reverence and affection and be treated as an *alter ego*, transformed into the likeness of a critic-creator. Thus Dante, who lends himself to this process more readily than either Boccaccio or Petrarch, becomes a kind of super-Carlyle or a Ruskinian divinely inspired artificer. It is at this stage that the poet must be shown to have relevance for the critic's own age, a message which only his interpreter is sufficiently perceptive to discern.

This creative criticism is not based on original research, and few of its English practitioners have a perfect knowledge of Italian. It depends for its factual background on Italian and French secondary sources, and, as we have seen, several new directions in its course can be directly traced to publications on the Continent: De Sade's life of Petrarch, histories of literature by Ginguené and Sismondi, the Fraticelli edition of the *Vita Nuova.* Campbell is almost alone in attempting to evaluate his sources and to resolve or choose between discrepancies. Only Ruskin has a specialized knowledge of the Middle Ages, but his interest in medieval literature in general is so slight that he mentions Boccaccio by name nowhere in all his works, though he makes one reference to the gardens in the *Decameron.* Petrarch he seems to associate only with his own visit to Arquà, except that on one occasion he couples him with Raphael and issues a stern warning against imitating either.[34]

With Charles Eliot Norton the study of Dante passes into the universities, which with a certain cloistered indulgence open their doors to Petrarch and Boccaccio as well. "Tout finit en Sorbonne," said Paul Valéry; but Fortune is restless even in academic groves, and she, to give the final word to Dante (and Cary):

> Con l'altre prime creature lieta
> Volve sua spera, e beata si gode.
>
> [*Inf.* VII, 95–96]
>
> Amidst the other primal beings glad
> Rolls on her sphere, and in her bliss exults.

[34] *Works,* 22: 80–81.

A Note on the Texts The omission of a passage from the texts is indicated in the usual way by an ellipsis. Obsolete and superfluous notes in the original texts have been omitted. Editorial notes are indicated by square brackets. Italian and French quotations have been checked and corrected by standard texts. References for Petrarch quotations are to modern editions of the *Canzoniere*, unless otherwise indicated.

I

GIUSEPPE BARETTI

In Defence of Dante

I will select one of our epic poets, who hath been always read and admired amongst us, and will endeavour as well as I am able to give the candid reader an idea of his beauties and show that he deserves neither that contemptuous silence of monsieur de Voltaire in his *Essay*, nor the insolent abuse the French writers lavish in general on us. The poet of whom I am going to speak is Dante, among the Italians called "*il padre della lingua e poesia toscana*," "the father of Tuscan language and poetry."

All the face of Europe was still overspread with gothic barbarism when the inhabitants of Florence bought their liberty of the northern emperors with sums of gold.

As soon as their Republic was settled, they turned their minds to the cultivation of arts and letters; assisting themselves with that little learning that was then creeping among the Sicilians and Provençals, which consisted in a few notions of laws and poetry.

Accursio and Brunetto Latini early among their citizens gave the first blow to ignorance. The Muses began to free themselves from their rusty shackles in the schools of these two men. Many other Florentines, putting their helping hand to the work, brightened a little the face of reason; but Dante appeared and like a morning-sun, almost dispersed the mists that hovered for so many ages over the Parnassean mountain.

This man was of a very noble and rich family of Florence, called Alighieri. He was of an haughty and inflexible disposition and obtained very early, both in the field and in the magistracy, the most eminent posts of the new commonwealth, which in his time was engaged in a war against most of its neighbours.

He was, while yet a youth, one of the principal leaders of the Florentine troops, and not contented with commanding them,

Reprinted from *Prefazioni e polemiche*, a cura di Luigi Piccioni (Bari: Gius. Laterza & Figli, 1911), pp. 97–109.

he exposed himself bravely in all encounters with the enemies like a common soldier, and with his own hand killed many of their men. But seeing himself endowed with all the literature of his time, as well sacred as profane, very well skilled in Latin, Greek and Hebrew; having capacity enough to be leader of his countrymen and a supreme degree of courage accompanied by uncommon strength and agility of body, he not only despised his fellow-citizens and the most venerable members of the Republic, but made little account of any of his contemporaries.

He one day in the counsel (so the Florentines then called their Senate) gave a too lively proof of his frequently expressed contempt for others and high opinion of himself. It being debated amongst them whom they should send ambassador to Rome on a very important occasion, the senators proposed Dante for that employment. "*E s' io vado, chi resta?*" "And if I go, who stays?" said he. Then stay, answered they. "*E s' io sto, chi va?*" "And if I stay, who goes?" replied the poet.

This insolent and contemptuous behavior soon alienated the affection of his countrymen from him, and, although they acknowledged that his merit was superior to many others, they hated and persecuted him and at last banished him from their territories.

Dante was obliged to fly and retire to Ravenna, where he was kindly received and entertained by the counts Polenta's, lords of that city. There it was that he wrote many things in Latin; but not entirely satisfied with his performances in that language, he undertook to write an epic poem in his own, which was at that time called in Italy "*lingua volgare*," "vulgar tongue."

The argument that he chose was well adapted to his own nature and gave him an opportunity of venting all that rancour and rage that boiled in his bosom and devoured him in his exile. Hell, Purgatory and Paradise were his theme; so he had the conveniency of throwing into the profoundest parts of Hell many of his fellow-citizens, against whom he was enraged, as also many other persons ancient or contemporaries whom he disliked. Emperors, kings, popes, cardinals, noblemen and plebeyans, his vehement pen respected none. Nay, having received some displeasure from the lords Polenta's, protectors and benefactors, he plunged two of them as adulterers in the mansion of the damned, and thus cast an indelible blemish on the honour of an illustrious family, to which he had been obliged for his safety and for a quiet and splendid retreat; and what is more remarkable (but for what reason is unknown) he immerged in Hell, and in the most infamous part of it, Brunetto Latini, who had been his preceptor and instructed him in his tender years with more than paternal affection.

Those who found grace were only confined in Purgatory, which, according to our Catholic notions, is a place of redemption, and those that are fortunate enough to be sent there are certain of arriving, soon or late, at celestial glory. But it is remarkable that Dante took the liberty to depart from the general belief of the church in which he was born and educated, since the first person he meets in Purgatory is a pagan, Cato of Utica.

In the third and last part of his poem, in which he paints Paradise, he exalts all his friends and all the famous men and great writers of Christian antiquity, his favourites; but above all them one Beatrix, the lady he was in love with, whom he feigns to be his guide from one circle of glory to another.

If I was desirous of finding some resemblance between Homer and Dante, I might say that his poem is an imitation of the *Odyssey*, since it is only the travels of a person over Hell, Purgatory, and Paradise, as the *Odyssey* is the travel of Ulysses through many seas and lands, poetically described. But this resemblance, which has been carried very far by some Italians, hath always seemed to me very much strained. So I will content myself with only extracting some passages from this Tuscan poet to give an idea of his poetical genius, without drawing by vain ostentation of erudition any parallel between him and the Greek.

The principal hero in the poem is Dante himself, if the shade of Virgil (who acts the same part for him as Mentor does for Telemachus) may not dispute the first place.

He begins his poem with relating that in the strength of his age he found himself in a horrid forest among terrible wild beasts, who, seeing him, came forward with open mouths to devour him; to avoid them he fled over a desert plain; there he met the shade of Virgil, who conducted him to the gate of Tartarus, over which these tremendous words were written:

> Per me si va nella cittá dolente,
> per me si va nell'eterno dolore, ecc.
>
> [*Inf.* III, 1–9]

Thus englished: "Through me lies the way to the doleful city. Through me lies the way to everlasting woe. Through me lies the way to those doomed to perdition. Eternal justice, omnipotent power, consummate wisdom, and all-creating love moved the Almighty to make me. Me, except his angels, the eldest of created things. I am to all eternity. Ye who enter here, quit hope for ever."

Not far from the infernal gate he comes to a place where the souls of indolent and slothful people are imprisoned, together with those angels who kept themselves neutral in the war between the Omnipotent and his rebel angels:

> Quivi sospiri, pianti ed alti guai
> risonavan per l'aer senza stelle, ecc.
> [*Inf.* III, 22 ff.]

> There sighs and tears and loud-resounding woes filled the dark air unblest with even a star. There different languages all horrid and confused, complaining words, accents of rage, loud shreeks and whispered anguish, heightened with clashing hands, form a harsh tumult in the ever-darkened air. Such is the sound as when a whirl-wind's furious blast drives the loose sands in clouds of whirling dust. Those have no hope of death, and their dull lives are spent in such a shameful obscurity, that every other fate they wish and envy. Lost in oblivion, their whole lives are blanks. Eternal mercy and justice disdain them. Let us not speak of them, but look and pass.

From thence, Dante and Virgil come to the infernal river, on the other side of which are the dreary habitations of the wicked. On the shore of the fatal flood stand innumerable souls waiting to be wafted to the opposite side:

> . . . quell'anime, ch'eran lasse e nude,
> cangiár colore e dibattero i denti, ecc.
> [*Inf.* III. 100 ff.]

> Those shivering souls moved slowly on. Pale were their looks and their trembling teeth clashed against each other. . . . Blaspheming God, execrating their parents, their country, their fore-fathers, the hour of their birth and the whole human race. Then clustering all in crowds with horrid yells, they reach the cursed shore, to which every mortal is doomed who fears not God.

Virgil and Dante pass the river also and enter the infernal regions, in the description of which the poet exerts a wonderful imagination. He divides Hell into many places of punishment, each of which contains a distinct class of sinners and transgressors of the laws of God. But his usual uncatholic vein transports him into a corner of it, where there is a place designed for the souls of the ancient sages and pagan heroes, who were virtuous and pious when in the world. The place, although it is in Hell, is nevertheless most delightful; and there he finds that Brutus, who delivered Rome from the tyranny of the Tarquins, with Socrates, Plato, Anaxagoras, Thales, Hipocrates, Tully, Lavinia, Lucretia, Portia and many other ancient men and women, who dwell there in happiness.

The episodes of the poem in this part, called *Hell*, are made up of several stories related by the damned, one of which I will transcribe.

Dante meets with a Florentine count, named Ugolino, who is furiously gnawing the scull of a human body. He asks him the cause of his canine rage, and

> La bocca sollevò dal fero pasto
> quel peccator, forbendola a' capelli, ecc.
> [*Inf*. XXXIII, 1 ff.]

Thus englished: "Then the fell wretch, taking his mouth from the horrible repast, and wiping it with the hairs of that head, that with his teeth he had all crashed behind, began:—Must I then renew my black despair and speak what tears my heart but in reflection only? Yet, if my words will fix eternal infamy on the memory of the villain, whose head I am gnawing thus, I shall speak and weep at once. . . . Know then that I am the count Ugolino, and this scull that thou beholdest was once the archbishop Ruggieri's. . . ."

The count then succinctly relates when and in what manner he was cast in a horrible dungeon with his four sons by the above-mentioned archbishop and thus goes on:

> Quand'io fui desto innanzi la dimane,
> pianger senti' fra'l sonno i miei figliuoli, ecc.

Thus englished:

> The next day, when it was yet scarce light, I heard my children weeping before their sleep was well dissipated. They were in the same place with me, and desired me to give them bread. Ah, if thou weepest not at the reflection of what I felt that cruel

moment, thy heart must be proof to every sentiment of compassion.... The fourth day being come, Gaddo falling extended at my feet cried:—My father, why do not you help me?—and died. The other three expired one after the other between the fifth and sixth days, famished as thou seest me now. And I, being seized with blindness, began to go groping upon them with my hands and feet. I continued calling them by their names during three days after they were dead. Then hunger vanquished my grief!—Saying this, with eyes all fierce and wild, he took again that detested scull between his teeth, crashing it as a hungry mastiff does his prey.

The poet rap'd as in an enthusiastic fit of rage by the horrible relation of Ugolino, closeth this story with this most heavy malediction on the city of Pisa, of which the barbarous Ruggieri was archbishop:

> Ahi Pisa, vituperio delle genti
> del bel paese lá, dove il sí sona! ecc.

Thus englished: "Ah Pisa, disgrace of the blest Italian land! since thy neighbors are slow in punishing thee, oh may Capraia and Gorgona move from their foundations and blocking up the river Arno, force back its streams to overwhelm the cursed race in thee!"

I have cited these few passages of Dante not only to give the English reader, who is not acquainted with him in the original, some idea of his poetry; but also to shew him that the Italian is falsely accused of effeminacy by Mr. Voltaire, or rather by those from whom he has humbly copied this opinion. The verses I have transcribed are so little effeminate, that every one who hears them read by a person who gives them their proper emphasis, although they do not understand them, will be convinced by the sound that they are as strong and sonorous as those in any other language. And if the reader would have a still greater proof of the strength of our tongùe, he needs only read the thirty-three first lines of the sixth canto of that poem, which I do not quote, to avoid too great length, or rather, because I believe it is impossible to translate them with energy equal to the original.

To sum up all I have to say on this head, the thirty-four cantos of Dante's *Hell* are wrote with more virility of thought and vigour of style than any other poem ancient or modern; and in this particular no nation has produced its equal, except the *Paradise lost* of Milton. The most nervous scenes of the great Corneille himself (a poet the least effeminate among the French) do not come near the strength of Dante.

I shall not dwell long on those two parts of the poem, called *Purgatory* and *Paradise;* but only say that the thoughts and style of *Purgatory* have neither too much strength nor too much softness. It is one continued picture of supportable grief; and supportable, because it is mixed with hope, according to the idea the Catholics have of that place. But there is no poet in Italy (deservedly called the mother of sweet poets) so sweet, so harmonious and so affecting as Dante in his description of *Paradise.* Nor is this a French exaggeration for which any allowance is to be made: it is a certain truth, that Petrarca himself, in the most pathetic descriptions of his passion for the beautiful Laura, does not equal the sweetness of the hymns which Dante makes the angels and blessed spirits sing in the third part of his poem. All the images, all the comparisons, all the descriptions of this part are as they ought to be; that is to say the very reverse of those of his *Hell*, as his *Purgatory* judiciously partakes of both.

I shall not quote any of the lines to prove the truth of what I say, because I do not think it possible to give them the same sweetness in a translation as they have in the original. All the world allows that the music of our syllables cannot be transfused into another language. But there have been so many editions of this poem in Italy and in other countries, that it is not difficult to find it; and every stranger may easily convince himself of what I say, by reading it himself, or if he does not understand Italian, making it only be read to him.

However, I will not neglect to take notice of two remarkable passages of this ancient poet, for the sake of a relation they have to the modern system of astronomy.

One of these passages is in the first canto of the *Purgatory*, to illustrate which I shall transcribe part of a letter written from Spain in the year 1500 by the famous Amerigo Vespucci of Florence to Lorenzo di Pierfrancesco d' Medici after his return from the countries he had discovered, which were called America from his name. These are Vespucci's words in English:[1]

> We sailed so far under the torrid-zone towards the east, that we found ourselves under the equinoxial line, having both the

[1] [Baretti first gives the Italian version.]

poles at the extremities of our horizon. We passed the line six degrees and quite lost the north-star. We could scarcely perceive the stars of the lesser bear. Desirous to be the discoverer and namer of the pole-star in the other hemisphere, I lost many times my sleep in contemplating the stars in the opposite pole, to discover which of them had least motion. Yet, notwithstanding the troublesome nights I had and the instruments I used, that is to say the quadrant and the astrolabe, I could not perceive any star that had less than ten degrees of motion. So that I had not the satisfaction of naming any one. While I was busying myself in these observations, I remembered a passage in our poet Dante, in the first canto of *Purgatory*, when feigning to ascend from this hemisphere, he finds himself in the other and describing the anthartic pole says:

I turned to the right-hand and fixed my eyes in the other pole, where I saw four stars that no person had even seen but our first parents. The sky smiled with their lustre. Oh! unhappy north that art deprived of beholding them!

In my judgment the poet in these verses intends by the four stars to describe the pole of the other firmament. And I do not despair but Dante's opinion will be found to be true, because I observed four stars in the form of an almond, that had but little motion. And if God gives me life and health, I hope to return to that hemisphere, and not come back without marking out the pole.

Although Dante, as appears by his poem, knew as much of astronomy as it was possible to know before the appearance of Galileo and Newton, nevertheless I cannot help thinking it strange, that he should have any certainty of the constellation of the opposite pole, at a time when we had but slight notions either of the circular or of the oblate figure of this globe, and were not quite sure in our hemisphere of the existence of an opposite one. But it is not without some reason that Lorenzo Giacomini, a learned Tuscan, in a dissertation upon poetical fury, wondered that Dante, by mere force of enthusiasm, should have thus hit upon a truth so remote from the knowledge of his time, as he has done in the abovequoted verses, that afforded matter for speculation to so great and singular a man as Vespucci.

The other passage is the following, in the 28th. canto of *Paradise*, where after having poetically said that the globes form a circle round the throne of the divinity, and are moved and ruled by the Dominations, Virtues, Principalities, Powers, Archangels and Angels, divided into several Hyerarchies according to their degrees of Dignity, he adds:

Quest'ordini di su tutti rimirano
e di giú vincon sí, che verso Dio
tutti tirati sono, e tutti tirano.

Thus englished: "These globes arranged in order divinely wonderful, all tend upwards by attraction, and downward by their gravity. They at once attract and are attracted towards God, the everlasting sun."

The abbot Tagliazucchi, a great mathematician and professor of the Greek and Tuscan languages in the University of Turin, who died two years ago and of whom I had the good fortune to be many years a pupil, endeavoured to prove in a dissertation that he wrote *On the manner of educating youth in the belle-letters*, that in this triplet of Dante are clearly expressed sir Isaac Newton's notions of attraction. I will leave the English reader to judge if my honoured preceptor was in the right in his assertion.

If Dante is wonderful in painting the passions and making lively representations of objects, as in my opinion may be plainly seen by the above-quoted passages of his *Inferno*, he is still more so in the justness of his similes, which are the nerves and soul of the poetry. There no poet is superior, or even equal to him.

Another of his peculiar beauties I must take notice of: and that is, his having interspersed in his poem several words, phrases and whole lines and triplets in pure Latin. This he hath done with infinite grace and judgment, which might perhaps appear ridiculous in any other of the living languages; but in Italian, and particularly in Dante's poem, it has a beautiful effect and adds great force and dignity to his style, not only because Dante knew well how to select those Latin words and phrases which have a similitude of sound with the Tuscan, but also because no other of the living languages hath so much affinity with the Latin tongue as ours hath. And it is observable also that what Latin he hath spread through his poem, is all taken from the sacred writings, in the style of which he hath always endeavoured to write.

I will not pretend to say that Dante has no defects. He is justly taxed with meanness of style in some few places and blamed with having made a medley of names and fables of the heathen mythology with the names and stories most venerable and holy of the Christian religion. But this fault may be extenuated if we reflect that he wrote in a time when they had no other models of good poetry but the works of the pagans, with which he was so well acquainted, that he could not avoid to fill his fancy with their thoughts and phrases. That spirit of method and geometry that hath taken possession, for more than an age, of the poetry of the principal European nations, hath been the consequence of rigid observation and exact criticism, and could not be found in the time of Dante, as he was the first great poet and great writer. Before him Italy had not produced a man worthy of immortality, by works of genius, after the fall of the empire of our predecessors.

To these poetic faults of Dante may be added a moral one: that is the having ridiculed and satirized, with as much bitterness as Luther himself, the priests and friars and generally all the supporters of the church in which he lived. Too many of our poets who came after him followed his imprudent and dangerous example.

II

THOMAS WARTON

Dante's Italian Poem

Nothing more fully illustrates and ascertains the respective merits and genius of different poets, than a juxtaposition of their performances on similar subjects. Having examined at large Sackville's Descent into Hell, for the sake of throwing a still stronger light on his manner of treating a fiction which gives so large a scope to fancy, I shall employ the remainder of this Section in setting before my reader a general view of Dante's Italian poem, entitled COMMEDIA, containing a description of Hell, Paradise, and Purgatory, and written about the year 1310. In the mean time, I presume that most of my readers will recollect and apply the sixth Book of Virgil: to which, however, it may be necessary to refer occasionally.

Although I have before insinuated that Dante has in his poem used the ghost of Virgil for a mystagogue, in imitation of Tully, who in the SOMNIUM Scipionis supposes Scipio to have been shewn the other world by his ancestor Africanus, yet at the same time in the invention of his introduction, he seems to have had an eye on the exordium of an old forgotten Florentine poem called TESORETTO, written in *Frottola*, or a short irregular measure, exhibiting a cyclopede of theoretic and practic philosophy, and composed by his preceptor Brunetto Latini about the year 1270. Brunetto supposes himself lost in a wood, at the foot of a mountain covered with animals, flowers, plants, and fruits of every species, and subject to the supreme command of a wonderful Lady, whom he thus describes. "Her head touched the heavens, which served at once for a veil and an ornament. The sky grew dark or serene at her voice, and her arms extended to the extremities of the earth." This bold personification, one of the earliest of the rude ages of poetry, is NATURE. She converses

Reprinted from *The History of English Poetry from the Close of the Eleventh to the Commencement of the Eighteenth Century* (London: Thomas Tegg, 1824), 4: 60–78.

with the poet, and describes the creation of the world. She enters upon a most unphilosophical and indeed unpoetical detail of the physical system: develops the head of man, and points out the seat of intelligence and of memory. From physics she proceeds to morals: but her principles are here confined to theology and the laws of the church, which she couches in technical rhymes.

Dante, like his master Brunetto, is bewildered in an unfrequented forest. He attempts to climb a mountain, whose summit is illuminated by the rising sun. A furious leopard, pressed by hunger, and a lion, at whose aspect the *air is affrighted*, accompanied by a she-wolf, oppose his progress; and force him to fly precipitately into the profundities of a pathless valley, where, says the poet, *the sun was silent.*

> Mi ripingeva là, dove il Sol tace.
> [*Inf.* I, 60.]

In the middle of a vast solitude he perceives a spectre, of whom he implores pity and help. The spectre hastens to his cries: it was the shade of Virgil, whom Beatrix, Dante's mistress, had sent, to give him courage, and to guide him into the regions of hell. Virgil begins a long discourse with Dante; and expostulates with him for chusing to wander through the rough obscurities of a barren and dreary vale, when the top of the neighbouring mountain afforded every delight. The conversation of Virgil, and the name of Beatrix, by degrees dissipate the fears of the poet, who explains his situation. He returns to himself, and compares this revival of his strength and spirits to a flower smitten by the frost of a night, which again lifts its shrinking head, and expands its vivid colours, at the first gleamings of the morning-sun.

> Quali i fioretti dal notturno gelo
> Chinati e chiusi, . . .
> [*Inf.* II, 127–28]

Dante, under the conduct of Virgil, penetrates hell. But he does not on this occasion always avail himself of Virgil's descriptions and mythologies. At least the formation of Dante's imageries are of another school. He feigns his hell to be a prodigious and almost bottomless abyss, which from its aperture to its lowest depth preserves a rotund shape: or rather, an immense perpendicular cavern, which opening as it descends into different circles, forms so many distinct subterraneous regions. We are struck with horror at the commencement of this dreadful adventure.

The first object which the poet perceives is a gate of brass, over which were inscribed in characters of a dark hue, *di colore oscuro,* these verses.

> Per me si và nella città dolente:
> Per me si và nell' eterno dolore:
> Per me si và trà la perduta gente.
> Giustizia mosse il mio alto fattore:
> Fecemi la divina potestate,
> La somma Sapienzia, e 'l primo Amore.
> Dinanzi a me non fur cose create
> Se non eterne, ed io eterno duro:[1]
> Lasciate ogni speranza voi ch' entrate.
> [*Inf.* III, 1–9]

That is, "By me is the way to the woeful city. By me is the way to the eternal pains. By me is the way to the damned race. My mighty maker was divine Justice and Power, the Supreme Wisdom, and the First Love. Before me nothing was created. If not eternal, I shall eternally remain. Put away all hope, ye that enter."

There is a severe solemnity in these abrupt and comprehensive sentences, and they are a striking preparation to the scenes that ensue. But the idea of such an inscription on the brazen portal of hell, was suggested to Dante by books of chivalry; in which the gate of an impregnable castle, is often inscribed with words importing the dangers or wonders to be found within. Over the door of every chamber in Spenser's necromantic palace of Busyrane, was written a threat to the champions who presumed to attempt to enter. This total exclusion of hope from hell, here so finely introduced and so forcibly expressed, was probably remembered by Milton, a disciple of Dante, where he describes

> Regions of sorrow, dolefull shades, where peace
> And rest can never dwell, HOPE NEVER COMES
> THAT COMES TO ALL.
> [*Par. L.* I, 65]

[1] [Warton has *duro eterno,* which destroys the rhyme.]

I have not time to follow Dante regularly through his dialogues and adventures with the crouds of ghosts, antient and modern, which he meets in the course of this infernal journey. In these interviews, there is often much of the party and politics of his own times, and of allusion to recent facts. Nor have I leisure particularly to display our author's punishments and phantoms. I observe in general, that the ground-work of his hell is classical, yet with many Gothic and extravagant innovations. The burning lakes, the fosses, and fiery towers which surround the city of DIS, and the three Furies which wait at its entrance, are touched with new strokes. The Gorgons, the Hydra, the Chimera, Cerberus, the serpent of Lerna, and the rest of Virgil's, or rather Homer's, infernal apparitions, are dilated with new touches of the terrible, and sometimes made ridiculous by the addition of comic or incongruous circumstances, yet without any intention of burlesque. Because Virgil had mentioned the Harpies in a single word only, in one of the loathsome groves which Dante passes, consisting of trees whose leaves are black, and whose knotted boughs are hard as iron, the Harpies build their nests.

> Non fronde verdi, ma di color fosco,
> Non rami schietti, ma nodosi e 'nvolti,
> Non pomi v' eran, ma stecchi con tosco.
>
> [*Inf.* XIII, 4–6]

Cacus, whom Virgil had called *Semifer* in his seventh book, appears in the shape of a Centaur covered with curling snakes, and on whose neck is perched a dragon hovering with expanded wings. It is supposed Dante took the idea of his INFERNO from a magnificent nightly representation of hell, exhibited by the pope in honour of the bishop of Ostia on the river Arno at Florence, in the year 1304. This is mentioned by the Italian critics in extenuation of Dante's choice of so strange a subject. But why should we attempt to excuse any absurdity in the writings or manners of the middle ages? Dante chose this subject as a reader of Virgil and Homer. The religious MYSTERY represented on the river Arno, however magnificent, was perhaps a spectacle purely orthodox, and perfectly conformable to the ideas of the church. And if we allow that it might hint the subject, with all its inconsistencies, it never could have furnished any considerable part of this wonderful compound of classical and romantic fancy, of pagan and christian theology, of real and fictitious history, of tragical and comic incidents, of familiar and heroic manners, and of satirical and sublime poetry. But the grossest improprieties of this poem discover an originality of invention, and its absurdities often border on sublimity. We are surprised that a poet should write one hundred cantos on hell, paradise and purgatory. But this prolixity is partly owing to the want of art and method; and is common to all early compositions, in which every thing is related circumstantially and without rejection, and not in those general terms which are used by modern writers.

Dante has beautifully enlarged Virgil's short comparison of the souls lingering on the banks of Lethe, to the numerous leaves falling from the trees in Autumn.

> Come d'autunno si levan le foglie
> L'una appresso dell'altra, infin che il ramo
> Vede alla terra tutte le sue spoglie,
> Similmente il mal seme d'Adamo;
> Gittansi di quel lito ad una ad una,
> Per cenni, come augel per suo richiamo.
> [*Inf.* III, 112–17]

In the Fields inhabited by unhappy lovers he sees Semiramis, Achilles, Paris, and Tristan, or sir Tristram. One of the old Italian commentators on this poem says, that the last was an English knight born in *Cornovaglio*, or Cornwall, a city of England.

Among many others of his friends, he sees Francisca the daughter of Guido di Polenta, in whose palace Dante died at Ravenna, and Paulo one of the sons of Malatesta lord of Rimini. This lady fell in love with Paulo; the passion was mutual, and she was betrothed to him in marriage: but her family chose rather that she should be married to Lanciotto, Paulo's eldest brother. This match had the most fatal consequences. The injured lovers could not dissemble or stifle their affection: they were surprised, and both assassinated by Lanciotto. Dante finds the shades of these distinguished victims of an unfortunate attachment at a distance from the rest, in a region of his INFERNO desolated by the most violent tempests. He accosts them both, and Francisca relates their history: yet the conversation is carried on with some difficulty, on account of the impetuosity of the storm which was perpetually raging. Dante, who from many circumstances of his own amours, appears to have possessed the most refined sensibilities about the delicacies of love, inquires in what manner, when in the other world, they first communicated their passion to each other. Francisca answers, that they were one day sitting together, and reading the romance of LANCELOT; where two lovers were represented in the same critical situation with themselves. Their changes of colour and countenance, while they were reading, often tacitly betrayed their yet undiscovered feelings. When they came to that passage in the romance, where the lovers, after many tender approaches, are gradually drawn by one uniform reciprocation of involuntary attraction to kiss each other, the book dropped from their hands. By a sudden impulse and an irresistible sympathy, they are tempted to do the same. Here was the commencement of their tragical history.

> Noi leggevam un giorno per diletto
> Di Lancilotto, come amor lo strinse:
> Soli eravamo, e senza alcun sospetto.
> Per più fiate gli occhi ci sospinse
> Quella lettura, e scolorocci il viso:
> Ma solo un punto fu quel che ci vinse.
> Quando leggemmo il disiato riso
> Esser baciato da cotanto amante,
> Questi, che mai da me non fia diviso,
> La bocca mi baciò tutto tremante:
> Galeotto fu il libro e chi lo scrisse:
> Quel giorno più non vi leggemmo avante.
>
> [*Inf.* V, 127–38]

But this picture, in which nature, sentiment, and the graces are concerned, I have to contrast with scenes of a very different nature. Salvator Rosa has here borrowed the pencil of Correggio. Dante's beauties are not of the soft and gentle kind.

> –Through many a dark and dreary vale
> They pass'd, and many a region dolorous,
> O'er many a frozen, many a fiery Alp.
>
> [*Par. L.*, II, 618]

A hurricane suddenly rising on the banks of the river Styx is thus described.

E già venia su per le torbid'onde
Un fracasso d'un suon pien di spavento,
Per cui tremavano ambo e due le sponde;
Non altrimenti fatto che d'un vento
Impetuoso per gli avversi ardori,
Che fier la selva, e senza alcun rattento
Li rami schianta, abbatte, e porta fuori.
Dinanzi polveroso va superbo,
E fa fuggir le fiere e li pastori.
[*Inf.* IX, 64–72]

Dante and his mystagogue meet the monster Geryon. He has the face of a man with a mild and benign aspect, but his human form ends in a serpent with voluminous tail of immense length, terminated by a sting, which he brandishes like a scorpion. His hands are rough with bristles and scales. His breast, back, and sides have all the rich colours displayed in the textures of Tartary and Turkey, or in the labours of Arachne. To speak in Spenser's language, he is,

A dragon, horrible and bright.
[*F. Q.* i, ix, 52]

No monster of romance is more savage or superb.

Lo dosso, e'l petto, ed amendue le coste,
Dipinte avea di nodi, e di rotelle.
Con più color sommesse e soppraposte,
Non fer mai drappo Tartari nè Turchi,
Nè fur tai tele per Aragne imposte.[2]
[*Inf.* XVII, 14–18]

The conformation of this heterogeneous beast, as a fabulous hell is the subject, perhaps immediately gave rise to one of the *formidable shapes* which sate on either side of the gates of hell in Milton. Although the fiction is founded in the classics.

The one seem'd woman to the waste and fair,
But ended foul in many a scaly fold
Voluminous and vast, a serpent arm'd
With mortal sting.
[*Par. L.* II, 649]

[2] [Dante says that he lay on the banks of a river like a Beaver, the Castor. But this foolish comparison is affectedly introduced by our author for a display of his natural knowledge from Pliny, or rather from the *Tesoro* of his master Brunetto.]

Virgil, seeming to acknowledge him as an old acquaintance, mounts the back of Geryon. At the same time Dante mounts, whom Virgil places before, "that you may not," says he, "be exposed to the monster's venomous sting." Virgil then commands Geryon not to move too rapidly, "for, consider, what a new burthen you carry!" . . .

In this manner they travel in the air through Tartarus: and from the back of the monster Geryon, Dante looks down on the burning lake of Phlegethon. This imagery is at once great and ridiculous. But much later Italian poets have fallen into the same strange mixture. In this horrid situation says Dante,

> Io sentia già dalla man destra il gorgo
> Far sotto noi un orribile scroscio:
> Perchè con gli occhi in giù la testa sporgo.[3]
>
> Allor fu'io più timido allo scoscio:
> Perocch'io vidi fuochi, e sentii pianti;
> Ond'io tremando tutto mi raccoscio.
> [*Inf.* XVII, 118–21]

This airy journey is copied from the flight of Icarus and Phaeton, and at length produced the Ippogrifo of Ariosto. Nor is it quite improbable, that Milton, although he has greatly improved and dignified the idea, might have caught from hence his fiction of Satan soaring over the infernal abyss. At length Geryon, having circuited the air like a faulcon towering without prey, deposits his burthen and vanishes.

While they are wandering along the banks of Phlegethon, as the twilight of evening approaches, Dante suddenly hears the sound of a horn more loud than thunder, or the horn of Orlando. . . . He descries through the gloom, what he thinks to be many high and vast towers, *molte alte torri*. These are the giants who warred against heaven, standing in a row, half concealed within and half extant without an immense abyss or pit.

> Gli orribili giganti, cui minaccia
> Giove del cielo ancora quando tuona.
> [*Inf.* XXXI, 44–45]

But Virgil informs Dante that he is deceived by appearances, and that these are not towers but the giants.

[3] [Warton has *sporsi.*]

Sappi che non son torri ma giganti,
E son nel pozzo intorno dalla ripa
Dall' umbilico in giuso tutti quanti.
[*Ibid.*, 31–33]

One of them cries out to Dante with horrible voice. Another, Ephialtes, is cloathed in iron and bound with huge chains. Dante wishes to see Briareus: he is answered, that he lies in an interior cavern biting his chain. Immediately Ephialties arose from another cavern, and shook himself like an earthquake.

Non fu tremoto già tanto rubesto,
Che scotesse una torre così forte,
Come Fialte a scotersi fu presto.
[*Ibid.*, 106–8]

Dante views the horn which had sounded so vehemently hanging by a leathern thong from the neck of one of the giants. Antaeus, whose body stands ten ells high from the pit, is commanded by Virgil to advance. They both mount on his shoulders, and are thus carried about Cocytus. The giant, says the poet, moved off with us like the mast of a ship. One cannot help observing, what has been indeed already hinted, how judiciously Milton, in a similar argument, has retained the just beauties, and avoided the childish or ludicrous excesses of these bold inventions. At the same time we may remark, how Dante has sometimes heightened, and sometimes diminished by improper additions or misrepresentations, the legitimate descriptions of Virgil.

One of the torments of the Damned in Dante's INFERNO, is the punishment of being eternally confined in lakes of ice.

Eran l'ombre dolenti nella ghiaccia
Mettendo i denti in nota di cicogna.
[*Inf.* XXXII, 35–36]

The ice is described to be like that of the Danube or Tanais. This species of infernal torment, which is neither directly warranted by scripture, nor suggested in the systems of the Platonic fabulists, and which has been adopted both by Shakespeare and Milton, has its origin in the legendary hell of the monks. The hint seems to have been taken from an obscure text in the Book of JOB, dilated by Saint Jerom and the early commentators. The torments of hell, in which the punishment by cold is painted at large, had formed a visionary romance, under the name of Saint Patrick's Purgatory or Cave, long before Dante wrote. The venerable Bede, who lived in the seventh century, has framed a future mansion of existence for departed souls with this mode of torture. In the hands of Dante it has assumed many fantastic and grotesque circumstances, which make us laugh and shudder at the same time.

In another department, Dante represents some of his criminals rolling themselves in human ordure. If his subject led him to such a description, he might at least have used decent expressions. But his diction is not here less sordid than his imagery. I am almost afraid to transcribe this gross passage, even in the disguise of the old Tuscan phraseology.

> Quindi giù nel fosso
> Vidi gente attuffata in uno sterco,
> Che dagli uman privati parea mosso:
> Et mentre ch'io là giù con l'occhio cerco,
> Vidi un, col capo sì da merda lordo,
> Che non *parea s'era laico, o cherco.*
> [*Inf.* XVIII, 112–17]

The humour of the last line does not make amends for the nastiness of the image.

It is not to be supposed, that a man of strong sense and genius, whose understanding had been cultivated by a most exact education, and who had passed his life in the courts of sovereign princes, would have indulged himself in these disgusting fooleries, had he been at all apprehensive that his readers would have been disgusted. But rude and early poets describe every thing. They follow the public manners: and if they are either obscene or indelicate, it should be remembered that they wrote before obscenity or indelicacy became offensive.

Some of the Guilty are made objects of contempt by a transformation into beastly or ridiculous shapes. This was from the fable of Circe. In others, the human figure is rendered ridiculous by distortion. There is one set of criminals whose faces are turned round towards their backs,

> che il pianto de gli occhi
> Le natiche bagnava per lo fesso.
> [*Inf.* XX, 23–24]

But Dante has displayed more true poetry in describing a real event than in the best of his fictions. This is in the story of Ugolino count of Pisa, the subject of a very capital picture by Reynolds. . . . It is not improbable, that the shades of unfortunate men, who, described under peculiar situations and with their proper attributes, are introduced relating at large their histories in hell to Dante, might have given the hint to Boccace's book DE CASIBUS VIRORUM ILLUSTRIUM, On the Misfortunes of Illustrious Personages, the original model of the MIRROUR OF MAGISTRATES.

Dante's PURGATORY is not on the whole less fantastic than his HELL. As his hell was a vast perpendicular cavity in the earth, he supposes Purgatory to be a cylindric mass elevated to a prodigious height. At intervals are recesses projecting from the outside of the cylinder. In these recesses, some higher and some lower, the wicked expiate their crimes, according to the proportion of their guilt. From one department they pass to another by steps of stone exceedingly steep. On the top of the whole, or the summit of Purgatory, is a platform adorned with trees and vegetables of every kind. This is the Terrestrial Paradise, which has been transported hither we know not how, and which forms an avenue to the Paradise Celestial. It is extraordinary that some of the Gothic painters should not have given us this subject.

Dante describes not disagreeably the first region which he traverses on leaving hell. The heavens are tinged with sapphire, and the star of love, or the sun, makes all the orient laugh. He sees a venerable sage approach. This is a Cato of Utica, who, astonished to see a living man in the mansion of ghosts, questions Dante and Virgil about the business which brought them hither. Virgil answers: and Cato advises Virgil to wash Dante's face, which was soiled with the smoke of hell, and to cover his head with one of the reeds which grew on the borders of the neighbouring river. Virgil takes his advice; and having gathered one reed, sees another spring up in its place. This is the golden bough of the Eneid, *uno avulso non deficit alter*. The shades also, as in Virgil, crowd to be ferried over Styx: but an angel performs the office of Charon, admitting some into the boat, and rejecting others. This confusion of fable and religion destroys the graces of the one and the majesty of the other.

Through adventures and scenes more strange and wild than any in the Pilgrim's Progress, we at length arrive at the twenty-first Canto. A concussion of the earth announces the deliverance of the soul from Purgatory. This is the soul of Statius, the favourite poet of the dark ages. Although a very improper companion for Virgil, he immediately joins our adventurers, and accompanies them in their progress. It is difficult to discover what pagan or christian idea regulates Dante's dispensation of rewards and punishments. Statius passes from Purgatory to Paradise, Cato remains in the place of expiation, and Virgil is condemned to eternal torments.

Dante meets his old acquaintance Forese, a debauchee of Florence. On finishing the conversation, Forese asks Dante when he shall have the pleasure of seeing him again. This question in Purgatory is diverting enough. Dante answers with much serious gravity, "I know not the time of death: but it cannot be too near. Look back on the troubles in which my country is involved!" The dispute between the pontificate and the empire appears to have been the predominant topic of Dante's mind. This circumstance has filled Dante's poem with strokes of satire. Every reader of Voltaire must remember that lively writer's paraphrase from the INFERNO, of the story of count Guido, in which are these inimitable lines. A Franciscan friar abandoned to Beelzebub thus exclaims:

> . . . "Monsieur de Lucifer,
> Je suis un saint, voyez ma robe grise:
> Je fus absous par le chef de l'Église."
> "J'aurai toujours," répondit le démon,
> "Un grand respect pour l'absolution;
> On est lavé de ses vieilles sottises,
> Pourvu qu'après autres ne soient commises.
> J'ai fait souvent cette distinction
> À tes pareils: et grâce à l'Italie
> Le Diable fait la théologie.
> Il dit et rit: je ne répliquai rien
> À Belzebuth, il raisonait trop bien.
> Lors il m'empoigne, et d'un bras roide et ferme
> Il appliqua sur ma triste épiderme
> Vingt coups de fouet, dont bien fort il me cuit:
> Que Dieu le rende à Boniface Huit.
>
> [*Dictionnaire Philosophique*, art. Dante]

Dante thus translated would have had many more readers than at present. I take this opportunity of remarking, that our author's perpetual reference to recent facts and characters is in imitation of Virgil, yet with this very material difference: The persons recognised in Virgil's sixth book, for instance the chiefs of the Trojan war, are the cotemporaries of the hero not of the poet. The truth is, Dante's poem is a satirical history of his own times.

Dante sees some of the ghosts of Purgatory advancing forward, more meagre and emaciated than the rest. He asks how this could happen in a place where all live alike without nourishment. Virgil quotes the example of Meleager, who wasted with a firebrand, on the gradual extinction of which his life depended. He also produces the comparison of a mirror reflecting a figure. These obscure explications do not satisfy the doubts of Dante. Statius, for his better instruction, explains how a child grows in the womb of the mother, how it is enlarged, and by degrees receives life and intellect. The drift of our author is apparent in these profound illustrations. He means to shew his skill in a sort of metaphysical anatomy. We see something of this in the TESORETTO of Brunetto. Unintelligible solutions of a similar sort, drawn from a frivolous and mysterious philosophy, mark the writers of Dante's age.

The PARADISE of Dante, the third part of this poem, resembles his PURGATORY. Its fictions, and its allegories which suffer by being explained, are all conceived in the same chimerical spirit. The poet successively views the glory of the saints, of angels, of the holy Virgin, and at last of God himself.

Heaven as well as hell, among the monks, had its legendary description; which it was heresy to disbelieve, and which was formed on perversions or misinterpretations of scripture. Our author's vision ends with the Deity, and we know not by what miraculous assistance he returns to earth.

It must be allowed, that the scenes of Virgil's sixth book have many fine strokes of the terrible. But Dante's colouring is of a more gloomy temperature. There is a sombrous cast in his imagination: and he has given new shades of horror to the classical hell. We may say of Dante, that

——Hell
GROWS DARKER at his FROWN.——
[*Par. L.*, II, 720]

The sensations of fear impressed by the Roman poet are less harassing to the repose of the mind: they have a more equable and placid effect. The terror of Virgil's tremendous objects is diminished by correctness of composition and elegance of style. We are reconciled to his Gorgons and Hydras, by the grace of expression, and the charms of versification.

In the mean time, it may seem a matter of surprise, that the Italian poets of the thirteenth century, who restored, admired, and studied the classics, did not imitate their beauties. But while they possessed the genuine models of antiquity, their unnatural and eccentric habits of mind and manners, their attachments to system, their scholastic theology, superstition, ideal love, and above all their chivalry, had corrupted every true principle of life and literature, and consequently prevented the progress of taste and propriety. They could not conform to the practices and notions of their own age, and to the ideas of the antients, at the same time. They were dazzled with the imageries of Virgil and Homer, which they could not always understand or apply: or which they saw through the mist of prejudice and misconception. Their genius having once taken a false direction, when recalled to copy a just pattern, produced only constraint and affectation, a distorted and unpleasing resemblance. The early Italian poets disfigured, instead of adorning their works, by attempting to imitate the classics. The charms which we so much admire in Dante, do not belong to the Greeks and Romans. They are derived from another origin, and must be traced back to a different stock. Nor is it at the same time less surprising, that the later Italian poets, in more enlightened times, should have paid so respectful a compliment to Dante as to acknowledge no other model, and with his excellencies, to transcribe and perpetuate all his extravagancies.

III

WILLIAM HAZLITT

Sismondi and the Trecentisti

We have hitherto followed M. Sismondi in his account of the progress of modern literature, before the Italian language had been made the vehicle of poetical composition, and before the revival of letters. The details which he gives on the last subject, and the extraordinary picture he presents of the pains and labour undergone by the scholars of that day in recovering antient manuscripts, and the remains of antient art, are highly interesting. It is from this important event, and also from the work of Dante, the first lasting monument of modern genius, that we should strictly date the origin of modern literature; and, indeed, it would not be difficult to show, that it is still the emulation of the antients, working, indeed, on very different materials, from different principles, and with very different results, that has been the great moving spring of the grandest efforts of human genius in our own times. Our author next follows the progress of the Italian language, particularly at the court of the Sicilian Monarchs, to the period of which we are speaking. He thus introduces his account of the first great name in modern literature.

> Nevertheless, no poet had as yet powerfully affected the mind, no philosopher had penetrated the depths of thought and sentiment, when the greatest of the Italians, the father of their poetry, Dante, appeared, and showed to the world how a powerful genius is able to arrange the gross materials prepared for him, in such a manner as to rear from them an edifice, magnificent as the universe, of which it was the image. Instead of love songs, addressed to an imaginary mistress,—instead of madrigals, full of cold conceits,—of sonnets painfully harmonious,—or allegories false and forced, the only models which Dante had before his eyes in any modern tongue, he conceived in his mind an image of the whole invisible world, and unveiled it to the

Reprinted from *The Complete Works of William Hazlitt*, edited by P. P. Howe (London: J. M. Dent & Sons, 1932), 16: 40–48.

eyes of his astonished readers. In the country, indeed, of Dante, that is, at Florence, on the 1st of May, 1304, (our author says), all the sufferings of hell were placed before the eyes of the people, at a horrible representation appointed for a festival day; the first idea of which was no doubt taken from the Inferno. The bed of the river Arno was to represent the gulf of hell; and all the variety of torments which the imagination of monks or of the poet had invented, streams of boiling pitch, flames, ice, serpents, were inflicted on real persons, whose cries and groans rendered the illusion complete to the spectators.

The subject, then, which Dante chose for his immortal poem, when he undertook to celebrate the invisible world, and the three kingdoms of the dead, hell, purgatory, and paradise, was in that age the most popular of all; at once the most profoundly religious, and the most closely allied to the love of country, of glory, and of party-feelings, inasmuch as all the illustrious dead were to appear on this extraordinary theatre; and in short, by its immensity, the most loftily sublime of any which the mind of man has ever conceived. The commentaries on Dante, left us by Boccace and others, furnish a new proof of the superiority of this great man. We are there astonished to find his professed admirers unable to appreciate his real grandeur. Dante himself, as well as his commentators, attaches his excellence to purity and correctness yet he is neither pure nor correct; but he is *a creator*. His characters walk and breathe; his pictures are nature itself; his language always speaks to the imagination, as well as to the understanding; and there is scarcely a stanza in his poem, which might not be represented with the pencil.[1]

M. Sismondi seems to have understood the great poet of Italy little better than his other commentators; and indeed the *Divine Comedy* must completely baffle the common rules of French criticism, which always seeks for excellence in the external image, and never in the internal power and feeling. But Dante is nothing but power, passion, self-will. In all that relates to the imitative part of poetry, he bears no comparison with many other poets; but there is a gloomy abstraction in his conceptions, which lies like a dead-weight upon the mind; a benumbing stupor from the intensity of the impression; a terrible obscurity like that which oppresses us in dreams; an identity of interest which moulds every object to its own purposes, and clothes all things

[1] [This passage, like that on page 63 is a paraphrase of Sismondi, not a quotation.]

with the passions and imaginations of the human soul, that make amends for all other deficiencies. Dante is a striking instance of the essential excellences and defects of modern genius. The immediate objects he presents to the mind, are not much in themselves;—they generally want grandeur, beauty, and order; but they become every thing by the force of the character which he impresses on them. His mind lends its own power to the objects which it contemplates, instead of borrowing it from them. He takes advantage even of the nakedness and dreary vacuity of his subject. His imagination peoples the shades of death, and broods over the barren vastnesses of illimitable space. In point of diction and style, he is the severest of all writers, the most opposite to the flowery and glittering—who relies most on his own power, and the sense of power in the reader—who leaves most to the imagination.[2]

Dante's only object is to interest; and he interests only by exciting our sympathy with the emotion by which he is himself possessed. He does not place before us the objects by which that emotion has been excited; but he seizes on the attention, by showing us the effect they produce on his feelings; and his poetry accordingly frequently gives us the thrilling and overwhelming sensation which is caught by gazing on the face of a person who has seen some object of horror. The improbability of the events, the abruptness and monotony in the Inferno, are excessive; but the interest never flags, from the intense earnestness of the author's mind. Dante, as well as Milton, appears to have been indebted to the writers of the Old Testament for the gloomy tone of his mind, for the prophetic fury which exalts and kindles his poetry. But there is more deep-working passion in Dante, and more imagination in Milton. Milton, more perhaps than any other poet, elevated his subject, by combining image with image in lofty gradation. Dante's great power is in combining internal feelings with familiar objects. Thus the gate of Hell, on which that withering inscription is written, seems to be endowed with speech and consciousness, and to utter its dread warning, not without a sense of mortal woes. The beauty to be found in Dante is of the same severe character, or mixed with deep sentiment. The story of Geneura [Francesca] to

[2] See, among a thousand instances, the conclusion of the story of Geneura [Francesca.]—"And all that day we read no more!"

which we have just alluded, is of this class. So is the affecting apostrophe, addressed to Dante by one of his countrymen, whom he meets in the other world.

> "Sweet is the dialect of Arno's vale!
> "Though half consumed, I gladly turn to hear."

And another example, even still finer, if any thing could be finer, is his description of the poets and great men of antiquity, whom he represents "serene and smiling," though in the shades of death, "because on earth their names

> "In fame's eternal records shine for aye."

This is the finest idea ever given of the love of fame.

Dante habitually unites the absolutely local and individual with the greatest wildness and mysticism. In the midst of the obscure and shadowy regions of the lower world, a tomb suddenly rises up, with this inscription, "I am the tomb of Pope Anastasius the Sixth:"—and half the personages whom he has crowded into the Inferno are his own acquaintance. All this tends to heighten the effect by the bold intermixture of realities, and the appeal, as it were, to the individual knowledge and experience of the reader. There are occasional striking images in Dante—but these are exceptions; and besides, they are striking only from the weight of consequences attached to them. The imagination of the poet retains and associates the objects of nature, not according to their external forms, but their inward qualities or powers; as when Satan is compared to a cormorant. It is not true, then, that Dante's excellence consists in natural description or dramatic invention. His characters are indeed 'instinct with life' and sentiment; but it is with the life and sentiment of the poet. In themselves they have little or no dramatic variety, except what arises immediately from the historical facts mentioned; and they afford, in our opinion, very few subjects for picture. There is indeed one gigantic one, that of Count Ugolino, of which Michael Angelo made a bas-relief, and which Sir Joshua Reynolds ought not to have painted. Michael Angelo was naturally an admirer of Dante, and has left a sonnet to his memory.

The Purgatory and Paradise are justly characterized by our author as "a falling off" from the Inferno. He however points out a number of beautiful passages in both these divisions of the poem. That in which the poet describes his ascent into heaven, completely marks the character of his mind. He employs no machinery, or supernatural agency, for this purpose; but mounts aloft 'by the sole strength of his desires—fixing an intense regard on the orbit of the sun!' This great poet was born at Florence in 1265, of the noble family of the Alighieri—and died at Ravenna, September 14th, 1321. Like Milton, he was unfortunate in his political connexions, and, what is worse, in those of his private life. He had a few imitators after his death, but none of any eminence.

M. Sismondi professes to have prejudice against Petrarch. In this he is not, as he supposes, singular; but we suspect that he is wrong. He seems to have reasoned on a very common, but very false hypothesis, that because there is a great deal of false wit and affectation in Petrarch's style, he is therefore without sentiment. The sentiment certainly does not consist in the conceits; —but is it not there in spite of them? The fanciful allusions, and the quaintnesses of style lie on the surface; and it is sometimes found convenient to make these an excuse for not seeking after that which lies deeper and is of more value.[3] It has been well observed, by a contemporary critic, that notwithstanding the adventitious ornaments with which their style is encumbered, there is more truth and feeling in Cowley and Sir Philip Sidney, than in a host of insipid and merely natural writers. It is not improbable, that if Shakespeare had written nothing but his sonnets and smaller poems, he would, for the same reason, have been assigned to the class of cold, artificial writers, who had no genuine sense of nature or passion. Yet, taking his plays for a guide to our decision, it requires no very great sagacity or boldness to discover that his other poems contain a rich vein of thought and sentiment. We apprehend it is the same with Petrarch. Then sentiments themselves are often of the most pure and natural kind, even where the expression is the most laboured and far-fetched. Nor does it follow, that this artificial and scholastic style was the result of affectation in the author. All pedantry is not affectation. Inveterate habit is not affectation. The technical jargon of professional men is not affectation in them:

[3] The late Mr. Blake was a writer of a very splendid imagination, and great command of words. This was, with many persons, a sufficient ground for concluding that he was a mere rhetorician, without depth of thought or solidity of judgment.

for it is the language with which their ideas have the strongest associations. Milton's Classical Pedantry was perfectly involuntary: it was the style in which he was accustomed to think and feel; and it would have required an effort to have expressed himself otherwise. The scholastic style is not indeed the natural style of the passion or sentiment of love; but it is quite false to argue, that an author did not feel this passion because he expressed himself in the usual language in which this and all other passions were expressed, in the particular age and country in which he lived. On the contrary, the more true and profound the feeling itself was, the more it might be supposed to be identified with his other habits and pursuits—to tinge all his thoughts, and to put in requisition every faculty of his soul—to give additional perversity to his wit, subtlety to his understanding, and extravagance to his expressions. Like all other strong passions, it seeks to express itself in exaggerations, and its characteristic is less to be simple than emphatic. The language of love was never more finely expressed than in the play of Romeo and Juliet; and yet assuredly the force or beauty of that language does not arise from its simplicity. It is the fine rapturous enthusiasm of youthful sensibility, which tries all ways to express its emotions, and finds none of them half tender or extravagant enough. The sonnet of Petrarch lamenting the death of Laura, which is quoted

> Gli occhi di ch' io parlai sì caldamente
> E le braccia, e le maní, e i piedi, e 'l viso
> Che m' havean sì da me stesso diviso,
> E fatto singular da l' altra gente;
> Le crispe chiome d' or puro lucente,
> E 'l lampeggiar de l' angelico riso,
> Che solean far in terra un paradiso,
> [CCXCII]

by M. Sismondi, and of which he complains as having 'too much wit,' would be a justification of these remarks; not to mention numberless others.

M. Sismondi wishes that the connexion between Petrarch and Laura had been more intimate, and his passion accompanied with more interesting circumstances. The whole is in better keeping as it is. The love of a man like Petrarch would have been less in character, if it had been less ideal. For the purposes of inspiration, a single interview was quite sufficient. The smile which sank into his heart the first time he ever beheld her, played round her lips ever after: the look with which her eyes first met his, never passed away. The image of his mistress still haunted his mind, and was recalled by every object in nature. Even death could not dissolve the fine illusion: for that which exists in the imagination is alone imperishable. As our feelings become more ideal, the impression of the moment indeed becomes less violent; but the effect is more general and permanent. The blow is felt only by reflection; it is the rebound that is fatal. We are not here standing up for this kind of Platonic attachment; but only endeavouring to explain the way in which the passions very commonly operate in minds accustomed to draw their strongest interests from constant contemplation.

Petrarch is at present chiefly remembered for his sonnets, and the passion which they celebrate: he was equally distinguished in his lifetime by his Latin Poems, and as one of the great restorers of learning. . . .

> Poca polvere son che nulla sente.
> Ed io pur vivo; onde mi doglio e sdegno,
> Rimaso, senza 'l lume ch' amai tanto,
> In gran fortuna e 'n disarmato legno.
> Or sia qui fine al mio amoroso canto:
> Secca è la vena de l' usato ingegno,
> E la cetera mia rivolta in pianto.'
> [CCXCII]

Literally as follows.

Those eyes of which I spoke so warmly, and the arms, and the hands, and the feet, and the face, which have robbed me of myself, and made me different from others; those crisped locks of pure shining gold, and the lightning of that angelical smile, which used to make a heaven upon earth, are now a little dust which feels nothing!—And I still remain! whence I lament and disdain myself, left without the light which I loved so much, in a troubled sea, and with dismantled bark. Here then must end all my amorous songs. Dry is the vein of my exhausted genius, and my lyre answers only in lamentations!

Boccacio was also one of the most indefatigable and successful of the restorers of ancient learning; and is classed by Mr. Sismondi as one of the three inventors of modern letters,—having done for Italian prose what Dante and Petrarch had done for

Italian poetry. He was born at Paris in 1313, the son of a Florentine merchant; and died at Certaldo, in Tuscany, in the house of his forefathers, 21st December 1375, at the age of sixty-two years. He wrote epic poems and theology: But his Tales are his great work.

The Decameron, says our author,

> the work to which, in the present day, Boccacio owes his highest celebrity, is a collection of a hundred novels, which he has arranged in an ingenious manner, by supposing, that in the dreadful plague in 1348, a society of men and women, who had retired into the country to avoid the contagion, had imposed on themselves an obligation, for ten days together, to recite each a novel a day. The company consisted of ten persons; and the number of novels is, of course, a hundred. The description of the delicious country round Florence, where these joyous hermits took up their abode,—that of their walks—their festivals—their repasts, has given Boccacio an opportunity to display all the riches of a style the most flexible and graceful. The novels themselves, which are varied with infinite art, both as to the subject and manner, from the most touching and tender to the most playful, and unfortunately also to the most licentious, demonstrate his talent for recounting in every style and tone. His description of the plague of Florence, which serves as the introduction, ranks as one of the finest historical portraits which any age has left us. Finally, that which constitutes the glory of Boccacio, is the perfect purity of the language, the elegance, the grace, and above all, the *naïveté* of the style, which is the highest merit of this class of writing, and the peculiar charm of the Italian language.

All this is true; though it might be said of many other authors: But what ought to have been said of him is, that there is in Boccacio's serious pieces a truth, a pathos, and an exquisite refinement of sentiment, which is not to be met with in any other prose writer whatever. We think M. Sismondi has missed a fine opportunity of doing the author of the Decameron that justice which has not been done him by the world. He has in general passed for a mere narrator of lascivious tales or idle jests. This character probably originated in the early popularity of his attacks on the monks, and has been kept up by the grossness of mankind, who revenged their own want of refinement on Boccacio, and only saw in his writings what suited the coarseness of their own tastes. But the truth is, that he has carried sentiment of every kind to its very highest purity and perfection. By sentiment we would here understand the habitual workings of some one powerful feeling, where the heart reposes almost entirely upon itself, without the violent excitement of opposing duties or untoward circumstances. In this way, nothing ever came up to the story of Frederigo Alberigi and his falcon. The perseverance in attachment, the spirit of gallantry and generosity displayed in it, has no parallel in the history of heroical sacrifices. The feeling is so unconscious too, and involuntary, is brought out in such small, unlooked-for, and unostentatious circumstances, as to show it to have been woven into the very nature and soul of the author. The story of Isabella is scarcely less fine, and is more affecting in the circumstances and the catastrophe. Dryden has done justice to the impassioned eloquence of the Tancred and Sigismunda; but has not given an adequate idea of the wild preternatural interest of the story of Honoria. Cimon and Iphigene is by no means one of the best, notwithstanding the popularity of the subject. The proof of unalterable affection given in the story of Jeronymo, and the simple touches of nature and picturesque beauty in the story of the two holiday lovers, who were poisoned by tasting of a leaf in the garden at Florence, are perfect masterpieces.[4] The epithet of Divine was well bestowed on this great painter of the human heart. The invention implied in his different tales is immense: but we are not to infer that it is all his own. He probably availed himself of all the common traditions which were floating in his time, and which he was the first to appropriate. Homer appears the most original of all authors—probably for no other reason than that we can trace the plagiarism no farther. Several of Shakespeare's plots are taken from Boccacio; and indeed he has furnished subjects to numberless writers since his time, both dramatic and narrative. The story of Guselda [Griselda] is borrowed from the Decameron by Chaucer; as is the Knight's Tale (Palamon and Arcite) from his poem of the Theseid.

[4] [Federigo degli Alberighi appears in *Dec.* V, 9. Isabella is the name given by Keats to Boccaccio's Isabetta (IV, 5). Sigismunda is Boccaccio's Ghismunda (IV, 1). Honoria is the name Dryden gives to the unnamed heroine of V, 8. Cimone and Efigenia are in V, 1. Jeronymo is the Girolamo of IV, 8. The form Jeronimo appears in the 1620 translation. Boccaccio's name is misspelled throughout.]

IV

SAMUEL TAYLOR COLERIDGE

From the Lectures

In the present Lecture [III] I must introduce you to a species of poetry, which had its birth-place near the centre of Roman glory, and in which, as might be anticipated, the influences of the Greek and Roman muse are far more conspicuous,–as great, indeed, as the efforts of intentional imitation on the part of the poets themselves could render them. But happily for us and for their own fame, the intention of the writers as men is often at complete variance with the genius of the same men as poets. To the force of their intention we owe their mythological ornaments, and the greater definiteness of their imagery; and their passion for the beautiful, the voluptuous, and the artificial, we must in part attribute to the same intention, but in part likewise to their natural dispositions and tastes. For the same climate and many of the same circumstances were acting on them, which had acted on the great classics, whom they were endeavoring to imitate. But the love of the marvellous, the deeper sensibility, the higher reverence for womanhood, the characteristic spirit of sentiment and courtesy,–these were the heirlooms of nature, which still regained the ascendant, whenever the use of the living mother-language enabled the inspired poet to appear instead of the toilsome scholar.

From this same union, in which the soul (if I may dare so express myself) was Gothic, while the outward forms and a majority of the words themselves, were the reliques of the Roman, arose the Romance, or romantic language, in which the Troubadours or Love-singers of Provence sang and wrote, and the different dialects of which have been modified into the modern Italian, Spanish, and Portuguese; while the language of the Trouveurs, Trouveres, or Norman-French poets, forms the intermediate link between the Romance or modified Roman, and

Reprinted from *Literary Remains*, collected and edited by Henry Nelson Coleridge (London: William Pickering, 1836–39), 4: 240–42; 287–97.

the Teutonic, including the Dutch, Danish, Swedish, and the upper and lower German, as being the modified Gothic. And as the northernmost extreme of the Norman-French, or that part of the link in which it formed on the Teutonic, we must take the Norman-English minstrels and metrical romances, from the greater predominance of the Anglo-Saxon Gothic in the derivation of the words. I mean, that the language of the English metrical romance is less romanized, and has fewer words, not originally of a northern origin, than the same romances in the Norman-French; which is the more striking, because the former were for the most part translated from the latter; the authors of which seem to have eminently merited their name of Trouveres, or inventors. Thus then we have a chain with two rings or staples: —at the southern end there is the Roman, or Latin; at the northern end the Keltic, Teutonic, or Gothic; and the links beginning with the southern end, are the Romance, including the Provençal, the Italian, Spanish, and Portuguese, with their different dialects, then the Norman-French, and lastly the English.

My object in adverting to the Italian poets, is not so much for their own sakes, in which point of view Dante and Ariosto alone would have required separate Lectures, but for the elucidation of the merits of our countrymen, as to what extent we must consider them as fortunate imitators of their Italian predecessors, and in what points they have the higher claims of original genius. Of Dante, I am to speak elsewhere. Of Boccaccio, who has little interest as a metrical poet in any respect, and none for my present purpose, except, perhaps, as the reputed inventor or introducer of the octave stanza in his Teseide, it will be sufficient to say, that we owe to him the subjects of numerous poems taken from his famous tales, the happy art of narration, and the still greater merit of a depth and fineness in the workings of the passions, in which last excellence, as likewise in the wild and imaginative character of the situations, his almost neglected romances appear to me greatly to excel his far-famed Decameron. To him, too, we owe the more doubtful merit of having introduced into the Italian prose, and by the authority of his name and the influence of his example, more or less throughout Europe, the long interwoven periods, and architectural structure which arose from the very nature of their language in the Greek writers, but which already in the Latin orators and historians, had betrayed a species of effort, a foreign something, which had been superinduced on the language, instead of growing out of it; and which was far too alien from that individualizing and confederating, yet not blending, character of the North, to become permanent, although its magnificence and stateliness were objects of admiration and occasional imitation. This style diminished the control of the writer over the inner feelings of men, and created too great a chasm between the body and the life; and hence especially it was abandoned by Luther.

But lastly, to Boccaccio's sanction we must trace a large portion of the mythological pedantry and incongruous paganisms, which for so long a period deformed the poetry, even of the truest poets. To such an extravagance did Boccaccio himself carry this folly, that in a romance of chivalry he has uniformly styled God the Father Jupiter, our Saviour Apollo, and the Evil Being Pluto. But for this there might be some excuse pleaded. I dare make none for the gross and disgusting licentiousness, the daring profaneness, which rendered the Decameron of Boccaccio the parent of a hundred worse children, fit to be classed among the enemies of the human race; which poisons Ariosto—(for that I may not speak oftener than necessary of so odious a subject, I mention it here once for all)—which interposes a painful mixture in the humor of Chaucer, and which has once or twice seduced even our pure-minded Spenser into a grossness, as heterogeneous from the spirit of his great poem, as it was alien to the delicacy of his morals. . . .

LECTURE X

As I remarked in a former Lecture on a different subject (for subjects the most diverse in literature have still their tangents), the Gothic character, and its good and evil fruits, appeared less in Italy than in any other part of European Christendom. There was accordingly much less romance, as that word is commonly understood; or, perhaps, more truly stated, there was romance instead of chivalry. In Italy, an earlier imitation of, and a more evident and intentional blending with, the Latin literature took place than elsewhere. The operation of the feudal system, too, was incalculably weaker, of that singular chain of independent interdependents, the principle of which was a confederacy for the preservation of individual, consistently with general, freedom. In short, Italy, in the time of Dante, was an after-birth of eldest Greece, a renewal or a reflex of the old Italy under its kings and first Roman consuls, a net-work of free little republics, with the same domestic feuds, civil wars, and party spirit—the same vices and virtues produced on a similarly narrow theatre—the existing state of things being, as in all small democracies, under the working and direction of certain individuals, to whose will even the laws were swayed;—whilst at the same time the singular spectacle was exhibited amidst all this confusion of the flourishing of commerce, and the protection and encouragement of letters and arts. Never was the commercial spirit so well reconciled to the nobler principles of social polity as in Florence. It tended there to union and permanence and elevation—not as the overbalance of it in England is now doing, to dislocation, change and moral degradation. The intensest patriotism reigned in these communities, but confined and attached exclusively to the small locality of the patriot's birth and residence; whereas in the true Gothic feudalism, country was nothing but the preservation of personal independence. But then, on the other hand, as a counterbalance to these disuniting elements, there was in Dante's Italy, as in Greece, a much greater uniformity of religion common to all than amongst the northern nations.

Upon these hints the history of the republican æras of ancient Greece and modern Italy ought to be written. There are three kinds or stages of historic narrative;—1. that of the annalist or chronicler, who deals merely in facts and events arranged in order of time, having no principle of selection, no plan of arrangement, and whose work properly constitutes a supplement to the poetical writings of romance or heroic legends:—2. that of the writer who takes his stand on some moral point, and selects a series of events for the express purpose of illustrating it, and in whose hands the narrative of the selected events is modified by the principle of selection;—as Thucydides, whose object was to describe the evils of democratic and aristocratic partisanships;—or Polybius, whose design was to show the social benefits resulting from the triumph and grandeur of Rome, in public institutions and military discipline;—or Tacitus, whose secret aim was to exhibit the pressure and corruptions of despotism; in all which writers and others like them, the ground-object of the historian colors with artificial lights the facts which he relates:—3. and which in idea is the grandest—the most truly founded in philosophy—there is the Herodotean history, which is not composed with reference to any particular causes, but attempts to describe human nature itself on a great scale as a portion of the drama of providence, the free will of man resisting the destiny of events—for the individuals often succeeding against it, but for the race always yielding to it, and in the resistance itself invariably affording means towards the completion of the ultimate result. Mitford's history is a good and useful work; but in his zeal against democratic government, Mitford forgot, or never saw, that ancient Greece was not, nor ought ever to be considered, a permanent thing, but that it existed, in the disposition of providence, as a proclaimer of ideal truths, and that everlasting proclamation being made, that its functions were naturally at an end.

However, in the height of such a state of society in Italy, Dante was born and flourished; and was himself eminently a picture of the age in which he lived. But of more importance even than this, to a right understanding of Dante, is the consideration that the scholastic philosophy was then at its acme even in itself; but more especially in Italy, where it never prevailed so exclusively as northward of the Alps. It is impossible to understand the genius of Dante, and difficult to understand his poem, without some knowledge of the characters, studies, and writings of the schoolmen of the twelfth, thirteenth, and fourteenth centuries. For Dante was the living link between religion and philosophy; he philosophized the religion and Christianized the philosophy of Italy; and, in this poetic union of religion and philosophy, he became the ground of transition into the mixed Platonism and Aristotelianism of the Schools, under which, by numerous minute articles of faith and ceremony, Christianity became a craft of hair-splitting, and was ultimately degraded into a complete *fetish* worship, divorced from philosophy, and made up of a faith without thought, and a credulity directed by passion. Afterwards, indeed, philosophy revived under condition of defending this very superstition; and, in so doing, it necessarily led the way to its subversion, and that in exact proportion to the influence of the philosophic schools. Hence it did its work most completely in Germany, then in England, next in France, then in Spain, least of all in Italy. We must, therefore, take the poetry of Dante as Christianized, but without the further Gothic accession of proper chivalry. It was at a somewhat later period, that the importations from the East, through the Venetian commerce and the crusading armaments, exercised a peculiarly strong influence on Italy.

In studying Dante, therefore, we must consider carefully the differences produced, first, by allegory being substituted for polytheism; and secondly and mainly, by the opposition of Chrisitanity to the spirit of pagan Greece, which receiving the very names of its gods from Egypt, soon deprived them of all that was universal. The Greeks changed the ideas into finites, and these finites into *anthropomorphi*, or forms of men. Hence their religion, their poetry, nay, their very pictures, became statuesque. With them the form was the end. The reverse of this was the natural effect of Christianity; in which finites, even the human form, must, in order to satisfy the mind, be brought into connection with, and be in fact symbolical of, the infinite; and must be considered in some enduring, however shadowy and indistinct, point of view, as the vehicle or representative of moral truth.

Hence resulted two great effects; a combination of poetry with doctrine, and, by turning the mind inward on its own essence instead of letting it act only on its outward circumstances and communities, a combination of poetry with sentiment. And it is this inwardness or subjectivity, which principally and most fundamentally distinguishes all the classic from all the modern poetry. Compare the passage in the Iliad (Z'. vi. 119–36) in which Diomed and Glaucus change arms,

Χεῖράς τ' ἀλλήγων λαβέτην καὶ πιστώσαντο . . .
They took each other by the hand, and pledged friendship . . .

with the scene in Ariosto (Orlando Furioso, c. i. st. 20–22), where Rinaldo and Ferrauto fight and afterwards make it up:

> Al Pagan la proposta non dispiacque:
> Così fu differita la tenzone;
> E tal tregua tra lor subito nacque,
> Sì l' odio e l' ira va in oblivione,
> Che 'l Pagano al partir dalle fresche acque
> Non lasciò a piede il buon figliuol d' Amone;
> Con preghi invita, e al fin lo toglie in groppa,
> E per l' orme d' Angelica galoppa.

Here Homer would have left it. But the Christian poet has his own feelings to express, and goes on:

Oh gran bontà de' cavalieri antiqui!
Eran rivali, eran di fè diversi,
E si sentian degli aspri colpi iniqui
Per tutta la persona anco dolersi;
E pur per selve oscure e calli obbliqui
Insieme van senza sospetto aversi!

And here you will observe, that the reaction of Ariosto's own feelings on the image or act is more fore-grounded (to use a painter's phrase) than the image or act itself.

The two different modes in which the imagination is acted on by the ancient and modern poetry, may be illustrated by the parallel effects caused by the contemplation of the Greek or Roman-Greek architecture, compared with the Gothic. In the Pantheon, the whole is perceived in a perceived harmony with the parts which compose it; and generally you will remember that where the parts preserve any distinct individuality, there simple beauty, or beauty simply, arises; but where the parts melt undistinguished into the whole, there majestic beauty, or majesty, is the result. In York Minster, the parts, the grotesques, are in themselves very sharply distinct and separate, and this distinction and separation of the parts is counterbalanced only by the multitude and variety of those parts, by which the attention is bewildered;—whilst the whole, or that there is a whole produced, is altogether a feeling in which the several thousand distinct impressions lose themselves as in a universal solvent. Hence in a Gothic cathedral, as in a prospect from a mountain's top, there is indeed a unity, an awful oneness;—but it is, because all distinction evades the eye. And just such is the distinction between the Antigone of Sophocles and the Hamlet of Shakespeare.

The Divina Commedia is a system of moral, political, and theological truths, with arbitrary personal exemplifications, which are not, in my opinion, allegorical. I do not even feel convinced that the punishments in the Inferno are strictly allegorical. I rather take them to have been in Dante's mind *quasi*-allegorical, or conceived in analogy to pure allegory.

I have said, that a combination of poetry with doctrines, is one of the characteristics of the Christian muse; but I think Dante has not succeeded in effecting this combination nearly so well as Milton.

This comparative failure of Dante, as also some other peculiarities of his mind, *in malam partem*, must be immediately attributed to the state of North Italy in his time, which is vividly represented in Dante's life; a state of intense democratical partisanship, in which an exaggerated importance was attached to individuals, and which whilst it afforded a vast field for the intellect, opened also a boundless arena for the passions, and in which envy, jealousy, hatred, and other malignant feelings, could and did assume the form of patriotism, even to the individual's own conscience.

All this common, and, as it were, natural partisanship, was aggravated and colored by the Guelf and Ghibelline factions; and, in part explanation of Dante's adherence to the latter, you must particularly remark, that the Pope had recently territorialized his authority to a great extent, and that this increase of territorial power in the church, was by no means the same beneficial movement for the citizens of free republics, as the parallel advance in other countries was for those who groaned as vassals under the oppression of the circumjacent baronial castles.[1]

By way of preparation to a satisfactory perusal of the Divina Commedia, I will now proceed to state what I consider to be Dante's chief excellences as a poet. And I begin with

I. Style—the vividness, logical connection, strength and energy of which can not be surpassed. In this I think Dante superior to Milton; and his style is accordingly more imitable than Milton's, and does to this day exercise a greater influence on the literature of his country. You can not read Dante without feeling a gush of manliness of thought within you. Dante was very sensible of his own excellence in this particular, and speaks of poets as guardians of the vast armory of language, which is the intermediate something between matter and spirit:—

> Or se' tu quel Virgilio, e quella fonte,
> Che spande di parlar sì largo fiume?
> Risposi lui con vergognosa fronte.
> O degli altri poeti onore e lume,
> Vagliami 'l lungo studio e 'l grande amore,
> Che m' han fatto cercar lo tuo volume.
> Tu se' lo mio maestro, e 'l mio autore:
> *Tu se' solo colui, da cu' io tolsi*
> *Lo bello stile, che m' ha fatto onore.*
> [*Inf.* I, 79–87]

[1] [Coleridge noted here that he would add historical comments, and compliment Henry Hallam.]

"And art thou then that Virgil, that well-spring,
From which such copious floods of eloquence
Have issued?" I, with front abash'd, replied:
"Glory and light of all the tuneful train!
May it avail me, that I long with zeal
Have sought thy volume, and with love immense
Have conn'd it o'er. My master, thou, and guide!
Thou he from whom I have alone deriv'd
That style, which for its beauty into fame
Exalts me."

CARY

Indeed there was a passion and a miracle of words in the twelfth and thirteenth centuries, after the long slumber of language in barbarism, which gave an almost romantic character, a virtuous quality and power, to what was read in a book, independently of the thoughts or images contained in it. This feeling is very often perceptible in Dante.

II. The Images in Dante are not only taken from obvious nature, and are all intelligible to all, but are ever conjoined with the universal feeling received from nature, and therefore affect the general feelings of all men. And in this respect, Dante's excellence is very great, and may be contrasted with the idiosyncrasies of some meritorious modern poets, who attempt an eruditeness, the result of particular feelings. Consider the simplicity, I may say plainness, of the following simile, and how differently we should in all probability deal with it at the present day:

Quale i fioretti dal notturno gelo
Chinati e chiusi, poi che 'l sol gl' imbianca,
Si drizzan tutti aperti in loro stelo,
Tal mi fec' io di mia virtute stanca:

[*Inf.* II, 127–30]

As florets, by the frosty air of night
Bent down and clos'd, when day has blanch'd their leaves,
Rise all unfolded on their spiry stems,—
So was my fainting vigor new restor'd.

CARY[2]

III. Consider the wonderful profoundness of the whole third canto of the Inferno; and especially of the inscription over Hellgate:

2 [It was here that Coleridge made a note to speak of Cary's translation and so give it the public commendation it deserved.]

Per me si va, . . .

which can only be explained by a meditation on the true nature of religion; that is,—reason *plus* the understanding. I say profoundness rather than sublimity; for Dante does not so much elevate your thoughts as send them down deeper. In this canto all the images are distinct, and even vividly distinct; but there is a total impression of infinity; the wholeness is not in vision or conception, but in an inner feeling of totality, and absolute being.

IV. In picturesqueness, Dante is beyond all other poets, modern, or ancient, and more in the stern style of Pindar, than of any other. Michel Angelo is said to have made a design for every page of the Divina Commedia. As super-excellent in this respect, I would note the conclusion of the third canto of the Inferno:

Ed ecco verso noi venir per nave
Un vecchio bianco per antico pelo
Gridando: guai a voi anime prave!
[82–84]

And lo! toward us in a bark
Comes on an old man, hoary white with eld,
Crying, "Woe to you, wicked spirits!"
CARY

Caron dimonio con occhi di bragia
Loro accennando, tutte le raccoglie: . . .[3]
Similemente il mal seme d' Adamo,
Gittansi di quel lito ad una ad una
Per cenni, com' augel per suo richiamo.
[109–17]

Charon, demoniac form,
With eyes of burning coal, collects them all,
Beck'ning, and each that lingers, with his oar
Strikes. As fall off the light autumnal leaves,
One still another following, till the bough
Strews all its honors on the earth beneath;—
E'en in like manner Adam's evil brood
Cast themselves one by one down from the shore
Each at a beck, as falcon at his call.
CARY

[3] [Coleridge quotes the whole passage in Italian which has been abridged here. The following quotations have also been abridged.]

And this passage, which I think admirably picturesque:

> Ma poco i valse, chè l' ali al sospetto
> Non potero avanzar: quegli andò sotto,
> E quei drizzò, volando suso, il petto....
> Ma però di levarsi era niente,
> Sì aveano inviscate l' ali sue.
> [*Inf.* XXII, 127–44]

> But little it avail'd: terror outstripp'd
> His following flight: the other plung'd beneath,
> And he with upward pinion rais'd his breast:
> E'en thus the water-fowl, when she perceives
> The falcon near, dives instant down, while he
> Enrag'd and spent retires. That mockery
> In Calcabrina fury stirr'd, who flew
> After him, with desire of strife inflam'd;
> And, for the barterer had 'scap'd, so turn'd
> His talons on his comrade. O'er the dyke
> In grapple close they join'd; but th' other prov'd
> A goshawk, able to rend well his foe;
> And in the boiling lake both fell. The heat
> Was umpire soon between them, but in vain
> To lift themselves they strove, so fast were glued
> Their pennons.
> CARY

V. Very closely connected with this picturesqueness, is the topographic reality of Dante's journey through Hell. You should note and dwell on this as one of his great charms, and which gives a striking peculiarity to his poetic power. He thus takes the thousand delusive forms of a nature worse than chaos, having no reality but from the passions which they excite, and compels them into the service of the permanent. Observe the exceeding truth of these lines:

> Noi ricidemmo 'l cerchio all' altra riva,
> Sovr' una fonte che bolle e riversa,
> Pér un fossato che da leí diriva. . . .
> Così girammo della lorda pozza
> Grand' arco tra la ripa secca e 'l mezzo,
> Con gli occhi volti a chi del fango ingozza:
> *Venimmo appiè d' una torre al dassezzo.*
> [*Inf.* VII, 100–14, 127–30]

> ———We the circle cross'd

To the next steep, arriving at a well,
That boiling pours itself down to a foss
Sluic'd from its source. Far murkier was the wave
Than sablest grain: and we in company
Of th' inky waters, journeying by their side,
Enter'd, though by a different track, beneath.
Into a lake, the Stygian nam'd, expands
The dismal stream, when it hath reach'd the foot
Of the gray wither'd cliffs. Intent I stood
To gaze, and in the marsh sunk, descried
A miry tribe, all naked, and with looks
Betok'ning rage. They with their hands alone
Struck not, but with the head, the breast, the feet,
Cutting each other piecemeal with their fangs. . . .
Our route
Thus compass'd, we a segment widely stretch'd
Between the dry embankment and the cove
Of the loath'd pool, turning meanwhile our eyes
Downward on those who gulp'd its muddy lees;
Nor stopp'd, till to a tower's low base we came.
CARY

VI. For Dante's power,—his absolute mastery over, although rare exhibition of, the pathetic, I can do no more than refer to the passages on Francesca di Rimini (*Inf.* V, 73 to the end), and on Ugolino (*Inf.* XXXIII, 1 to 75). They are so well known, and rightly so admired, that it would be pedantry to analyze their composition; but you will note that the first is the pathos of passion, the second that of affection; and yet even in the first, you seem to perceive that the lovers have sacrificed their passion to the cherishing of a deep and rememberable impression.

VII. As to going into the endless subtle beauties of Dante, that is impossible; but I can not help citing the first triplet of the twenty-ninth canto of the Inferno:

La molta gente e le diverse piaghe
Avean le luci mie sì inebriate,
Che dello stare a piangere eran vaghe.

So were mine eyes inebriate with the view
Of the vast multitude, whom various wounds
Disfigur'd, that they long'd to stay and weep.
CARY

Nor have I now room for any specific comparison of Dante with Milton. But if I had, I would institute it upon the ground of the last canto of the Inferno from the 1st to the 69th line, and from the 106th to the end. And in this comparison I should notice Dante's occasional fault of becoming grotesque from being too graphic without imagination; as in his Lucifer compared with Milton's Satan. Indeed he is sometimes horrible rather than terrible,—falling into the μιση τὸν instead of the δεινὸν of Longinus; in other words, many of his images excite bodily disgust, and not moral fear. But here, as in other cases, you may perceive that the faults of great authors are generally excellencies carried to an excess.

V

UGO FOSCOLO

An Essay on the Poetry of Petrarch

. . . non ho se non quest'una
Via da celare il mio angoscioso pianto.
[CII, 13–14]

The vision of the spirit of Laura was written, as appears by the expressions at the close of it, when Petrarch was far advanced in years. He revised it four months before his death and inserted it as an episode in a moral poem which he called TRIONFI—a series of allegorical visions on the powers of Love, Chastity, Death, Talents, Fame, Time, and the Eternity. Several Provençal poems written before his time, and the *Dream*, the *Flower and the Leaf*, and the *House of Fame*, of his contemporary Chaucer, are of the same description.

Perhaps the models of them may be traced in the visions which the monks preached in imitation of those of Ezekiel and St. John's Revelation. The last canto of the *Trionfi* is called *Della Divinità*, and begins, "Since, then, I behold nothing certain beneath the heavens, I look fearfully around me, and ask myself, in what then canst thou trust? I answered, in God."—It concludes with Laura: "If he who beheld her on earth was blessed, what shall he not be on beholding her again in heaven!"

Se fu beato chi la vide in terra,
Or che fia dunque a rivederla in Cielo!
[*Trionfi* X, 144–45]

He considered this work as a great undertaking; and he gave it up from the fear that he would be unable to finish it.[1] He

Reprinted from the *Edizone Nazionale delle Opere di Ugo Foscolo*, vol. 10: *Saggi e discorsi critici*, a cura di Cesare Foligno (Firenze: La Monnier, 1953), pp. 37–78.

[1] Magnum opus inceperam in eo genere, sed aetatem respiciens, substiti.—Ad Joh. Bocac. Sen. Lib. V. Ep. 3.

betook to it again, however: he perceived that he had failed; but he persevered nevertheless, and left it so disfigured with various readings, that to complete a copy after his death, it was necessary to supply much by conjecture. It is only when he is speaking of Laura in this poem, that his heart communicates its fire to his genius, which had languished more under the disgust of life than the burthen of years. He records his melancholy feelings on the margins of his manuscript: "The more I reflect on what I am, the more I feel ashamed of this work: It is no longer myself, it is another who writes."[2]—He was born to create with anxiety, and to dissipate in despair, the illusions which were necessary to his repose, and he was thus often tempted to destroy even the lyric poetry which he had addressed to Laura.[3] He does not even mention it in his LETTER TO POSTERITY, though, if it had not been for this very poetry, the other literary merits of this great man would not have been remembered with so much gratitude. To his intimate friends, he expresses himself ashamed of having devoted his talents to the amusement of ballad-singers, and lovers,—lamenting that his verses had been too generally dispersed to be recalled; and complaining that they had sometimes been partially disfigured, and sometimes entirely forged by professional singers, who took great merit to themselves for collecting them.[4] He offers the same apology to the world, in the first sonnet of his collection,[5] which he resolved to prepare in his old age, rejecting those pieces which were apocryphal, and those which he considered unworthy of him.[6]

The pleasure of living his youth over again, of meeting Laura in every line, of examining the history of his own heart; and

[2] *Dum quid sum cogito, pudet haec scribere—scribo enim non tanquam ego, sed quasi alius.*—This memorandum was copied by the Archbishop Beccadelli from the autograph copy then in the possession of Cardinal Bembo.

[3] Famil. Lib. 8. Ep. 3.—Senil. Lib. 5. Ep. 3

[4] Senil. Lib. 13. Epist. 4.

[5] Quand'era in parte altr'uom da quel che or sono—
Ma ben vegg'io siccome al popol tutto
Favola fui gran tempo—
Or del mio vaneggiar vergogna è il frutto
E il pentirsi.

[6] They are to be found in almost all the editions, at the end of the volume, under the titles of *Giunta*, or *Rime rifiutate*.

perhaps the consciousness which, after all, rarely misleads authors respecting the best of their works, induced the poet in his old age to give to his love-verses a perfection, which has never been attained by any other Italian writer, and which he thinks "he could not himself have carried farther."[7] If the manuscripts did not still exist, it would be impossible to imagine or believe the unwearied pains he has bestowed on the correction of his verses. They are curious monuments, although they afford little aid in exploring by what secret workings the long and laborious meditation of Petrarch has spread over his poetry all the natural charms of sudden and irresistible inspiration.

The following is a literal translation of a succession of memorandums in Latin, at the head of one of his sonnets "I began this by the impulse of the Lord (*Domino jubente*), 10th September, at the dawn of the day, after my morning prayers."

"I must make these two verses over again, singing them (*cantando*), and I must transpose them; 3 o'clock, A. M. 19th October."

"I like this (*hoc placet*), 30th October, 10 o'clock in the morning."

"No; this does not please me. 20th December in the evening"—

And in the midst of his corrections he writes, on laying down his pen, "I shall return to this again; I am called to supper."

"February 18th, towards noon; this is now well; however, look at it again (*vide tamen adhuc*)."

Sometimes he notes the town where he happens to be—"1364, *Veneris mane*, 19 *Jan. dum invitus Patavii ferior.*"—It might seem rather a curious than useful remark, that it was generally on Friday that he occupied himself with the painful labour of correction, did we not also know that it was to him a day of fast and penitence.

When any thought occurred to him, he noted it in the midst of his verses thus, "Consider this—I had some thoughts of transposing these lines, and of making the first verse the last, but I have not done so for the sake of harmony—the first would be more sonorous, and the last less so, which is against rule; for the end should be more harmonious than the beginning." Sometimes

[7] *Pietro Paolo Vergerio intese da Colucio Salutato amico del Petrarca che aveva detto, "come le sue composizioni tutte potevano migliorare, fuorchè le Rime nelle quali s'era tanto alzato, che più non gli dava l'animo d'arrivarle.* BECCADELLI, *Vit. del Petrar.*

he says, "The commencement is good, but it is not pathetic enough." In some places he suggests to himself to repeat the same words rather than the same ideas. In others he judges it better not to multiply the ideas, but to amplify them with other expressions. Every verse is turned in several different ways; above each phrase and each word he frequently places equivalent expressions, in order to examine them again; and it requires a profound knowledge of Italian to perceive, that after such perplexing scruples, he always adopts those words which combine at once most harmony, elegance, and energy.

These laborious corrections gave rise to an opinion, even in the life-time of Petrarch, that his verses were the work less of a lover than of a poet.[8] It is indubitably true that, that passion cannot be very strong, which we are at leisure to describe.—But a man of genius feels more intensely and suffers more strongly than another; and for this very reason, when the force of his passion has subsided, he retains for a longer period the recollection of what it has been, and can more easily imagine himself again under its influence; and, in my conception, what we call the power of imagination is chiefly the combination of strong feelings and recollections. Thus a man of genius is peculiarly gifted with the faculty of observing the secret workings of human nature, as she prevails in his own heart, and in the hearts of all mankind; and is enabled to describe those feelings, and bring them home to every reader. The great secret of the poet's art is, to make us feel our existence by the force of sympathy; but at the moment that he groans under his own sufferings, it is impossible for him to examine the workings of his heart, or those of others—and the lyrical poetry of Petrarch, which may be read in the course of a few days, was written during a period of thirty-two years. Many of the pieces, no doubt, were conceived at moments when he was under the immediate influence of his passion; but were written many days, perhaps many months, and certainly perfected many years, afterwards. The 48th sonnet of the first part of his collection was written eleven years after his acquaintance with Laura:

Or volge Signor mio, l'*undecim'anno*
Ch'io fui sommesso al dispietato giogo—
[LXII, 9–10]

[8] Epist. Famil. Lib. 2. Ep. 7.

Four years after this last epoch he wrote the 85th sonnet:

> Fuggir vorrei; ma gli amorosi rai
> Che dì e notte nella mente stanno
> Risplendon sì che al *quintodecim*'anno
> M'abbaglian più che il primo giorno assai–
> [CVIII, 5–8]

During the course of this year, and the whole of the next, he composed only eleven sonnets; for the 96th began

> Rimansi adietro il *sestodecim*'anno–
> [CXVIII, 1]

and the 97th

> *Dicesett*' anni ha già rivolto il Cielo
> [CXXII, 1]

Thus in these *twelve* months he wrote only fourteen verses to Laura. Indeed if his mind had experienced no intervals of calm, he would never have been able to execute those conceptions, and still less to correct them. He would not have lived so long; or, if he had lived, it would have been in that state of disquietude and inaction, inseparable from agitated feelings. The harmony, elegance, and perfection of his poetry are the result of long labour; but its original conceptions and pathos always sprang from the sudden inspiration of a deep and powerful passion. By an attentive perusal of all the writings of Petrarch, it may be reduced almost to a certainty–that by dwelling perpetually on the same ideas, and by allowing his mind to prey incessantly on itself, the whole train of his feelings and reflections acquired one strong character and tone; and if he was ever able to suppress them for a time, they returned to him with increased violence–that, to tranquillize this agitated state of his mind, he, in the first instance, communicated in a free and loose manner all that he thought and felt, in his correspondence with his intimate friends–that he afterwards reduced these narratives, with more order and description, into Latin verse–and that he, lastly, perfected them with a greater profusion of imagery and more art, in his Italian poetry, the composition of which at first served only, as he frequently says, "to divert and mitigate all his afflictions."

We may thus understand the perfect concord which prevails in Petrarch's poetry between nature and art; between the accuracy of fact and the magic of invention; between depth and perspicuity; between devouring passion and calm meditation. In three or four verses of Italian he often condenses the description, and concentrates the fire, which fill a page of his elegies and letters in Latin. It is precisely because the poetry of Petrarch originally sprang from his heart, that his passion never seems fictitious or cold, notwithstanding the profuse ornament of his style, or the metaphysical elevation of his thoughts. In the movement of Laura's eyes he sees a light which points out the way to heaven—

> Gentil mia donna, io veggio
> Nel mover de' vostri occhi un dolce lume
> Che mi mostra la via ch' al Ciel conduce.
> [LXXII, 1–3]

He exclaims "that the atmosphere becomes smiling, luminous, and serene, at her approach"—

> Il Ciel di vaghe e lucide faville
> S'accende intorno; e in vista si rallegra
> D'esser fatto seren da sì begli occhi—
> [CXCII, 12–14]

"that the air which is breathed around her, is so purified by the celestial radiance of her countenance, that while he fixes eyes upon her, every sensual desire is extinguished"—

> L'aer percosso da'lor dolci rai
> S'infiamma d'onestate—
> Basso desir non è ch' ivi si senta;
> Ma d'onor, di virtute. Or quando mai
> Fu per somma beltà vil voglia spenta?
> [CLIV, 9–10, 12–14]

Still he is always natural. Few lovers, indeed, could have conceived these ideas; yet the fire and the facility with which they are expressed, render them instantly familiar to the imagination of almost every reader. In the art of forming new and evident images, either of the most simple or abstract ideas, through the means of metaphor, Petrarch is as happy as he is original. To express the common-place thought, that his poetry and the beauty of Laura would be remembered after their death—"I see in fancy," says he, "a silent tongue, and two fair eyes, though closed, still beaming with light, surviving us—"

Ch'io veggio nel pensier, dolce mio foco,
Fredda una lingua e duo begli occhi chiusi
Rimaner dopo noi, pien' di faville —
[CCIII, 12–14]

and he has been imitated in this passage by an English poet, who combines in a great degree severity of taste, with boldness of expression:

"Ev'n in our ashes live their wonted fires."
GRAY

If Petrarch had not too unsparingly made use of antitheses—if he had not too frequently repeated his hyperboles—if he had not too often compared Laura to the sun—his numerous plagiarists, who, however, have never been able to imitate his beauties, would not have been so much noticed for their faults; nor would Salvator Rosa have had occasion to complain in his satires that "*These metaphors had exhausted the sun.*"—His play upon the words *Lauro* and *L'aura*, signifying *the laurel*, and *the air;* and the conceits afforded by the transformation of Apollo's Daphne into the immortal laurel, are still admired by some foreigners, on the authority of one of the most celebrated critics of Italy,[9] who nevertheless was delighted with the *Italia Liberata* of Trissino, and would never allow that Tasso's *Jerusalem* was the work of a poet. For my own part, I feel some pity towards a great poet, who with such extreme delicacy and ardour of mind—with a judgment so difficult, and a taste so refined—with a heated imagination, and an impassioned heart, could condescend, for the amusement of Laura and his readers, to such cold affectations. Still even Petrarch was bound to discharge the unfortunate duty of almost all writers, by sacrificing his own taste to that of his contemporaries. . . .

The elevated strain of piety and love which breathes through his works, borders occasionally on profaneness—

Baciale il piede, e la man bella e bianca;
Dille, e il baciar sia in vece di parole,
Lo spirto è pronto, ma la carne è stanca.
[CCVIII, 12–14]

Her lovely feet and gentle hands salute,
Wafting a poor reply with semblance mute,

[9] [Gian Vincenzo Gravina.]

Mourning and humble—signs that seem to speak
"The spirit is willing, but the flesh is weak."
Matth. c. XXVI. v. 41

To dissipate Laura's jealousy, he compares the eagerness with which he sought her resemblance in the face of beautiful women, to the devotion of a pilgrim gazing at the image of his Saviour—

Movesi il vecchierel canuto, e bianco,
Dal dolce loco ov'ha sua età fornita,
E dalla famigliuola sbigottita,
Che vede il caro Padre venir manco:
Indi, traendo poi l'antico fianco
Per l'estreme giornate di sua vita,
Quanto più può col buon voler s'aita,
Rotto da gli anni e dal cammino stanco;
E viene a Roma seguendo 'l desio
Per mirar la sembianza di Colui
Ch'amor lassù nel Ciel vedere spera:
Così, lasso, talor vo cercand'io,
Donna, quant'è possibile, in altrui
La desïata vostra forma vera.
[XVI]

The palmer bent, with locks of silver gray,
Quits the sweet spot where he has pass'd his years,
Quits his poor family whose anxious fears
Paint the loved father fainting on his way;
And trembling, on his aged limbs slow borne,
In these last days that close his earthly course,
He, in his soul's strong purpose, finds new force,
Though weak with age, though by long travel worn:
Thus reaching Rome, led on by pious love,
He seeks the image of that Saviour Lord
Whom soon he hopes to meet in bliss above:
So, oft in other forms I seek to trace
Some charm, that to my heart may yet afford
A faint resemblance of thy matchless grace.
Lady Dacre[10]

Love, alluding to the creation of the first man in Genesis, directs the poet to write that "Since the eyes of Adam were

10 [Foscolo dedicated the 1823 edition of the *Essays on Petrarch* to Barberina Lady Dacre. The last forty-five pages contain some of her translations from Petrarch. She had begun to publish translations of the sonnets privately about 1815, and in 1836 included many in her *Translations from the Italian Poets*, also privately printed.]

unclosed, mankind had never contemplated such beauty as Laura bore with her to the grave":

> Forma par non fu mai dal dì che Adamo
> Aperse gli occhi prima; e basti or questo:
> Piangendo il dico, e tu piangendo scrivi.
> [CCCLIV, 12–14]

The grand and solemn forms under which Love is represented by the Italian poets, belong more to the mystic philosophy, than to the popular mythology of the ancients. . . . The blind child, of whose wantoness Anacreon and Horace delight to complain, becomes in Petrarch "a Godhead in the full vigour of manhood, whose sight is deep and clear, and whose wounds are not inflicted by chance or by caprice" . . . severe and inexorable, he commands resignation, because "he executes those laws to which heaven and earth are alike subject"—

> Dura legge d'Amor! ma benchè obbliqua,
> Servar conviensi; però ch'ella aggiunge
> Di cielo in terra, universale, antiqua.
> [*Trionfi*, II, 148–50]

At the same time that he excites the spiritual, he cannot avoid exciting the material, portion of our nature; and that we desire the body as much as the soul of the object of our affections, must be ascribed to the grossness of our senses, and not to the viciousness of our passion. He is thus not the tyrant of Petrarch, but his "master and preceptor"—"the director of his conduct and the depositary of his secrets"—nor does he disdain "to render an account of the exercise of this power."—"Thou knowest that I feed upon tears; but thou knowest also, that at this price thou hast been able to respect the purity of that beauty which thou adorest, to raise thy mind to that Being who created her, and to render thyself like unto her"—

> Amor mi manda quel dolce pensiero,
> Che secretario antico è fra noi due,
> E mi conforta. . . .
> [XLXVIII, 1–3]

These conversations often pass between Love and the Poet on the banks of the Sorga; and they wander together through the valley of Vaucluse, after the death of Laura, consoling each other for her loss—

Amor, che meco al buon tempo ti stavi
In queste rive a' pensier nostri amiche,
E per saldar le ragion nostre antiche,
Meco, e col fiume ragionando andavi.
[CCCIII, 1–4]

Sì aspre vie nè sì selvagge
Cercar non so, che Amor non venga sempre
Ragionando con meco, ed io con lui.
[XXXV, 12–14]

Petrarch's love poetry may be considered as the intermediate link between that of the classics and the moderns. . . . He both feels like the ancient and philosophizes like the modern poets. When he paints after the manner of the classics, he is equal if not superior to them. The spirit of Laura soars to heaven, angels and blessed souls descend to meet her, and while she looks back upon earth to see if Petrarch follows her, she seems to pause in her aërial way—

Ad or ad or si volge a tergo
Mirando s'io la seguo; e par che aspetti.
[CCCXLVI, 11–12]

These few words contain a sublime and impassioned picture, requiring only the colouring of Titian. The poet could not give us a greater proof of the force and purity of Laura's passion than by delaying her flight to heaven in the expectation of her lover. It is true that these are inferences which we must ourselves draw; but those hearts which are not at once capable of supplying them, do not deserve to have them suggested. When Petrarch complies with the taste of his age, love and religion sometimes give warmth and solemnity even to the coldest antithesis: "Do not lament my fate," says the spirit of Laura to her lover; "for in dying, my days become eternal, and when I appeared to close my eyes, it was then that they were first opened"—

Di me non pianger tu, chè i miei dì fersi,
Morendo, eterni; e nell'eterno lume[11]
Quando mostrai di chiuder gli occhi apersi.
[CCIXXIX, 12–14]

The lady, whose translations are the fairest ornaments of these pages, has thus admirably rendered this passage:

[11] [The modern reading is *interno lume*.]

No longer mourn my fate! through death my days
Become eternal!—to eternal light
These eyes, which seems in darkness closed, I raise!

LADY DACRE

But whenever he has occasion to express abstract ideas, or to dive into the depths of the heart, Petrarch does not stop to define or expand; he uses every effort of his art that his observations may pass across the mind of his reader with the flash and rapidity of lightning.—"I know," says he, "how eagerly we pursue her who flies from us, and yet how we fear to overtake her." As every person who has loved, has found himself in this situation, he is the more ready to acquiesce in an observation which follows it, equally just, though not equally familiar—"I know that a lover may become so completely imbued with the thoughts of his mistress, as to believe almost in his identity with her—"

So della mia nemica cercar l'orme,
E temer di trovarla—e so in qual guisa
L'amante nell'amato si trasforme.

[*Trionfi* II, 160–62]

A modern writer, bound to construct poetry less on the poetical principles of Petrarch, than on the analytical taste of his own times, could not render this passage but with double the number of lines—

I know what hope and fear assail the mind
When I pursue my love, yet dread to find;
I know the strange and sympathetic tie,
When, soul in soul transfused, a fond ally
For ever seems another and the same,
Or change with mutual love their mortal frame.

BOYD's Transl.

But, besides this amplification, these lines have nothing to do with *mutual love;* for the poet expressly calls Laura *his enemy* in them: and it would seem that his translator had rather in view a passage of the Epistle of Eloisa—

Oh! happy state! when souls each other draw,
When love is liberty, and nature law:
All then is full, possessing and possest,
No craving void left aching in the breast;
Ev'n thought meets thought, ere from the lips it part;
And each warm wish springs mutual from the heart;

This sure is bliss (if bliss on earth there be),
And once the lot of Abelard and me.
[*Eloïsa to Abelard,* 91–98]

This school of poetical analysis, which the admirable taste of Pope brought to such perfection, belongs, if I may venture to give an opinion, more exclusively to the English, and is of early date. The notion expressed by Petrarch in the single line,

L'amante nell'amato si trasforme,

Ben Jonson has thus amplified into metaphysical detail:

It is a flame and ardour of the mind,
Dead in the proper corpse, quick in another's:
Transfers the lover into the [be-]loved:
That he or she, that loves, engraves or stamps
The idea of what they love, first in themselves;
Or, like the glasses, so their minds take in
The forms of their beloved, and them reflect.
[*The New Inn,* III, 2]

Some passages in Petrarch are, no doubt, too compressed and obscure; yet so much is the reader hurried along by the warmth and passion of the lover, that he fancies he understands what in reality demands some meditation to unravel. It would seem that if we do not conceive very distinctly the thoughts of a poet his lines must lose much of their effect; still whatever is deeply felt, we think is distinctly conceived by us,—and it is just when we are doubting whether we can soar with him above the precincts of the earth, that Petrarch contrives to insinuate himself into the inmost folds of our hearts; and the moment we feel with him, we are willing to admit the truth of his visions. He exclaims that "Heaven and Nature have united their efforts to exhibit their fairest work in Laura"—

Chi vuol veder quantunque può Natura,
E il Ciel fra noi, venga a mirar costei—
[CCXLVIII, 1–2]

Again,

Le stelle, il Cielo e gli elementi a prova
Tutte lor arti ed ogni estrema cura
Poser nel vivo lume, in cui Natura
Si specchia—
[CLIV, 1–4]

"That Laura came invested with all her virtues from the planet which she inhabited before she descended on earth"—

> In tale stella due begli occhi vidi
> Tutti pien' d' onestate, e di dolcezza—
> [CCLX, 1–2]

"That Laura's beauty existed in the conception of the Divinity before the creation of the universe"—

> In qual parte del Cielo, in quale Idea
> Era l'esempio?
> [CLIX, 1–2]

Yet in this very sonnet which developes the Platonic theory—"that all objects which fall under the senses of mankind are only copies of models more or less perfect, which have existed from all eternity in the mind of the Divinity,"—the poet abruptly exclaims—"Yet all her celestial beauties conspire only to my guilty death!"

> Benchè la somma è di mia morte rea!
> [CLIX, 8]

Thus the brilliancy of the description is masterly shadowed forth with a single line, which reminds us that, if Laura be an angel, her lover at least is a mortal, who suffers like ourselves.

One of those few poets whose inspirations are combined with the sober and deep insight into the mysteries of their art, has observed, "that we have a pleasure in the poet's representations of life, from our attachment to life itself: all imitations of objects have a certain value to the mind, as the resemblances and records of a perishable existence"[12]—The truth of this remark, and its application to works of imagination, may be fully understood by any person who considers, that our attachment to life springs from the consciousness of our existence:—that such consciousness is produced by the action of our faculties:—that this action fatigues and exhausts us:—and that we, therefore, oppose to it a constant desire of repose. We can thus explain our conflicting propensities to restlessness and inaction under which all men, more or less, occasionally labour. I believe that the motion and the equilibrium of our intellectual faculties is sustained, like the

[12] CAMPBELL's Lectures on Poetry. [Published in the *New Monthly Magazine*, January, 1821.]

palpitation of our heart, by a continual oscillation towards contrary directions; and that as soon as that oscillation stops, life ceases. We are always seeking repose, and for this very reason can never obtain it. When we do obtain it by absolute inactivity, our existence is rendered wearisome; and it is then that we tremble at the thought that life is passing away, and at the approach of the only real calm, which is death. Yet, as the complete repose of our faculties stupifies us, so the violent agitation of our own passions overwhelms us:—the representation of the passions of others, therefore, is agreable, because it renders us conscious of our existence by exciting but not distressing us, and conveys to us at once the pleasures of agitation and repose. The representation of love has the greatest influence upon mankind, because the other passions, the seeds of which are contained in every human breast, require the aid of circumstances, which to many persons never occur, to develope them; whereas love and death are, as Dante says of the sun, "the greatest ministers of Nature"; it is by love only that she can reproduce her creations which death is perpetually destroying. But love is seen, by almost all writers, under those outward appearances with which it may be incidentally clothed by the peculiar manners of each nation and age. Thus novels seldom please the next generation, because they represent rather the accidental and transitory forms, than the inward nature, of love. But when a great poet describes his own heart, his picture of love will draw tears from the eyes of every man in every age. Although Petrarch raises this passion to the level of his own mind, and adorns it according to the metaphysical theories and the manners of his time, he still brings before our eyes many resemblances and records of our own feelings. Perhaps he is the most successful among those poets, "who surprise us with traits of nature that have escaped our observation, or faded from our memories, and affect us as if they restored to us a lost or absent friend, with all the tender illusion, though without the indistinctness, of a dream." In Petrarch's poetry we meet with every little circumstance of our passion—the pains—the pleasures—the hopes—the fears we have experienced; and sometimes by a single line he transports us back again to live with the person who was once dearest to us, and who may have long ago disappeared from our eyes, and almost from our recollection. The loftiness of his style and the ornament of his images, so far from repelling us, draw us to him, because he seems to employ every effort of his talents to make us the spectators and companions of his happiness or of his misery.—"Here she sang so sweetly; and here she sat. Here she turned, and there she paused; here her beautiful eyes penetrated my soul, and here she spoke to me—there she smiled, and there her countenance changed. With such thoughts does Love, who is thy master and mine, fill my mind both night and day"—

> Qui cantò dolcemente; e qui s'assise;
> Qui si rivolse, e qui rattenne il passo;
> Qui co' begli occhi mi trafisse il core;
> Qui disse una parola, e qui sorrise;
> Qui cangiò il viso. In questi pensier, lasso,
> Notte e dì tiemmi il signor nostro, Amore.
> [CXII, 9–14]

It is chiefly in the expression of grief that Petrarch enters into every heart, and that all hearts enter into his. Neatness of diction—delicacy of sentiment—Platonic ecstasy, all yield to the violence of his grief; and we witness the dreadful conflict of reason with despair—of passion with religion. The remembrance of his love, and the remorse of his guilty desires, penetrate his heart; and whilst he seems ready to destroy himself, he is checked by the fear only of passing from one misery to a greater—

> Se sapessi per Morte essere scarco
> Del pensier amoroso che mi atterra,
> Con le mie mani avrei già posto in terra,
> Queste membra dogliose e quello incarco:
> Ma perch'io temo che sarebbe un varco
> Di pianto in pianto, e d'una in altra guerra—
> [XXXVI, 1–6]
>
> Oh! if this cankering thought—this torturing dream
> In endless death these hands might hope to close;
> Soon should my wearied limbs on earth repose,
> And the damp sod a welcome bed I'd deem.
> But still I fear to tempt the awful stream,
> To fly from strife to strife—from woe to woes.

When he seeks consolation from Heaven, from mankind, and from all the objects that surround him, our sympathy with the man makes us almost forget our admiration of the poet; because we see, that, like every creature who feels extremely miserable, he fancies that he has inspired all nature with his own affliction—

Poor solitary bird, that pour'st thy lay,
Or haply mournest the sweet season gone:
As chilly night and winter hurry on,
And day-light fades, and summer flies away;
If as the cares that swell thy little throat,
Thou knew'st alike the woes that wound my rest,
Oh, thou wouldst house thee in this kindred breast,
And mix with mine thy melancholy note.
Yet little know I our's are kindred ills:
She still may live the object of thy song:
Not so for me stern Death or Heaven wills!
But the sad season, and less grateful hour,
And of past joy and sorrow thoughts that throng
Prompt my full heart this idle lay to pour.—

LADY DACRE

Vago augelletto, che cantando vai,
Ovver piangendo il tuo tempo passato,
Veggendoti la notte e 'l verno a lato,
E 'l dì dopo le spalle, e i mesi gai;
Se come i tuoi gravosi affanni sai,
Così sapessi il mio simile stato;
Verresti in grembo a questo sconsolato
A partir seco i dolorosi guai.
I 'non so se le parti sarian pari;
Chè quella cui tu piangi è forse in vita;
Di ch'a me Morte e 'l Ciel son tanto avari:
Ma la stagione e l'ora men gradita,
Col membrar de' dolci anni e degli amari,
A parlar teco con pietà m'invita.

[CCCLIII]

His poetry about Laura finishes with one of his most beautiful odes. It is addressed to the blessed Virgin, whom as she had known human affections, and had combined in herself the three gentlest dearest names on earth—of mother, daughter, and wife—he hopes will be merciful to him—

Tre dolci e cari nomi hai in te raccolti,
Madre, Figliuola, e Sposa.

[CCCLXVI, 46–47]

Then with a sublimity and pathos which no poet has ever surpassed, he implores, through her assistance, that he may cease in his old age to lament over the ashes of one who had filled his life with dangers and with tears. . . .

Little as the *Sonetti* and *Canzoni* may appear to our modern composers of operas to be susceptible of music, it is not on that account the less true, that these terms are derived from *Suono* and *Canto*, and that poets often added notes of music to their stanzas. In the manuscripts which are still preserved at Florence, of Franco Sacchetti and other contemporaries of Petrarch, the following note is to be found at the head of some of their sonnets: *Intonatum per Francum–Scriptor dedit sonum.* The system of Italian music, by counterpoint, had been created three centuries before their age by Guido d'Arezzo; and it is only in our days that it has been rendered refined and complicated, by the followers of the German school. Poetry was not then in Italy the mere *caput mortuum* of music; and the human voice, instead of being a subordinate accessory to the orchestra, filled the most prominent part, and was accompanied by inanimate instruments only so far as was necessary to support it, and to regulate its modulations. The words might then strike the ear with less astonishment than the tunes; but they spoke more forcibly to the heart and more usefully to the mind. Petrarch poured forth his verses to the sound of his lute, which he bequeathed in his will to a friend;[13] and his voice was sweet, flexible, and of great compass.[14] All the love-poetry of his predecessors, except that of Cino, wants sweetness of numbers; but the sweetness of Petrarch is enlivened with a variety, a rapidity, and a glow, which no Italian lyric has ever possessed in an equal degree. The power of preserving, and at the same time of diversifying the rhythm, belongs to him alone–his melody is perpetual, and yet never wearies the ear. His *canzoni* (a species of composition partaking of the ode and the elegy, the character and form of which are exclusively Italian) contain stanzas sometimes of twenty lines. He has placed the cadences, however, in such a manner as to allow the voice to rest at the end of every three or four verses, and has fixed the recurrence of the same rhyme and the same musical pauses at intervals sufficiently long to avoid monotony, and sufficiently short to preserve harmony. It is not difficult, therefore, to give credit to Filippo Vilani, when he

13 *Magistro Thomae Bombasio de Ferraria lego leutum meum bonum, ut eum sonet, non pro vanitate saeculi fugacis, sed ad laudem Dei aeterni.* –Petr. Testam.

14 *Doctus insuper Lyra mire cecinit / Fuit vocis sonorae atque redundantis suavitatis tantae atque dulcedinis.–Phil.* VILLANI, *Vit. Petr.*

assures us, "that the musical modulation of the verses which Petrarch addressed to Laura flowed so melodiously, that even the most grave could not refrain from repeating them."[15]

Metastasio, to please the court of Vienna, the musicians, and the public of his day, and to gratify the delicacy of his own feminine taste, has reduced his language and versification to so limited a number of words, phrases, and cadences, that they seem always the same, and in the end produce only the effect of a flute, which conveys rather delightful melody than quick and distinct sensations. Petrarch, on the contrary, has not only vigorously grasped and beautifully used all the abundance of words—all the variety of numbers—all the graces and energy and idioms of his own language, but he has naturalized those of the Provençal and Spanish poets. No term which he has employed is become obsolete; and each of his phrases may be, and still is, written without quaintness. At the same time that he improves the materials in which the Italian language already abounded, he seems to create it afresh, for it was in reality both native and foreign to him. When he was only nine years old, he was taken into France, where he passed his youth, and the greater portion of his life. His parents, from whom he might have acquired the Tuscan idiom, died when he was still a youth. In the frequent journeys which he made into Italy, he lived every where for considerable periods except at Florence, where he passed only three or four weeks. In order to form a style which should be quite his own, he assures us that he never possessed a copy of Dante's great poem, whose diction he affects to despise.[16] It was only near the close of his life that Petrarch began to repent of not having availed himself of the "vulgar language," —"a new-discovered field which had fallen into the hands of unskilful husbandmen, and which still remained to be cleared."[17] I am indebted to the library and liberality of my Lord Holland, for the only specimen I have ever seen of the Italian prose of Petrarch. It is a manuscript in Petrarch's own hand,[18] of two letters, which, far from possessing the elegance

[15] *Tanta siquidem dulcedine rithmi fluunt, ut ab eorum pronunciatione et sonis, gravissimi nesciebant abstinere.* PHIL. VILLANI, *Vit. Petr.*

[16] See the Epistle of Boccace to Petrarch: *Italiae jam certus honor.*

[17] *Hic vulgaris stylus modo inventus vastatoribus crebris, et nullo squallidus colono.*—Senilium Lib. 5. Ep. 2, 3.

[18] [These letters later were proved not to be autographs.]

and grammatical correctness of Dante and Boccaccio, or indeed of their minor contemporaries, are remarkable only for the warmth of feeling and perspicuity of thought peculiar to his style. If, instead of devoting his life to an ancient language, in which there were already so many inimitable authors, he had written his numerous works in Italian, he might have left models for every sort of composition. His great power in the poetry of a language which he had cultivated so little, is one of those secret wonders which genius works unconsciously even to him who possesses it; as seeds which chance has scattered in some congenial spot, will sometimes spontaneously quicken to greater luxuriance, than the most industrious art could have affected a less favoured soil.

In the numerous letters written by Petrarch towards the decline of life, and arranged by him under the title of EPISTOLAE SENILES, the old solitary man, while conversing with his most intimate friends, intended to be heard by the world. They are full of pathos and wisdom; of pedantry and eloquence; of christian self-denial and puerile self-complacency: and there is a continual struggle between his natural frankness and the caution of age. However, his correspondents were indebted to him for a profusion of quotations, which, in the scarcity of books in that age, made them acquainted with many passages of classical writers. Possibly they indulged almost as much as we do, in gossiping about all the concerns, great and small, public and personal, historical and fabulous, of their celebrated contemporaries; but editors of monthly and quarterly publications, of daily newspapers, and of biographical dictionaries of the dead and the living, had not as yet either the professional inducements or the means to penetrate into the privacy of domestic retirement. Petrarch, allured by the idea that his celebrity would magnify into importance all the ordinary occurrences of his life, satisfied the curiosity both of his friends and foes by seriously telling them, how

> He did all natural functions of a man,
> Ate, drank, and slept, and put his raiment on—
> [*Inf*. XXXIII, 141. Cary's version]

which has afforded this advantage at any rate, that our information is not apocryphal, and that we possess the materials for the most interesting of histories—the history of the mind of a man of genius,—but he still requires, what he has never yet had the good fortune to find, a man of genius for his historian. In Petrarch's letters as well as in his poems and treatises, we always identify the author with the man who felt himself irresistibly impelled to develope his own intense feelings. Being endowed with almost all the noble, and with some of the paltry passions, of our nature, and having attempted to conceal them, he awakens us to reflection upon ourselves, while we contemplate in him a being of our own species, yet different from every other, and whose originality excites even more sympathy than admiration.

VI

UGO FOSCOLO

Boccaccio

Amongst the books which have been the most frequently republished since the invention of printing, and which will probably continue to be multiplied in this and all succeeding ages, few, if any, can be mentioned, as surpassing the tales of Boccaccio, in the rarity or number of editions, in the constant and assiduous criticism, or the typographical elegance bestowed upon them. A single copy of some of the earlier editions has sometimes fetched a price which would purchase a useful collection of books sufficient for the purposes of a man of letters. A new one has lately appeared, embellished with designs by Stothard. However great may be the artist's merit, as it has nothing to do with the present subject of our considerations,—the moral tendency of the book,—it appears advisable to leave it to the discussion of lovers of bibliographical elegancies. In the Historical Illustrations, however, which are prefixed to it, we have met with many very curious remarks—the more valuable from their novelty, though relating to an author and to a book which have enjoyed five centuries of celebrity.

The critical examination of the Decameron, considered as a literary work, is placed in a new point of view by the author [Foscolo himself] of the Illustrations. Perhaps neither the enthusiastic admirers of Boccaccio, nor his severe censors, will be satisfied with the terms to which he reduces the question. But the anger of litigants against the judge who would put an end to their differences is no slight proof of the equity of his sentence. In these Illustrations the causes of the celebrity of the Decameron are traced through the political and religious history of Italy, and illustrated by anecdotes unknown to the numerous compilers of new and old literary curiosities, which are often new and curious only because they are furbished up by those who copy them, in such a manner as to engage the admiration,

Reprinted from the *Opere* (Firenze: Le Monnier, 1953), 10: 377–96.

and to impose on the credulity of idle readers. Lastly, in the Illustrations before us, we gain a nearer insight into the heart and mind of a celebrated author, of whom we are naturally led to form an idea corresponding with his book; and we discover, not without wonder, that the character of the book was entirely opposed to the tenor of the writer's life.

Considering the Novelle as a work of genius, their greatest merit consists in the variety of characters they contain. The author, with a skill and felicity truly wonderful, has adapted his style to princes, matrons, youths, maidens, friars, and thieves, without ever falling into exaggeration; and if his characters are deficient in force of expression, they always abound in fidelity and in grace; and the illusion is perfect, precisely because the author never appears to try to produce it. His most devoted commentators are however of opinion, that Boccaccio was a more dignified narrator than any ancient historian; that the discourses he puts into the mouths of his actors are more powerful than the orations of Cicero or Demosthenes; that his representations of strong minds struggling against passion or calamity, are more pathetic and touching than the tragedies of Æschylus or of any other writer; and that his wit and sarcasm are more pungent than those of Lucian. Admiration like this is mere fanaticism. Boccaccio, without being pre-eminent in any one of these various kinds of style, was felicitous in all; which can scarcely be said of any other writer whatever. Nevertheless, M. Ginguené, one of the most elegant and celebrated critics of our times, thinks that Boccaccio, having before his eyes the history of Thucydides and the poem of Lucretius, aspired to the imitation of their respective merits so successfully, that he not only equalled, but surpassed them both; and described the plague like an historian, a philosopher, and a poet.[1]

It is not known whether Boccaccio had read both these writers; the Roman was however sufficient, since he follows precisely in the footsteps of Thucydides. Many passages in the Italian appear paraphrases, not only of the events which happened in Athens or in Florence respectively, in consequence of the same dreadful epidemy, but of reflexions and minute details in which it is improbable that writers should agree by mere accident. The merit of the description of the pestilence in the

[1] Ginguené, *Hist. Litt. d'Italie.* Tom. III. p. 87, seq.

Decameron does not arise so much from the style—which, in comparison with those of Thucydides and Lucretius, is extremely cold—as from the contrast between the disease, the funerals, and the desolation of the city, and the tranquil pleasures, the dances and the banquets, the songs and tales of the villa. In this respect, Boccaccio, even if he were a copier of the main incident, copied it in the spirit of an inventor. But if we consider each description separately, we shall find that the words of the Greek historian excite powerful emotions either of sympathy or horror, which press with combined yet distinct force upon our hearts, because he follows the order marked out by nature in the beginning, progress, and consequences of such a calamity. He puts together twice as many circumstances as Boccaccio, and paints them forcibly in a few words, so that they combine to occupy every faculty of our minds.

Boccaccio pauses leisurely on one circumstance after another, and adorns them with that light touch which painters call *piazzoso*, and amplifies them in such a manner, as to make us think he exaggerates: "Maravigliosa cosa è ad udire quello che io debbo dire; il che se dagli occhi di molti e da' miei non fosse stato veduto appena che io ardissi di crederlo non che di scriverlo, quantunque da fededegno udito l'avessi."—"Wonderful to hear is that which I have to relate; which if it had not been seen by the eyes of many, as well as by my own, scarcely should I dare to believe, much less to write, although I had heard it from a trustworthy person." Nor is this all. "Di che gli occhi miei (siccome poco davante è detto) presero trall'altre volte un dì così fatta esperienza, nella via pubblica."[2]—"Of which my eyes (as has been just now said) had one day, among other times, so full an evidence in the public street." Thucydides, it is true, relates with more effect, because his experience was still more positive. "I have also suffered from this disease myself, and have seen others suffering under it." But he abstains from all rhetorical declamation, and from any protestations of veracity. The different temper of their minds, and the diversity of their pursuits, led them to describe and to colour the same object in styles perfectly distinct. In the age of Thucydides the meretricious ornaments of style which Boccaccio acquired from the admired masters of Roman rhetoric, were not yet fashioned by Isocrates

[2] *Introduzione.*

and other declaimers, nor had they attained to any authority in Athens. He is the least Attic of the Athenians because he modelled his maternal dialect upon the universal and simple language which had come down from Homer. This was not a Mosaic, formed of different dialects, as is generally imagined, but was studied by poets and historians, for the purpose of infusing a literary character into the dialects of their respective cities, in order that by the use of it they might be the more easily read throughout Greece. And because that primitive language was national and living, the dialects acquired beauty from it, while they lost nothing in vigour. Boccaccio, moulding the Florentine idiom on the dead language of the Latins, raised it in dignity, but deadened its native energy. Lastly, Thucydides employs words as passive matters, and compels them to give form and being to passions, imaginations, and reflections, almost more numerous than they can contain or express; he appears the tyrant of his language. Boccaccio courts his like a lover; every word seems, in his eyes, instinct with life, not needing to be animated by intellect; and therefore, for a medium of continuous narration, he desired "lingua d'eloquenza splendida e di vocaboli eccellenti faconda."[3] He judged of their excellence by his ear, which was most delicate for the construction of prose. Certain it is that the exterior and permanent beauty of every language depends on sounds, because these are natural properties, and the only ones which can be perpetual and unchangeable in words. All other qualities they acquire from common consent and usage, which are often inconstant; or from the various modifications of feeling and thinking among writers. It is not, however, the less true that the greater is the number of words by which a thought is represented, the smaller is the portion of intellect which necessarily belongs to each of them, although the variety occasioned by this copiousness is productive of harmony. Hence every style consisting rather of sounds than of signification, glides smoothly and agreeably over the mind: it keeps it in a state of gentle excitement without fatiguing it. But if harmony compensates for languor, it often retards the rapidity of thought; and ideas which owe their clearness to periphrasis, do not carry that conviction which results from appropriateness and precision of expression. Writers of this de-

[3] *Fiammetta,* lib. iv.

scription shine but do not warm; whenever they are impassioned they appear rather skilful in the use of language than naturally eloquent; the reader cannot persuade himself that they feel what they write; their narrations describe but do not paint; nor does it ever happen to them to condense their sentences into one utterance of fact, reason, imagination, and passion; to dart them like an arrow, whose course is visible only in the line of warmth and light it leaves, and which flies, without noise of flame, straight to the mark. They are nevertheless exquisite writers in their way, but one cannot see how others can admire in them a union of the highest qualities of style which characterize philosophers, historians, and poets. They are incompatible qualities—unless we mistake those of Boccaccio—and the proof of this is, that when abused they degenerate into perfectly contrary defects. Thucydides fatigues us by imposing on us an incessant labour of thought, while Boccaccio, perhaps, wearies us like a man who should incessantly entertain our ears with sweet music. It is a style in every respect most happily appropriate to gay and sprightly ladies and enamoured youths, who sit amusing themselves with telling stories.

The black-letter scholars of Italy have ransacked every library and archive, to discover the ancient authors and anecdotes which furnished Boccaccio with the materials for his tales. And if genius consists rather in the invention of facts than in the novelty and skill with which they are related, Boccaccio has certainly no claim to originality. But for the same reason all tragic poets, not even excepting Shakespeare must be considered as copyists, since they founded the action of their dramas on circumstances and characters described by historians. The first origin of dramas and of tales is of little importance to criticism. What is important is to observe the impulse given by every great writer to that department of literature in which he particularly excelled. In the middle ages story-tellers (novellatori) were regularly salaried to amuse the tables and the idle hours of the great; in some cases they were even regarded as officers of the court. The telling of stories being then a regular vocation, rendered the writing of them more easy and common, even in those barbarous time when princes could scarcely read. The first rude and primitive specimens of the infant Italian language, in prose, are to be met with among compositions of this kind.

The following tale was written more than a century before the time of Boccaccio:—

> The damsel loved Lancelot so much that at length she lay dying, and commanded that when her soul should have departed from his body, a rich boat should be made ready, covered with a scarlet stuff, and having a rich bed therein, with rich and noble coverings of silk, adorned with rich precious stones; and that her body should be laid upon this bed, clad in her most noble garments, and with a beautiful crown on her head, rich with much gold, and with many rich precious stones; and with a rich girdle and purse, and in this purse there was a letter of the following tenor. But first let us tell concerning that which goes before the letter. The damsel died of the love sickness, and that was done which she had commanded, as to the boat without a sail and without oars, and without any one therein; and it was placed upon the sea. The sea guided it to Camalot, and it stopped at the shore. The cry of it went through all the court. The knights and barons came down from their palaces, and the noble King Arthur came thither, wondering very greatly that this boat had thus been brought thither without any steersman. The king entered therein; saw the damsel and the clothing. He caused the purse to be opened; they found this letter. He caused it to be read, and it said thus:—To all the Knights of the Round Table, this damsel of Scalot sends health, as to the best company of the world. And if you would know wherefore at my end I am come hither, it is for the best knight in the world, and the most cruel, that is, my Lord Sir Lancelot of the Lake, whom I knew not how so far to entreat for love, as that he should have pity upon me. And therefore, alas! I have died for loving well, as you may see.

If Boccaccio had chosen to amplify and embellish this story with the variety, the incidents, the passions, and characters, and the richness of style with which he adorned many others borrowed from old romances, he would certainly have made a wonderful use of the strange obsequies chosen by the damsel, and would have arranged and coloured the circumstances in such a manner as to give an air of verisimilitude to so new an invention; unless, perhaps, by too great a desire to describe the damsel being dead, clad as for a marriage feast, and wandering over the deep without any certainty of finding burial, or by making her discourse in her last moments, comforting herself with the hope of showing the world that the knight by his cruelty had caused her death, he had chilled the fancy of the reader by his rhetoric, and dissipated all those images and emotions which arise spontaneously on the mere relation of touching incidents in simple language. "The damsel died of the love sickness, and that was done which she had commanded, as to the boat without sail and without oars, and without any one therein; and it was placed upon the sea." The barrenness of almost all these early narrators is sometimes compensated by the liberty in which they leave the mind of the reader to think and feel for itself. Having now taken from the illustrations before us whatever has seemed to us necessary for appreciating the true value of the Novelle, as a literary work, we shall proceed to give an historical account of the causes which have led them to be regarded and adopted for so many ages, as the sole model of style, the sole grammatical authority of Italy. This phenomenon has never yet been explained.

The author died not only without the hope, but without the desire, that his Decameron should outlive him. His autograph copy has never been found, and from what we shall presently have occasion to observe about his hand-writing, we derive very strong presumptive evidence that he destroyed it himself. A young friend of his, eight or ten years after his death, transcribed it with the most scrupulous exactness, frankly confessing that the copy he used was full or errors. After the introduction of printing, copies and editions were multiplied with mistakes, which, it was clear, were partly taken from the manuscripts of wretched copiers, and partly accumulated by the negligence of printers, while their art was yet in its infancy. But from the age of Boccaccio to that of Lorenzo de Medici, and the Pontificate of Leo X., the Italian language was so barbarized that it seemed lost to the learned men of Italy, and for more than a century they wrote in Latin which had fixed rules, and was common to all Europe. The critics of that illustrious epoch, strove by every means to form the language spoken by Italians into a literary language, well adapted for written composition, and for being understood by the whole nation, and in the penury of authors who could furnish observations, and examples, and principles, from which a right method might be derived, they had recourse, with common consent, to the tales of Boccaccio; they found words at once vernacular and perfectly elegant, distinct and expressive, skilful construction, musical periods, and diversity of style; nor perhaps could any expedient at that time have been found better adapted for obviating numerous difficulties which presented themselves. But the maxims and the practice of the literary men of that age, consisted not so much in constructing rules from observations, as in imitating punctually, servilely, and childishly, the most admired writers. In poetry they were implicit copiers of Petrarch, and sang of pure and sacred love. In Latin they imitated Virgil and Cicero, and treated sacred things in profane words. Thus the system of restricting a whole dead language to the works of a few writers was still more absurdly applied to the living tongue of Italy, and critics were almost unanimous in decreeing that no example was to be adduced from any poem except the Canzoniere Amoroso of Petrarch.

From this circumstance, the Protestants took occasion to impute to the literary men of that time very small regard to manners, and no sense of religion. The first accusation is exaggerated, and was common to them with all orders of society in Europe; the other is most absurd, but has prevailed in Protestant universities from that day, and has been handed down by long tradition, on the testimony of the first religious reformers, who, in order to open every possible way for the reception of their doctrines, imputed infidelity to all the learned men of the court of Leo X. But most, if not all of these men, believed the faith they professed, and which was then attacked by hostile superstition. Some made a vow never to read a profane book, but being unable long to observe it, got absolution from the pope; others, that they might not contaminate Christian things with the impure latinity of monks and friars, tried to translate the Bible into the language of the age of Augustus. This system of servilely imitating excellent authors, did not prevent some men of genius, particularly historians, from attempting to relate in a style at once original, dignified, and energetic, the events of their country. But they were living writers, nor had long celebrity and prescriptive authority yet stamped them as models. To this reason, which holds good of every age and country, was added, that the liberty of the numerous republics of Italy which had sprung up in the barbarism of the middle ages, declined in the most fertile and splendid period of her literature, and the historians who were witnesses of the misfortunes and degradation of their country, wrote in a manner which was not agreeable to her tyrants. Hence Machiavelli, Guicciardini, Segni, and others who are now studied as masters of style, were not then read, except by a few; their works were hardly known in manuscript, and if published they were mutilated; nor were any complete editions of their histories printed until two centuries after they were written. Thus the Novelle of Boccaccio held the field, and their popularity was greatly increased by the abhorrence and contempt which they inspired against the wickedness of the monks.

Certain young men of Florence conspired against Duke Alexander, bastard of Clement VII, with the design of driving him from their country, and re-establishing the republic. They held meetings under colour of amending the text of Boccaccio by the collation of manuscripts, and by critical examination. Such was the source, and such the authors, of the celebrated edition of Giunti, in 1527, now regarded as one of the rarest curiosities of bibliography, and preserved from that time as a record of the Florentine republic, almost all those young men having fought against the house of Medici, and died at the siege of Florence, or in exile. The work subsequently became more scarce, because it was constantly exposed to the danger of being mutilated or prohibited through the interest of the monks. Leo X made a jest of those things, and crowned the abbot of Gaeta, seated on an elephant, with laurel and cabbage-leaves. Adrian VI who succeeded him, had been immured in a cloister, and the cardinals of his school shortly after proposed that the Colloquies of Erasmus, and every popular book injurious to the clergy, should be prohibited. Paul III was of opinion that the threat was sufficient, nor was it at that time put in execution; but when the Decameron, which had already been translated into several languages, was quoted by the Anti-Papists, the church ceased to confine herself to threats, and began actually to prohibit the reprinting and the reading of Boccaccio's tales; nor could any one have a copy in his possession without a licence from his confessor. The Protestant Reformation provoked a reform in the Catholic church, which though less apparent, was perhaps greater and more solid. The Protestants took as the basis of their's, the liberty of interpreting the oracles of the Holy Spirit by the aid of human reason; while the Catholics admitted no interpretations but those inspired by God as represented by the popes. Which of these two was the most beneficial to the interest of religion, is a difficult question. Perhaps every religion which is much subjected to the scrutiny of reason, ceases to be faith; while every creed, inculcated without the concurrence of the reason, degenerates into blind superstition. But, as far as literature was concerned, liberty of conscience, in many countries, prepared the way for civil liberty, and for the free expression of thoughts and opinions; while in Italy, passive obedience to the religious power strengthened political tyranny, and increased the debasement and long servitude of the public mind. The Protestant Reformation was principally confined to dogmas—the Catholic wholly to discipline; and, therefore, all speculations on the lives and manners of ecclesiastics were then repressed as leading to new heresies. The Council of Trent saw that the people of Germany did not stop short at complaining that the monks were traders in Indulgencies, but went on to deny the sacrament of confession, the celibacy of the clergy, and the infallibility and spiritual power of the pope. It therefore decreed, that any attack upon, or insinuations against, the clergy, should be followed by immediate registration of the book containing them in the index of prohibited works; and that the reading, or the possession of any such book, without licence from a bishop, should be regarded both as a sin and as an offence punishable in virtue of the anathema. These laws, of ecclesiastical origin, were thenceforth interpreted and administered by civil tribunals subjected to the presidency of inquisitors of the order of St. Dominick; who, moreover, by the consent of the Italian governments, were invested with authority to examine, alter, mutilate, and suppress every book, whether ancient or modern, previously to its being printed.

The Spanish domination in Italy, the long reign of Philip II (the most tyrannical of tyrants), and the Council of Trent, had imposed silence upon genius. Cosmo I Grand Duke of Tuscany, kept in his pay one or two historians of the house of Medici; he caused all books of a less servile character to be collected together from every part and burnt. The Decameron was, therefore, by an absolute political necessity, resorted to by literary men as the sole rule and standard of the written prose language. To cancel every memorial of freedom, Cosmo I suppressed all the academies instituted in Tuscany during the republican government of its cities; the only indulgence he showed was towards an assembly of grammarians, who afterwards became rather famous than illustrious under the name of the Academy della Crusca; and then, when the indolence of slavery deadened and chilled the passions; when education, committed to the jesuits, had enfeebled all intellect; when men of letters became the furniture of courts, often of foreign courts; when universities were in the pay of kings, and under the direction of inquisitors;—then did the academy Della Crusca begin to claim supremacy over Italian literature, and to establish the tales of Boccaccio as the sole text and rule for every dictionary or grammar, and the basis of every philosophical theory regarding the language.

Nevertheless, the academicians found that the Decameron had never been printed in a genuine and correct form, fitted to serve as the ground-work of language. After many years spent in consulting, correcting, and collating manuscripts, they prepared an edition which they hoped to consacrate as an oracle in all grammatical questions: but the Holy Office interposed in the most furious manner, and did not allow it to be printed. They therefore consented, as they could do no better, to publish a mutilated edition. The grand dukes of Tuscany, in order to put an end to these difficulties, deputed certain learned men to negotiate with the Master of the Sacred Palace in the Vatican, one of whom was a bishop, and nearly all dignified ecclesiastics. The Master of the Sacred Palace, a Dominican friar and a Spaniard, attended their meetings in his own right. Writing his opinions in a bastard language, he gave his advice as an official grammarian: they did not, however, come to any conclusion.

At length an Italian Dominican, of a more facile character, was added to the council, and having been confessor to Pius V he prevailed on Gregory XIII to allow the Decameron to be printed without any other alteration than what was necessary for the good fame of the ecclesiastics. Thus, abbesses and nuns in love with their gardeners were transformed into matrons and young ladies; friars who got up impostures and miracles into necromancers; and priests who intrigued with their parishioners' wives into soldiers; and by dint of a hundred other inevitable transformations and mutilations, the academy, after four years' labour, succeeded in publishing the Decameron in Florence, illustrated by their researches. But Sextus V ordered that even this edition, though approved by his predecessor, should be infamized in the Index. It was therefore necessary to have recourse to fresh mangling and interpolation, and of texts so fabricated, therefore, the academicians of La Crusca weighed every word and every syllable of the Novelle, exaggerated every minute detail, and described every thing under the high-sounding names of the richness, propriety, grace, elegance, the figures, laws, and principles of language.

These facts, which our limits compel us to condense and to strip of those circumstances which render them infinitely more diverting, would appear the inventions of a satirist, if the author of the Illustrations did not confirm his narrative, step by step, by authorities and documents. From the various reflections which he deduces from them, we shall select but one—that the literary language of Italy was founded on a collection of tales, not of the most edifying description, at the same period that the literary language of England was fixed by the translation of the Holy Scriptures.

This singular destiny of a work composed as a mere pastime, threw into comparative oblivion its other literary merits, which were more useful to the civilization of Europe, and stamped upon the name of its author an infamous celebrity, which has always hidden from the world the true character of his mind. The Illustrations before us are extremely interesting from the light they throw on the human heart. It is unquestionable, that if Petrarch had expended on writing Italian prose, the tenth part of the labour which he bestowed on his poetry, he would not have been able to write so much as he did. This reason, among many others, contributed to induce him to write in Latin: the chief motive, however, was the glory which then attached to the Latin poets, and which, in the universities and the courts of the princes, was scarcely granted to those who wrote in Italian. Few however, if any, had any real conception of the spirit and merits of the Latin tongue. Coluccio Salutato was a man of great learning, and enjoyed a high reputation among the scholars of that age; yet he pronounced that the pastoral poems of Boccaccio, written in Latin, were only inferior to Petrarch, and that Petrarch was superior to Virgil![4] Erasmus, a critic of another age, and of a different turn of mind, when commenting on the literature of the fourteenth century, detracts a little from the

[4] *Colutius Salutatus. Epis. ad Bocc.*

praises bestowed upon Petrarch, and enhances those of Boccaccio, whose Latinity he esteems the less barbarous of the two.[5]

The injury which Petrarch did to his native tongue, by his ambition of writing in Latin, was compensated by his indefatigable and generous perseverance in restoring to Europe the most noble remains of human intellect. No monument of antiquity, no series of medals, or manuscript of Roman literature was neglected by him wherever he had the least hope of rescuing the one from oblivion, or of multiplying copies of the other. He acquired a claim to the gratitude of all Europe, and is still deservedly called the first restorer of classical literature. Boccaccio, however, is entitled not only to a share, but to an equal share, to say the least, of this honour. We are perfectly aware that our opinion on this subject will be at first regarded as a paradox put forth from a mere ambition of novelty; the proofs, however, which we shall briefly adduce, will convert the surprise of our readers at our temerity, into wonder at the scanty recompense which Boccaccio has hitherto received, in spite of his gigantic and successful endeavours to dispel the ignorance of the middle ages.

The allegorical mythology, together with the theology and metaphysics of the ancients, the events of the history of ages less remote, and even geography, were illustrated by Boccaccio in his voluminous Latin Treatises, now little read, but at that time studied by all as the chiefest and best works of solid learning. Petrarch knew nothing of Greek; and whatever acquaintance, in Tuscany or Italy, they had with the writers of that language, they owed entirely to Boccaccio. He went to Sicily, where there were still some remains of a Greek dialect, and masters who taught the language, and put himself under two preceptors of the greatest merit, Barlaamus and Leontius. Under them he studied several years; he afterwards prevailed on the republic of Florence to establish a chair of Greek literature for Leontius. Had it not been for Boccaccio, the poems of Homer would have remained long undiscovered. The story of the Trojan War was read in the celebrated romance called the History of Guido delle Colonne, from which also were derived many wild inventions and apocryphal records of the Homeric times, and various dramas, like Shakspeare's Troilus and

[5] *Ciceronianus.*

Cressida, containing not a single circumstance to be met with in the Iliad or Odyssey. Nor should it be forgotten, that undertakings like these demanded affluence, which Petrarch possessed; while Boccaccio's whole life was passed in the midst of difficulties and privations. He compensated for the want of pecuniary resources by indefatigable industry; he submitted to mechanical labours, wholly unsuited to the bent of his character and genius, and copied manuscripts with his own hand. Leonardo Bruni, who was born before the death of Boccaccio, was astonished when he saw the multitude of authors' copies transcribed by him.[6] Benvenuto da Imola, who was a disciple of Boccaccio, relates a curious anecdote on this subject, which as we do not recollect that it is anywhere to be met with, except in the great collection of the writers of the middle ages, by Muratori, a work inaccessible to the greater number of our readers, we shall insert.[7]—Going once to the abbey of Monte Cassino, celebrated for the number of manuscripts which lay there, unknown and neglected, Boccaccio humbly requested to be shown into the library of the monastery. A monk dryly replied, "Go, it stands open," and pointed to a very high staircase. The good Boccaccio found every book he opened torn and mutilated; lamenting that all these fruits of the labours of the great men of antiquity had fallen into the hands of such masters, he went away weeping. Coming down the staircase he met another monk, and asked him "How those books could possibly have been so mutilated?"—"We make covers for little Prayer-books out of the parchment leaves of those volumes," said he, coolly, "and sell them for twopence, threepence, and sometimes fivepence each."—"And now go," concludes the pupil of Boccaccio, "go, you unfortunate author, and distract your brain in composing more books." Such were the obstacles opposed by the imperfect civilization of his age which this admirable man, together with Petrarch, had to surmount; and it is an act of tardy and religious justice to show that the tribute of grateful recollection to which they were both entitled to receive from posterity, was almost also [alone] awarded to his more fortunate contemporary. We cannot conclude our remarks, without paying another debt to the memory of Boccaccio. The

[6] Leonardo Aretino. *Vita del Petrarca* in fine.

[7] *Benvenutus Imolensis apud Muratorium Script.* Rer. Ital.

indecency of the Novelle, and their immoral tendency, can neither be justified nor extenuated; but from the herd of writers in England, who confidently repeat this merited censure of Boccaccio, year after year, it appears but too much as if the study of the language and of the style had been made a pretext for feeding the imaginations of the readers with ideas which all are prone to indulge, but compelled to conceal; and that the tales of Boccaccio would not have predominated so much over all other literature, if they had been more chaste. The art of suggesting thoughts, at once desired and forbidden, flatters while it irritates the passions, and is an efficacious instrument for governing the consciences of boys, and of the most discreet old men. The jesuits, therefore, no sooner made themselves masters of the schools of Italy, than they adopted this book, mutilated in the same manner as some of the licentious Latin poets, well knowing that the expunged passages are the most coveted, precisely because they *are* expunged, and that the imaginations of youth supply ideas worse than they would have formed had the books been left entire.

In order to excuse the use they made of the Decameron in their colleges, the jesuits succeeded in persuading Bellarmine to justify, in his controversies, the intentions of the author. Perhaps, indeed, they interpolated these arguments as they did soon many others, in the edition of Bellarmine, wherever the doctrines did not accord with the interests of their order.[8] It is, moreover, probable that they favoured a book famous for its invectives against the rules of the cloister, and written long before their order had arisen to acquire a jurisdiction over all. Bellarmine was much less indulgent than Boccaccio to the reputations of the old congregations; and although some writers who have undertaken their defence have called his Gemitus Columbae apocryphal, it was, at all events, printed among his works during his life. To return to Boccaccio. Before he died he had atoned for his want of respect for decorum; he felt that men thought him culpable, and he expiated his tales by a punishment heavier, perhaps, than the offence. There is some reason to believe that he wrote them when under the influence of a lady whom he abjured just before, and whom he defames in his Laberinto d'Amore. However this may be, he conjured fathers of families

[8] Fuligatus, in *Vita Bellarmini.*

not to suffer the Decameron to go into the hands of any who had not already lost the modesty of youth.—"Do not let that book be read; and if it is true that you love me, and weep for my afflictions, have pity, were it only for my honour's sake."

With remorse of conscience which does more honour to the excellence of his intentions than to the strength of his mind, he even tried to atone for the ridicule he had poured upon the priests and their infamous superstitions. No writer, perhaps, since Aristophanes, has so bitterly satirized the effrontery of ignorant preachers, and the credulity of their ignorant hearers, as Boccaccio in the Novelle, which are written in a spirit of implacable hostility to monks. In one of them he introduces one of these vagabonds boasting from the pulpit, that he had wandered through all countries in the terraqueous globe, and even beyond it, in search of relics of saints, and making the people in the church pay to adore them. And yet, in spite of this, he said, on his death-bed, that he had been long in search of holy relics through various parts of the world, and he left them, for the devotion of the people, to a convent of friars. This desire was found expressed in a will, written in Italian in his own hand; and in another in Latin, drawn up many years afterwards by a notary, and signed and approved by Boccaccio a short time before he died. In both these wills he bequeathed all his books and manuscripts to his confessor and to the convent of the Santo Spirito, in order that the monks might pray to God for his soul, and that his fellow-citizens might read and copy them for their instruction. It is therefore more than probable, that there was among these books no copy of the Decameron; and from the following anecdote, which being found in books which are read by very few is little known, it appears that the original manuscript of the Novelle was destroyed long before by the author; it is, in fact, as we have already remarked, impossible to find it.

Towards the end of his life, poverty, which is rendered more grievous by old age, and the turbulent state of Florence, made social life a burden to him, so that he fled to solitude; but his generous and amiable soul was debased and depressed by religious terrors. There lived at that time two Sienese, who were afterwards canonized. One of them was a man of letters and a Carthusian monk, mentioned by Fabricius as Sanctus Petrus Petronus; the other was Giovanni Colombini, who founded another order of monks, and wrote the life of St. Pietro Petroni by divine inspiration. The Bollandists allege that the manuscript of the new saint, after having been lost for two centuries and a half, fell miraculously into the hands of a Carthusian, who translated it from Italian into Latin, and in 1619 dedicated it to a Cardinal de Medici. It is possible that Colombini never wrote, and that the biographer of the saints, who wrote in the seventeenth century, drew his descriptions of miracles from those recorded in the chronicles and other documents of the fourteenth century; and in order to exaggerate the miraculous conversion of Boccaccio, he perverted a letter of Petrarch, entitled De Vaticinio Morientium, which is to be found in his Latin works. The blessed Petroni, at his death, which happened about the year 1360, charged a monk to advise Boccaccio to desist from his studies and to prepare for death. Boccaccio wrote in terror to Petrarch, who replied: "My brother, your letter filled my mind with horrible fantasies, and I read it assailed by great wonder and great affliction. And how could I, without tearful eyes, behold you weeping and calling to mind your near-approaching death; whilst I, not well informed of the fact, most anxiously explored the meaning of your words? But now that I have discovered the cause of your terrors, and have reflected somewhat upon them, I have no longer either sadness or surprise. You write that an–I know not what–Pietro di Siena, celebrated for his piety, and also for his miracles, predicted to us two, many future occurrences; and in the witness of the truth of them, sent to signify to us certain past things which you and I had kept secret from all men, and which he, who never knew us, nor was known by us, knew as if he had seen them with his mind's eye. This is a great thing, if indeed it be true. But the art of covering and adorning impostures with the veil of religion and of sanctity, is most common and old. Those who use it explore the age, the countenance, the eyes, the manners of the man; his daily customs, his motions, his standing, his sitting, his voice, his speech, and above all, his intentions and affections; and draw predictions which they ascribe to divine inspiration. Now if he, dying, foretold your death, so also did Hector in former times to Achilles; and Orodes to Mezentius, in Virgil; and Cheramenes to Eritia, in Cicero; and Calamus to Alexander; and Possidonius, the illustrious philosopher, when dying, named six of his contemporaries who were soon to follow him, and told who should die first, and who afterwards. It matters not to dispute now concerning the truth or the origin of such-like predictions; nor to you, if even this your alarmer (terrificator hic tuus) had told you the truth, would it avail any thing to afflict yourself. How then? If this man had not sent to let you know, would you have been ignorant that there remains not to you a long space of life? and even if you were young, is death any respecter of age?" But neither these, nor all the other arguments in Petrarch's letter, which is very long, nor the eloquence with which he combines the consolations of the Christian religion with the manly philosophy of the ancients, could deliver his friend from superstitious terrors.

Boccaccio survived the prediction more than twelve years, and the older he grew the more did he feel the seeds scattered in his mind by his grandmother and his nurse, spring up like thorns. He died in 1375, aged sixty-two, and not more than twelve or fourteen months after Petrarch. Nor did Petrarch himself always contemplate death with a stedfast eye. Such was the character of those times; and such, under varied appearances, will always be the nature of man.

VII

THOMAS BABINGTON MACAULAY

Criticisms on the Principal Italian Writers

NO. I. DANTE

> Fairest of stars, last in the train of night,
> If better thou belong not to the dawn,
> Sure pledge of day, that crown'st the smiling morn
> With thy bright circlet.
>
> MILTON

In a review of Italian literature, Dante has a double claim to precedency. He was the earliest and the greatest writer of his country. He was the first man who fully descried and exhibited the powers of his native dialect. The Latin tongue, which, under the most favourable circumstances, and in the hands of the greatest masters, had still been poor, feeble, and singularly unpoetical, and which had, in the age of Dante, been debased by the admixture of innumerable barbarous words and idioms, was still cultivated with superstitious veneration, and received, in the last stage of corruption, more honours than it had deserved in the period of its life and vigour. It was the language of the cabinet, of the university, of the church. It was employed by all who aspired to distinction in the higher walks of poetry. In compassion to the ignorance of his mistress, a cavalier might now and then proclaim his passion in Tuscan or Provençal rhymes. The vulgar might occasionally be edified by a pious allegory in the popular jargon. But no writer had conceived it possible that the dialect of peasants and market-women should possess sufficient energy and precision for a majestic and durable work. Dante adventured first. He detected the rich treasures of thought and diction which still lay latent in their ore. He refined them

Reprinted from *The Works of Lord Macaulay* (London: Longmans Green & Co., 1898), 11: 254–96. (Vol. 1 of *Speeches, Poems and Miscellaneous Writings*).

into purity. He burnished them into splendour. He fitted them for every purpose of use and magnificence. And he has thus acquired the glory, not only of producing the finest narrative poem of modern times, but also of creating a language, distinguished by unrivalled melody, and peculiarly capable of furnishing to lofty and passionate thoughts their appropriate garb of severe and concise expression.

To many this may appear a singular panegyric on the Italian tongue. Indeed the great majority of the young gentlemen and young ladies, who, when they are asked whether they read Italian, answer "yes," never go beyond the stories at the end of their grammar,—The Pastor Fido,—or an act of Artaserse.[1] They could as soon read a Babylonian brick as a canto of Dante. Hence it is a general opinion, among those who know little or nothing of the subject, that this admirable language is adapted only to the effeminate cant of sonneteers, musicians, and connoisseurs.

The fact is that Dante and Petrarch have been the Oromasdes and Arimanes of Italian literature. I wish not to detract from the merits of Petrarch. No one can doubt that his poems exhibit, amidst some imbecility and more affectation, much elegance, ingenuity, and tenderness. They present us with a mixture which can only be compared to the whimsical concert described by the humorous poet of Modena:

> S' udian gli usignuoli, al primo albore,
> E gli asini cantar versi d' amore.
>
> Tassoni; Secchia Rapita, canto i. stanza 6.

I am not, however, at present speaking of the intrinsic excellencies of his writings, which I shall take another opportunity to examine, but of the effect which they produced on the literature of Italy. The florid and luxurious charms of his style enticed the poets and the public from the contemplation of nobler and sterner models. In truth, though a rude state of society is that in which great original works are most frequently produced, it is also that in which they are worst appreciated. This may appear paradoxical; but it is proved by experience, and is consistent with reason. To be without any received canons of taste is good for the few who can create, but bad for the many who can only imitate and judge. Great and active minds cannot re-

[1] [By Guarini and Metastasio, respectively.]

main at rest. In a cultivated age they are too often contented to move on in the beaten path. But where no path exists they will make one. Thus the Iliad, the Odyssey, the Divine Comedy, appeared in dark and half barbarous times: and thus of the few original works which have been produced in more polished ages we owe a large proportion to men in low stations and of uninformed minds. I will instance, in our own language, the Pilgrim's Progress and Robinson Crusoe. Of all the prose works of fiction which we possess, these are, I will not say the best, but the most peculiar, the most unprecedented, the most inimitable. Had Bunyan and Defoe been educated gentlemen, they would probably have published translations and imitations of French romances "by a person of quality." I am not sure that we should have had Lear if Shakspeare had been able to read Sophocles.

But these circumstances, while they foster genius, are unfavourable to the science of criticism. Men judge by comparison. They are unable to estimate the grandeur of an object when there is no standard by which they can measure it. One of the French philosophers . . . who accompanied Napoleon to Egypt tells us that, when he first visited the great Pyramid, he was surprised to see it so diminutive. It stood alone in a boundless plain. There was nothing near it from which he could calculate its magnitude. But when the camp was pitched beside it, and the tents appeared like diminutive specks around its base, he then perceived the immensity of this mightiest work of man. In the same manner, it is not till a crowd of petty writers has sprung up that the merit of the great masterspirits of literature is understood.

We have indeed ample proof that Dante was highly admired in his own and the following age. I wish that we had equal proof that he was admired for his excellencies. But it is a remarkable corroboration of what has been said, that this great man seems to have been utterly unable to appreciate himself. In his treatise *De Vulgari Eloquentia* he talks with satisfaction of what he has done for Italian literature, of the purity and correctness of his style. "*Cependant,*" says a favourite[2] writer of mine, "*il n'est ni pur, ni correct, mais il est créateur.*" Considering the difficulties with which Dante had to struggle, we may perhaps be more in-

[2] Sismondi; Littérature du Midi de l'Europe.

clined than the French critic to allow him this praise. Still it is by no means his highest or most peculiar title to applause. It is scarcely necessary to say that those qualities which escaped the notice of the poet himself were not likely to attract the attention of the commentators. The fact is, that, while the public homage was paid to some absurdities with which his works may be justly charged, and to many more which were falsely imputed to them, —while lecturers were paid to expound and eulogize his physics, his metaphysics, his theology, all bad of their kind,—while annotators laboured to detect allegorical meanings of which the author never dreamed, the great powers of his imagination, and the imcomparable force of his style, were neither admired nor imitated. Arimanes had prevailed. The Divine Comedy was to that age what Saint Paul's Cathedral was to Omai.[3] The poor Otaheitean stared listlessly for a moment at the huge cupola, and ran into a toyshop to play with beads. Italy, too, was charmed with literary trinkets, and played with them for four centuries.

From the time of Petrarch to the appearance of Alfieri's tragedies, we may trace in almost every page of Italian literature the influence of those celebrated sonnets which, from the nature both of their beauties and their faults, were peculiarly unfit to be models for general imitation. Almost all the poets of that period, however different in the degree and quality of their talents, are characterized by great exaggeration, and, as a necessary consequence, great coldness of sentiment; by a passion for frivolous and tawdry ornament; and, above all, by an extreme feebleness and diffuseness of style. Tasso, Marino, Guarini, Metastasio, and a crowd of writers of inferior merit and celebrity, were spell-bound in the enchanted gardens of a gaudy and meretricious Alcina, who concealed debility and deformity beneath the deceitful semblance of loveliness and health. Ariosto, the great Ariosto himself, like his own Ruggiero, stooped for a time to linger amidst the magic flowers and fountains, and to caress the gay and painted sorceress. But to him, as to his own

[3] [This precedes by sixteen years the more famous passage in the *Essay on Von Ranke* about the New Zealander surveying the ruins of St. Paul's. Omai was brought from Tahiti to London in 1774 by Captain Furneaux, the companion of Captain Cook in his expedition to the South Seas. He was mentioned in Cook's *Voyage to the South Pole* (1777), and an article on him appeared in the *Gentleman's Magazine*, 51 (1781): 232–34.]

Ruggiero, had been given the omnipotent ring and the winged courser, which bore him from the paradise of deception to the regions of light and nature.

The evil of which I speak was not confined to the graver poets. It infected satire, comedy, burlesque. No person can admire more than I do the great masterpieces of wit and humour which Italy has produced. Still I cannot but discern and lament a great deficiency, which is common to them all. I find in them abundance of ingenuity, of droll naïveté, of profound and just reflection, of happy expression. Manners, characters, opinions, are treated with "a most learned spirit of human dealing." But something is still wanting. We read, and we admire, and we yawn. We look in vain for the bacchanalian fury which inspired the comedy of Athens, for the fierce and withering scorn which animates the invectives of Juvenal and Dryden, or even for the compact and pointed diction which adds zest to the verses of Pope and Boileau. There is no enthusiasm, no energy, no condensation, nothing which springs from strong feeling, nothing which tends to excite it. Many fine thoughts and fine expressions reward the toil of reading. Still it is a toil. The Secchia Rapita, in some points the best poem of its kind, is painfully diffuse and languid. The Animali Parlanti of Casti is perfectly intolerable. I admire the dexterity of the plot, and the liberality of the opinions. I admit that it is impossible to turn to a page which does not contain something that deserves to be remembered; but it is at least six times as long as it ought to be. And the garrulous feebleness of the style is a still greater fault than the length of the work.

It may be thought that I have gone too far in attributing these evils to the influence of the works and the fame of Petrarch. It cannot, however, be doubted that they have arisen, in a great measure, from a neglect of the style of Dante. This is not more proved by the decline of Italian poetry than by its resuscitation. After the lapse of four hundred and fifty years, there appeared a man capable of appreciating and imitating the father of Tuscan literature—Vittorio Alfieri. Like the prince in the nursery tale, he sought and found the Sleeping Beauty within the recesses which had so long concealed her from mankind. The portal was indeed rusted by time;—the dust of ages had accumulated on the hangings;—the furniture was of antique fashion;—and the gorgeous colour of the embroidery had faded. But the living charms which were well worth all the rest remained in the bloom of eternal youth, and well rewarded the bold adventurer who roused them from their long slumber. In every line of the Philip and the Saul, the greatest poems, I think, of the eighteenth century, we may trace the influence of that mighty genius which has immortalized the ill-starred love of Francesca, and the paternal agonies of Ugolino. Alfieri bequeathed the sovereignty of Italian literature to the author of the Aristodemus[4]—a man of genius scarcely inferior to his own, and a still more devoted disciple of the great Florentine. It must be acknowledged that this eminent writer has sometimes pushed too far his idolatry of Dante. To borrow a sprightly illustration from Sir John Denham, he has not only imitated his garb, but borrowed his clothes. He often quotes his phrases; and he has, not very judiciously, as it appears to me, imitated his versification. Nevertheless, he has displayed many of the higher excellencies of his master; and his works may justly inspire us with a hope that the Italian language will long flourish under a new literary dynasty, or rather under the legitimate line, which has at length been restored to a throne long occupied by specious usurpers.

The man to whom the literature of his country owes its origin and its revival was born in times singularly adapted to call forth his extraordinary powers. Religious zeal, chivalrous love and honour, democratic liberty, are the three most powerful principles that have ever influenced the character of large masses of men. Each of them singly has often excited the greatest enthusiasm, and produced the most important changes. In the time of Dante all the three, often in amalgamation, generally in conflict, agitated the public mind. The preceding generation had witnessed the wrongs and the revenge of the brave, the accomplished, the unfortunate Emperor Frederic the Second,—a poet in an age of schoolmen,—a philosopher in an age of monks,—a statesman in an age of crusaders. During the whole life of the poet, Italy was experiencing the consequences of the memorable struggle which he had maintained against the Church. The finest works of imagination have always been produced in times of political convulsion, as the richest vineyards and the sweetest flowers always grow on the soil which has been fertilized by the fiery deluge of a volcano. To look no further than the literary

4 [Vincenzo Monti.]

history of our own country, can we doubt that Shakspeare was in a great measure produced by the Reformation, and Wordsworth by the French Revolution? Poets often avoid political transactions; they often affect to despise them. But, whether they perceive it or not, they must be influenced by them. As long as their minds have any point of contact with those of their fellow-men, the electric impulse, at whatever distance it may originate, will be circuitously communicated to them.

This will be the case even in large societies, where the division of labour enables many speculative men to observe the face of nature, or to analyze their own minds, at a distance from the seat of political transactions. In the little republic of which Dante was a member the state of things was very different. These small communities are most unmercifully abused by most of our modern professors of the science of government. In such states, they tell us, factions are always most violent: where both parties are cooped up within a narrow space, political difference necessarily produces personal malignity. Every man must be a soldier; every moment may produce a war. No citizen can lie down secure that he shall not be roused by the alarum-bell, to repel or avenge an injury. In such petty quarrels Greece squandered the blood which might have purchased for her the permanent empire of the world, and Italy wasted the energy and the abilities which would have enabled her to defend her independence against the Pontiffs and the Cæsars.

All this is true: yet there is still a compensation. Mankind has not derived so much benefit from the empire of Rome as from the city of Athens, nor from the kingdom of France as from the city of Florence. The violence of party feeling may be an evil; but it calls forth that activity of mind which in some states of society it is desirable to produce at any expense. Universal soldiership may be an evil; but where every man is a soldier there will be no standing army. And is it no evil that one man in every fifty should be bred to the trade of slaughter; should live only by destroying and by exposing himself to be destroyed; should fight without enthusiasm and conquer without glory; be sent to a hospital when wounded, and rot on a dunghill when old? Such, over more than two-thirds of Europe, is the fate of soldiers. It was something that the citizen of Milan or Florence fought, not merely in the vague and rhetorical sense in which the words are often used, but in sober truth, for his parents, his children, his lands, his house, his altars. It was something that he marched forth to battle beneath the Carroccio, which had been the object of his childish veneration; that his aged father looked down from the battlements on his exploits; that his friends and his rivals were the witnesses of his glory. If he fell, he was consigned to no venal or heedless guardians. The same day saw him conveyed within the walls which he had defended. His wounds were dressed by his mother; his confession was whispered to the friendly priest who had heard and absolved the follies of his youth; his last sigh was breathed upon the lips of the lady of his love. Surely there is no sword like that which is beaten out of a ploughshare. Surely this state of things was not unmixedly bad: its evils were alleviated by enthusiasm and by tenderness; and it will at least be acknowledged that it was well fitted to nurse poetical genius in an imaginative and observant mind.

Nor did the religious spirit of the age tend less to this result than its political circumstances. Fanaticism is an evil, but it is not the greatest of evils. It is good that a people should be roused by any means from a state of utter torpor;—that their minds should be diverted from objects merely sensual, to meditations, however erroneous, on the mysteries of the moral and intellectual world; and from interests which are immediately selfish to those which relate to the past, the future, and the remote. These effects have sometimes been produced by the worst superstitions that ever existed; but the Catholic religion, even in the time of its utmost extravagance and atrocity, never wholly lost the spirit of the Great Teacher, whose precepts form the noblest code, as his conduct furnished the purest example, of moral excellence. It is of all religions the most poetical. The ancient superstitutions furnished the fancy with beautiful images, but took no hold on the heart. The doctrines of the Reformed Churches have most powerfully influenced the feelings and the conduct of men, but have not presented them with visions of sensible beauty and grandeur. The Roman Catholic Church has united to the awful doctrines of the one what Mr. Coleridge calls the "fair humanities" of the other. It has enriched sculpture and painting with the loveliest and most majestic forms. To the Phidian Jupiter it can oppose the Moses of Michael Angelo; and to the voluptuous beauty of the Queen of Cyprus, the serene and pensive loveliness of the Virgin Mother. The legends of its martyrs and its saints may vie in ingenuity and interest with the mythological fables of Greece; its ceremonies and processions were the delight of the vulgar; the huge fabric of secular power with which it was connected attracted the admiration of the statesman. At the same time, it never lost sight of the most solemn and tremendous doctrines of Christianity,–the incarnate God,–the judgment,–the retribution,–the eternity of happiness or torment. Thus, while, like the ancient religions, it received incalculable support from policy and ceremony, it never wholly became, like those religions, a merely political and ceremonial institution.

The beginning of the thirteenth century was, as Machiavelli has remarked, the era of a great revival of this extraordinary system. The policy of Innocent,–the growth of the inquisition and the mendicant orders,–the wars against the Albigenses, the Pagans of the East, and the unfortunate princes of the house of Swabia, agitated Italy during the two following generations. In this point Dante was completely under the influence of his age. He was a man of a turbid and melancholy spirit. In early youth he had entertained a strong and unfortunate passion, which, long after the death of her whom he loved, continued to haunt him. Dissipation, ambition, misfortunes had not effaced it. He was not only a sincere, but a passionate, believer. The crimes and abuses of the Church of Rome were indeed loathsome to him; but to all its doctrines and all its rites he adhered with enthusiastic fondness and veneration; and, at length, driven from his native country, reduced to a situation the most painful to a man of his disposition, condemned to learn by experience that no food is so bitter as the bread of dependence, and no ascent so painful as the staircase of a patron,–his wounded spirit took refuge in visionary devotion. Beatrice, the unforgotten object of his early tenderness, was invested by his imagination with glorious and mysterious attributes; she was enthroned among the highest of the celestial hierarchy: Almighty Wisdom had assigned to her the care of the sinful and unhappy wanderer who had loved her with such a perfect love. By a confusion, like that which often takes place in dreams, he has sometimes lost sight of her human nature, and even of her personal existence, and seems to consider her as one of the attributes of the Deity.

But those religious hopes which had released the mind of the sublime enthusiast from the terrors of death had not rendered his speculations on human life more cheerful. This is an inconsistency which may often be observed in men of a similar temperament. He hoped for happiness beyond the grave: but he felt none on earth. It is from this cause, more than from any other, that his description of Heaven is so far inferior to the Hell or the Purgatory. With the passions and miseries of the suffering spirits he feels a strong sympathy. But among the beatified he appears as one who has nothing in common with them,—as one who is incapable of comprehending, not only the degree, but the nature of their enjoyment. We think that we see him standing amidst those smiling and radiant spirits with that scowl of unutterable misery on his brow, and that curl of bitter disdain on his lips, which all his portraits have preserved, and which might furnish Chantrey with hints for the head of his projected Satan.

There is no poet whose intellectual and moral character are so closely connected. The great source, as it appears to me, of the power of the Divine Comedy is the strong belief with which the story seems to be told. In this respect, the only books which approach to its excellence are Gulliver's Travels and Robinson Crusoe. The solemnity of his asseverations, the consistency and minuteness of his details, the earnestness with which he labours to make the reader understand the exact shape and size of every thing that he describes, give an air of reality to his wildest fictions. I should only weaken this statement by quoting instances of a feeling which pervades the whole work, and to which it owes much of its fascination. This is the real justification of the many passages in his poem which bad critics have condemned as grotesque. I am concerned to see that Mr. Cary, to whom Dante owes more than ever poet owed to translator, has sanctioned an accusation utterly unworthy of his abilities. "His solicitude," says that gentleman, "to define all his images in such manner as to bring them within the circle of our vision, and to subject them to the power of the pencil, renders him little better than grotesque, where Milton has since taught us to expect sublimity." It is true that Dante has never shrunk from embodying his conceptions in determinate words, that he has even given measures and numbers, where Milton would have left his images to float undefined in a gorgeous haze of language. Both were right. Milton did not profess to have been in heaven or hell. He might therefore reasonably confine himself to magnificent generalities. Far different was the office of the lonely traveller who had wandered through the nations of the dead. Had he described the abode of the rejected spirits in language resembling the splended lines of the English poet,—had he told us of—

> An universe of death, which God by curse
> Created evil, for evil only good,
> Where all life dies, death lives, and Nature breeds
> Perverse all monstrous, all prodigious things,
> Abominable, unutterable, and worse
> Than fables yet have feigned, or fear conceived,
> Gorgons, and hydras, and chimæras dire,—
> [*Par. L.* II, 622–27]

this would doubtless have been noble writing. But where would have been that strong impression of reality, which, in accordance with his plan, it should have been his great object to produce? It was absolutely necessary for him to delineate accurately "all monstrous, all prodigious things,"—to utter what might to others appear "unutterable,"—to relate with the air of truth what fables had never feigned,—to embody what fear had never conceived. And I will frankly confess that the vague sublimity of Milton affects me less than these reviled details of Dante. We read Milton; and we know that we are reading a great poet. When we read Dante, the poet vanishes. We are listening to the man who has returned from "the valley of the dolorous abyss";—we seem to see the dilated eye of horror, to hear the shuddering accents with which he tells his fearful tale. Considered in this light, the narratives are exactly what they should be,—definite in themselves, but suggesting to the mind ideas of awful and indefinite wonder. They are made up of the images of the earth:—they are told in the language of the earth.—Yet the whole effect is, beyond expression, wild and unearthly. The fact is, that supernatural beings, as long as they are considered merely with reference to their own nature, excite our feelings very feebly. It is when the great gulf which separates them from us is passed, when we suspect some strange and undefinable relation between the laws of the visible and the invisible world, that they rouse, perhaps, the strongest emotions of which our nature is capable. How many children, and how many men, are afraid of ghosts, who are not afraid of God! And this, because, though they entertain a much stronger conviction of the existence of a Deity than of the reality of apparitions, they have no apprehension that he will manifest himself to them in any sensible manner. While this is the case, to describe super-human beings in the language, and to attribute to them the actions, of humanity may be grotesque, unphilosophical, inconsistent; but it will be the only mode of working upon the feelings of men, and, therefore, the only mode suited for poetry. Shakspeare understood this well, as he understood every thing that belonged to his art. Who does not sympathize with the rapture of Ariel, flying after sunset on the wings of the bat, or sucking in the cups of flowers with the bee? Who does not shudder at the caldron of Macbeth? Where is the philosopher who is not moved when he thinks of the strange connection between the infernal spirits and "the sow's blood that hath eaten her nine farrow"? But this difficult task of representing supernatural beings to our minds, in a manner which shall be neither unintelligible to our intellects nor wholly inconsistent with our ideas of their nature, has never been so well performed as by Dante. I will refer to three instances, which are, perhaps, the most striking—the description of the transformations of the serpents and the robbers, in the twenty-fifth canto of the Inferno,—the passage concerning Nimrod, in the thirty-first canto of the same part,—and the magnificent procession in the twenty-ninth canto of the Purgatorio.

The metaphors and comparisons of Dante harmonize admirably with that air of strong reality of which I have spoken. They have a very peculiar character. He is perhaps the only poet whose writings would become much less intelligible if all illustrations of this sort were expunged. His similes are frequently rather those of a traveller than of a poet. He employs them not to display his ingenuity by fanciful analogies,—not to delight the reader by affording him a distant and passing glimpse of beautiful images remote from the path in which he is proceeding,—but to give an exact idea of the objects which he is describing, by comparing them with others generally known. The boiling pitch in Malebolge was like that in the Venetian arsenal:—the mound on which he travelled along the banks of Phlegethon was like that between Ghent and Bruges, but not so large:—the cavities where the Simoniacal prelates are confined resemble the fonts in the Church of John at Florence. Every reader of Dante will recall many other illustrations of this description, which add to the appearance of sincerity and earnestness from which the narrative derives so much of its interest.

Many of his comparisons, again, are intended to give an exact idea of his feelings under particular circumstances. The delicate shades of grief, of fear, of anger, are rarely discriminated with sufficient accuracy in the language of the most refined nations. A rude dialect never abounds in nice distinctions of this kind. Dante therefore employs the most accurate and infinitely the most poetical mode of marking the precise state of his mind. Every person who has experienced the bewildering effect of sudden bad tidings,—the stupefaction,—the vague doubt of the truth of our own perceptions which they produce,—will understand the following simile:—"I was as he is who dreameth his own harm,—who, dreaming, wishes that it may be all a dream, so that he desires that which is as though it were not." This is only one out of a hundred equally striking and expressive similitudes. The comparisons of Homer and Milton are magnificent digressions. It scarcely injures their effect to detach them from the work. Those of Dante are very different. They derive their beauty from the context, and reflect beauty upon it. His embroidery cannot be taken out without spoiling the whole web. I cannot dismiss this part of the subject without advising every person who can muster sufficient Italian to read the simile of the sheep, in the third canto of the Purgatorio. I think it the most perfect passage of the kind in the world, the most imaginative, the most picturesque, and the most sweetly expressed.

No person can have attended to the Divine Comedy without observing how little impression the forms of the external world appear to have made on the mind of Dante. His temper and his situation had led him to fix his observation almost exclusively on human nature. The exquisite opening of the eighth[5] canto of the Purgatorio affords a strong instance of this. He leaves to others the earth, the ocean, and the sky. His business is with man. To other writers, evening may be the season of dews and stars and radiant clouds. To Dante it is the hour of fond recol-

[5] I cannot help observing that Gray's imitation of that noble line,

"Che paia 'l giorno pianger che si muore,"

is one of the most striking instances of injudicious plagiarism with which I am acquainted. Dante did not put this strong personification at the beginning of his description. The imagination of the reader is so well prepared for it by the previous lines, that it appears perfectly natural and pathetic. Placed as Gray has placed it, neither preceded nor followed by any thing that harmonizes with it, it becomes a frigid conceit. Woe to the unskilful rider who ventures on the horses of Achilles.

lection and passionate devotion,—the hour which melts the heart of the mariner and kindles the love of the pilgrim,—the hour when the toll of the bell seems to mourn for another day which is gone and will return no more.

The feeling of the present age has taken a direction diametrically opposite. The magnificence of the physical world, and its influence upon the human mind, have been the favourite themes of our most eminent poets. The herd of blue-stocking ladies and sonneteering gentlemen seem to consider a strong sensibility to the "splendour of the grass, the glory of the flower," as an ingredient absolutely indispensable in the formation of a poetical mind. They treat with contempt all writers who are unfortunately

nec ponere lucum
Artifices, nec rus saturum laudare.

The orthodox poetical creed is more Catholic. The noblest earthly object of the contemplation of man is man himself. The universe, and all its fair and glorious forms, are indeed included in the wide empire of the imagination; but she has placed her home and her sanctuary amidst the inexhaustible varieties and the impenetrable mysteries of the mind.

In tutte parti impera, e quivi regge;
Quivi è la sua cittade, e l' alto seggio.
[*Inf.* I, 127–28]

Othello is perhaps the greatest work in the world. From what does it derive its power? From the clouds? From the ocean? From the mountains? Or from love strong as death, and jealousy cruel as the grave? What is it that we go forth to see in Hamlet? Is it a reed shaken with the wind? A small celandine? A bed of daffodils? Or is it to contemplate a mighty and wayward mind laid bare before us to the inmost recesses? It may perhaps be doubted whether the lakes and the hills are better fitted for the education of a poet than the dusky streets of a huge capital. Indeed who is not tired to death with pure description of scenery? Is it not the fact, that external objects never strongly excite our feelings but when they are contemplated in reference to man, as illustrating his destiny, or as influencing his character? The most beautiful object in the world, it will be allowed, is a beautiful woman. But who that can analyse his feelings is not sensible that she owes her fascination less to grace of outline and delicacy of colour, than to a thousand associations which, often unperceived by ourselves, connect those qualities with the source of our existence, with the nourishment of our infancy, with the passions of our youth, with the hopes of our age, with elegance, with vivacity, with tenderness, with the strongest of natural instincts, with the dearest of social ties?

To those who think thus, the insensibility of the Florentine poet to the beauties of nature will not appear an unpardonable deficiency. On mankind no writer, with the exception of Shakspeare, has looked with a more penetrating eye. I have said that his poetical character had derived a tinge from his peculiar temper. It is on the sterner and darker passions that he delights to dwell. All love, excepting the half mystic passion which he still felt for his buried Beatrice, had palled on the fierce and restless exile. The sad story of Rimini is almost a single exception. I know not whether it has been remarked, that, in one point, misanthropy seems to have affected his mind as it did that of Swift. Nauseous and revolting images seem to have had a fascination for his mind; and he repeatedly places before his readers, with all the energy of his incomparable style, the most loathsome objects of the sewer and the dissecting-room.

There is another peculiarity in the poem of Dante, which, I think, deserves notice. Ancient mythology has hardly ever been successfully interwoven with modern poetry. One class of writers have introduced the fabulous deities merely as allegorical representatives of love, wine, or wisdom. This necessarily renders their works tame and cold. We may sometimes admire their ingenuity; but with what interest can we read of beings of whose personal existence the writer does not suffer us to entertain, for a moment, even a conventional belief? Even Spenser's allegory is scarcely tolerable, till we contrive to forget that Una signifies innocence, and consider her merely as an oppressed lady under the protection of a generous knight.

Those writers who have, more judiciously, attempted to preserve the personality of the classical divinities have failed from a different cause. They have been imitators, and imitators at a disadvantage. Euripides and Catullus believed in Bacchus and Cybele as little as we do. But they lived among men who did. Their imaginations, if not their opinions, took the colour of the age. Hence the glorious inspiration of the Bacchæ and the Atys.

Our minds are formed by circumstances: and I do not believe that it would be in the power of the greatest modern poet to lash himself up to a degree of enthusiasm adequate to the production of such works.

Dante alone, among the poets of later times, has been, in this respect, neither an allegorist nor an imitator; and, consequently, he alone has introduced the ancient fictions with effect. His Minos, his Charon, his Pluto, are absolutely terrific. Nothing can be more beautiful or original than the use which he has made of the river of Lethe. He has never assigned to his mythological characters any functions inconsistent with the creed of the Catholic Church. He has related nothing concerning them which a good Christian of that age might not believe possible. On this account, there is nothing in these passages that appears puerile or pedantic. On the contrary, this singular use of classical names suggests to the mind a vague and awful idea of some mysterious revelation, anterior to all recorded history, of which the dispersed fragments might have been retained amidst the impostures and superstitions of later religions. Indeed the mythology of the Divine Comedy is of the elder and more colossal mould. It breathes the spirit of Homer and Æschylus, not of Ovid and Claudian.

This is the more extraordinary, since Dante seems to have been utterly ignorant of the Greek language; and his favourite Latin models could only have served to mislead him. Indeed, it is impossible not to remark his admiration of writers far inferior to himself; and, in particular, his idolatry of Virgil, who, elegant and splendid as he is, has no pretensions to the depth and originality of mind which characterize his Tuscan worshipper. In truth, it may be laid down as an almost universal rule that good poets are bad critics. Their minds are under the tyranny of ten thousand associations imperceptible to others. The worst writer may easily happen to touch a spring which is connected in their minds with a long succession of beautiful images. They are like the gigantic slaves of Aladdin, gifted with matchless power, but bound by spells so mighty than when a child whom they could have crushed touched a talisman, of whose secret he was ignorant, they immediately became his vassals. It has more than once happened to me to see minds, graceful and majestic as the Titania of Shakspeare, bewitched by the charms of an ass's head, bestowing on it the fondest caresses, and crowning it with the sweetest flowers. I need only mention the poems attributed to Ossian. They are utterly worthless, except as an edifying instance of the success of a story without evidence, and of a book without merit. They are a chaos of words which present no image, of images which have no archetype:—they are without form and void; and darkness is upon the face of them. Yet how many men of genius have panegyrized and imitated them!

The style of Dante is, if not his highest, perhaps his most peculiar excellence. I know nothing with which it can be compared. The noblest models of Greek composition must yield to it. His words are the fewest and the best which it is possible to use. The first expression in which he clothes his thoughts is always so energetic and comprehensive that amplification would only injure the effect. There is probably no writer in any language who has presented so many strong pictures to the mind. Yet there is probably no writer equally concise. This perfection of style is the principal merit of the Paradiso, which, as I have already remarked, is by no means equal in other respects to the two preceding parts of the poem. The force and felicity of the diction, however, irresistibly attract the reader through the theological lectures and the sketches of ecclesiastical biography, with which this division of the work too much abounds. It may seem almost absurd to quote particular specimens of an excellence which is diffused over all his hundred cantos. I will, however, instance the third canto of the Inferno, and the sixth of the Purgatorio, as passages incomparable in their kind. The merit of the latter is, perhaps, rather oratorical than poetical; nor can I recollect any thing in the great Athenian speeches which equals it in force of invective and bitterness of sarcasm. I have heard the most eloquent statesman of the age [Edmund Burke] remark that, next to Demosthenes, Dante is the writer who ought to be most attentively studied by every man who desires to attain oratorical eminence.

NO. II. PETRARCH

> Et vos, o lauri, carpam, et te, proxima myrte,
> Sic positæ quoniam suaves miscetis odores.
>
> VIRGIL

It would not be easy to name a writer whose celebrity, when both its extent and its duration are taken into the account, can be considered as equal to that of Petrarch. Four centuries and a half have elapsed since his death. Yet still the inhabitants of every nation throughout the western world are as familiar with his character and his adventures as with the most illustrious names, and the most recent anecdotes, of their own literary history. This is indeed a rare distinction. His detractors must acknowledge that it could not have been acquired by a poet destitute of merit. His admirers will scarcely maintain that the unassisted merit of Petrarch could have raised him to that eminence which has not yet been attained by Shakspeare, Milton, or Dante,–that eminence, of which perhaps no modern writer, excepting himself and Cervantes, has long retained possession,–an European reputation.

It is not difficult to discover some of the causes to which this great man has owed a celebrity, which I cannot but think disproportioned to his real claims on the admiration of mankind. In the first place, he is an egotist. Egotism in conversation is universally abhorred. Lovers, and, I believe, lovers alone, pardon it in each other. No services, no talents, no powers of pleasing, render it endurable. Gratitude, admiration, interest, fear, scarcely prevent those who are condemned to listen to it from indicating their disgust and fatigue. The childish uncle, the powerful patron, can scarcely extort this compliance. We leave the inside of the mail in a storm, and mount the box, rather than hear the history of our companion. The chaplain bites his lips in the presence of the archbishop. The midshipman yawns at the table of the First Lord. Yet, from whatever cause, this practice, the pest of conversation, gives to writing a zest which nothing else can impart. Rousseau made the boldest experiment of this kind; and it fully succeeded. In our own time Lord Byron, by a series of attempts of the same nature, made himself the object of general interest and admiration. Wordsworth wrote with egotism more intense, but less obvious; and he has been rewarded with a sect of worshippers, comparatively small in number, but far more enthusiastic in their devotion. It is needless to multiply instances. Even now all the walks of literature are infested with mendicants for fame, who attempt to excite our interest by exhibiting all the distortions of their intellects, and stripping the covering from all the putrid sores of their feelings. Nor are there wanting many who push their imitation of the beggars whom they resemble a step further, and who find it easier to extort a pittance from the spectator, by simulating deformity and debility from which they are exempt, than by such honest labour as their health and strength enable them to perform. In the meantime the credulous public pities and pampers a nuisance which requires only the tread-mill and the whip. This art, often successful when employed by dunces, gives irresistible fascination to works which possess intrinsic merit. We are always desirous to know something of the character and situation of those whose writings we have perused with pleasure. The passages in which Milton has alluded to his own circumstances are perhaps read more frequently, and with more interest, than any other lines in his poems. It is amusing to observe with what labour critics have attempted to glean from the poems of Homer some hints as to his situation and feelings. According to one hypothesis, he intended to describe himself under the name of Demodocus. Others maintain that he was the identical Phemius whose life Ulysses spared. This propensity of the human mind explains, I think, in a great degree, the extensive popularity of a poet whose works are little else than the expression of his personal feelings.

In the second place, Petrarch was not only an egotist, but an amatory egotist. The hopes and fears, the joys and sorrows, which he described, were derived from the passion which of all passions exerts the widest influence, and which of all passions borrows most from the imagination. He had also another immense advantage. He was the first eminent amatory poet who appeared after the great convulsion which had changed, not only the political, but the moral, state of the world. The Greeks, who, in their public institutions and their literary tastes, were diametrically opposed to the oriental nations, bore a considerable resemblance to those nations in their domestic habits. Like them, they despised the intellects and immured the persons of their women; and it was among the least of the frightful evils to which this pernicious system gave birth, that all the accomplishments of mind, and all the fascinations of manner, which, in a highly cultivated age, will generally be necessary to attach men to their female associates, were monopolized by the Phrynes and the Lamias. The indispensable ingredients of honourable and chivalrous love were nowhere to be found united. The matrons and their daughters, confined in the harem,–insipid, uneducated, ignorant of all but the mechanical arts, scarcely seen till they were married,—could rarely excite interest; while their brilliant rivals, half graces, half harpies, elegant and informed, but fickle and rapacious, could never inspire respect.

The state of society in Rome was, in this point, far happier; and the Latin literature partook of the superiority. The Roman poets have decidedly surpassed those of Greece in the delineation of the passion of love. There is no subject which they have treated with so much success. Ovid, Catullus, Tibullus, Horace, and Propertius, in spite of all their faults, must be allowed to rank high in this department of the art. To these I would add my favourite Plautus; who, though he took his plots from Greece, found, I suspect, the originals of his enchanting female characters at Rome.

Still many evils remained: and, in the decline of the great empire, all that was pernicious in its domestic institutions appeared more strongly. Under the influence of governments at once dependent and tyrannical, which purchased, by cringing to their enemies, the power of trampling on their subjects, the Romans sunk into the lowest state of effeminacy and debasement. Falsehood, cowardice, sloth, conscious and unrepining degradation, formed the national character. Such a character is totally incompatible with the stronger passions. Love, in particular, which, in the modern sense of the word, implies protection and devotion on the one side, confidence on the other, respect and fidelity on both, could not exist among the sluggish and heartless slaves who cringed around the thrones of Honorius and Augustulus. At this period the great renovation commenced. The warriors of the north, destitute as they were of knowledge and humanity, brought with them, from their forests and marshes, those qualities without which humanity is a weakness, and knowledge a curse,—energy—independence—the dread of shame—the contempt of danger. It would be most interesting to examine the manner in which the admixture of the savage conquerors and the effeminate slaves, after many generations of darkness and agitation, produced the modern European character;—to trace back, from the first conflict to the final amalgamation, the operation of that mysterious alchemy which, from hostile and worthless elements, has extracted the pure gold of human nature—to analyse the mass, and to determine the proportions in which the ingredients are mingled. But I will confine myself to the subject to which I have more particularly referred. The nature of the passion of love had undergone a complete change. It still retained, indeed, the fanciful and voluptuous character which it had possessed among the southern nations of antiquity. But it was tinged with the superstitious veneration with which the northern warriors had been accustomed to regard women. Devotion and war had imparted to it their most solemn and animating feelings. It was sanctified by the blessings of the Church, and decorated with the wreaths of the tournament. Venus, as in the ancient fable, was again rising above the dark and tempestuous waves which had so long covered her beauty. But she rose not now, as of old, in exposed and luxurious loveliness. She still wore the cestus of her ancient witchcraft; but the diadem of Juno was on her brow, and the ægis of Pallas in her hand. Love might, in fact, be called a new passion; and it is not astonishing that the first poet of eminence who wholly devoted his genius to this theme should have excited an extraordinary sensation. He may be compared to an adventurer who accidentally lands in a rich and unknown island; and who, though he may only set up an ill-shaped cross upon the shore, acquires possession of its treasures, and gives it his name. The claim of Petrarch was indeed somewhat like that of Amerigo Vespucci to the continent which should have derived its appellation from Columbus. The Provençal poets were unquestionably the masters of the Florentine. But they wrote in an age which could not appreciate their merits; and their imitator lived at the very period when composition in the vernacular language began to attract general attention. Petrarch was in literature what a Valentine is in love. The public preferred him, not because his merits were of a transcendent order, but because he was the first person whom they saw after they awoke from their long sleep.

Nor did Petrarch gain less by comparison with his immediate successors than with those who had preceded him. Till more than a century after his death Italy produced no poet who could be compared to him. This decay of genius is doubtless to be ascribed, in a great measure, to the influence which his own works had exercised upon the literature of his country. Yet it has conduced much to his fame. Nothing is more favourable to the reputation of a writer than to be succeeded by a race inferior to himself; and it is an advantage, from obvious causes, much more frequently enjoyed by those who corrupt the national taste than by those who improve it.

Another cause has co-operated with those which I have mentioned to spread the renown of Petrarch. I mean the interest which is inspired by the events of his life—an interest which must have been strongly felt by his contemporaries, since, after an interval of five hundred years, no critic can be wholly exempt from its influence. Among the great men to whom we owe the resuscitation of science he deserves the foremost place; and his enthusiastic attachment to this great cause constitutes his most just and splendid title to the gratitude of posterity. He was the votary of literature. He loved it with a perfect love. He worshipped it with an almost fanatical devotion. He was the missionary, who proclaimed its discoveries to distant countries—the pilgrim, who travelled far and wide to collect its reliques—the hermit, who retired to seclusion to meditate on its beauties—the champion, who fought its battles—the conqueror, who, in more than a metaphorical sense, led barbarism and ignorance in triumph, and received in the Capitol the laurel which his magnificent victory had earned.

Nothing can be conceived more noble or affecting than that ceremony. The superb palaces and porticoes, by which had rolled the ivory chariots of Marius and Cæsar, had long mouldered into dust. The laurelled fasces—the golden eagles—the shouting legions—the captives and the pictured cities—were indeed wanting to his victorious procession. The sceptre had passed away from Rome. But she still retained the mightier influence of an intellectual empire, and was now to confer the prouder reward of an intellectual triumph. To the man who had extended the dominion of her ancient language—who had erected the trophies of philosophy and imagination in the haunts of ignorance and ferocity—whose captives were the hearts of admiring nations enchained by the influence of his song—whose spoils were the treasures of ancient genius rescued from obscurity and decay—the Eternal City offered the just and glorious tribute of her gratitude. Amidst the ruined monuments of ancient and the infant erections of modern art, he who had restored the broken link between the two ages of human civilization was crowned with the wreath which he had deserved from the moderns who owed to him their refinement—from the ancients who owed to him their fame. Never was a coronation so august witnessed by Westminster or by Rheims.

When we turn from this glorious spectacle to the private

chamber of the poet,—when we contemplate the struggle of passion and virtue—the eye dimmed, the cheek furrowed, by the tears of sinful and hopeless desire,—when we reflect on the whole history of his attachment, from the gay fantasy of his youth to the lingering despair of his age, pity and affection mingle with our admiration. Even after death had placed the last seal on his misery, we see him devoting to the cause of the human mind all the strength and energy which love and sorrow had spared. He lived the apostle of literature;—he fell its martyr:—he was found dead with his head reclined on a book.

Those who have studied the life and writings of Petrarch with attention, will perhaps be inclined to make some deductions from this panegyric. It cannot be denied that his merits were disfigured by a most unpleasant affectation. His zeal for literature communicated a tinge of pedantry to all his feelings and opinions. His love was the love of a sonneteer:—his patriotism was the patriotism of an antiquarian. The interest with which we contemplate the works, and study the history, of those who, in former ages, have occupied our country, arises from the associations which connect them with the community in which are comprised all the objects of our affection and our hope. In the mind of Petrarch these feelings were reversed. He loved Italy, because it abounded with the monuments of the ancient masters of the world. His native city—the fair and glorious Florence—the modern Athens, then in all the bloom and strength of its youth, could not obtain, from the most distinguished of its citizens, any portion of that passionate homage which he paid to the decrepitude of Rome. These and many other blemishes, though they must in candour be acknowledged, can but in a very slight degree diminish the glory of his career. For my own part, I look upon it with so much fondness and pleasure that I feel reluctant to turn from it to the consideration of his works, which I by no means contemplate with equal admiration.

Nevertheless, I think highly of the poetical powers of Petrarch. He did not possess, indeed, the art of strongly presenting sensible objects to the imagination;—and this is the more remarkable, because the talent of which I speak is that which peculiarly distinguishes the Italian poets. In the Divine Comedy it is displayed in its highest perfection. It characterizes almost every celebrated poem in the language. Perhaps this is to be attributed to the circumstances, that painting and sculpture had attained a high degree of excellence in Italy before poetry had been extensively cultivated. Men were debarred from books, but accustomed from childhood to contemplate the admirable works of art, which, even in the thirteenth century, Italy began to produce. Hence their imaginations received so strong a bias that, even in their writings, a taste for graphic delineation is discernible. The progress of things in England has been in all respects different. The consequence is, that English historical pictures are poems on canvass; while Italian poems are pictures painted to the mind by means of words. Of this national characteristic the writings of Petrarch are almost totally destitute. His sonnets indeed, from their subject and nature, and his Latin poems, from the restraints which always shackle one who writes in a dead language, cannot fairly be received in evidence. But his Triumphs absolutely required the exercise of this talent, and exhibit no indications of it.

Genius, however, he certainly possessed, and genius of a high order. His ardent, tender, and magnificent turn of thought, his brilliant fancy, his command of expression, at once forcible and elegant, must be acknowledged. Nature meant him for the prince of lyric writers. But by one fatal present she deprived her other gifts of half their value. He would have been a much greater poet had he been a less clever man. His ingenuity was the bane of his mind. He abandoned the noble and natural style, in which he might have excelled, for the conceits which he produced with a facility at once admirable and disgusting. His muse, like the Roman lady in Livy, was tempted by gaudy ornaments to betray the fastnesses of her strength, and, like her, was crushed beneath the glittering bribes which had seduced her.

The paucity of his thoughts is very remarkable. It is impossible to look without amazement on a mind so fertile in combinations, yet so barren of images. His amatory poetry is wholly made up of a very few topics, disposed in so many orders, and exhibited in so many lights, that it reminds us of those arithmetical problems about permutations, which so much astonish the unlearned. The French cook, who boasted that he could make fifteen different dishes out of a nettle-top, was not a greater master of his art. The mind of Petrarch was a kaleidoscope. At every turn it presents us with new forms, always fantastic, occasionally beautiful; and we can scarcely believe that all these varieties have been produced by the same worthless fragments of glass. The sameness of his images is, indeed, in some degree, to be attributed to the sameness of his subject. It would be unreasonable to expect perpetual variety from so many hundred compositions, all of the same length, all in the same measure, and all addressed to the same insipid and heartless coquette. I cannot but suspect also that the perverted taste, which is the blemish of his amatory verses, was to be attributed to the influence of Laura, who, probably, like most critics of her sex, preferred a gaudy to a majestic style. Be this as it may, he no sooner changes his subject than he changes his manner. When he speaks of the wrongs and degradation of Italy, devastated by foreign invaders, and but feebly defended by her pusillanimous children, the effeminate lisp of the sonneteer is exchanged for a cry, wild, and solemn, and piercing as that which proclaimed "Sleep no more" to the bloody house of Cawdor. "Italy seems not to feel her sufferings," exclaims her impassioned poet; "decrepit, sluggish, and languid, will she sleep for ever? Will there be none to awake her? Oh that I had my hands twisted in her hair!"

Nor is it with less energy that he denounces against the Mahometan Babylon the vengeance of Europe and of Christ. His magnificent enumeration of the ancient exploits of the Greeks must always excite admiration, and cannot be perused without the deepest interest, at a time when the wise and good, bitterly disappointed in so many other countries, are looking with breathless anxiety towards the natal land of liberty,—the field of Marathon,—and the deadly pass where the Lion of Lacedæmon turned to bay.

His poems on religious subjects also deserve the highest commendation. At the head of these must be placed the Ode to the Virgin. It is, perhaps, the finest hymn in the world. His devout veneration receives an exquisitely poetical character from the delicate perception of the sex and the loveliness of his idol, which we may easily trace throughout the whole composition.

I could dwell with pleasure on these and similar parts of the writings of Petrarch; but I must return to his amatory poetry: to that he entrusted his fame; and to that he has principally owed it.

The prevailing defect of his best compositions on this subject is the universal brilliancy with which they are lighted up. The natural language of the passions is, indeed, often figurative and fantastic; and with none is this more the case than with that of love. Still there is a limit. The feelings should, indeed, have their ornamental garb; but, like an elegant woman, they should be neither muffled nor exposed. The drapery should be so arranged, as at once to answer the purposes of modest concealment and judicious display. The decorations should sometimes be employed to hide a defect, and sometimes to heighten a beauty; but never to conceal, much less to distort, the charms to which they are subsidiary. The love of Petrarch, on the contrary, arrays itself like a foppish savage, whose nose is bored with a golden ring, whose skin is painted with grotesque forms and dazzling colours, and whose ears are drawn down his shoulders by the weight of jewels. It is a rule, without any exception, in all kinds of composition, that the principal idea, the predominant feeling, should never be confounded with the accompanying decorations. It should generally be distinguished from them by greater simplicity of expression; as we recognize Napoleon in the pictures of his battles, amidst a crowd of embroidered coats and plumes, by his grey cloak and his hat without a feather. In the verses of Petrarch it is generally impossible to say what thought is meant to be prominent. All is equally elaborate. The chief wears the same gorgeous and degrading livery with his retinue, and obtains only his share of the indifferent stare which we bestow upon them in common. The poems have no strong lights and shades, no background, no foreground;–they are like the illuminated figures in an oriental manuscript,–plenty of rich tints and no perspective. Such are the faults of the most celebrated of these compositions. Of those which are universally acknowledged to be bad it is scarcely possible to speak with patience. Yet they have much in common with their splendid companions. They differ from them, as a May-day procession of chimney-sweepers differs from the Field of Cloth of Gold. They have the gaudiness but not the wealth. His muse belongs to that numerous class of females who have no objection to be dirty, while they can be tawdry. When his brilliant conceits are exhausted, he supplies their place with metaphysical quibbles, forced antitheses, bad puns, and execrable charades. In his fifth sonnet he may, I think, be said to have sounded the lowest chasm of the Bathos. Upon the whole, that piece may be safely pronounced to be the worst attempt at poetry, and the worst attempt at wit, in the world.

A strong proof of the truth of these criticisms is, that almost all the sonnets produce exactly the same effect on the mind of the reader. They relate to all the various moods of a lover, from joy to despair:—yet they are perused, as far as my experience and observation have gone, with exactly the same feeling. The fact is, that in none of them are the passion and the ingenuity mixed in just proportions. There is not enough sentiment to dilute the condiments which are employed to season it. The repast which he sets before us resembles the Spanish entertainment in Dryden's Mock Astrologer, at which the relish of all the dishes and sauces was overpowered by the common flavour of spice. Fish,—flesh,—fowl,—every thing at table tasted of nothing but red pepper.

The writings of Petrarch may indeed suffer undeservedly from one cause to which I must allude. His imitators have so much familiarized the ear of Italy and of Europe to the favourite topics of amorous flattery and lamentation, that we can scarcely think them original when we find them in the first author; and, even when our understandings have convinced us that they were new to him, they are still old to us. This has been the fate of many of the finest passages of the most eminent writers. It is melancholy to trace a noble thought from stage to stage of its profanation; to see it transferred from the first illustrious wearer to his lacqueys, turned, and turned again, and at last hung on a scare-crow. Petrarch has really suffered much from this cause. Yet that he should have so suffered is a sufficient proof that his excellencies were not of the highest order. A line may be stolen; but the pervading spirit of a great poet is not to be surreptitiously obtained by a plagiarist. The continued imitation of twenty-five centuries has left Homer as it found him. If every simile and every turn of Dante had been copied ten thousand times, the Divine Comedy would have retained all its freshness. It was easy for the porter in Farquhar to pass for Beau Clincher, by borrowing his lace and his pulvilio. It would have been more difficult to enact Sir Harry Wildair.

Before I quit this subject I must defend Petrarch from one accusation, which is in the present day frequently brought against him. His sonnets are pronounced by a large sect of critics not to possess certain qualities which they maintain to be indispensable to sonnets, with as much confidence, and as much reason, as their prototypes of old insisted on the unities of the drama. I am an exoteric—utterly unable to explain the mysteries of this new poetical faith. I only know that it is a faith, which except a man do keep pure and undefiled, without doubt he shall be called a blockhead. I cannot, however, refrain from asking what is the particular virtue which belongs to fourteen as distinguished from all other numbers. Does it arise from its being a multiple of seven? Has this principle any reference to the sabbatical ordinance? Or is it to the order of rhymes that these singular properties are attached? Unhappily the sonnets of Shakspeare differ as much in this respect from those of Petrarch, as from a Spenserian or an octave stanza. Away with this unmeaning jargon! We have pulled down the old regime of criticism. I trust that we shall never tolerate the equally pedantic and irrational despotism, which some of the revolutionary leaders would erect upon its ruins. We have not dethroned Aristotle and Bossu [Boileau] for this.

These sonnet-fanciers would do well to reflect that, though the style of Petrarch may not suit the standard of perfection which they have chosen, they lie under great obligations to these very poems,—that, but for Petrarch, the measure, concerning which they legislate so judiciously, would probably never have attracted notice;—and that to him they owe the pleasure of admiring, and the glory of composing, pieces, which seem to have been produced by Master Slender, with the assistance of his man Simple.

I cannot conclude these remarks without making a few observations on the Latin writings of Petrarch. It appears that, both by himself and by his contemporaries, these were far more highly valued than his compositions in the vernacular language. Posterity, the supreme court of literary appeal, has not only reversed the judgment, but, according to its general practice, reversed it with costs, and condemned the unfortunate works to pay, not only for their own inferiority, but also for the injustice of those who had given them an unmerited preference. And it must be owned that, without making large allowances for the circumstances under which they were produced, we cannot pronounce a very favourable judgment. They must be considered as exotics, transplanted to a foreign climate, and reared in an unfavourable situation; and it would be unreasonable to expect from them the health and the vigour which we find in the indigenous plants around them, or which they might themselves have possessed in their native soil. He has but very imperfectly imitated the style of the Latin authors, and has not compensated for the deficiency by enriching the ancient language with the graces of modern poetry. The splendour and ingenuity, which we admire, even when we condemn it, in his Italian works, is almost totally wanting, and only illuminates with rare and occasional glimpses the dreary obscurity of the Africa. The eclogues have more animation; but they can only be called poems by courtesy. They have nothing in common with his writings in his native language, except the eternal pun about Laura and Daphne. None of these works would have placed him on a level with Vida or Buchanan. Yet, when we compare him with those who preceded him, when we consider that he went on the forlorn hope of literature, that he was the first who perceived, and the first who attempted to revive, the finer elegancies of the ancient language of the world, we shall perhaps think more highly of him than of those who could never have surpassed his beauties if they had not inherited them.

He has aspired to emulate the philosophical eloquence of Cicero, as well as the poetical majesty of Virgil. His essay on the Remedies of Good and Evil Fortune is a singular work in a colloquial form, and a most scholastic style. It seems to be framed upon the model of the Tusculan Questions,—with what success those who have read it may easily determine. It consists of a series of dialogues: in each of these a person is introduced who has experienced some happy or some adverse event: he gravely states his case; and a reasoner, or rather Reason personified, confutes him; a task not very difficult, since the disciple defends his position only by pertinaciously repeating it, in almost the same words, at the end of every argument of his antagonist. In this manner Petrarch solves an immense variety of cases. Indeed, I doubt whether it would be possible to name any pleasure or any calamity which does not find a place in this dissertation. He gives excellent advice to a man who is in expectation of discovering the philosopher's stone;—to another, who has formed a fine aviary;—to a third, who is delighted with the tricks of a favourite monkey. His lectures to the unfortunate are equally singular. He seems to imagine that a precedent in point is a sufficient consolation for every form of suffering. "Our town is taken," says one complainant; "So was Troy," replies his comforter. "My wife has eloped," says another; "If it has happened to you once, it happened to Menelaus twice." One poor fellow is in great distress at having discovered that his wife's son is none of his. "It is hard," says he, "that I should have had the expense of bringing up one who is indifferent to me." "You are a man," returns his monitor, quoting the famous line of Terence; "and nothing that belongs to any other man ought to be indifferent to you." The physical calamities of life are not omitted; and there is in particular a disquisition on the advantages of having the itch, which, if not convincing, is certainly very amusing.

The invectives on an unfortunate physician, or rather upon the medical science, have more spirit. Petrarch was thoroughly in earnest on this subject. And the bitterness of his feelings occasionally produces, in the midst of his classical and scholastic pedantry, a sentence worthy of the second Philippic. Swift himself might have envied the chapter on the causes of the paleness of physicians.

Of his Latin works the Epistles are the most generally known and admired. As compositions they are certainly superior to his essays. But their excellence is only comparative. From so large a collection of letters, written by so eminent a man, during so varied and eventful a life, we should have expected a complete and spirited view of the literature, the manners, and the politics of the age. A traveller—a poet—a scholar—a lover—a courtier—a recluse—he might have perpetuated, in an imperishable record, the form and pressure of the age and body of the time. Those who read his correspondence, in the hope of finding such information as this, will be utterly disappointed. It contains nothing characteristic of the period or of the individual. It is a series, not of letters, but of themes; and, as it is not generally known, might be very safely employed at public schools as a magazine of common-places. Whether he write on politics to the Emperor and the Doge, or send advice and consolation to a private friend, every line is crowded with examples and quotations, and sounds big with Anaxagoras and Scipio. Such was the interest excited by the character of Petrarch, and such the admiration which was felt for his epistolary style, that it was with difficulty that his letters reached the place of their destination. The poet describes, with pretended regret and real complacency, the importunity of the curious, who often opened, and sometimes stole, these favourite compositions. It is a remarkable fact that, of all his epistles, the least affected are those which are addressed to the dead and the unborn. Nothing can be more absurd than his whim of composing grave letters of expostulation and commendation to Cicero and Seneca; yet these strange performances are written in a far more natural manner than his communications to his living correspondents. But of all his Latin works the preference must be given to the Epistle to Posterity; a simple, noble, and pathetic composition, most honourable both to his taste and his heart. If we can make allowance for some of the affected humility of an author, we shall perhaps think that no literary man has left a more pleasing memorial of himself.

In conclusion, we may pronounce that the works of Petrarch were below both his genius and his celebrity; and that the circumstances under which he wrote were as adverse to the development of his powers as they were favourable to the extension of his fame.

VIII

THOMAS CAMPBELL

The Literary Character of Petrarch

One circumstance fills me with distrust of being able to render entire justice to the Italian poet, in so many respects exquisite, which is, that I can make no atonement for any fault that I may find with him by any counter-manifestation of his beauties. A reader will take the critic's word, with slender proving, for any fault alleged against a poet; but, in order to be penetrated with a sense of his super-prevailing merits, he must have evidence in some adequate translation of the works of that foreign poet, if the reader be an Englishman little or not at all imbued with the foreign language. Now, where shall we apply for the means of rendering such justice to Petrarch? We have Homer and Dante transferred, as it were, soul and body into English; but who has succeeded in fully transferring Petrarch's graces into our tongue? The very genius of the two languages seems unpropitious to the task of translating an Italian into an English sonnet. The former seems a flower too delicate to prosper in the stormy climate of our speech.

Nevertheless, though I shall never pretend to be the translator of Petrarch, I recoil not, after writing his Life, from giving a sincere account of the impression which his poetry produces on my mind. I have studied the Italian language with assiduity, though perhaps at a later period of my life than enables the ear to be *perfectly* sensitive to its harmony, for it is in youth, nay, almost in childhood alone, that the melody and felicitous expressions of any tongue can touch our deepest sensibility; but still I have studied it with pains—I can relish Dante, I think, to his highest value; I can perceive much in Petrarch that is elevated and tender; and I approach the subject unconscious of the slightest splenetic prejudice.

Reprinted from *Life and Times of Petrarch: With Notices of Boccaccio and His Illustrious Contemporaries*, by Thomas Campbell, 2d ed. (London: Henry Colburn, 1843), 2: 346–69.

M. Sismondi, I am quite sure, no more wrote about Petrarch in haste or spleen, or the love of singularity, than I do. Yet he says something about being ashamed at his dissenting from the general enthusiasm respecting Petrarch's amatory poetry. I may have, upon the whole, a higher idea of this poet than Sismondi; yet I agree so cordially with some of his remarks, that, when he blushes for his own opinions, I should desire him to blush for mine by proxy, unless I thought conscientious opinions above all blame or shame.

I have certainly felt, in the perusal of Petrarch's amatory sonnets, sensations exceedingly different in the degree of respect for him which they inspire. When I found him describing himself haunted, not metaphorically, but optically and corporeally, by the image of his absent mistress, and comparing the sacredness of her birthplace to the Bethlehem, where our Saviour was born, I have not been able to banish a momentary suspicion that this was madness, which, if it had not run upon love, would have taken some other subject. The passages, however, which excited this conception, are not numerous, and the entranced features of his muse seldom lose their loveliness in these sybilline contortions. Laura ever and anon presents herself, a minute picture, to the mind's eye—her very veil and mantle, her features, her smile, her step—and we are in love with Laura. I must say, however, that we are rather smitten by her outward beauty than rapt into interest with her mind. Dante contrives, one scarcely can tell by what insensible traits, to make us the fond friends of his Beatrice, as well as to admire her; but what do we know of the secrets of Laura's heart? Her being too pure to be seduced might arise, as I suspect it did, from coldness towards Petrarch, and poetry coming to the aid of her discretion; but what struggles of sensibility she had to encounter, or whether she had any sensibility at all, is very much left to our conjecture.

Again, there is a sameness in the fluctuations of his amatory feelings, which is scarcely more amusing than if they had no fluctuations at all. His heart is a love-thermometer of hope and despair, which rises and falls between their extreme points, though generally inclining to the melancholy zero. A spice of jealousy for a suspected rival, or a tone of anger, methinks, would sometimes relieve this monotony, like a discord in harmony, that makes music seem more natural. There are times when all lovers are naturally enemies.

I demur to calling him the first of modern poets who refined and dignified the language of love. Dante had certainly set him the example. It is true that, compared with his brothers of classical antiquity in love-poetry, he appears like an Abel of purity offering innocent incense at the side of so many Cains making their carnal sacrifices. Tibullus alone anticipates his tenderness. At the same time, while Petrarch is purer than those classical lovers, he is never so natural as they sometimes are when their passages are least objectionable, and the sun-bursts of his real, manly, and natural human love seem to me often to come to us struggling through the clouds of Platonism.

I will not expatiate on the *concetti* that may be objected to in many of his sonnets, for they are so often in such close connexion with exquisitely fine thoughts, that, in tearing away the weed, we might be in danger of snapping the flower.

I feel little inclined, besides, to dwell on Petrarch's faults with that feline dilation of vision which sees in the dark what would escape other eyes in daylight, for, if I could make out the strongest critical case against him, I should still have to answer this question, "How comes it that Petrarch's poetry, in spite of all these faults, has been the favourite of the world for nearly five hundred years?"

We know, to be sure, that false belief, with all the perverted feelings which it entails, may reign among mankind for thousands of years. False religions have had that permanence. It is, moreover, too true that there is not only a conscientious religion in our taste for poetry, a pure, devoted love of truth, but sometimes also, and more than sometimes, in vulgar minds, an hereditary bigotry and a spiteful contentment in mistake, so that false poetical reputations may last a long time. But still false literary taste has no strong basis for its continuance. It has no established church, and no state payments or persecutions to support it. It leaves the enlightened votary of taste without the alternative of being crowned with a mitre for his faith, or having his disbelieving tongue bored for blasphemy with a red-hot iron. There is, therefore, every probability of poetical taste being sincere in proportion to its duration, and of being true in proportion to its sincerity.

So strong a regard for Petrarch is rooted in the mind of Italy, that his renown has grown up like an oak which has reached maturity amidst the storms of ages, and fears not decay from revolving centuries. One of the high charms of his poetical language is its pure and melting melody, a charm untransferable to any more northern tongue. Even in German, a still harsher language than English, the ear often luxuriates in the *singbarkeit*, or singableness, if we might coin such an English word, which the poet's art can elicit, and he wonders that the collocation of syllables can produce a mosaic of sounds so sweet to the ear. But the vocal Ausonian speech carries this spell of melody still higher. It is true that no conformation of words will charm the ear unless they bring silent thoughts of corresponding sweetness to the mind; nor could the most sonorous, vapid verses be changed into poetry if they were set to the music of the Spheres. It is scarcely necessary, however, to say that Petrarch has intellectual graces of thought and spiritual felicities of diction, without which his tactics in the mere march of words would be a worthless skill.

The love of Petrarch was misplaced, but its utterance was at once so fervid and delicate, and its enthusiasm so enduring, that the purest minds feel justified in abstracting from their consideration the unhappiness of the attachment, and attending only to its devout fidelity. Among his deepest admirers we shall find women of virtue above suspicion, who are willing to forget his Laura being married, or to forgive the circumstances for the eloquence of his courtship and the unwavering faith of his affection. Nor is this predilection for Petrarch the result of female vanity and the mere love of homage. No; it is a wise instinctive consciousness in women that the offer of love to them, without enthusiasm, refinement, and *constancy*, is of no value at all. Without these qualities in their wooers, they are the slaves of the stronger sex. It is no wonder, therefore, that they are grateful to Petrarch for holding up the perfect image of a lover, and that they regard him as a friend to that passion, on the delicacy and constancy of which the happiness, the most hallowed ties, and the very continuance of the species depend.

In modern Italian criticism there are two schools of taste, whose respective partizans may be called the Petrarchists and the Danteists. The latter allege that Petrarch's amatory poetry, from its platonic and mystic character, was best suited to the age of cloisters, of dreaming voluptuaries, and of men living under tyrannical governments, whose thoughts and feelings were oppressed and disguised. The genius of Dante, on the other hand, they say, appeals to all that is bold and natural in the human breast, and they trace the grand revival of his popularity in our own times to the re-awakened spirit of liberty. On this side of the question the most eminent Italian scholars and poets are certainly ranged. The most gifted man of that country with whom I was ever personally acquainted, Ugo Foscolo, was a vehement Danteist. Yet his copious memory was well stored with many a sonnet of Petrarch's, which he could repeat by heart; and, with all his Danteism, he infused the deepest tones of admiration into his recitation of the Petrarchan sonnets. . . .

I despair of ever seeing in English verse a translation of Petrarch's Italian poetry that shall be adequate and popular. The term adequate, of course, always applies to the translation of genuine poetry in a subdued sense. It means the best that can be expected, after making allowance for that escape of etherial spirit which is inevitable in the transfer of poetic thoughts from one language to another. The word popular is also to be taken in a limited meaning regarding all translations. Cowper's ballad of John Gilpin is twenty times more popular than his Homer; yet the latter work is deservedly popular in comparison with the bulk of translations from antiquity. The same thing may be said of Carey's Dante; it is like Cowper's Homer, as adequate and popular as translated poetry can be expected to be. Yet I doubt if either of those poets could have succeeded so well with Petrarch. Lady Dacre has shewn much grace and ingenuity in the passages of our poet, which she has versified; but she could not transfer into English those graces of Petrarchan diction, which are mostly intransferable. She could not bring the Italian language along with her.

Is not this, it may be asked, a proof that Petrarch is not so genuine a poet as Homer and Dante, since his charm depends upon the delicacies of diction that evaporate in the transfer from tongue to tongue, more than on hardy thoughts that will take root in any language to which they are transplanted? In a general view, I agree with this proposition; yet, what we call felicitous diction can never have a potent charm without refined thoughts, which, like essential odours, may be too impalpable to bear transfusion. Burns has the happiest imaginable Scottish diction; yet, what true Scotsman would bear to see him *done* into French? And, with the exception of German, what language has done justice to Shakespeare?

The reader must be a true Petrarchist who is unconscious of a general similarity in the character of his sonnets, which, in the long perusal of them, amounts to monotony. At the same time, it must be said that this monotonous similarity impresses the mind of Petrarch's reader exactly in proportion to the slenderness of his acquaintance with the poet. Does he approach Petrarch's sonnets for the first time, they will probably appear to him all as like to each other as the sheep of a flock; but, when he becomes more familiar with them, he will perceive an interesting individuality in every sonnet, and will discriminate their individual character as precisely as the shepherd can distinguish every single sheep of his flock by its voice and face. It would be rather tedious to pull out, one by one, all the sheep and lambs of our poet's flock of sonnets, and to enumerate the varieties of their bleat; and though, by studying the subject half his lifetime, a man might classify them by their main characteristics, he would find them defy a perfect classification, as they often blend different qualities. Some of them have a uniform expression of calm and beautiful feeling. Others breathe ardent and almost hopeful passion. Others again shew him jealous, despondent, or despairing; sometimes gloomily, and sometimes with touching resignation. But a great many of them have a mixed character, where, in the space of a line, he passes from one mood of mind to another.

As an example of pleasing and calm reflection, I would cite the first of his sonnets, according to the order in which they are usually printed. It is singular to find it confessing the poet's shame at the retrospect of so many years spent,

Fra le vane speranze e'l van dolore.

[I, *6*]

Ye who shall hear amidst my scattered lays
The sighs with which I fanned and fed my heart,
When, young and glowing, I was but in part
The man I am become in later days;
Ye who have marked the changes of my style
From vain despondency to hope as vain,
From him among you, who has felt love's pain,
I hope for pardon, ay, and pity's smile,
Though conscious, now, my passion was a theme,

Long, idly dwelt on by the public tongue,
I blush for all the vanities I've sung,
And find the world's applause a fleeting dream.

The following sonnet [CLIX] is such a gem of Petrarchan and Platonic homage to beauty that I subjoin my translation of it with the most sincere avowal of my conscious inability to do it justice.

In what ideal world or part of heaven
Did Nature find the model of that face
And form, so fraught with loveliness and grace,
In which, to our creation, she has given
Her prime proof of creative power above?
What fountain nymph or goddess ever let
Such lovely tresses float of gold refined
Upon the breeze, or in a single mind,
Where have so many virtues ever met,
E'en though those charms have slain my bosom's weal?
He knows not love who has not seen her eyes
Turn when she sweetly speaks, or smiles, or sighs,
Or how the power of love can hurt or heal.

Sonnet [XC] is remarkable for the fineness of its closing thought.

Time was her tresses by the breathing air
Were wreath'd to many a ringlet golden bright,
Time was her eyes diffused unmeasured light,
Though now their lovely beams are waxing rare,
Her face methought that in its blushes shew'd
Compassion, her angelic shape and walk,
Her voice that seem'd with Heaven's own speech to talk,
At these, what wonder that my bosom glowed!
A living sun she seemed—a spirit of Heaven.
Those charms decline: but does my passion? No!
I love not less—the slackening of the bow
Assuages not the wound its shaft has given.

The following sonnet [CCLIX] is remarkable for its last four lines having puzzled all the poet's commentators to explain what he meant by the words "A la man, ond'io scrivo, è fatta amica, a questa volta." I agree with De Sade in conjecturing that Laura in receiving some of his verses had touched the hand that presented them, in token of her gratitude.

In solitudes I've ever loved to abide
By woods and streams, and shunn'd the evil-hearted,
Who from the path of heaven are foully parted,
Sweet Tuscany has been to me denied,
Whose sunny realms I would have gladly haunted,
Yet still the Sorgue his beauteous hills among
Has lent auxiliar murmurs to my song,
And echoed to the plaints my love has chanted.
Here triumph'd too the poet's hand that wrote
These lines—the power of love has witness'd this.
Delicious victory! I know my bliss,
She knows it too—the saint on whom I doat.

Of Petrarch's poetry that is not amatory Ugo Foscolo says with justice, that his three political canzoni, exquisite as they are in versification and style, do not breathe that enthusiasm which opened to Pindar's grasp all the wealth of imagination, all the treasures of historic lore and moral truth, to illustrate and dignify his strain. Yet the vigour, the arrangement, and the perspicuity of the ideas in these canzoni of Petrarch, the tone of conviction and melancholy in which the patriot upbraids and mourns over his country, strike the heart with such force, as to atone for the absence of grand and exuberant imagery, and of the irresistible impetus which peculiarly belongs to the ode. The exhaustion consequent on long continued civil feuds was now precipitating Italy into that state of inaction and dependence from which she has never risen. Petrarch saw no salvation but in the union of those few lofty spirits who love their country.

Fra magnanimi pochi a chi 'l ben piace, . . .
I' vo gridando: Pace, Pace, Pace.
[CXXVIII, 120, 121]

But he found too few of those lofty spirits, and went about invoking peace in vain.

Petrarch's principal Italian poem that is not thrown into the shape of the sonnet is his Trionfi, or Triumphs, in five parts. Though not consisting of sonnets, however, it has the same amatory and constant allusions to Laura as the greater part of his poetry. Here, as elsewhere, he recurs from time to time to the history of his passion, its rise, its progress, and its end. For this purpose he describes human life in its successive stages, omitting no opportunity of introducing his mistress and himself.

1. Man in his youthful state is the slave of love. 2. As he

advances in age he feels the inconveniences of his amatory propensities, and endeavours to conquer them by chastity. 3. Amidst the victory which he obtains over himself, Death steps in, and levels alike the victor and the vanquished. 4. But Fame arrives after death, and makes man as it were live again after death, and survive it for ages by his fame. 5. But man even by fame cannot live for ever; if God has not granted him a happy existence throughout eternity. Thus Love triumphs over Man; Chastity triumphs over Love; Death triumphs over both; Fame triumphs over Death; Time triumphs over Fame; and Eternity triumphs over Time.

The subordinate parts and imagery of the Trionfi have a beauty rather arabesque than classical, and resembling the florid tracery of the later oriental Gothic architecture. But the whole effect of the poem is pleasing from the general grandeur of its design.

In summing up Petrarch's character, moral, political, and poetical, I should not stint myself to the equivocal phrase used by Tacitus respecting Agricola: *Bonum Virum facile dixeris, magnum lubenter*, but should at once claim for his memory the title both of great and good. A restorer of ancient learning, a rescuer of its treasures from oblivion, a despiser of many contemporary superstitions, a man, who, though no reformer himself, certainly contributed to the reformation, (if Luther himself were to rise from the dead, and deny my latter position, I would not believe him) an Italian patriot who was above provincial partialities, a poet who still lives in the hearts of his country, and who is shielded from oblivion by more generations than there were hides in the seven-fold shield of Ajax—if this was not a great man, many who are so called must bear the title unworthily. He was a faithful friend, and a devoted lover, and appears to have been one of the most fascinating beings that ever existed. Even when his failings were admitted, it must still be said that *even his failings leaned to virtue's side*, and, altogether, we may pronounce that

> His life was gentle, and the elements
> So mix'd in him that Nature might stand up
> And say to all the world "This was a man!"

IX

WALTER SAVAGE LANDOR

Francesco Petrarca

Scarcely on any author, of whatever age or country, has there so much been written, spoken, and thought, by both sexes, as on the subject of this criticism, Petrarca.

The compilation by Mr. Campbell is chiefly drawn together from the French.[1] It contains no criticism on the poetry of his author, beyond a hasty remark or two in places which least require it. He might have read Sismondi and Ginguené more profitably; the author of the *Introduction to the Literature of Europe* [Henry Hallam] had already done so; but neither has *he* thrown any fresh light on the character or the writings of Petrarca, or, in addition to what had already been performed by those two judicious men, furnished us with a remark in any way worth notice. The readers of Italian, if they are suspicious, may even suspect that Mr. Campbell knows not very much of the language. Among the many apparent causes for this suspicion, we shall notice only two. Instead of *Friuli*, he writes the French word *Frioul;* and, instead of the *Marca* di Ancona, the *Marshes.* In Italian, a *marsh* is *palude* or *padule:* whereas *marca* is the origin of *marchese:* the one a *confine;* the other a *defender* of a *confine*, or lord of such a territory.

Whoever is desirous of knowing all about Petrarca, will consult Muratori and De Sade: whoever has been waiting for a compendious and sound judgment on his works at large, will listen attentively to Ginguené: whoever can be gratified by a rapid glance at his works and character, will be directed by the clear-sighted follower of truth, Sismondi; and whoever reads only English, and is contented to fare on a small portion of recocted criticism in a long excursion, may be accommodated by Mrs. Dobson, Mr. Hallam, and Mr. Campbell.

Reprinted from *The Complete Works of Walter Savage Landor*, edited by T. Earle Welby (London: Chapman & Hall, 1931), 12: 25–60.

[1] [Campbell had prefaced his *Life* with a "Review of the Biographers of Petrarch," and constantly refers to Italian as well as to French sources.]

Francesco Petrarca

It may seem fastidious and affected to write, as I have done, his Italian name in preference to his English one; but I think it better to call him as he called himself, as Laura called him, as he was called by Colonna and Rienzi and Boccaccio, and in short by all Italy: for I pretend to no vernacular familiarity with a person of his distinction, and should almost be as ready to abbreviate Francesco into Frank, as Petrarca into Petrarch. Beside, the one appellation is euphonious, the other quite the reverse. . . .

Francesco Petrarca, if far from the greatest, yet certainly the most celebrated of poets, was born in the night between the nineteenth and twentieth day of July, 1304. His father's name was Petracco, his mother's Eletta Canigiani. Petracco left Florence under the same sentence of banishment as his friend Dante Alighieri, and joined with him and the other exiles of the Bianchi army in the unsuccessful attack on that city, the very night when, on his return to Arezzo, he found a son born to him: it was his first. To this son, afterward so illustrious, was given the name of Francesco di Petracco. In after life the sound had something in it which he thought ignoble; and he converted it into Petrarca. The wise and virtuous Gravina, patron of one who has written much good poetry, and less of bad than Petrarca, changed in like manner the name of Trapasso to Metastasio. I can not agree with him that the sound of the Hellenized name is more harmonious: the reduplication of the syllable *tas* is painful: but I do agree with Petrarca, whose adopted form has only one fault, which is, that there is no meaning in it. . . .

He had attained his tenth year when his father took him with a party of friends to the fountain of Vaucluse. Even at that early age his enthusiasm was excited by the beauty and solitude of the scene. The waters then flowed freely: habitations there were none but the most rustic: and indeed one only near the rivulet. Such was then Vaucluse; and such it remained all his lifetime, and long after. The tender heart is often moulded by localities. Perhaps the purity and singleness of Petrarca's, his communion with it on one only altar, his exclusion of all images but one, result from this early visit to the gushing springs, the eddying torrents, the insurmountable rocks, the profound and inviolate solitudes, of Vaucluse.

The time was now come when his father saw the necessity of beginning to educate him for a profession: and he thought the canon law was likely to be the most advantageous. Consequently he was sent to Montpelier, the nearest university, where he resided four years; not engaged, as he ought to have been, among the jurisconsults, but among the classics. Information of this perversity soon reached Petracco, who hastened to the place, found the noxious books, and threw them into the fire: but, affected by the lamentations of his son, he recovered the Cicero and the Virgil, and restored them to him, partially consumed. At the age of eighteen he was sent from Montpelier to Bologna, where he found Cino da Pistoja, to whom he applied himself in good earnest, not indeed for his knowledge as a jurisconsult, in which he had acquired the highest reputation, but for his celebrity as a poet. After two more years he lost his father: and the guardians, it is said, were unfaithful to their trust. Probably there was little for them to administer. He now returned to Avignon, where, after the decease of Clement V., John XXII. occupied the popedom. Here his Latin poetry soon raised him into notice, for nobody in Avignon wrote so good; but happily, both for himself and many thousand sensitive hearts in every age and nation, he soon desired his verses to be received and understood by one to whom the Latin was unknown.

> Benedetto sia il giorno, e 'l mese, e 'l anno!
> [LXI, 1]
> Blest be the day, and month, and year!

Laura, daughter of Audibert de Noves, was married to Hugh de Sade; persons of distinction. She was younger by three years than Petrarca. They met first on Good Friday, in the convent-church of St. Claire, at six in the morning. That hour she inspired such a passion, by her beauty and her modesty, as years only tended to strengthen, and death to sanctify. The incense which burnt in the breast of Petrarca before his Laura, might have purified, one would have thought, even the court of Avignon; and never was love so ardent breathed into ear so chaste. The man who excelled all others in beauty of person, in dignity of demeanour, in genius, in tenderness, in devotion, was perhaps the only one who failed in attaining the object of his desires. But cold as Laura was in temperament, rigid as she was in her sense of duty, she never was insensible to the merits of her lover. A light of distant hope often shone upon him, and tempted him onward, through surge after surge, over the depths of passion. Laura loved admiration, as the most retired and most diffident of women do: and the admiration of Petrarca drew after it the admiration of the world. She also, what not all women do, looked forward to the glory that awaited her, when those courtiers, and those crowds, and that city should be no more, and when of all women, the Madonna alone should be so glorified on earth.

Perhaps it is well for those who delight in poetry that she was inflexible and obdurate; for the sweetest song ceases when the feathers have lined the nest. Incredible as it may seem, Petrarca was capable of quitting her: he was capable of believing that absence could moderate, or perhaps extinguish, his passion. Generally the lover who can think so, has almost succeeded; but Petrarca had contracted the habit of writing poetry; and now writing it on Laura, and Laura only, he brought the past and the future into a focus on his breast. All magical powers, it is said, are dangerous to the possessor: none is more dangerous than the magic of the poet, who can call before him at will the object of his wishes; but her countenance and her words remain her own, and beyond his influence.

It is wonderful how extremely few, even of Italian scholars, and natives of Italy, have read his letters or his poetry entirely through. I am not speaking of his Latin; for it would indeed be a greater marvel if the most enterprising industry succeeded there. The thunderbolt of war—"Scipiades fulmen belli"—has always left a barren place behind. No poet ever was fortunate in the description of his exploits; and the least fortunate of the number is Petrarca. . . . I can not well believe that any man living has read beyond five hundred lines of *Africa:* I myself, in sundry expeditions, have penetrated about thus far into its immeasurable sea of sand.[2] But the wonder is that neither the poetry nor the letters of Petrarca seem to have been, even in his own country, read thoroughly and attentively; for surely his commentators ought to have made themselves masters of these, before they agitated the question, some whether Laura really existed, and others whether she was flexible to the ardour of her lover. . . .

It is censured as the worst of conceits in Petrarca that he played so often on the name of Laura; and many have suspected that there could be little passion in so much allusion. A purer

[2] [Coleridge claimed to be "almost the only Englishman who has ever levied so heavy a subsidy on his own time and patience," *Miscellaneous Criticism*, edited by Thomas Middleton Raysor (Cambridge: Harvard University Press, 1936), p. 24.]

taste might indeed have corrected in the poetry the outpourings of tenderness in the name; but surely there is a true and a pardonable pleasure in cherishing the very sound of what we love. If it belongs to the heart, as it does, it belongs to poetry, and is not easily to be cast aside. The shrub recalling the idea of Laura was planted by his hand; often, that he might nurture it, was the pen laid by; the leaves were often shaken by his sighs, and not unfrequently did they sparkle with his tears. He felt the comfort of devotion as he bent before the image of her name. But he now saw little of her, and was never at her house: it was only in small parties, chiefly of ladies, that they met. She excelled them all in grace of person and in elegance of attire. Probably her dress was not the more indifferent to her on her thinking whom she was about to meet: yet she maintained the same reserve: the nourisher of love, but not of hope. . . .

At Vaucluse Petrarca purchased a poor cottage and a small meadow; hither he transferred his books; and hither also that image which he could nowhere leave behind. Summer, autumn, winter, he spent among these solitudes; a fisherman was his only attendant, but occasionally a few intimate friends came from Avignon to visit him. The Bishop of Cavaillon, Philippe de Cabassoles, in whose diocese was Vaucluse, and who had a villa not far off, here formed with him a lasting friendship, and was worthy of it. During these months the poet wrote the three canzoni on the eyes of Laura, which some have called the "Three Graces," but which he himself called the "Three Sisters." The Italians, the best-tempered and the most polite of nations, look rather for beauties than faults, and imagine them more easily. A brilliant thought blinds them to improprieties, and they are incapable of resisting a strong expression. Enthusiastic criticism is common in Italy, ingenious is not deficient, correct is yet to come.

About this time Simone Memmi of Siena, whom some without any reason whatsoever have called a disciple of Giotto, was invited by the Pope to Avignon, where he painted an apartment in the pontifical palace, just then completed. Petrarca has celebrated him, not only in two sonnets, but also in his letters, in which he says, "Duos ego novi pictores egregios: Joctium Florentinum civem, cujus inter modernos fama ingens est, et Simonem Senensem."

Had so great an artist been the scholar of Giotto, it would have added to the reputation of even this illustrious man, a triumvir with Ghiberti and Michel-Agnolo. These, although indeed not flourishing together, may be considered as the first triumvirate in the republic of the arts; Raffael, Correggio, and Titian the second. There is no resemblance to Giotto in the manner of Simone; nor does Ghiberti mention him as the disciple of the Florentine. No man knew better than Ghiberti how distinct are the Siennese and the Florentine schools. Simone Memmi, the first of the moderns who gave roundness and beauty to the female face, neglected not the graceful air of Laura. Frequently did he repeat her modest features in the principal figure of his sacred compositions; and Petrarca was alternately tortured and consoled by the possession of her portrait from the hand of Memmi. It was painted in the year 1339, so that she was thirty-two years old; but, whether at the desire of her lover, or guided by his own discretion, or that in reality she retained the charms of youth after bearing eight or nine children, she is represented youthful, and almost girlish, whenever he introduces her. . . .

I will not discuss the question, how great or how little was the glory of his coronation; a glory which Homer and Dante, which Shakespeare and Milton, never sought, and never would have attained. Merit has rarely risen of itself, but a pebble or a twig is often quite sufficient for it to spring from to the highest ascent. There is usually some baseness before there is any elevation. After all, no man can be made greater by another, although he may be made more conspicuous by title, dress, position, and acclamation. The powerful can only be ushers to the truly great; and in the execution of this office, they themselves approach to greatness. But Petrarca stood far above all the other poets of his age; and, incompetent as were his judges, it is much to their praise that they awarded due honour to the purifier both of language and of morals. With these indeed to solicit the wife of another may seem inconsistent; but such was always the custom of the Tuscan race; and not always with the same chastity as was enforced by Laura. As Petrarca loved her,

Id, Manli! non est turpe, magis miserum est.

Love is the purifier of the heart; its depths are less turbid than its shallows. In despite of precepts and arguments, the most sedate and the most religious of women think charitably, and even reverentially, of the impassioned poet. Constancy is the antagonist of frailty, exempt from the captivity and above the assaults of sin.

There is much resemblance in the character of Petrarca to that of Abeillard.[3] Both were learned, both were disputatious, both were handsome, both were vain; both ran incessantly backward and forward from celebrity to seclusion, from seclusion to celebrity; both loved unhappily; but the least fortunate was the most beloved.

Devoted as Petrarca was to the classics, and prone as the Italian poets are to follow and imitate them, he stands apart with Laura; and if some of his reflections are to be found in the sonnets of Cino da Pistoja, and a few in the more precious reliquary of Latin Elegy, he seems disdainful of repeating in her ear what has ever been spoken in another's. Although a cloud of pure incense rises up and veils the intensity of his love, it is such love as animates all creatures upon earth, and tends to the same object in all. Throughout life we have been accustomed to hear of the Platonic: absurd as it is everywhere, it is most so here. Nothing in the voluminous works of Plato authorizes us to affix this designation to simple friendship, to friendship exempt from passion. On the contrary, the philosopher leaves us no doubt whatever that his notion of love is sensual.[4] He says expressly what species of it, and from what bestowers, should be the reward of sages and heroes.

Dii meliora piis!

[3] [Landor's version of Abélard or Abailard.]

[4] A mysterious and indistinct idea, not dissipated by the closest view of the original, led the poetical mind of Shelley into the labyrinth that encompassed the garden of Academus. He has given us an accurate and graceful translation of the most eloquent of Plato's dialogues. Consistently with modesty he found it impossible to present the whole to his readers; but as the subject is entirely on the nature of love, they will discover that nothing is more unlike Petrarca's. The trifles, the quibbles, the unseasonable jokes, of what is exhibited in very harmonious Greek, and in English nearly as harmonious, pass uncensured and unnoticed by the fascinated Shelley. So his gentleness and warmth of heart induced him to look with affection on the poetry of Petrarca; poetry by how many degrees inferior to his own! Nevertheless, with justice and propriety he ranks Dante higher in the same department, who indeed has described love more eloquently than any other poet, excepting (who always must be excepted) Shakespeare. Francesca and Beatrice open all the heart, and fill it up with tenderness and with pity.—W.S.L.

Beside Sonnets and Canzoni Petrarca wrote "Sestine"; so named because each stanza contains six verses, and each poem six stanzas, to the last of which three lines are added. If the terza-rima is disagreeable to the ear, what is the sestina, in which there are only six rhymes to thirty-six verses, and all these respond to the same words! Cleverness in distortion can proceed no further. Petrarca wearied the Popes by his repeated solicitations that they would abandon Avignon: he never thought of repeating a sestina to them: it would have driven the most obtuse and obstinate out to sea; and he never would have removed his hands from under the tiara until he entered his port of Civita-Vecchia. While our poet was thus amusing his ingenuity by the most intolerable scheme of rhyming that the poetry of any language has exhibited, his friend Boccaccio was occupied in framing that very stanza, the ottava-rima, which so delights us in Berni, Ariosto, and Tasso. But Tasso is most harmonious when he expatiates most freely, "numerisque fertur lege solutis": for instance, in the *Aminta*, where he is followed by Milton in his *Lycidas*.

We left Petrarca not engaged in these studies of his retirement, but passing in triumph through the capital of the world. On his way toward Avignon, where he was ambitious of displaying his fresh laurels, he stayed a short time at Parma with Azzo da Correggio, who had taken possession of that city. Azzo was among the most unprincipled, ungrateful, and mean, of the numerous petty tyrants who have infested Italy. Petrarca's love of liberty never quite outrivalled his love of princes: for which Boccaccio mildly expostulates with him; and Sismondi, as liberal, wise, and honest as Boccaccio, severely reprehends him. But what other, loving as he loved, would have urged incessantly the return to Italy, the abandonment of Avignon? At times, beyond a doubt, he preferred his imperfect hopes to the complete restoration of Italian glory; but he shook them like dust from his bosom, and Laura was less than Rome. Shall we refuse the name of patriot to such a man? No; those alone will do it who have little to lose or leave. Sismondi, who never judges harshly, never hastily, passes no such sentence on him. . . .

Laura, pleased by his return to her, was for a time less rigorous. Within the year, Charles of Luxemburg, soon after made emperor, went to Avignon. Knowing the celebrity of Laura, and finding her at a ball, he went up to her and kissed her forehead and her eyes. "This sweet and strange action," says her lover, "filled me with envy." Surely, to him at least, the sweetness must have been somewhat less than the strangeness. She was now indeed verging on her fortieth year: but love is forgetful of arithmetic. The following summer, Francesco for the first time visited his only brother Gherardo, who had taken the monastic habit in the Chartreuse of Montrieu. On his return he went to Vaucluse, where he composed a treatise *De Otio Religiosorum*, which he presented to the monastery.

Very different thoughts and feelings now suddenly burst upon him. Among the seventeen who accompanied him in the deputation, inviting the Pope to Rome, there was another beside Petrarca chosen for his eloquence. It was Cola Rienzi. The love of letters and the spirit of patriotism united them in friendship. This extraordinary man, now invested with power, had driven the robbers and assassins, with their patrons the Orsini and Colonnas, out of Rome, and had established (what rarely are established together) both liberty and order. The dignity of tribune was conferred on him; by which title Petrarca addressed him, in a letter of sound advice and earnest solicitation. Now the bishop of Lombes was dead he little feared the indignation of the other Colonnas, but openly espoused and loudly pleaded the cause of the resuscitated commonwealth. The cardinal was probably taught by him to believe that, by his influence with Rienzi, he might avert from his family the disaster and disgrace into which the mass of the nobility had fallen. "No family on earth," says he, "is dearer to me; but the republic, Rome, Italy, are dearer."

He took leave of the prelate, with amity on both sides undiminished: he also took leave of Laura. He could not repress, he could not conceal, he could not moderate his grief, nor could he utter one sad adieu. A look of fondness and compassion followed his parting steps; and the lover and the beloved were separated for ever. He did not think it; else never could he have gone; but he thought a brief absence might be endured once more, rewarded as it would be with an accession to his glory; and, precluded from other union with him, in his glory Laura might participate.

Retired, and thinking of her duties and her home, sat Laura; not indifferent to the praises of the most celebrated man alive (for her heart in all its regions was womanly) but tepidly tranquil, or moved invisibly, and retaining her purity amidst the uncleanly stream that deluged Avignon. We may imagine that she sometimes drew out, and unfolded on her bed, the apparel long laid apart and carefully preserved by her, in which she first had captivated the giver of her immortality; we may imagine that she sometimes compared with him an illiterate, coarse, morose husband; and perhaps a sigh escaped her, and perhaps a tear, as she folded up again the cherished gown she wore on that Good Friday.

On his arrival at Genoa, Petrarca heard of the follies and extravagances committed by Rienzi, and, instead of pursuing his journey to Rome, turned off to Parma. Here he learnt that the greater part of the Roman nobility, and many of the Colonnas, had been exterminated by order of the tribune. . . . In January the poet left Parma for Verona, where on the 25th (1348) he felt the shock of an earthquake. In the preceeding month a column of fire was observed above the pontifical palace. After these harbingers of calamity came that memorable plague, to which we owe the immortal work of Boccaccio; a work occupying the next station, in continental literature, to the *Divina Commedia*, and displaying a greater variety of powers. The pestilence had now penetrated into the northern parts of Italy, and into the southern of France; it had ravaged Marseilles; it was raging in Avignon. Petrarca sent messenger after messenger for intelligence. Their return was tardy; and only on the 19th of May was notice brought to him that Laura had departed on the 6th of April, at six in the morning; the very day, the very hour, he met her first. Beloved by all about her for her gentleness and serenity, she expired in the midst of relatives and friends. But did never her eyes look round for one who was away? And did not love, did not glory tell him, that in that chamber he might at least have died?

Other friends were also taken from him. Two months after this event he lost Cardinal Colonna; and then Sennuccio del Bene, the depository of his thoughts and the interpreter of Laura's.

The Lord of Mantua, Luigi Gonzaga, had often invited him to his court, and he now accepted the invitation. From this residence he went to visit the hamlet of Pietola, formerly Andes, the birthplace of Virgil. At the cradle of her illustrious poet the glories of ancient Rome burst again upon him; and, hearing that

Charles of Luxemburg was about to cross the Alps, he addressed to him an eloquent exhortation, *Dê pacificandâ Italiâ.* After three years the emperor sent him an answer. The testy republican may condemn him, as Dante was condemned before, for inviting a stranger to become supreme in Italy; but how many evils would this step have obviated! Recluses, and idlers, and often the most vicious, had been elevated to the honours of demigods; and incense had been wafted before the altar, among the most solemn rites of religion, to pilferers and impostors. As the Roman empire, with all the kingdoms of the earth, was sold under the spear by the Pretorian legion, so now, with title-deeds more defective, was the kingdom of Heaven knocked down to the best bidder. It was not a desire of office and emolument, it was a love of freedom and of Roman glory, which turned the eyes of Petrarca, first in one quarter, then in another, to seek for the deliverance and regeneration of his native land.

No preferment, no friendship, stood before this object. In the beginning he exhorted Rienzi to the prosecution of his enterprise, and augured its success. But the vanity of the tribune, like Buonaparte's, precipitated his ruin. Both were so improvident as to be quite unaware, that he who continues to play at *double or quits* must at last lose all. Rienzi, different from that other, was endowed by nature with manly, frank, and generous sentiments. Meditative but communicative, studious but accessible, he would have followed, we may well believe, the counsels of Petrarca, had they been given him personally. Cautious but not suspicious, severe but not vindictive, he might perhaps have removed a D'Enghien by the axe, but never a L'Ouverture by famine. He would not have banished, he would not have treated with insolence and indignity, the greatest writer of the age, from a consciousness of inferiority in intellect, as that other did in Madame de Staël. With that other, similarity of views and sentiments was no bond of union: he hated, he maligned, he persecuted, the wisest and bravest who would not serve his purposes: patriotism was a ridicule, honour was an insult to him, and veracity a reproach. The *heart* of Rienzi was not insane. Instead of ordering the murder, he would have condemned to the gallows the murderer, of such a man as Hofer. In his impetuous and eccentric course he carried less about him of the middle ages, than the pestilent meteor that flamed forth in ours. Petrarca had too much wisdom, too much virtue, to praise or countenance him in his pride and insolence; but his fall was regretted by him, and is even still to be regretted by his country. It is indeed among the greatest calamities that have befallen the human race, condemned for several more centuries to lie in chains and darkness.

In the year of the jubilee (1350) he went again to Rome. Passing through Florence, he there visited Boccaccio, whom he had met at Naples. What was scarcely an acquaintance grew rapidly into friendship; and this friendship, honourable to both, lasted throughout life, unbroken and undiminished. Both were eloquent, both richly endowed with fancy and imagination; but Petrarca, who had incomparably the least of these qualities, had a readier faculty of investing them with verse, in which Boccaccio, fond as he was of poetry, ill succeeded. There are stories in the *Decameron* which require more genius to conceive and execute than all the poetry of Petrarca, and indeed there is in Boccaccio more variety of the mental powers than in any of his countrymen, greatly more deep feeling, greatly more mastery over the human heart, than in any other but Dante. Honesty, manliness, a mild and social independence, rendered him the most delightful companion and the sincerest friend. . . .

[In 1358] he settled at Garignano, a village three miles from Milan, to which residence he gave the name of Linterno, from the villa of Scipio on the coast of Naples. Fond as he was of the great and powerful, he did not always give them preference. Capra, a goldsmith of Bergamo, enthusiastic in admiration of his genius, invited him with earnest entreaties to honour that city with a visit. On his arrival, the governor and nobility contended which should perform the offices of hospitality toward so illustrious a guest: but he went at once to the house of Capra, where he was treated by his worthy host with princely magnificence, and with delicate attentions which princely magnificence often overlooks. The number of choice volumes in the library, and the conversation of Capra, were evidences of a cultivated understanding and a virtuous heart. In the winter following (1359) Boccaccio spent several days at Linterno, and the poet gave him his Latin Eclogues in his own handwriting. On his return to Florence, Boccaccio sent his friend the *Divina Commedia*, written out likewise by himself, and accompanied with profuse commendations.

Incredible as it may appear this noble poem, the glory of Italy, and admitting at that time but one other in the world to a proximity with it, was wanting to the library of Petrarca. His reply was cold and cautious: the more popular man, it might be thought, took umbrage at the loftier. He was jealous even of the genius which had gone by, and which bore no resemblance to his own, excepting in the purity and intensity of love: for this was a portion of the genius in both. He was certainly the very best man that ever was a very vain one: and vanity has a better excuse for itself in him than in any other, since none was more admired by the world at large, and particularly by that part of it which the wisest are most desirous to conciliate, turning their wisdom in full activity to the elevation of their happiness. Laura, it is true, was sensible of little or no passion for him; but she was pleased with his; and stood like a beautiful Caryatid of stainless marble, at the base of an image on which the eyes of Italy were fixt.

Petrarca, like Boccaccio, regretted at the close of life, not only the pleasure he had enjoyed, but also the pleasure he had imparted to the world. Both of them, as their mental faculties were diminishing, and their animal spirits were leaving them apace, became unconscious how incomparably greater was the benefit than the injury done by their writings. In Boccaccio there are certain tales so coarse that modesty casts them aside, and those only who are irreparably contaminated can receive any amusement from them. But in the greater part, what truthfulness, what tenderness, what joyousness, what purity! Their levities and gaieties are like the harmless lightnings of a summer sky in the delightful regions they were written in. Petrarca, with a mind which bears the same proportion to Boccaccio's as the Sorga bears to the Arno, has been the solace of many sad hours to those who probably were more despondent. It may be that, at the time when he was writing some of his softest and most sorrowful complaints, his dejection was caused by dalliance with another, far more indulgent than Laura. But his ruling passion was ungratified by her; therefore she died unsung, and, for aught we know to the contrary, unlamented. He had forgotten what he had declared in Sonnet 17.

> E, se di lui fors' altra donna spera,
> Vive in speranza debile e fallace;
> Mio, perchè sdegno ciò ch' a voi dispiace, . . .
> [XXI, 5–7]

> If any other hopes to find
> That love in me which you despise,

Ah! let her leave the hope behind:
I hold from all what you alone should prize.

It can only be said that he ceased to be a visionary: and we ought to rejoice that an inflammation, of ten years' recurrence, sank down into a regular fit, and settled in no vital part. Yet I can not but wish that he had been as zealous in giving instruction and counsel to his only son, a youth whom he represents in one of his letters to have been singularly modest and docile, as he had been in giving it to princes, emperors, and popes, who exhibited very little of those characters. While he was at his villa at Linterno, the unfortunate youth robbed the house in Milan, and fled. We may reasonably suppose that home had become irksome to him, and that neither the eye nor the heart of a father was over him. Giovanni was repentant, was forgiven, and died.

The tenderness of Petrarca, there is too much reason to fear, was at all times concentrated in self. A nephew of his early patron Colonna, in whose house he had spent many happy hours, was now deprived of house and home, and, being reduced to abject poverty, had taken refuge in Bologna. He had surely great reason to complain of Petrarca, who never in his journeys to and fro had visited or noticed him, or, rich as he was in benefices by the patronage of his family, offered him any succour. This has been excused by Mr. Campbell: it may be short of turpitude; but it is farther, much farther, from generosity and from justice. Never is mention made by him of Laura's children, whom he must have seen with her, and one or other of whom must have noticed with the pure delight of unsuspicious childhood his fond glances at the lovely mother. Surely in all the years he was devoted to Laura, one or other of her children grieved her by ill-health, or perhaps by dying; for virtue never set a mark on any door so that sickness and sorrow must not enter. But Petrarca thought more about her eyes than about those tears that are usually the inheritance of the brightest, and may well be supposed to have said, in some inedited canzone,

What care I what tears there be,
If the tears are not for me?

His love, when it administered nothing to his celebrity, was silent. Of his two children, a son and a daughter, not a word is uttered in any of his verses. How beautifully does Ovid, who is thought in general to have been less tender, and was probably less chaste, refer to the purer objects of his affection!

Unica nata, mei justissima causa doloris, . . .

Petrarca's daughter lived to be the solace of his age, and married happily. Boccaccio, in the most beautiful and interesting letter in the whole of Petrarca's correspondence, mentions her kind reception of him, and praises her beauty and demeanour. Even the unhappy boy appears to have been by nature of nearly the same character. According to the father's own account, his disposition was gentle and tractable; he was modest and shy, and abased his eyes before the smart witticisms of Petrarca on the defects his own negligence had caused. A parent should never excite a blush, nor extinguish one. . . .

On the 18th of July, 1374, Petrarca was found in his library, his brow upon a book he had been reading: he was dead.

There is no record of any literary man, or perhaps of any man whatsoever, to whom such honours, honours of so many kinds, and from such different quarters and personages, have been offered. They began in his early life; and we are walking at this hour in the midst of the procession. Few travellers dare to return from Italy until they can describe to the attentive ear and glistening eye the scenery of the Euganean hills. He who has loved truly, and, above all, he who has loved unhappily, approaches, as holiest altars are approached, the cenotaph on the little columns at Arquà. . . .

Petrarca in all his Latin poetry, and indeed in all his Latin compositions, is an imitator, and generally a very unsuccessful one; but his versification is more harmonious, and his language has more the air of antiquity, and more resembles the better models, than any had done since Boethius.

We now come to his Italian poetry. In this he is less deficient in originality, though in several pieces he has imitated too closely Cino da Pistoja. "Mille dubj in un dì," for instance, in his seventh canzone. Cino is crude and enigmatical: but there is a beautiful sonnet by him addressed to Dante, which he wrote on passing the Apennines, and stopping to visit the tomb and invoke the name of Selvaggia. Petrarca, late in life, made a collection of sonnets on Laura; they are not printed in the order in which they were written. The first is a kind of prologue to the rest, as the first ode of Horace is. There is melancholy grace in this preliminary piece. The third ought to have been the second; for, after having in the first related his errors and regrets, we might have expected to find the cause of them in the following; we find it in the third. "Di pensier in pensier," "Chiare dolci e fresche acque," "Se il pensier che mi strugge," "Benedetto sia il giorno," "Solo e pensoso," are incomparably better than the "Tre Sorelle," by which the Italians are enchanted, and which the poet himself views with great complacency.[5] These three are upon the eyes of Laura. The second of the "Sorelle," or, as they have often been styled, the "Grazie," is the most admired of them. In this however the ear is offended at "*Qual all' alta*." The critics do not observe this sad cacophony. And nothing is less appropriate than

> Ed al fuoco *gentil* ond' io *tutto ardo*.

The close is,

> Canzon! l' una Sorella è poco inanzi,
> E l' altra sento in quel medesmo albergo
> Apparecchiarsi; *ond' io più carta vergo*.
> [LXXII]

This ruins the figure. What becomes of the *Sorella*, and the *albergo*, and the *apparecchiarsi?* The third is less celebrated than the two elder sisters.

Muratori, the most judicious of Italian commentators, gives these canzoni the preference over the others: but it remained for a foreigner to write correctly on them, and to demonstrate that they are very faulty. I find more faults and graver than Ginguené has found in them: but I do not complain with him so much that the commencement of the third is heavy and languid, as that serious thoughts are interested with quibbles, and spangled with conceits. I will here remark freely, and in some detail, on this part of the poetry of Petrarca.

Sonetto 21. It will be difficult to find in all the domains of poetry so frigid a conceit as in the conclusion of this sonnet,

> E far delle sue braccia a sè stess' ombra.
> [XXXIV, 14]

Strange that it should be followed by the most beautiful he ever wrote:

5[LXXI, LXXII, LXXIII.]

Solo e pensoso, . . .
[XXXV]

Canzone 1.

Nè meno ancor m' agghiaccia
L' esser coperto poi di bianche piume,
Ond' io presi col suon color di cigno!
[XXIII, 50, 51, 60]

How very inferior is this childish play to Horace's ode, in which he also becomes a swan.

Canzone 3. Among the thousand offices which he attributes to the eyes is *carrying the keys.* Here he talks of the *sweet eyes* carrying the keys of his *sweet thoughts* [XXXVIV]. Again he has a peep at the keyhole in the seventh [LXXII].

Quel cuor ond' hanno i begli occhi la chiave.
[LXXII, 30]

He also lets us into the secret that he is really *fond* of complaining, and that he *takes pains* to have his eyes always full of tears.

Ed io son un di quei ch' il pianger *giova;*
E par ben ch' io m' *ingegna*
Che di lagrime pregni
Sien gli occhi miei.
[XXXVII, 69–72]

Sonetto 20. Here are Phœbus, Vulcan, Jupiter, *Cæsar*, Janus, Saturn, Mars, Orion, Neptune, Juno, and a chorus of *Angels:* and they have only fourteen lines to turn about in [XLI].

Sonetto 39. In this beautiful sonnet, as in almost every one, there is a redundancy of words: for instance,

Benedetto sia il giorno, e 'l mese, e l' anno,
E la stagion, e 'l tempo.
[LXI, 1–2]

Sonetto 40 is very serious. It is a prayer to God that his heart may be turned to other desires, and that it may remember how on that day He was crucified [LXII].

Sestina 3. With what derision would a poet of the present day be treated who had written such stuff as,

E *nel bel* petto l' *indurato* ghiaccio
Che trae del mio sì *dolorosi venti.*
[LXVI, 29–30]

Canzone 8. As far as we know it has never been remarked (nor indeed is an Italian Academia worth a remark) that the motto of the Academia della Crusca, "Il più bel fior ne coglie" is from

> E, le onorate
> Cose cercando, il più bel fior ne colse.
> [LXXIII, 35–36]

Sonetto 46. Here he wonders whence all the ink can come with which he fills his paper on Laura [LXXIV].

Sonetto 51. In the fourteenth year of his passion, his ardour is increasing to such a degree, that, he says, "Death approaches . . . *and life flies away*."

> Che la morte s' appressa *e 'l viver fugge.*
> [LXXIX, 14]

We believe there is no instance where life has resisted the encounter.

Sonetto 59. This is very different from all his others. The first part is poor enough: the last would be interesting if we could believe it to be more than imaginary. Here he boasts of the impression he had made on Laura, yet in his last canzone he asks her whether he ever had. The words of this sonnet are,

> Era ben forte la nemica mia,
> E lei vid' io ferita in *mezzo 'l core.*
> [LXXXVIII, 13–14]

But we may well take all this for ideal, when we read the very next, in which he speaks of being free from the thraldom that had held him so many years. . . .

Canzone 9. It would be difficult to find anywhere, except in the rarest and most valuable books, so wretched a poem as this. The rhymes occur over and over again, not only at the close, but often at the fifth and sixth syllables, and then another time. Metastasio has managed best the redundant rhymes. . . .

Canzone 11. This is incomparably the most elaborate work of the poet, but it is very far from the perfection of "Solo e pensoso." The second and third stanzas are inferior to the rest; and the *fera bella e mansueta* is quite unworthy of the place it occupies [CXVI]. . . .

Sonetto 98. Four verses are filled with the names of rivers, excepting the monosyllables *non* and *e*. He says that all these rivers can not slake the fire that is the anguish of his heart: no, nor even ivy, fir, pine, beech, or juniper. It is by no means a matter of wonder that these subsidiaries lend but little aid to the exertions of the fireman [CXLVIII].

Sonetto 110.

O anime gentili ed amorose
[CLXI, 12]

has been imitated and improved upon by Redi, in his

Donne gentili, divote d' amore.

Sonetto 111. No extravagance ever surpassed the invocation to the rocks in the water, requiring that henceforward there would not be a single one which had neglected to learn how to burn with his flames [CLXII]. He himself can only go farther in

Sonetto 119, where he tells us that Laura's eyes can burn up the Rhine when it is most frozen, and crack its hardest rocks [CLXXI].

Sonetto 132. In the precarious state of her health, he fears more about the disappointment of his hopes in love than about her danger [CLXXXIV].

Sonetto 148. His descriptions of beauty are not always distinct and correct: for example,

Gli occhi sereni e le *stellanti* ciglia,
La bella bocca angelica, di perle
Piena, e di rose e di dolci *parole.*
[CC, 9–11]

In this place we shall say a little about *occhi* and *ciglia.* First, the sense would be better and the verse equally good, if, transposing the epithets, it were written

Gli occhi stellanti e le serene ciglia.

The Italian poets are very much in the habit of putting the *eyelashes* for the *eyes,* because *ciglia* is a most useful rhyme. The Latin poets, contented with *oculi, ocelli,* and *lumina,* never employ *cilia,* of which indeed they appear to have made but little account. Greatly more than a hundred times has Petrarca inserted eyes into the first part of his sonnets; it is rarely that we find one without its *occhi.* They certainly are very ornamental things; but it is not desirable for a poet to resemble an Argus.

Canzone 15. The versification here differs from the others, but is no less beautiful than in any of them. However, where Love appears in person, we would rather that Pharaoh, Rachel, &c., were absent [CCVI].

Sonetto 157. He tells us on what day he entered the labyrinth of love.

> Mille trecento ventisette *appunto*
> Sull' ora prima il dì sesto d' Aprile.
> [CCXI, 12–13]

This poetry has very unfairly been taken advantage of, in a book

> Written by William Prynne Esquier, the
> Year of our Lord sixteen hundred thirty-three. . . .

Sonetto 161. The first verse is rendered very inharmonious by the cesura and the final word having syllables that rhyme. Tutto 'l dì *piango*, e per la notte *quan*do, lagri*mando*, and consu*mando*, are considered as rhymes, although rhymes should be formed by similarity of sound and not by identity. The Italians, the Spaniards, and the French, reject this canon [CCXVI]. . . .

Sonetto 192. He fears he may never see Laura again. Probably this was written after her death. He dreams of her saying to him, "do you not remember the last evening, when I left you with your eyes in tears? Forced to go away from you, I would not tell you, nor could I, what I tell you now. *Do not hope to see me again on earth.*" This most simple and beautiful sonnet has been less noticed than many which a pure taste would have rejected. The next is a vision of Laura's death [CCL, CCLI]. There are verses in Petrarca which will be uttered by many sorrowers through many ages. Such, for instance, are

> Non la connobbe il mondo mentre l' ebbe,
> Conobbil' io ch' a pianger quì rimasi.
> [CCCXXXVIII, 12–13]

But we are hard of belief when he says

> Pianger cercai, *non già dal pianto onore.*
> [CCXCIII, 12]

There are fourteen more Sonnets, and one more Canzone in the first series of the *Rime;* but we must here close it. Of the second, third, and fourth series we must be contented with fewer notices, for already we have exceeded the limits we proposed. They were written after Laura's death, and contain altogether somewhat more than the first alone. Many of the poems in them are grave, tender, and beautiful. There are the same faults, but fewer in number, and less in degree. He never talks again, as he does in the last words of the first, of carrying a laurel and a column in his bosom, the one for fifteen, the other for eighteen years.

Ginguené seems disinclined to allow a preference to this second part of the Canzoniere. But surely it is in general far more pathetic, and more exempt from the importunities of petty fancies. He takes the trouble to translate the wretched sonnet (33, part 2) in which the waters of the river are increased by the poet's tears, and the fish (as they had a right to expect) are spoken to [CCCI]. But the next is certainly a most beautiful poem, and worthy of Dante himself, whose manner of thinking and style of expression it much resembles. There is a canzone in dialogue which also resembles it in sentiment and feeling:

> Quando il soave mio fido conforto, . . .
> [CCCLIX]

The next again is imitated from Cino da Pistoja: what a crowd of words at the opening!

> Quell' antico mio dolce empio signore.
> [CCCLX]

It is permitted in no other poetry than the Italian to shovel up such a quantity of trash and triviality before the doors. But rather than indulge in censure, we will recommend to the especial perusal of the reader another list of admirable compositions. "Alma felice," "Anima bella," "Ite rime dolenti," "Tornami a mente," "Quel rossignol," "Vago augelletto," "Dolce mio caro," "Gli angeli," "Ohime! il bel viso," "Che debbo io far," "Amor! se vuoi," "O aspettata," "Anima, che dimostra," "Spirto gentil," "Italia mia." Few indeed, if any, of these are without a flaw; but they are of higher worth than those on which the reader, unless forewarned, would spend his time unprofitably. It would be a great blessing if a critic deeply versed in this literature, like Cary, would publish the Italian poets with significant marks before the passages worth reading; the more worth, and the less. Probably it would not be a mark of admiration, only that surprise and admiration have but one between them, which would follow the poet's declaration in Can. 18

[LXXI], that "if he does not melt away it is because fear holds him together." After this foolery he becomes a true poet again, "O colli!" &c.,[6] then again bad, "You see how many colours love paints my face with."

Nothing he ever wrote is so tender as a reproach of Laura's, after ten years' admiration, "You are *soon* grown tired of loving me!"

There is poetry in Petrarca which we have not yet averted to, in which he has changed the chords καὶ τὴν λυρήν ἅπασαν: such as "Fiamma del ciel," "L' avara Babilonia," "Fontana di dolor." The volumes close with the "Trionfi." The first, as we might have anticipated, is "Il Trionfo d' Amore." The poem is a vile one, stuffed with proper names. The "Triumph of Chastity" is shorter, as might also be anticipated, and not quite so full of them. At the close, Love meets Laura, who makes him her captive, and carries him in triumph among the virgins and matrons most celebrated for purity and constancy. The "Triumph of Death" follows.

This poem is truly admirable. Laura is returning from her victory over Love; suddenly there appears a black flag, followed by a female in black apparel, and terrible in attitude and voice. She stops the festive procession, and strikes Laura. The poet now describes her last moments, and her soft sleep of death, in which she retains all her beauty. In the second part she comes to him in a dream, holds out her hand, and invites him to sit by her on the bank of a rivulet, under the shade of a beech and a laurel. Nothing, in this most beautiful of languages, is so beautiful, excepting the lines of Dante on Francesca, as these.

E quella man' già tanto desiata,
A me, parlando e sospirando, porse.

Their discourse is upon death, which she tells him should be formidable only to the wicked, and assures him that the enjoyment she receives from it, is far beyond any which life has to bestow. He then asks her a question, which he alone had a right to ask her, and only in her state of purity and bliss.

She sigh'd and said, "No; nothing could dissever
My heart from thine, and nothing shall there ever.

[6] [Landor misquotes. The original is "O poggi" (l. 37).]

If, thy fond ardour to repress,
I sometimes frown'd (and how could I do less?)
If, now and then, my look was not benign,
'Twas but to save my fame, and thine.
And, as thou knowest, when I saw thy grief
A glance was ready with relief."

Scarce with dry cheek
These tender words I heard her speak.
"Were they but true!" I cried. She bent the head,
Not unreproachfully, and said,
"Yes, I did love thee: and whene'er
I turn'd away mine eyes, 'twas shame and fear;
A thousand times to thee did they incline,
But sank before the flame that shot from thine."

He who, the twentieth time, can read unmoved this canzone, never has experienced a love which could not be requited, and never has deserved a happy one.

X

SAMUEL GRAY WARD

Letters from Italy on the Representatives of Italy

I have promised to write to you from Italy of the Italians. Not of those of to-day, late and imperfectly ripened fruits of the great tree, beneath which the nations once feasted in the shade, but of the great ones who represent the June day in the garden of the world.

When we were most devoted to the literature of Italy, and found no repose from the bustle and noise of every-day life, so sweet and profound as in the solitudes of Vaucluse, or the garden of Boccaccio, you would say, after declaiming some favorite passage with a superabundant emphasis, which would, perhaps have called a smile to the lip even of the Italian most addicted to the *issimos:* "But, after all, we do not entirely feel the beauty of this. No work of literature or art can be felt as it ought, except in those relations of climate and scenery, in which it was produced. This, true of all countries, it is peculiarly so of Italy; for the Italian is educated by his climate, and lives in the open air. The Italian sun paints this description, the Italian breeze breathes in these cadences, the happy constitution of the people gives a smoothness and subtle delicacy to this witticism, which we cannot appreciate beside a coal fire, and with the keen wind of our hills blowing the snow drifts before our eyes."

I often laughed at this theory; yet here upon the spot I find it true. The Italian sonnet is another thing to me, since I heard the language day by day; and the wine and honey of the Italian prose never, I find, were tasted in their true flavor till my eye became acquainted with the sky beneath which it grew up.

Of none is this truer than of our friend Boccaccio. And I will begin the promised correspondence by noting down a few thoughts suggested by my new acquaintance with the Decam-

Reprinted from *The Dial,* 1 (January, 1841): 386–400.

eron. They are not many, for I do not read or think much; in this climate mere living is enjoyment enough.

Giovanni Boccaccio; it is a famous name, and yet how few seem to appreciate or even know anything about him, except that he is one of three whose names we are in the habit of jingling together,—Dante, Petrarch, and Boccaccio. Neither is there much chance of his being better known, for the world grows more and more delicate as it grows older, and Boccace is nature itself, and the most unclad nature withal. And here, once for all, let me say what occurs to me on this subject. When we see a picture or statue, on what is our judgment of it founded? We look to see if the sentiment is true to nature, if the drawing is correct, if the *nature* is beautiful and true, if the spirit in which it is conceived be refined, and if we find these we are satisfied. But do we ask ourselves, when we see a drunken and sensual faun carved in Parian stone, whether the subject is moral, whether it is decent? Thank Heaven! I believe not, naturally,—such an inquiry is always suggested to the mind by the habit of using a conventional standard. When a Michael Angelo carves a Bacchus, (and his was no ideal Bacchus, but the deity of drunkenness,) do we ask such a question? Never. The art is its own reason. We recognise the presence of a wider law than that of our conventions, and, self-forgetful, are lost in the power of design. We recognise in the artist, not a law-giver to man, but a seer of the law of God. I saw, not long since, an engraving of an ancient marble, which represented a sea-monster, half-fish, half-man, carrying away a woman over the ocean, who seems to struggle and look back in vain, and rarely have I received from any design more pure delight. For the whole was full of Grecian grace; you could fancy the gentle waves, curling about the group, the blue sky above, all the earth young and loving about them. The genius of the artist so carried you at once to his ideal world, that it required an effort of thought to remember the actual subject, or figure to yourself that some Philistine, with no idea of any world beyond the one present at this moment, might say, "What a disgusting subject!" And so, Giovanni Boccaccio, do I think of thee! In thy noble mind this world was no decrepid debauchee, shunning the light, and hiding his unseemly person; but young, as if fresh from creation, not ashamed to utter all the thoughts that came into its head, sad or gay, tragic or fantastic. And this leads me to speak of a characteristic of Boccaccio; it is this perpetual youth. If he would describe a delicious scene, it is always with the dewy freshness of sunrise on every leaf,—his descriptions of morning are unrivalled. His persons are always "giovani, e costumati, e piacevoli assai"; young and fair to look upon, gentle, and of good manners, but frank and free; so that, if you were now to see such an one, fresh and full of fun and feeling, you would say, "There is one of Boccaccio's young men." His characters have not those minute and delicate traits, marking man from man as an individual, which Shakspeare, and, in a less degree, so many moderns have taught us to look for. Rather are they all drawn after one noble pattern; not like the work of a mannerist, but as if the author had lived in an early stage of society, when the lines are rather between class and class than between man and man. But I am afraid of making my distinction too marked, without making plain enough what it consists in. You will understand me, if I recall to your mind some of the painters whose figures have no mannerism, and yet seem all of one homogeneous race.

Dante, Petrarch, and Boccaccio,—I repeated to myself; and then asked what is it that entitles the author of the Decameron to such companionship? For I need not tell you in what estimation I hold the two first, and how they seem to me, with Shakspeare, to make the great Three in modern literature. Now, I will own Boccaccio as a not unworthy fourth. For I should say that it belongs to them more than any other modern writers, to have sprung from the earth,—original, titanic, the first of their race. We like to trace back the filiations of genius, to see how circumstances, or the contact with other minds, have influenced its growth; to trace an idea growing toward perfection through many minds, till at last it comes to flower in one, but we look in vain for the progenitors of these. Most men are the sons of time,—these are its "prophetic lords." Many a poet has expressed what his century taught him. These wrote as if they stood at the beginning of time, and had the centuries to teach. To sympathize with me here, you must look through the costume, the manners of their times, their systems of religion and morals, to the elemental forms they cover. In Boccaccio, what delights me is his constant freedom. He saw through the spirit of his time. He understood its littleness and bigotry. He despised its prejudices. What is mean, or low, or vicious, he attacks, sometimes with bitter and unsparing reproof (as in his denunciation of the Florentines, for their treatment of Dante), with grave irony, or, more often, and this suits better his cheerful nature, with overpowering wholesale ridicule. At what is deformed or vicious he will rather laugh than weep, but what is true or beautiful finds no more sincere lover and interpreter than he.

At a time when the church was preëminent; when all Europe was filled with monks and monasteries; he feared not their power nor their enmity; but gaily and gravely, decorously and indecorously, attacked their saintly and respected hypocrisy in the most vulnerable parts. Dante's bitter, though often veiled denunciation, had opened the minds of the few; the gay and fearless assaults of Boccaccio dragged the cowl from the satyr, and exposed him to the ridicule of the mob. He had no compassion for a class, or for a sanctity that was cut off by its very nature from the common sympathies of humanity; and yet true religion never encountered an enemy in him. As a proof of this, I translate the opening of the first novel,[1] which seems to me admirable and most truly christian in its spirit, at once devout and liberal.

> It is meet, O dearest ladies! that whatsoever work a man enters upon, should be prefaced with the wondrous and holy name of him who was the Creator of all. Wherefore, since I am to begin our story-telling, I mean to make a beginning with one of his wonderful truths, so that by hearing it our faith in Him, as in something not to be changed, may become stronger, and we may always give praises to his name. . . . Still more does his compassion and goodness towards us become manifest, when we consider that since the brightness of mortal eye cannot pierce the secrets of the divine mind, it may happen that we, deceived in our estimation, have chosen as our intercessor before his face, one who is driven thence into eternal banishment; and still, He from whom nothing is hidden, regarding the purity of him that prays, and not his ignorance, or the absence of his intercessor, hears the prayers, as if he through whom it is addressed were among the happy in his presence. The which will appear plainly in the novel I mean to relate,—plainly, I mean, to judgment of man—not to that of God.

[1] [The story of Ser Ciappelletto, who though a consummate sinner receives popular canonization after his death. It is one of the stories that endeared Boccaccio to Protestants.]

One must know the narrow and unsparing dogmatism of the church in those times, to appreciate the liberality of this,—and how far he was in advance of his time. And is not the doctrine of the intercession of saints beautiful in this simple statement? The same liberality may be seen in his treatment of the Jews. It seems as if prejudice against them were inborn in the nations. Scott has a Rebecca to be sure, and Shakspeare a Jessica; and among a thousand heroines in modern fictions, we now and then see an amiable Jewess; but here liberality stops,—and we remember with how little tenderness Shylock and Isaac are pictured by their creators. Not so Boccaccio, whose Jews are noble figures, and the only novels in which, so far as I remember, he has introduced them, he has chosen to set forth lessons that we too have not come so late into the world that we can derive no profit from them. The first of these relates to a Jew, by name Abraham, who lived in Paris, and who, as the story goes, was in all things an upright, and honorable man. Now he had a Christian friend, —Giannotto da Civigni, a great merchant and excellent man, who was much attached to him, and who, seeing the life he led, sought by every means in his power, to turn him from his belief, and make him a Christian. The Jew, after a while, began to take a pleasure in hearing him, but was not to be shaken in his faith. At last he announced his intention of going to Rome, to see and judge for himself how far their faith rendered the pastors of the church more excellent than other men. Now was Giannotto at his wit's end; for, thinks he, if Abraham goes to Rome and sees what the heads of the church really are, alas! It is all over with making him into a Christian. However, the Jew was not to be moved from his purpose, and accordingly goes to Rome; when he finds the vices and depravity of the clergy beyond belief,—finds them sensual, avaricious, and given without remorse to more sins than he can number. When he has satisfied himself, he returns home and tells Giannotto what he has seen, and how all seem to be striving to destroy the faith from its foundation. "And yet," he says, "I do not see that they succeed, but day by day your religion grows, and becomes more clear, so that I plainly perceive that, by its truth and holiness, it has a deeper foundation and support in the divine spirit than any other. So that I, who before so stiffly opposed your arguments, and would not become a Christian, would now by all means become so."

The power of the Roman Church has passed away. The clergy, among ourselves, are not possessed of wealth and power. We cannot accuse them of avarice, or luxury, or pride; we are, beside, too little rather than too much given to cherishing things sacred. Still, when we recollect that a class set apart from the rest to satisfy one want of humanity, must always be in danger of one-sidedness and narrowness, and when we know that, in being thus divided from the rest, they are not necessarily made better than the rest, not certainly made sacred in being separated, we feel the force of Abraham's words, and say with him, Let us cherish the priest, but believe the religion.

The other story is the well-known one of the "Three Rings."

The true commentary on the writings of an author is his life, if we can but get at it as a whole. That of Boccaccio, in the mere outline I have before me, speaks plainly enough. His father was a Tuscan of the little town of Certaldo, his mother born in Paris. Their condition was neither high nor low, but of that middle class, in which the heart's blood of society flows with strongest pulse. He received a tolerable education, and was then by his father introduced to trade, and remained a merchant till his eight-and-twentieth year. During this time he led a life of travelling, which, in those days, must have been one of continual adventure; above all, to the romantic, bold, fun-loving and woman-loving Boccaccio. This is the life best suited to bring a man closely in contact with the realities as well as the romance of his time. The history goes on to say that, by his father's command, he established himself at Naples, and that, walking one day alone, he came to the place where lie the ashes of Virgil. There he fell to meditating on the glory acquired by this great poet, and thereat took so great a despite to traffic, that, returning home, he gave himself entirely to the study of poetry.

This seems an extravagance, till we feel who it was that took this sudden determination, one of no weak or doubting mind. For to one of his "altezza d'animo," to know his course false to himself, and to forsake it, is but one act. And his stories contain many examples of characters of the same large and simple mould; there is, for instance, the story of a miser, who, reproved by a single word of a wise and witty man, saw so clearly the baseness of his avarice and discourtesy, that from that day forward, he abandoned them. The story of Abraham, which I have given above, is of the same sort; and this largeness and singleness of soul, which he who so felt could so well paint, gives a charm to the story of Ghismonda, which makes it a sublime tragedy.

The life goes on to say, that he gave his time to the study of the ancients, and became one of the most learned men of his time. He wrote, in Latin, a genealogy of the gods, and a list of ancient names of rivers and mountains; these are tasks, which seem even pedantic, and yet so free and incapable of fetters was his spirit, that his Decameron, is perhaps, the first book of modern times which is completely modern, showing no trace of the study of the classics, unless in the amenity and uniformity of its design.

I do not know that I can better confirm my thought, than by giving you here a translation of the Preface to the Fourth Day.

> Dearest ladies; from all that I had heard of the words of the wise, and all that I myself had seen or read, I had judged that the impetuous and fiery blast of envy should attack only the highest towers and most lofty tree-tops. But alas! how wofully has my judgment gone astray, since I, who have always bent my forces to avoid the fierce enmity of this rabid spirit; as you may plainly see, if you will consider these novels of mine, how I have written them not only in the vulgar Florentine, and in prose, and without a name, but also in the most humble and unambitious style I could, yet for all this could not escape being fiercely shaken, and torn almost up by the roots by this tempest, and all scarred by the teeth of envy. . . .
>
> Many, who show themselves most tender of my fame, say that I should do more wisely to stay with the Muses on Mount Parnassus, than to employ myself among you about these trifles; . . . That I should remain with the Muses on Mount Parnassus I allow is good counsel, and not amiss. But we may not dwell ever with the Muses, nor they with us. And when it happens that a man must leave their company, that he should delight himself with that which is nearest to their likeness, is this blameworthy? The Muses are women, and though women be not their peers, yet do they bear in their aspect a likeness to them, so that if they pleased me for nought else, here were a reason. Moreover, in past times women have been the cause of my making thousands of verses, but the Muses never of one. They have assisted me, indeed, and shown me how to compose those thousands; and perhaps also in the writing of these things, humble as they are, they have come sometimes to stand beside me, and lend their aid perchance in honor of the likeness between them-

selves and the subject of my stories. For while I weave them I leave neither Parnassus nor the Muses so far behind as many perhaps may think. . . .

A delicacy, a gentle irony, which seems to throw dust in the eyes of his bat-like adversaries, rather than take the trouble to confute them, charms me throughout this passage, and it seems to veil in its light grace an abounding wisdom. Thus, where he answers those who say that he should have remained with the Muses on Parnassus, rather than be looking to women for inspiration, his reply seems to say that we must leave the outworn traditions of the past, and seek our inspiration in the living world about us. I see running through the whole a defence of nature, a trust in natural impulses, a contempt for artificial distinctions and limitation. I am never tired of repeating to myself the image, so full of high wisdom, which occurs near the close, in which he likens himself and his labors to the impalpable dust, which the breeze may pass over and leave quiet on the ground, or which, borne aloft, may be left on the high palace tops, or the crowns of kings, but can fall no lower than its native home.

There is no truth which Boccaccio more delights in bringing forward than that there is no human condition so low, but that virtue may be found there; no outward disadvantage that mind, and heart, and soul, may not make null and void. . . .[2]

Since writing the above some days have passed, and I have nearly read through the Decameron. Naturally the subject has grown upon me, and I feel that it would be a work of time to give a complete account of my view of it. So take these imperfect notes in good part for the present.

Boccaccio did not act upon me with immediate attraction; to me he was not what we call "magnetic." My respect and liking for him grow each time I renew the acquaintance. Manliness, tenderness, nobleness, simplicity, nature, I find and admire in him. He is a true painter of man, *the creature of passion and circumstance*. "The plant man," he knows; but on the nobler side of this subject is unsatisfactory. With delicacy, refinement, *morbidezzu*, he has little to do, and it is because we are aware of his almost entire deficiency in these attributes, that the broad jokes and broad nature of Boccaccio do not disgust us. Here is

[2] [Ward here gives, partly in Italian, partly in translation, the story of Giotto and Messer Forese (*Dec.* VI, 5).]

both his wealth and his poverty. But for us moderns, who, inheriting the civilization of all past time, have run the gauntlet of sentiment and refinement, so busy in adjusting the drapery of feeling, that the bone and sinew it should cover are well nigh forgotten, it is well to come back to Boccaccio, and his healthy morning freshness. One feeling, of which I am often aware, yet am not sure, is this, that he is in a sense a mechanical artist. His figures seem too much made, too little conceived from within outwards. This effect may be attributable to the advanced age at which he embraced literature as a profession. What say you?

XI

THOMAS CARLYLE

The Hero as Poet: Dante

The Hero as Divinity, the Hero as Prophet, are productions of old ages; not to be repeated in the new. They presuppose a certain rudeness of conception, which the progress of mere scientific knowledge puts an end to. There needs to be, as it were, a world vacant, or almost vacant of scientific forms, if men in their loving wonder are to fancy their fellow-man either a god or one speaking with the voice of a god. Divinity and Prophet are past. We are now to see our Hero in the less ambitious, but also less questionable, character of Poet; a character which does not pass. The Poet is a heroic figure belonging to all ages; whom all ages possess, when once he is produced, whom the newest age as the oldest may produce;—and will produce, always when Nature pleases. Let Nature send a Hero-soul; in no age is it other than possible that he may be shaped into a Poet.

Hero, Prophet, Poet,—many different names, in different times and places, do we give to Great Men; according to varieties we note in them, according to the sphere in which they have displayed themselves! We might give many more names, on this same principle. I will remark again, however, as a fact not unimportant to be understood, that the different *sphere* constitutes the grand origin of such distinction; that the Hero can be Poet, Prophet, King, Priest or what you will, according to the kind of world he finds himself born into. I confess, I have no notion of a truly great man that could not be *all* sorts of men. The Poet who could merely sit on a chair, and compose stanzas, would never make a stanza worth much. He could not sing the Heroic warrior, unless he himself were at least a Heroic warrior too. I fancy there is in him the Politician, the Thinker, Legislator, Philosopher;—in one or the other degree, he could have been,

Reprinted from *Thomas Carlyle's Works*, "*The Ashburton Edition*," vol. 3: *Heroes and Hero-Worship* (Lecture III: "The Hero as Poet: Dante; Shakspeare") (London: Chapman & Hall, 1889), pp. 65–94.

he is all these. So too I cannot understand how a Mirabeau, with that great glowing heart, with the fire that was in it, with the bursting tears that were in it, could not have written verses, tragedies, poems, and touched all hearts in that way, had his course of life and education led him thitherward. The grand fundamental character is that of Great Man; that the man be great. Napoleon has words in him which are like Austerlitz Battles. Louis Fourteenth's Marshals are a kind of poetical men withal; the things Turenne says are full of sagacity and geniality, like sayings of Samuel Johnson. The great heart, the clear deep-seeing eye: there it lies; no man whatever, in what province soever, can prosper at all without these. Petrarch and Boccaccio did diplomatic messages, it seems, quite well: one can easily believe it; they had done things a little harder than these! Burns, a gifted song-writer, might have made a still better Mirabeau. Shakspeare,—one knows not what *he* could not have made, in the supreme degree. . . .

Poet and Prophet differ greatly in our loose modern notions of them. In some old languages, again, the titles are synonymous; *Vates* means both Prophet and Poet: and indeed at all times, Prophet and Poet, well understood, have much kindred of meaning. Fundamentally indeed they are still the same; in this most important respect especially, That they have penetrated both of them into the sacred mystery of the Universe; what Goethe calls 'the open secret'. "Which is the great secret?" asks one.—"The *open* secret,"—open to all, seen by almost none! That divine mystery, which lies everywhere in all Beings, 'the Divine Idea of the World, that which lies at the bottom of Appearance', as Fichte styles it; of which all Appearance, from the starry sky to the grass of the field, but especially the Appearance of Man and his work, is but the *vesture*, the embodiment that renders it visible. This divine mystery *is* in all times and in all places; veritably is. In most times and places it is greatly overlooked; and the Universe, definable always in one or the other dialect, as the realised Thought of God, is considered a trivial, inert, commonplace matter,—as if, says the Satirist, it were a dead thing, which some upholsterer had put together! It could do no good, at present, to *speak* much about this; but it is a pity for every one of us if we do not know it, live ever in the knowledge of it. Really a most mournful pity;–a failure to live at all, if we live otherwise!

But now, I say, whoever may forget this divine mystery, the *Vates*, whether Prophet or Poet, has penetrated into it; is a man sent hither to make it more impressively known to us. That always is his message; he is to reveal that to us,–that sacred mystery which he more than others lives ever present with. While others forget it, he knows it;–I might say, he has been driven to know it; without consent asked of *him*, he finds himself living in it, bound to live in it. Once more, here is no Hearsay, but a direct Insight and Belief; this man too could not help being a sincere man! Whosoever may live in the shows of things, it is for him a necessity of nature to live in the very fact of things. A man once more, in earnest with the Universe, though all others were but toying with it. He is a *vates*, first of all, in virtue of being sincere. So far Poet and Prophet, participators in the 'open secret', are one.

With respect to their distinction again: The *Vates* Prophet, we might say, has seized that sacred mystery rather on the moral side, as Good and Evil, Duty and Prohibition; the *Vates* Poet on what the Germans call the æsthetic side, as Beautiful, and the like. The one we may call a revealer of what we are to do, the other of what we are to love. But indeed these two provinces run into one another, and cannot be disjoined. The Prophet too has his eye on what we are to love: how else shall he know what it is we are to do? The highest Voice ever heard on this earth said withal, "Consider the lilies of the field; they toil not, neither do they spin: yet Solomon in all his glory was not arrayed like one of these." A glance, that, into the deepest deep of Beauty. 'The lilies of the field,'–dressed finer than earthly princes, springing-up there in the humble furrow-field; a beautiful *eye* looking-out on you, from the great inner Sea of Beauty! How could the rude Earth make these, if her Essence, rugged as she looks and is, were not inwardly Beauty? In this point of view, too, a saying of Goethe's, which has staggered several, may have meaning: 'The Beautiful', he intimates, 'is higher than the Good; the Beautiful includes in it the Good'. The *true* Beautiful; which however, I have said somewhere, 'differs from the *false* as Heaven does from Vauxhall!' So much for the distinction and identity of Poet and Prophet.–

In ancient and also in modern periods we find a few Poets

who are accounted perfect; whom it were a kind of treason to find fault with. This is noteworthy; this is right: yet in strictness it is only an illusion. At bottom, clearly enough, there is no perfect Poet! A vein of Poetry exists in the hearts of all men; no man is made altogether of Poetry. We are all poets when we *read* a poem well. The 'imagination that shudders at the Hell of Dante', is not that the same faculty, weaker in degree, as Dante's own? No one but Shakspeare can embody, out of *Saxo Grammaticus*, the story of *Hamlet* as Shakspeare did: but every one models some kind of story out of it; every one embodies it better or worse. We need not spend time in defining. Where there is no specific difference, as between round and square, all definition must be more or less arbitrary. A man that has *so* much more of the poetic element developed in him as to have become noticeable, will be called Poet by his neighbours. World-Poets too, those whom we are to take for perfect Poets, are settled by critics in the same way. One who rises *so* far above the general level of Poets will, to such and such critics, seem a Universal Poet; as he ought to do. And yet it is, and must be, an arbitrary distinction. All Poets, all men, have some touches of the Universal; no man is wholly made of that. Most Poets are very soon forgotten: but not the noblest Shakspeare or Homer of them can be remembered *forever*;—a day comes when he too is not!

Nevertheless, you will say, there must be a difference between true Poetry and true Speech not poetical: what is the difference? On this point many things have been written, especially by late German Critics, some of which are not very intelligible at first. They say, for example, that the Poet has an *infinitude* in him; communicates an *Unendlichkeit*, a certain character of 'infinitude', to whatsoever he delineates. This, though not very precise, yet on so vague a matter is worth remembering: if well meditated, some meaning will gradually be found in it. For my own part, I find considerable meaning in the old vulgar distinction of Poetry being *metrical*, having music in it, being a Song. Truly, if pressed to give a definition, one might say this as soon as anything else: If your delineation be authentically *musical*, musical not in word only, but in heart and substance, in all the thoughts and utterances of it, in the whole conception of it, then it will be poetical; if not, not.—Musical: how much lies in that! A *musical* thought is one spoken by a mind that has penetrated into the inmost heart of the thing; detected the inmost mystery of it, namely the *melody* that lies hidden in it; the inward harmony of coherence which is its soul, whereby it exists, and has a right to be, here in this world. All inmost things, we may say, are melodious; naturally utter themselves in Song. The meaning of Song goes deep. Who is there that, in logical words, can express the effect music has on us? A kind of inarticulate unfathomable speech, which leads us to the edge of the Infinite, and lets us for moments gaze into that!

Nay all speech, even the commonest speech, has something of song in it: not a parish in the world but has its parish-accent;—the rhythm or *tune* to which the people there *sing* what they have to say! Accent is a kind of chanting; all men have accent of their own,—though they only *notice* that of others. Observe too how all passionate language does of itself become musical,—with a finer music than the mere accent; the speech of a man even in zealous anger becomes a chant, a song. All deep things are Song. It seems somehow the very central essence of us, Song; as if all the rest were but wrappages and hulls! The primal element of us; of us, and of all things. The Greeks fabled of Sphere-Harmonies: it was the feeling they had of the inner structure of Nature; that the soul of all her voices and utterances was perfect music. Poetry, therefore, we will call *musical Thought.* The Poet is he who *thinks* in that manner. At bottom, it turns still on power of intellect; it is a man's sincerity and depth of vision that makes him a Poet. See deep enough, and you see musically; the heart of Nature *being* everywhere music, if you can only reach it.

The *Vates* Poet, with his melodious Apocalypse of Nature, seems to hold a poor rank among us, in comparison with the *Vates* Prophet; his function, and our esteem of him for his function, alike slight. The Hero taken as Divinity; the Hero taken as Prophet; then next the Hero taken only as Poet: does it not look as if our estimate of the Great Man, epoch after epoch, were continually diminishing? We take him first for a god, then for one god-inspired; and now in the next stage of it, his most miraculous word gains from us only the recognition that he is a Poet, beautiful verse-maker, man of genius, or suchlike!—It looks so; but I persuade myself that intrinsically it is not so. If we consider well, it will perhaps appear that in man still there is the *same* altogether peculiar admiration for the Heroic Gift, by what name soever called, that there at any time was.

I should say, if we do not now reckon a Great Man literally divine, it is that our notions of God, of the supreme unattainable Fountain of Splendour, Wisdom and Heroism, are ever rising *higher;* not altogether that our reverence for these qualities, as manifested in our like, is getting lower. This is worth taking thought of. Sceptical Dilettantism, the curse of these ages, a curse which will not last forever, does indeed in this the highest province of human things, as in all provinces, make sad work; and our reverence for great men, all crippled, blinded, paralytic as it is, comes out in poor plight, hardly recognisable. Men worship the shows of great men; the most disbelieve that there is any reality of great men to worship. The dreariest, fatalest faith; believing which, one would literally despair of human things. Nevertheless look, for example, at Napoleon! A Corsican lieutenant of artillery; that is the show of *him:* yet is he not obeyed, *worshipped* after his sort, as all the Tiaraed and Diademed of the world put together could not be? High Duchesses, and ostlers of inns, gather round the Scottish rustic, Burns;—a strange feeling dwelling in each that they never heard a man like this; that, on the whole, this is the man! In the secret heart of these people it still dimly reveals itself, though there is no accredited way of uttering it at present, that this rustic, with his black brows and flashing sun-eyes, and strange words moving laughter and tears, is of a dignity far beyond all others, incommensurable with all others. Do not we feel it so? But now, were Dilettantism, Scepticism, Triviality, and all that sorrowful brood, cast-out of us,—as, by God's blessing, they shall one day be; were faith in the shows of things entirely swept-out, replaced by clear faith in the *things,* so that a man acted on the impulse of that only, and counted the other non-extant; what a new livelier feeling towards this Burns were it!

Nay here in these ages, such as they are, have we not two mere Poets, if not deified, yet we may say beatified? Shakspeare and Dante are Saints of Poetry; really, if we will think of it, *canonised,* so that it is impiety to meddle with them. The unguided instinct of the world, working across all these perverse impediments, has arrived at such result. Dante and Shakspeare are a peculiar Two. They dwell apart, in a kind of royal solitude; none equal, none second to them: in the general feeling of the world, a certain transcendentalism, a glory as of complete perfection, invests these two. They *are* canonised, though no

Pope or Cardinals took hand in doing it! Such, in spite of every perverting influence, in the most unheroic times, is still our indestructible reverence for heroism.—We will look a little at these Two, the Poet Dante and the Poet Shakspeare: what little it is permitted us to say here of the Hero as Poet will most fitly arrange itself in that fashion.

Many volumes have been written by way of commentary on Dante and his Book; yet, on the whole, with no great result. His Biography is, as it were, irrecoverably lost for us. An unimportant, wandering, sorrowstricken man, not much note was taken of him while he lived; and the most of that has vanished, in the long space that now intervenes. It is five centuries since he ceased writing and living here. After all commentaries, the Book itself is mainly what we know of him. The Book;—and one might add that Portrait commonly attributed to Giotto, which, looking on it, you cannot help inclining to think genuine, whoever did it. To me it is a most touching face; perhaps of all faces that I know, the most so. Lonely there, painted as on vacancy, with the simple laurel wound round it; the deathless sorrow and pain, the known victory which is also deathless;—significant of the whole history of Dante! I think it is the mournfulest face that ever was painted from reality; an altogether tragic, heart-affecting face. There is in it, as foundation of it, the softness, tenderness, gentle affection as of a child; but all this is as if congealed into sharp contradiction, into abnegation, isolation, proud hopeless pain. A soft ethereal soul looking-out so stern, implacable, grim-trenchant, as from imprisonment of thick-ribbed ice! Withal it is a silent pain too, a silent scornful one: the lip is curled in a kind of godlike disdain of the thing that is eating-out his heart,—as if it were withal a mean insignificant thing, as if he whom it had power to torture and strangle were greater than it. The face of one wholly in protest, and life-long unsurrendering battle, against the world. Affection all converted into indignation: an implacable indignation; slow, equable, silent, like that of a god! The eye too, it looks-out as in a kind of *surprise*, a kind of inquiry, Why the world was of such a sort? This is Dante: so he looks, this 'voice of ten silent centuries', and sings us 'his mystic unfathomable song'.

The little that we know of Dante's Life corresponds well

enough with this Portrait and this Book. He was born at Florence, in the upper class of society, in the year 1265. His education was the best then going; much school-divinity, Aristotelean logic, some Latin classics,—no inconsiderable insight into certain provinces of things: and Dante, with his earnest intelligent nature, we need not doubt, learned better than most all that was learnable. He has a clear cultivated understanding, and of great subtlety; this best fruit of education he had contrived to realise from these scholastics. He knows accurately and well what lies close to him; but, in such a time, without printed books or free intercourse, he could not know well what was distant: the small clear light, most luminous for what is near, breaks itself into singular *chiaroscuro* striking on what is far off. This was Dante's learning from the schools. In life, he had gone through the usual destinies; been twice out campaigning as a soldier for the Florentine State, been on embassy; had in his thirty-fifth year, by natural gradation of talent and service, become one of the Chief Magistrates of Florence. He had met in boyhood a certain Beatrice Portinari, a beautiful little girl of his own age and rank, and grown-up thenceforth in partial sight of her, in some distant intercourse with her. All readers know his graceful affecting account of this; and then of their being parted; of her being wedded to another, and of her death soon after. She makes a great figure in Dante's Poem; seems to have made a great figure in his life. Of all beings it might seem as if she, held apart from him, far apart at last in the dim Eternity, were the only one he had ever with his whole strength of affection loved. She died: Dante himself was wedded; but it seems not happily, far from happily. I fancy, the rigorous earnest man, with his keen excitabilities, was not altogether easy to make happy.

We will not complain of Dante's miseries: had all gone right with him as he wished it, he might have been Prior, Podestà, or whatsoever they call it, of Florence, well accepted among neighbours,—and the world had wanted one of the most notable words ever spoken or sung. Florence would have had another prosperous Lord Mayor; and the ten dumb centuries continued voiceless, and the ten other listening centuries (for there will be ten of them and more) had no *Divina Commedia* to hear! We will complain of nothing. A nobler destiny was appointed for this Dante; and he, struggling like a man led towards death and crucifixion, could not help fulfilling it. Give *him* the choice of his happiness! He knew not, more than we do, what was really happy, what was really miserable.

In Dante's Priorship, the Guelf-Ghibelline, Bianchi-Neri, or some other confused disturbances rose to such a height, that Dante, whose party had seemed the stronger, was with his friends cast unexpectedly forth into banishment; doomed thenceforth to a life of woe and wandering. His property was all confiscated and more; he had the fiercest feeling that it was entirely unjust, nefarious in the sight of God and man. He tried what was in him to get reinstated; tried even by warlike surprisal, with arms in his hand: but it would not do; bad only had become worse. There is a record, I believe, still extant in the Florence Archives, dooming this Dante, wheresoever caught, to be burnt alive. Burnt alive; so it stands, they say: a very curious civic document. Another curious document, some considerable number of years later, is a Letter of Dante's to the Florentine Magistrates, written in answer to a milder proposal of theirs, that he should return on condition of apologising and paying a fine. He answers, with fixed stern pride: "If I cannot return without calling myself guilty, I will never return, *nunquam revertar*."

For Dante there was now no home in this world. He wandered from patron to patron, from place to place: proving, in his own bitter words, 'How hard is the path, *Come è duro calle*'. The wretched are not cheerful company. Dante, poor and banished, with his proud earnest nature, with his moody humours, was not a man to conciliate men. Petrarch reports of him that being at Can della Scala's court, and blamed one day for his gloom and taciturnity, he answered in no courtier-like way. Della Scala stood among his courtiers, with mimes and buffoons *(nebulones ac histriones)* making him heartily merry; when turning to Dante, he said: "Is it not strange, now, that this poor fool should make himself so entertaining; while you, a wise man, sit there day after day, and have nothing to amuse us with at all?" Dante answered bitterly: "No, not strange; your Highness is to recollect the Proverb, *Like to Like*";–given the amuser, the amusee must also be given! Such a man, with his proud silent ways, with his sarcasms and sorrows, was not made to succeed at court. By degrees, it came to be evident to him that he had no longer any resting-place, or hope of benefit, in this earth. The earthly world had cast him forth, to wander, wander; no living heart to love him now; for his sore miseries there was no solace here.

The deeper naturally would the Eternal World impress itself on him; that awful reality over which, after all, this Time-world, with its Florences and banishments, only flutters as an unreal shadow. Florence thou shalt never see: but Hell and Purgatory and Heaven thou shalt surely see! What is Florence, Can della Scala, and the World and Life altogether? ETERNITY: thither, of a truth, not elsewhither, art thou and all things bound! The great soul of Dante, homeless on earth, made its home more and more in that awful other world. Naturally his thoughts brooded on that, as on the one fact important for him. Bodied or bodiless, it is the one fact important for all men:—but to Dante, in that age, it was bodied in fixed certainty of scientific shape; he no more doubted of that *Malebolge* Pool, that it all lay there with its gloomy circles, with its *alti guai*, and that he himself should see it, than we doubt that we should see Constantinople if we went thither. Dante's heart, long filled with this, brooding over it in speechless thought and awe, bursts forth at length into 'mystic unfathomable song'; and this his *Divine Comedy*, the most remarkable of all modern Books, is the result.

It must have been a great solacement to Dante, and was, as we can see, a proud thought for him at times, That he, here in exile, could do this work; that no Florence, nor no man or men, could hinder him from doing it, or even much help him in doing it. He knew too, partly, that it was great; the greatest a man could do. 'If thou follow thy star, *Se tu segui tua stella*',—so could the Hero, in his forsakenness, in his extreme need, still say to himself: "Follow thou thy star, thou shalt not fail of a glorious haven!" The labour of writing, we find, and indeed could know otherwise, was great and painful for him; he says, This Book, 'which has made me lean for many years'. Ah yes, it was won, all of it, with pain and sore toil,—not in sport, but in grim earnest. His Book, as indeed most good Books are, has been written, in many senses, with his heart's blood. It is his whole history, this Book. He died after finishing it; not yet very old, at the age of fifty-six;— broken-hearted rather, as is said. He lies buried in his death-city Ravenna: *Hic claudor Dantes patriis extorris ab oris*. The Florentines begged back his body, in a century after; the Ravenna people would not give it. "Here am I Dante laid, shut-out from my native shores."

I said, Dante's Poem was a Song: it is Tieck who calls it 'a mystic unfathomable Song'; and such is literally the character of it. Coleridge remarks very pertinently somewhere, that wherever you find a sentence musically worded, of true rhythm and melody in the words, there is something deep and good in the meaning too. For body and soul, word and idea, go strangely together here as everywhere. Song: we said before, it was the Heroic of Speech! All *old* Poems, Homer's and the rest, are authentically Songs. I would say, in strictness, that all right Poems are; that whatsoever is not *sung* is properly no Poem, but a piece of Prose cramped into jingling lines,–to the great injury of the grammar, to the great grief of the reader, for most part! What we want to get at is the *thought* the man had, if he had any: why should he twist it into jingle, if he *could* speak it out plainly? It is only when the heart of him is rapt into true passion of melody, and the very tones of him, according to Coleridge's remark, become musical by the greatness, depth and music of his thoughts, that we can give him right to rhyme and sing; that we call him a Poet, and listen to him as the Heroic of Speakers,–whose speech *is* Song. Pretenders to this are many; and to an earnest reader, I doubt, it is for most part a very melancholy, not to say an insupportable business, that of reading rhyme! Rhyme that had no inward necessity to be rhymed;–it ought to have told us plainly, without any jingle, what it was aiming at. I would advise all men who *can* speak their thought, not to sing it; to understand that, in a serious time, among serious men, there is no vocation in them for singing it. Precisely as we love the true song, and are charmed by it as by something divine, so shall we hate the false song, and account it a mere wooden noise, a thing hollow, superfluous, altogether an insincere and offensive thing.

I give Dante my highest praise when I say of his *Divine Comedy* that it is, in all senses, genuinely a Song. In the very sound of it there is a *canto fermo;* it proceeds as by a chant. The language, his simple *terza rima,* doubtless helped him in this. One reads along naturally with a sort of *lilt.* But I add, that it could not be otherwise; for the essence and material of the work are themselves rhythmic. Its depth, and rapt passion and sincerity, makes it musical;–go *deep* enough, there is music everywhere. A true inward symmetry, what one calls an architectural harmony, reigns in it, proportionates it all: architectural; which also partakes of the character of music. The three kingdoms, *Inferno*, *Purgatorio*, *Paradiso*, look-out on one another like compartments of a great edifice; a great supernatural world-cathedral, piled-up there, stern, solemn, awful; Dante's World of Souls! It is, at bottom, the *sincerest* of all Poems; sincerity, here too, we find to be the measure of worth. It came deep out of the author's heart of hearts; and it goes deep, and through long generations, into ours. The people of Verona, when they saw him on the streets, used to say, "*Eccovi l' uom ch'è stato all'Inferno*, See, there is the man that was in Hell!" As yes, he had been in Hell;–in Hell enough, in long severe sorrow and struggle; as the like of him is pretty sure to have been. Commedias that come-out *divine* are not accomplished otherwise. Thought, true labour of any kind, highest virtue itself, is it not the daughter of Pain? Born as out of the black whirlwind;–true *effort*, in fact, as of a captive struggling to free himself: that is Thought. In all ways we are 'to become perfect through *suffering*'. But, as I say, no work known to me is so elaborated as this of Dante's. It has all been as if molten, in the hottest furnace of his soul. It had made him 'lean' for many years. Not the general whole only; every compartment of it is worked-out, with intense earnestness, into truth, into clear visuality. Each answers to the other; each fits in its place, like a marble stone accurately hewn and polished. It is the soul of Dante, and in this the soul of the middle ages, rendered forever rhythmically visible there. No light task; a right intense one: but a task which is *done*.

Perhaps one would say, *intensity*, with the much that depends on it, is the prevailing character of Dante's genius. Dante does not come before us as a large catholic mind; rather as a narrow, and even sectarian mind: it is partly the fruit of his age and position, but partly too of his own nature. His greatness has, in all senses, concentered itself into fiery emphasis and depth. He is world-great not because he is world-wide, but because he is world-deep. Through all objects he pierces as it were down into the heart of Being. I know nothing so intense as Dante. Consider, for example, to begin with the outermost development of his intensity, consider how he paints. He has a great power of vision; seizes the very type of a thing; presents that and nothing more. You remember that first view he gets of the Hall of Dite: *red* pinnacle, redhot cone of iron glowing through the dim immensity of gloom;–so vivid, so distinct, visible at once and forever! It is as an emblem of the whole genius of Dante. There is a brevity, an abrupt precision in him: Tacitus is not briefer, more condensed; and then in Dante it seems a natural condensation, spontaneous to the man. One smiting word; and then there is silence, nothing more said. His silence is more eloquent than words. It is strange with what a sharp decisive grace he snatches the true likeness of a matter: cuts into the matter as with a pen of fire. Plutus, the blustering giant, collapses at Virgil's rebuke; it is 'as the sails sink, the mast being suddenly broken'. Or that poor Brunetto Latini, with the *cotto aspetto*, 'face *baked*', parched brown and lean; and the 'fiery snow' that falls on them there, a 'fiery snow without wind', slow, deliberate, never-ending! Or the lids of those Tombs: square sarcophaguses, in that silent dim-burning Hall, each with its Soul in torment; the lids laid open there; they are to be shut at the Day of Judgment, through Eternity. And how Farinata rises; and how Cavalcante falls–at hearing of his Son, and the past tense '*fue*'*!* The very movements in Dante have something brief; swift, decisive, almost military. It is of the inmost essence of his genius this sort of painting. The fiery, swift Italian nature of the man, so silent, passionate, with its quick abrupt movements, its silent 'pale rages', speaks itself in these things.

For though this of painting is one of the outermost developments of a man, it comes like all else from the essential faculty of him; it is physiognomical of the whole man. Find a man whose words paint you a likeness, you have found a man worth something; mark his manner of doing it, as very characteristic of him. In the first place, he could not have discerned the object at all, or seen the vital type of it, unless he had, what we may call *sympathised* with it,–had sympathy in him to bestow on objects. He must have been *sincere* about it too; sincere and sympathetic: a man without worth cannot give you the likeness of any object; he dwells in vague outwardness, fallacy and trivial hearsay, about all objects. And indeed may we not say that intellect altogether expresses itself in this power of discerning what an object is? Whatsoever of faculty a man's mind may have will come out here. Is it even of business, a matter to be done? The gifted man is he who *sees* the essential point, and leaves all the rest aside as surplusage: it is his faculty too, the man of business's faculty, that he discern the true *likeness*, not the false superficial one, of the thing he has got to work in. And how much of *morality* is in the kind of insight we get of anything;

'the eye seeing in all things what it brought with it the faculty of seeing'! To the mean eye all things are trivial, as certainly as to the jaundiced they are yellow. Raphael, the Painters tell us, is the best of all Portrait-painters withal. No most gifted eye can exhaust the significance of any object. In the commonest human face there lies more than Raphael will take-away with him.

Dante's painting is not graphic only, brief, true, and of a vividness as of fire in dark night; taken on the wider scale, it is everyway noble, and the outcome of a great soul. Francesca and her Lover, what qualities in that! A thing woven as out of rainbows, on a ground of eternal black. A small flute-voice of infinite wail speaks there, into our very heart of hearts. A touch of womanhood in it too: *della bella persona, che mi fu tolta;* and how, even in the Pit of woe, it is a solace that *he* will never part from her! Saddest tragedy in these *alti guai.* And the racking winds, in that *aer bruno,* whirl them away again, to wail forever!—Strange to think: Dante was the friend of this poor Francesca's father; Francesca herself may have sat upon the Poet's knee, as a bright innocent little child. Infinite pity, yet also infinite rigour of law; it is so Nature is made; it is so Dante discerned that she was made. What a paltry notion is that of his *Divine Comedy's* being a poor splenetic impotent terrestrial libel; putting those into Hell whom he could not be avenged-upon on earth! I suppose if ever pity, tender as a mother's, was in the heart of any man, it was in Dante's. But a man who does not know rigour cannot pity either. His very pity will be cowardly, egoistic,—sentimentality, or little better. I know not in the world an affection equal to that of Dante. It is a tenderness, a trembling, longing, pitying love: like the wail of Æolean harps, soft, soft; like a child's young heart;—and then that stern, sore-saddened heart! These longings of his towards his Beatrice; their meeting together in the *Paradiso;* his gazing in her pure transfigured eyes, her that had been purified by death so long, separated from him so far:—one likens it to the song of angels; it is among the purest utterances of affection, perhaps the very purest, that ever came out of a human soul.

For the *intense* Dante is intense in all things; he has got into the essence of all. His intellectual insight as painter, on occasion too as reasoner, is but the result of all other sorts of intensity. Morally great, above all, we must call him; it is the beginning of all. His scorn, his grief are as transcendent as his love;—as indeed, what are they but the *inverse* or *converse* of his love? '*A Dio spiacenti ed a' nemici sui*, Hateful to God and to the enemies of God:' lofty scorn, unappeasable silent reprobation and aversion; '*Non ragionam di lor*, We will not speak of *them*, look only and pass.' Or think of this; 'They have not the *hope* to die, *Non han speranza di morte*.' One day, it had risen sternly benign on the scathed heart of Dante, that he, wretched, never-resting, worn as he was, would full surely *die;* 'that Destiny itself could not doom him not to die'. Such words are in this man. For rigour, earnestness and depth, he is not to be paralleled in the modern world; to seek his parallel we must go into the Hebrew Bible, and live with the antique Prophets there.

I do not agree with much modern criticism, in greatly preferring the *Inferno* to the two other parts of the Divine *Commedia*. Such preference belongs, I imagine, to our general Byronism of taste, and is like to be a transient feeling. The *Purgatorio* and *Paradiso*, especially the former, one would almost say, is even more excellent than it. It is a noble thing that *Purgatorio*, 'Mountain of Purification'; an emblem of the noblest conception of that age. If Sin is so fatal, and Hell is and must be so rigorous, awful, yet in Repentance too is man purified; Repentance is the grand Christian act. It is beautiful how Dante works it out. The *tremolar dell' onde*, that 'trembling' of the ocean-waves, under the first pure gleam of morning, dawning afar on the wandering Two, is as the type of an altered mood. Hope has now dawned; never-dying Hope, if in company still with heavy sorrow. The obscure sojourn of dæmons and reprobate is underfoot; a soft breathing of penitence mounts higher and higher, to the Throne of Mercy itself. "Pray for me," the denizens of that Mount of Pain all say to him. "Tell my Giovanna to pray for me," my daughter Giovanna; "I think her mother loves me no more!" They toil painfully up by that winding steep, 'bent-down like corbels of a building', some of them,—crushed-together so 'for the sin of pride'; yet nevertheless in years, in ages and æons, they shall have reached the top, which is Heaven's gate, and by Mercy shall have been admitted in. The joy too of all, when one has prevailed; the whole Mountain shakes with joy, and a psalm of praise rises, when one soul has perfected repentance and got its sin and misery left behind! I call all this a noble embodiment of a true noble thought.

But indeed the Three compartments mutually support one

another, are indispensable to one another. The *Paradiso*, a kind of inarticulate music to me, is the redeeming side of the *Inferno;* the *Inferno* without it were untrue. All three make-up the true Unseen World, as figured in the Christianity of the Middle Ages; a thing forever memorable, forever true in the essence of it, to all men. It was perhaps delineated in no human soul with such depth of veracity as in this of Dante's; a man *sent* to sing it, to keep it long memorable. Very notable with what brief simplicity he passes out of the every-day reality, into the Invisible one; and in the second or third stanza, we find ourselves in the World of Spirits; and dwell there, as among things palpable, indubitable! To Dante they *were* so; the real world, as it is called, and its facts, was but the threshold to an infinitely higher Fact of a World. At bottom, the one was as *preter*natural as the other. Has not each man a soul? He will not only be a spirit, but is one. To the earnest Dante it is all one visible Fact; he believes it, sees it; is the Poet of it in virtue of that. Sincerity, I say again, is the saving merit, now as always.

Dante's Hell, Purgatory, Paradise, are a symbol withal, an emblematic representation of his Belief about this Universe:—some Critic in a future age, like those Scandinavian ones the other day, who has ceased altogether to think as Dante did, may find this too all an 'Allegory', perhaps an idle Allegory! It is a sublime embodiment, or sublimest, of the soul of Christianity. It expresses, as in huge worldwide architectural emblems, how the Christian Dante felt Good and Evil to be the two polar elements of this Creation, on which it all turns; that these two differ not by *preferability* of one to the other, but by incompatibility absolute and infinite; that the one is excellent and high as light and Heaven, the other hideous, black as Gehenna and the Pit of Hell! Everlasting Justice, yet with Penitence, with everlasting Pity,—all Christianism, as Dante and the Middle Ages had it, is emblemed here. Emblemed: and yet . . . with what entire truth of purpose; how unconscious of any embleming! Hell, Purgatory, Paradise: these things were not fashioned as emblems; was there, in our Modern European Mind, any thought at all of their being emblems; Were they not indubitable awful facts; the whole of man taking them for practically true, all Nature everywhere confirming them? So is it always in these things. Men do not believe an Allegory. The future Critic, whatever his new thought may be, who considers this of Dante to have been all got-up as an Allegory, will commit one sore mistake!—Paganism we recognised as a veracious expression of the earnest awe-struck feeling of man towards the Universe; veracious, true once, and still not without worth for us. But mark here the difference of Paganism and Christianism; one great difference. Paganism emblemed chiefly the Operations of Nature; the destinies, efforts, combinations, vicissitudes of things and men in this world; Christianism emblemed the Law of Human Duty, the Moral Law of Man. One was for the sensuous nature: a rude helpless utterance of the *first* Thought of men,—the chief recognised virtue, Courage, Superiority to Fear. The other was not for the sensuous nature, but for the moral. What a progress is here, if in that one respect only!

And so in this Dante, as we said, had ten silent centuries, in a very strange way, found a voice. The *Divina Commedia* is of Dante's writing; yet in truth *it* belongs to ten Christian centuries, only the finishing of it is Dante's. So always. The craftsman there, the smith with that metal of his, with these tools, with these cunning methods,—how little of all he does is properly *his* work! All past inventive men work there with him;—as indeed with all of us, in all things. Dante is the spokesman of the Middle Ages; the Thought they lived by stands here, in everlasting music. These sublime ideas of his, terrible and beautiful, are the fruit of the Christian Meditation of all the good men who had gone before him. Precious they; but also is not he precious? Much, had not he spoken, would have been dumb; not dead, yet living voiceless.

On the whole, is it not an utterance, this mystic Song, at once of one of the greatest human souls, and of the highest thing that Europe had hitherto realised for itself? Christianism, as Dante sings it, is another than Paganism in the rude Norse mind; another than "Bastard Christianism' half-articulately spoken in the Arab Desert seven-hundred years before!— The noblest *idea* made *real* hitherto among men, is sung, and emblemed-forth abidingly, by one of the noblest men. In the one sense and in the other, are we not right glad to possess it? As I calculate, it may last yet for long thousands of years. For the thing that is uttered from the inmost parts of a man's soul, differs altogether from what is uttered by the outer part. The outer is of the day, under the empire of mode; the outer passes away, in swift endless changes; the inmost is the same yesterday, today and forever. True souls, in all generations of the world, who look on this Dante, will find a brotherhood in him; the deep sincerity of his thoughts, his woes and hopes, will speak likewise to their sincerity; they will feel that this Dante too was a brother. Napoleon in Saint-Helena is charmed with the genial veracity of old Homer. The oldest Hebrew Prophet, under a vesture the most diverse from ours, does yet, because he speaks from the heart of man, speak to all men's hearts. It is the one sole secret of continuing long memorable. Dante, for depth of sincerity, is like an antique Prophet too; his words, like theirs, come from his very heart. One need not wonder if it were predicted that his Poem might be the most enduring thing our Europe has yet made; for nothing so endures as a truly spoken word. All cathedrals, pontificalities, brass and stone, and outer arrangement never so lasting, are brief in comparison to an unfathomable heart-song like this: one feels as if it might survive, still of importance to men, when these had all sunk into now irrecognisable combinations, and had ceased individually to be. Europe has made much; great cities, great empires, encyclopædias, creeds, bodies of opinion and practice: but it has made little of the class of Dante's Thought. Homer yet *is*, veritably present face to face with every open soul of us; and Greece, where is *it?* Desolate for thousands of years; away, vanished; a bewildered heap of stones and rubbish, the life and existence of it all gone. Like a dream; like the dust of King Agamemnon! Greece was; Greece, except in the *words* it spoke, is not.

The uses of this Dante? We will not say much about his 'uses'. A human soul who has once got into that primal element of *Song*, and sung-forth fitly somewhat therefrom, has worked in the *depths* of our existence; feeding through long times the life-*roots* of all excellent human things whatsoever,—in a way that 'utilities' will not succeed well in calculating! We will not estimate the Sun by the quantity of gas-light it saves us; Dante shall be invaluable, or of no value. One remark I may make: the contrast in this respect between the Hero-Poet and the Hero-Prophet. In a hundred years, Mahomet, as we saw, had his Arabians at Grenada and at Delphi; Dante's Italians seem to be yet very much where they were. Shall we say, then, Dante's effect on the world was small in comparison? Not so: his arena is far more restricted; but also it is far nobler, clearer;—perhaps not less but more important. Mahomet speaks to great masses of men, in the coarse dialect adapted to such; a dialect filled with inconsistencies, crudities, follies: on the great masses alone can he act, and there with good and with evil strangely blended. Dante speaks to the noble, the pure and great, in all times and places. Neither does he grow obsolete, as the other does. Dante burns as a pure star, fixed there in the firmament, at which the great and the high of all ages kindle themselves: he is the possession of all the chosen of the world for uncounted time....

As Dante, the Italian man, was sent into our world to embody musically the Religion of the Middle Ages, the Religion of our Modern Europe, its Inner Life; so Shakspeare, we may say, embodies for us the Outer Life of our Europe as developed then, its chivalries, courtesies, humours, ambitions, what practical way of thinking, acting, looking at the world, men then had. As in Homer we may still construe Old Greece; so in Shakspeare and Dante, after thousands of years, what our modern Europe was, in Faith and in Practice, will still be legible. Dante has given us the Faith or soul; Shakspeare, in a not less noble way, has given us the Practice or body. This latter also we were to have; a man was sent for it, the man Shakspeare. Just when that chivalry way of life had reached its last finish, and was on the point of breaking down into slow or swift dissolution, as we now see it everywhere, this other sovereign Poet, with his seeing eye, with his perennial singing voice, was sent to take note of it, to give long-enduring record of it. Two fit men: Dante, deep, fierce as the central fire of the world; Shakspeare, wide, placid, far-seeing, as the Sun, the upper light of the world. Italy produced the one world-voice; we English had the honour of producing the other. . . .

Yes, truly, it is a great thing for a Nation that it get an articulate voice; that it produce a man who will speak-forth melodiously what the heart of it means! Italy, for example, poor Italy lies dismembered, scattered asunder, not appearing in any protocol or treaty as a unity at all; yet the noble Italy is actually *one:* Italy produced its Dante; Italy can speak! The Czar of all the Russias, he is strong, with so many bayonets, Cossacks and cannons; and does a great feat in keeping such a tract of Earth politically together; but he cannot yet speak. Something great in him, but it is a dumb greatness. He has had no voice of genius, to be heard of all men and times. He must learn to speak. He is a great dumb monster hitherto. His cannons and Cossacks will all have rusted into nonentity, while that Dante's voice is still audible. The Nation that has a Dante is bound together as no dumb Russia can be.—We must here end what we had to say of the *Hero-Poet*.

XII

LEIGH HUNT

Critical Notice of Dante's Life and Genius

Dante was a very great poet, a man of the strongest passions, a claimant of unbounded powers to lead and enlighten the world; and he lived in a semi-barbarous age, as favourable to the intensity of his imagination, as it was otherwise to the rest of his pretensions. Party zeal, and the fluctuations of moral and critical opinion, have at different periods over-rated and depreciated his memory; and if, in the following attempt to form its just estimate, I have found myself compelled, in some important respects, to differ with preceding writers, and to protest in particular against his being regarded as a proper teacher on any one point, poetry excepted, and as far as all such genius and energy cannot in some degree help being, I have not been the less sensible of the wonderful nature of that genius, while acting within the circle to which it belongs. Dante was indeed so great a poet, and at the same time exhibited in his personal character such a mortifying exception to what we conceive to be the natural wisdom and temper of great poets; in other words, he was such a bigoted and exasperated man, and sullied his imagination with so much that is contradictory to good feeling, in matters divine as well as human; that I should not have thought myself justified in assisting, however humbly, to extend the influence of his writings, had I not believed a time to have arrived, when the community may profit both from the marvels of his power and the melancholy absurdity of its contradictions.

Dante Alighieri, who has always been known by his Christian rather than surname (partly owing to the Italian predilection for Christian names, and partly to the unsettled state of patronymics in his time), was the son of a lawyer of good family in

Reprinted from *Stories from the Italian Poets: With the Lives of the Writers* (London: Chapman & Hall, 1846), 1: 3–77.

Florence, and was born in that city on the 14th of May 1265, sixty-three years after the birth of such men as Folco and St. Dominic. The tragical as well as "fantastic tricks" which

> Man, proud man,
> Drest in a little brief authority,

plays with his energy and bad passions under the guise of duty, is among the most perplexing of those spectacles, which, according to a greater understanding than Dante's, "make the angels weep." (Dante, by the way, has introduced in his heaven no such angels as those; though he has plenty that scorn and denounce.) Lope de Vega, though a poet, was an officer of the Inquisition, and joined the famous Armada that was coming to thumbscrew and roast us into his views of Christian meekness. Whether the author of the story of *Paulo and Francesca* could have carried the Dominican theories into practice, had he been the banisher instead of the banished, is a point that may happily be doubted; but at all events he revenged himself on his enemies after their own fashion; for he answered their decree of the stake by putting them into hell.

Dante entitled the saddest poem in the world a Comedy, because it was written in a middle style; though some, by a strange confusion of ideas, think the reason must have been because it "ended happily!" that is, because, beginning with hell (to some), it terminated with "heaven" (to others). As well might they have said, that a morning's work in the Inquisition ended happily, because, while people were being racked in the dungeons, the officers were making merry in the drawing-room. For the much-injured epithet of "Divine," Dante's memory is not responsible. He entitled his poem, arrogantly enough, yet still not with that impiety of arrogance, "The Comedy of Dante Alighieri, a Florentine by nation but not by habits." The word "divine" was added by some transcriber; and it heaped absurdity on absurdity, too much of it, alas! being literally infernal tragedy. I am not speaking in mockery, any further than the fact itself cannot help so speaking. I respect what is to be respected in Dante; I admire in him what is admirable; would love (if his infernalities would let me) what is loveable; but this must not hinder one of the human race from protesting against what is erroneous in his fame, when it jars against every best feeling, human and divine. Mr. Cary thinks that Dante had as much right to avail himself of "the popular creed in all its extravagance" as Homer had of his gods, or Shakspeare of his fairies. But the distinction is obvious. Homer did not personally identify himself with a creed, or do his utmost to perpetuate the worst parts of it in behalf of a ferocious inquisitorial church, and to the risk of endangering the peace of millions of gentle minds.

The great poem thus misnomered is partly a system of theology, partly an abstract of the knowledge of the day, but chiefly a series of passionate and imaginative pictures, altogether forming an account of the author's times, his friends, his enemies, and himself, written to vent the spleen of his exile, and the rest of his feelings, good and bad, and to reform church and state by a spirit of resentment and obloquy, which highly needed reform itself. It has also a design strictly self-referential. The author feigns, that the beatified spirit of his mistress has obtained leave to warn and purify his soul by shewing him the state of things in the next world. She deputes the soul of his master Virgil to conduct him through hell and purgatory, and then takes him herself through the spheres of heaven, where Saint Peter catechises and confirms him, and where he is finally honoured with sights of the Virgin Mary, of Christ, and even a glimpse of the Supreme Being!

His hell, considered as a place, is, to speak geologically, a most fantastical formation. It descends from beneath Jerusalem to the centre of the earth, and is a funnel graduated in circles, each circle being a separate place of torment for a different vice or its co-ordinates, and the point of the funnel terminating with Satan stuck into ice. Purgatory is a corresponding mountain on the other side of the globe, commencing with the antipodes of Jerusalem, and divided into exterior circles of expiation, which end in a table-land forming the terrestrial paradise. From this the hero and his mistress ascend by a flight, exquisitely conceived, to the stars; where the sun and the planets of the Ptolemaic system (for the true one was unknown in Dante's time) form a series of heavens for different virtues, the whole terminating in the empyrean, or region of pure light, and the presence of the Beatific Vision.

The boundaries of old and new, strange as it may now seem to us, were so confused in those days, and books were so rare, and the Latin poets held in such invincible reverence, that Dante, in one and the same poem, speaks of the false gods of Paganism, and yet retains much of its lower mythology; nay, invokes Apollo himself at the door of paradise. There was, perhaps, some mystical and even philosophical inclusion of the past in this medley, as recognising the constant superintendence of Providence; but that Dante partook of what may be called the literary superstition of the time, even for want of better knowledge, is clear from the grave historical use he makes of poetic fables in his treatise on Monarchy, and in the very arguments which he puts into the mouths of saints and apostles. There are lingering feelings to this effect even now among the peasantry of Italy; where, the reader need not be told, Pagan customs of all sorts, including religious and most reverend ones, are existing under the sanction of other names;—the heathenisms christened. A Tuscan postilion, once enumerating to me some of the native poets, concluded his list with Apollo; and a plaster-cast man over here, in London, appeared much puzzled, when conversing on the subject with a friend of mine, how to discrepate Samson from Hercules.

Dante accordingly, while, with the frightful bigotry of the schools, he puts the whole Pagan world into hell-borders (with the exception of two or three, whose salvation adds to the absurdity), mingles the hell of Virgil with that of Tertullian and St. Dominic; sets Minos at the door as judge; retains Charon in his old office of boatman over the Stygian lake; puts fabulous people with real among the damned, Dido, and Cacus, and Ephialtes, with Ezzelino and Pope Nicholas the Fifth; and associates the Centaurs and the Furies with the agents of diabolical torture. It has pleased him also to elevate Cato of Utica to the office of warder of purgatory, though the censor's poor good wife, Marcia, is detained in the regions below. By these and other far greater inconsistencies, the whole place of punishment becomes a *reductio ad absurdum*, as ridiculous as it is melancholy; so that one is astonished how so great a man, and especially a man who thought himself so far advanced beyond his age, and who possessed such powers of discerning the good and beautiful, could endure to let his mind live in so foul and foolish a region for any length of time, and there wreak and harden the unworthiest of his passions. Genius, nevertheless, is so commensurate with absurdity throughout the book, and there are even such sweet and balmy as well as sublime pictures in it occasionally, nay often, that not only will the poem ever be worthy of admiration, but when those increasing purifications of Christianity which our blessed reformers began, shall finally precipitate the whole dregs of the author into the mythology to which they belong, the world will derive a pleasure from it to an amount not to be conceived till the arrival of that day. Dante, meantime, with an impartiality which has been admired by those who can approve the assumption of a theological tyranny at the expense of common feeling and decency, has put friends as well as foes into hell: tutors of his childhood, kinsmen of those who treated him hospitably, even the father of his beloved friend, Guido Cavalcante—the last for not believing in a God: therein doing the worst thing possible in behalf of the belief, and totally differing both with the pious heathen Plutarch, and the great Christian philosopher Bacon, who were of opinion that a contumelious belief is worse than none, and that it is far better and more pious to believe in "no God at all," than in a God who would "eat his children as soon as they were born." And Dante makes him do worse; for the whole unbaptised infant world, Christian as well as Pagan, is in his Tartarus.

Milton has spoken of the "milder shades of Purgatory"; and truly they possess great beauties. Even in a theological point of view they are something like a bit of Christian refreshment after the horrors of the *Inferno.* The first emerging from the hideous gulf to the sight of the blue serenity of heaven, is painted in a manner inexpressibly charming. So is the sea-shore with the coming of the angel; the valley, with the angels in green; the repose at night on the rocks; and twenty other pictures of gentleness and love. And yet, special and great has been the escape of the Protestant world from this part of Roman Catholic belief; for Purgatory is the heaviest stone that hangs about the neck of the old and feeble in that communion. Hell is avoidable by repentance; but Purgatory, what modest conscience shall escape? Mr. Cary, in a note on a passage in which Dante recommends his readers to think on what follows this expiatory state, rather than what is suffered there, looks upon the poet's injunction as an "unanswerable objection to the doctrine of purgatory," it being difficult to conceive "how the best can meet death without horror, if they believe it must be followed by immediate and intense suffering." Luckily, assent is not belief; and mankind's feelings are for the most part superior to their opinions; otherwise the world would have been in a bad way indeed, and nature not been vindicated of her children. But let us watch and be on our guard against all resuscitations of superstition.

As to our Florentine's Heaven, it is full of beauties also, though sometimes of a more questionable and pantomimical sort than is to be found in either of the other books. I shall speak of some of them presently; but the general impression of the place is, that it is no heaven at all. He says it is, and talks much of its smiles and its beatitude; but always excepting the poetry—especially the similes brought from the more heavenly earth—we realise little but a fantastical assemblage of doctors and doubtful characters, far more angry and theological than celestial; giddy raptures of monks and inquisitors dancing in circles, and saints denouncing popes and Florentines; in short, a heaven libelling itself with invectives against earth, and terminating in a great presumption. Many of the people put there, a Calvinistic Dante would have consigned to the "other place"; and some, if now living, would not be admitted into decent society. At the beginning of one of the cantos, the poet congratulates himself, with a complacent superiority, on his being in heaven and occupied with celestial matters, while his poor fellow-creatures are wandering and blundering on earth. But he had never got there! A divine—worthy of that name—of the Church of England (Dr. Whichcote), has beautifully said, that "heaven is first in temper, and then a place." According to this truly celestial topography, the implacable Florentine had not reached its outermost court. Again, his heavenly mistress, Beatrice, besides being far too didactic to sustain the womanly part of her character properly, alternates her smiles and her sarcasms in a way that jars horribly against the occasional enchantment of her aspect. She does not scruple to burst into taunts of the Florentines in the presence of Jesus himself; and the spirit of his ancestor, Cacciaguida, in the very bosom of Christian bliss, promises him revenge on his enemies! Is this the kind of zeal that is to be exempt from objection in a man who objected to all the world? or will it be thought a profaneness against such profanity, to remind the reader of the philosopher in Swift, who "while gazing on the stars, was betrayed by his lower parts into a ditch!"

The reader's time need not be wasted with the allegorical and other mystical significations given to the poem; still less on the question whether Beatrice is theology, or a young lady, or both; and least of all on the discovery of the ingenious Signor Rossetti,[1] that Dante and all the other great old Italian writers meant nothing, either by their mistresses or their mythology, but attacks on the court of Rome. Suffice it, that besides all other possible meanings, Dante himself had told us that his poem has its obvious and literal meaning; that he means a spade by a spade, purgatory by purgatory, and truly and unaffectedly to devote his friends to the infernal regions whenever he does so. I confess I think it is a great pity that Guido Cavalcante did not live to read the poem, especially the passage about his father. The understanding of Guido, who had not the admiration for Virgil that Dante had (very likely for reasons that have been thought sound in modern times), was in all probability as good as that of his friend in many respects, and perhaps more so in one or two; and modern criticism might have been saved some of its pains of objection by the poet's contemporary.

The author did not live to publish, in any formal manner, his extraordinary poem, probably did not intend to do so, except under those circumstances of political triumph which he was always looking for; but as he shewed portions of it to his friends, it was no doubt talked of to a certain extent, and must have exasperated such of his enemies as considered him worth their hostility. No wonder they did all they could to keep him out of Florence. What would they have said of him, could they have written a counter poem? What would even his friends have said of him? for we see in what manner he has treated even those; and yet how could he possibly know, with respect either to friends or enemies, what passed between them and their consciences? or who was it that gave him his right to generate the boasted distinction between an author's feelings as a man and his assumed office as a theologian, and parade the latter at the former's expense? His own spleen, hatred, and avowed sentiments of vengeance, are manifest throughout the poem; and there is this, indeed, to be said for the moral and religious inconsistencies both of the man and his verse, that in those violent

[1] [Gabriele Rossetti (the father of Dante Gabriel) came to London as a political exile in 1824, and from 1831 taught Italian at King's College. Between 1826 and 1842 he wrote a series of works (in Italian but published in London) to prove that all Dante's poetry was a political anti-ecclesiastical allegory.]

times the spirit of Christian charity, and even the sentiment of personal shame, were so little understood, that the author in one part of it is made to blush by a friend for not having avenged him; and it is said to have been thought a compliment to put a lady herself into hell, that she might be talked of, provided it was for something not odious. An admirer of this infernal kind of celebrity, even in later times, declared that he would have given a sum of money (I forget to what amount) if Dante had but done as much for one of his ancestors. It has been argued, that in all the parties concerned in these curious ethics there is a generous love of distinction, and a strong craving after life, action, and sympathy of some kind or other. Granted; there are all sorts of half-good, half-barbarous feelings in Dante's poem. Let justice be done to the good half; but do not let us take the ferocity for wisdom and piety; or pretend, in the complacency of our own freedom from superstition, to see no danger of harm to the less fortunate among our fellow-creatures in the support it receives from a man of genius. Bedlams have been filled with such horrors; thousands, nay millions of feeble minds are suffering by them or from them, at this minute, all over the world. Dante's best critic, Foscolo, has said much of the heroical nature of the age in which the poet lived; but he adds, that its mixture of knowledge and absurdity is almost inexplicable. The truth is, that like everything else which appears harsh and unaccountable in nature, it was an excess of the materials for good, working in an over-active and inexperienced manner; but knowing this, we are bound, for the sake of the good, not to retard its improvement by ignoring existing impieties, or blind ourselves to the perpetuating tendencies of the bigotries of great men. Oh! had the first indoctrinators of Christian feeling, while enlisting the "divine Plato" into the service of diviner charity, only kept the latter just enough in mind to discern the beautiful difference between the philosopher's unmalignant and improvable evil, and their own malignant and eternal one, what a world of folly and misery they might have saved us! But as the evil has happened, let us hope that even this form of it has had its uses. If Dante thought it salutary to the world to maintain a system of religious terror, the same charity which can hope that it may once have been so, has taught us how to commence a better. But did he, after all, or did he not, think it salutary? Did he think so, believing the creed himself? or did he think it from an unwilling sense of its necessity? Or, lastly, did he write only as a mythologist, and care for nothing but the exercise of his spleen and genius? If he had no other object than that, his conscientiousness would be reduced to a low pitch indeed. . . . Thank heaven, his "Hell" has not embittered the mild reading-desks of the Church of England. If King George the Third himself, with all his arbitrary notions, and willing religious acquiescence, could not endure the creed of St. Athanasius with its damnatory enjoinments of the impossible, what would have been said to the inscription over Dante's hell-gate, or the account of Ugolino eating an archbishop, in the gentle chapels of Queen Victoria? May those chapels have every beauty in them, and every air of heaven, that painting and music can bestow—divine gifts, not unworthy to be set before their Divine Bestower; but far from them be kept the foul fiends of inhumanity and superstition!

It is certainly impossible to get at a thorough knowledge of the opinions of Dante even in theology; and his morals, if judged according to the received standard, are not seldom puzzling. He rarely thinks as the popes do; sometimes not as the Church does: he is lax, for instance, on the subject of absolution by the priest at death. All you can be sure of is, the predominance of his will, the most wonderful poetry, and the notions he entertained of the degrees of vice and virtue. Towards the errors of love he is inclined to be so lenient (some think because he had indulged in them himself), that it is pretty clear he would not have put Paulo and Francesca into hell, if their story had not been too recent, and their death too sudden, to allow him to assume their repentance in the teeth of the evidence required. He avails himself of orthodox license to put "the harlot Rahab" into heaven ("cette bonne fille de Jéricho," as Ginguené calls her); nay, he puts her into the planet Venus, as if to compliment her on her profession; and one of her companions there is a fair Ghibelline, sister of the tyrant Ezzelino, a lady famous for her gallantries, of whom the poet good-naturedly says, that she "was overcome by her star"—to wit, the said planet Venus; and yet he makes her the organ of the most unfeminine triumphs over the Guelphs. But both these ladies, it is to be understood, repented—for they had time for repentance; their good fortune saved them. Poor murdered Francesca had no time to repent;

therefore her mischance was her damnation! Such are the compliments theology pays to the Creator. . . .

If Dante had erred only on the side of indulgence, humanity could easily have forgiven him—for the excesses of charity are the extensions of hope; but, unfortunately, where he is sweet-natured once, he is bitter a hundred times. This is the impression he makes on universalists of all creeds and parties; that is to say, on men who having run the whole round of sympathy with their fellow-creatures, become the only final judges of sovereign pretension. It is very well for individuals to make a god of Dante for some encouragement of their own position or pretension; but a god for the world at large he never was, or can be; and I doubt if an impression to this effect was not always, from the very dawn of our literature, the one entertained of him by the genius of our native country, which could never long endure any kind of unwarrantable diction. . . .

Ugo Foscolo, an excellent critic where his own temper and violence did not interfere, sees nothing but jealousy in Petrarch's dislike of Dante, and nothing but Jesuitism in similar feelings entertained by such men as Tiraboschi. But all gentle and considerate hearts must dislike the rage and bigotry in Dante, even were it true (as the Dantesque Foscolo thinks) that Italy will never be regenerated till one-half of it is baptised in the blood of the other![2] Such men, with all their acuteness, are incapable of seeing what can be effected by nobler and serener times, and the progress of civilisation. They fancy, no doubt, that they are vindicating the energies of Nature herself, and the inevitable necessity of "doing evil that good may come." But Dante in so doing violated the Scripture he professed to revere; and men must not assume to themselves that final knowledge of results, which is the only warrant of the privilege, and the possession of which is to be arrogated by no earthly wisdom. One calm discovery of science may do away with all the boasted eternal necessities of the angry and the self-idolatrous. The passions that may be necessary to savages are not bound to remain so to civilised men, any more than the eating of man's flesh or the worship of Jugghernaut. When we think of the wonderful

[2] *Discorso sul Testo*, p. 226. The whole passage (sect. cx.) is very eloquent, horrible, and *self-betraying*.

things lately done by science for the intercourse of the world, and the beautiful and tranquil books of philosophy written by men of equal energy and benevolence, and opening the peacefulest hopes for mankind, and views of creation to which Dante's universe was a nutshell,—such a vision as that of his poem (in a theological point of view) seems no better than the dream of an hypochondriacal savage, and his nutshell a rottenness to be spit out of the mouth. . . .

It might have been thought of Dante, if he had not taken a part in the cruelty, that he detailed the horrors of his hell out of a wish to disgust the world with its frightful notions of God. This is certainly the effect of the worst part of his descriptions in an age like the present. Black burning gulfs, full of outcries and blasphemy, feet red-hot with fire, men eternally eating their fellow-creatures, frozen wretches malignantly dashing their iced heads against one another, other adversaries mutually exchanging shapes by force of an attraction at once irresistible and loathing, and spitting with hate and disgust when it is done—Enough, enough, for God's sake! Take the disgust out of one's senses, O flower of true Christian wisdom and charity, now beginning to fill the air with fragrance!

Many, indeed, of the absurdities of Dante's poem are too obvious now-a-days to need remark. Even the composition of the poem, egotistically said to be faultless by such critics as Alfieri, who thought they resembled him, partakes, as every body's style does, of the faults as well as good qualities of the man. It is nervous, concise, full almost as it can hold, picturesque, mighty, primeval; but it is often obscure, often harsh, and forced in its constructions, defective in melody, and wilful and superfluous in the rhyme. Sometimes, also, the writer is inconsistent in circumstance (probably from not having corrected the poem); and he is not above being filthy. Even in the episode of Paulo and Francesca, which has so often been pronounced faultless, and which is unquestionably one of the most beautiful pieces of writing in the world, some of these faults are observable, particularly in the obscurity of the passage about *tolta forma*, the cessation of the incessant tempest, and the non-adjuration of the two lovers in the manner that Virgil prescribes.

But truly it is said, that when Dante is great, nobody surpasses him. I doubt if anybody equals him, as to the constant intensity and incessant variety of his pictures; and whatever he paints, he throws, as it were, upon its own powers; as though an artist should draw figures that started into life, and proceeded to action for themselves, frightening their creator. Every motion, word, and look of these creatures becomes full of sensibility and suggestions. The invisible is at the back of the visible; darkness becomes palpable; silence describes a character, nay, forms the most striking part of a story; a word acts as a flash of lightning, which displays some gloomy neighbourhood, where a tower is standing, with dreadful faces at the window; or where, at your feet, full of eternal voices, one abyss is beheld dropping out of another in the lurid light of torment. In the present volume a story will be found which tells a long tragedy in half-a-dozen lines. Dante has the minute probabilities of a Defoe in the midst of the loftiest and most generalising poetry; and this feeling of matter-of-fact is impressed by fictions the most improbable, nay, the most ridiculous and revolting. You laugh at the absurdity; you are shocked at the detestable cruelty; yet, for the moment, the thing almost seems as if it must be true. You feel as you do in a dream, and after it;–you wake and laugh, but the absurdity seemed true at the time; and while you laugh you shudder.

Enough of this crueller part of his genius has been exhibited; but it is seldom you can have the genius without sadness. In the circle of hell, soothsayers walk along weeping, with their faces turned the wrong way, so that their tears fall between their shoulders. The picture is still more dreadful. Warton thinks it ridiculous. But I cannot help feeling with the poet, that it is dreadfully pathetic. It is the last mortifying insult to human pretension. Warton, who has a grudge against Dante natural to a man of happier piety, thinks him ridiculous also in describing the monster Geryon lying upon the edge of one of the gulfs of hell "like a beaver" (canto xvii.). He is of opinion that the writer only does it to shew his knowledge of natural history. But surely the idea of so strange and awful a creature (a huge mild-faced man ending in a dragon's body) lying familiarly on the edge of the gulf, as a beaver does by the water, combines the supernatural with the familiar in a very impressive manner. It is this combination of extremes which is the life and soul of the whole poem; you have this world in the next; the same persons, passions, remembrances, intensified by superhuman despairs or beatitudes; the speechless entrancements of bliss, the purgatorial trials of hope and patience; the supports of hate and anger (such as they are) in hell itself; nay, of loving despairs, and a self-pity made unboundedly pathetic by endless suffering. Hence there is no love-story so affecting as that of Paulo and Francesca thus told and perpetuated in another world; no father's misery so enforced upon us as Ugolino's, who, for hundreds of years, has not grown tired of the revenge to which it wrought him. Dante even puts his weight and continuity of feeling into passages of mere transient emotion or illustration, unconnected with the next world; as in the famous instance of the verses about evening. . . . His Heaven, it is true, though containing both sublime and lovely passages, is not so good as his Earth. The more unearthly he tried to make it, the less heavenly it became. When he is content with earth in heaven itself,—when he literalises a metaphor, and with exquisite felicity finds himself *arrived there* in consequence of fixing his eyes on the eyes of Beatrice, then he is most celestial. But his endeavors to express degrees of beatitude and holiness by varieties of flame and light,—of dancing lights, revolving lights, lights of smiles, of stars, of starry crosses, of didactic letters and sentences, of animal figures made up of stars full of blessed souls, with saints *forming an eagle's beak* and David in its *eye!*—such superhuman attempts become for the most part tricks of theatrical machinery, on which we gaze with little curiosity and no respect.

His angels, however, are another matter. Belief was prepared for those winged human forms, and they furnished him with some of his most beautiful combinations of the natural with the supernatural. Ginguené has remarked the singular variety as well as beauty of Dante's angels. Milton's, indeed, are commonplace in the comparison. In the eighth canto of the *Inferno*, the devils insolently refuse the poet and his guide an entrance into the city of Dis:—an angel comes sweeping over the Stygian lake to enforce it; the noise of his wings makes the shores tremble, and is like a crashing whirlwind such as beats down the trees and sends the peasants and their herds flying before it. The heavenly messenger, after rebuking the devils, touches the portals of the city with his wand; they fly open; and he returns the way he came without uttering a word to the two companions. His face was that of one occupied with other thoughts. This angel is announced by a tempest. Another, who brings the souls of the departed to Purgatory, is first discovered at a distance, gradually disclosing white splendours, which are his wings and garments. He comes in a boat, of which his wings are the sails; and as he approaches, it is impossible to look him in the face for its brightness. Two other angels have green wings and green garments, and the drapery is kept in motion like a flag by the vehement action of the wings. A fifth has a face like the morning star, casting forth quivering beams. A sixth is of a lustre so oppressive, that the poet feels a weight on his eyes before he knows what is coming. Another's presence affects the senses like the fragrance of a May-morning; and another is in garments dark as cinders, but has a sword in his hand too sparkling to be gazed at. Dante's occasional pictures of the beauties of external nature are worthy of these angelic creations, and to the last degree fresh and lovely. You long to bathe your eyes, smarting with the fumes of hell, in his dews. You gaze enchanted on his green fields and his celestial blue skies, the more so from the pain and sorrow in midst of which the visions are created.

Dante's grandeur of every kind is proportionate to that of his angels, almost to his ferocity; and that is saying every thing. It is not always the spiritual grandeur of Milton, the subjection of the material impression to the moral; but it is equally such when he chooses, and far more abundant. His infernal precipices —his black whirlwinds—his innumerable cries and claspings of hands—his very odours of huge loathsomeness—his giants at twilight standing up to the middle in pits, like towers, and causing earthquakes when they move—his earthquake of the mountain in Purgatory, when a spirit is set free for heaven—his dignified Mantuan Sordello, silently regarding him and his guide as they go by, "like a lion on his watch"—his blasphemer, Capaneus, lying in unconquered rage and sullenness under an eternal rain of flakes of fire (human precursor of Milton's Satan) —his aspect of Paradise, "as if the universe had smiled"—his inhabitants of the whole planet Saturn crying out *so loud*, in accordance with the anti-papal indignation of Saint Pietro Damiano, that the poet, though among them, *could not hear what they said*—and the blushing eclipse, like red clouds at sunset, which takes place at the apostle Peter's denunciation of the sanguinary filth of the court of Rome—all these sublimities, and many more, make us not know whether to be more astonished at the greatness of the poet or the raging littleness of the man. Grievous is it to be forced to bring two such opposites together; and I wish, for the honour and glory of poetry, I did not feel compelled to do so. But the swarthy Florentine had not the healthy temperament of his brethren, and he fell upon evil times. Compared with Homer and Shakspeare, his very intensity seems only superior to theirs from an excess of the morbid; and he is inferior to both in other sovereign qualities of poetry—to the one, in giving you the healthiest general impression of nature itself—to Shakspeare, in boundless universality—to most great poets, in thorough harmony and delightfulness. He wanted (generally speaking) the music of a happy and a happy-making disposition. Homer, from his large vital bosom, breathes like a broad fresh air over the world, amidst alternate storm and sunshine, making you aware that there is rough work to be faced, but also activity and beauty to be enjoyed. The feeling of health and strength is predominant. Life laughs at death itself, or meets it with a noble confidence—is not taught to dread it as a malignant goblin. Shakspeare has all the smiles as well as tears of nature, and discerns the "soul of goodness in things evil." He is comedy as well as tragedy—the entire man in all his qualities, moods, and experiences; and he beautifies all. And both those truly divine poets make nature their subject through her own inspiriting medium—not through the darkened glass of one man's spleen and resentment. Dante, in constituting himself the hero of his poem, not only renders her, in the general impression, as dreary as himself, in spite of the occasional beautiful pictures he draws of her, but narrows her very immensity into his pettiness. He fancied, alas, that he could build her universe over again out of the politics of old Rome and the divinity of the schools!

Dante, besides his great poem, and a few Latin eclogues of no great value, wrote lyrics full of Platonical sentiment, some of which anticipated the loveliest of Petrarch's; and he was the author of various prose works, political and philosophical, all more or less masterly for the time in which he lived, and all coadjutors of his poetry in fixing his native tongue. His account of his Early Life (the *Vita Nuova*) is a most engaging history of a boyish passion, evidently as real and true on his own side as love and truth can be, whatever might be its mistake as to its object. The treatise on the Vernacular Tongue (*de Vulgari Eloquio*) shews how critically he considered his materials for impressing the world, and what a reader he was of every production of his contemporaries. The Banquet (*Convito*) is but an abstruse commentary on some of his minor poems; but the book on Monarchy (*de Monarchia*) is a compound of ability and absurdity, in which his great genius is fairly overborne by the barbarous pedantry of the age. It is an argument to prove that the world must all be governed by one man; that this one man must be the successor of the Roman Emperor—God having manifestly designed the world to be subject for ever to the Roman empire; and lastly, that this Emperor is equally designed by God to be independent of the Pope—spiritually subject to him, indeed, but so far only as a good son is subject to the religious advice of his father; and thus making Church and State happy for ever in the two divided supremacies. And all this assumption of the obsolete and impossible the author gravely proves in all the forms of logic, by arguments drawn from the history of Æneas, and the providential cackle of the Roman geese!

How can the patriots of modern Italy, justified as they are in extolling the poet to the skies, see him plunge into such depths of bigotry in his verse and childishness in his prose, and consent to perplex the friends of advancement with making a type of their success out of so erring though so great a man? Such slavishness, even to such greatness, is a poor and unpromising thing, compared with an altogether unprejudiced and forward-looking self-reliance. To have no faith in names has been announced as one of their principles; and "God and Humanity" is their motto. What, therefore, has Dante's name to do with their principles? or what have the semi-barbarisms of the thirteenth century to do with the final triumph of "God and Humanity"? Dante's lauded wish for that union of the Italian States, which his fame has led them so fondly to identify with their own, was but a portion of his greater and prouder wish to see the whole world at the feet of his boasted ancestress, Rome. Not, of course, that he had no view to what he considered good and just government (for what sane despot purposes to rule without that?); but his good and just government was always to be founded on the *sine qua non* principle of universal Italian domination.

All that Dante said or did has its interest for us in spite of his errors, because he was an earnest and suffering man and a great genius; but his fame must ever continue to lie where his greatest blame does, in his principal work. He was a gratuitous logician, a preposterous politician, a cruel theologian; but his wonderful imagination, and (considering the bitterness that was in him) still more wonderful sweetness, have gone into the hearts of his fellow-creatures, and will remain there in spite of the moral and religious absurdities with which they are mingled, and of the inability which the best-natured readers feel to associate his entire memory, as a poet, with their usual personal delight in a poet and his name.

XIII

JOHN RUSKIN

Mediaeval Landscape and Dante

[§ 28.] . . . It is not possible for us to conceive, through the rigidity of the signs employed, what were the real feelings of the mediæval workman or spectator about the natural landscape. We see that the thing carved or painted is not intended in anywise to imitate the truth, or convey to us the feelings which the workman had in contemplating the truth. He has got a way of talking about it so definite and cold, and tells us with his chisel so calmly that the knight had a castle to attack, or the saint a river to cross dryshod, without making the smallest effort to describt pictorially either castle or river, that we are left wholly at fault as to the nature of the emotion with which he contemplated the real objects. But that emotion, as the intermediate step between the feelings of the Grecian and the modern, it must be our aim to ascertain as clearly as possible; and, therefore, finding it not at this period completely expressed in visible art, we must, as we did with the Greeks, take up the written landscape instead, and examine this mediæval sentiment as we find it embodied in the poem of Dante.

§ 29. The thing that must first strike us in this respect, as we turn our thoughts to the poem, is, unquestionably, the *formality* of its landscape.

Milton's effort, in all that he tells us of his Inferno, is to make it indefinite; Dante's, to make it *definite*. Both, indeed, describe it as entered through gates; but, within the gate, all is wild and fenceless with Milton, having indeed its four rivers,—the last vestige of the mediæval tradition,—but rivers which flow through a waste of mountain and moorland, and by "many a frozen, many a fiery Alp." But Dante's Inferno is accurately separated into circles drawn with well-pointed compasses;

Reprinted from *Modern Painters*, vol. 3 of *The Works of John Ruskin*, ed. E. T. Cook and Alexander Wedderburn (London: George Allen, 1903–12), pt. 4, chaps. 14–15, pp. 269–315.

mapped and properly surveyed in every direction, trenched in a thoroughly good style of engineering from depth to depth, and divided in the "*accurate* middle" (dritto mezzo) of its deepest abyss, into a concentric series of ten moats and embankments, like those about a castle, with bridges from each embankment to the next. . . . These larger fosses are of rock, and the bridges also; but as he goes farther into detail, Dante tells us of various minor fosses and embankments, in which he anxiously points out to us not only the formality, but the neatness and perfectness, of the stonework. For instance, in describing the river Phlegethon, he tells us that it was "paved with stone at the bottom, and at the sides, and *over the edges of the sides*," just as the water is at the baths of Bulicame; and for fear we should think this embankment at all *larger* than it really was, Dante adds, carefully, that it was made just like the embankments of Ghent or Bruges against the sea, or those in Lombardy which bank the Brenta, only "not so high, nor so wide," as any of these. And besides the trenches, we have two well-built castles; one, like Ecbatana, with seven circuits of wall (and surrounded by a fair stream), wherein the great poets and sages of antiquity live; and another, a great fortified city with walls of iron, red-hot, and a deep fosse round it, and full of "grave citizens,"—the city of Dis.

§ 30. Now, whether this be in what we moderns call "good taste," or not, I do not mean just now to inquire—Dante having nothing to do with taste, but with the facts of what he had seen; only, so far as the imaginative faculty of the two poets is concerned, note that Milton's vagueness is not the sign of imagination, but of its absence, so far as it is significative in the matter. For it does not follow, because Milton did not map out his Inferno as Dante did, that he *could* not have done so if he had chosen; only, it was the easier and less imaginative process to leave it vague than to define it. Imagination is always the seeing and asserting faculty; that which obscures or conceals may be judgment, or feeling, but not invention. The invention, whether good or bad, is in the accurate engineering, not in the fog and uncertainty.

§ 31. When we pass with Dante from the Inferno to Purgatory, we have indeed more light and air, but no more liberty; being now confined on various ledges cut into a mountain side, with a precipice on one hand and a vertical wall on the other;

and, lest here also we should make any mistake about magnitudes, we are told that the ledges were eighteen feet wide,[1] and that the ascent from one to the other was by steps, made like those which go up from Florence to the Church of San Miniato.[2]

Lastly, though in the Paradise there is perfect freedom and infinity of space, though for trenches we have planets, and for cornices constellations, yet there is more cadence, procession, and order among the redeemed souls than any other; they fly, so as to describe letters and sentences in the air, and rest in circles, like rainbows, or determinate figures, as of a cross and an eagle; in which certain of the more glorified natures are so arranged as to form the eye of the bird, while those most highly blessed are arranged with their white crowds in leaflets, so as to form the image of a white rose in the midst of heaven.

§ 32. Thus, throughout the poem, I conceive that the first striking character of its scenery is intense definition; precisely the reflection of that definiteness which we have already traced in pictorial art. But the second point which seems noteworthy is, that the flat ground and embanked trenches are reserved for the Inferno: and that the entire territory of the Purgatory is a mountain, thus marking the sense of that purifying and perfecting influence in mountains which we saw the mediæval mind was so ready to suggest. The same general idea is indicated at the very commencement of the poem, in which Dante is overwhelmed by fear and sorrow in passing through a dark forest, but revives on seeing the sun touch the top of a hill, afterwards called by Virgil "the pleasant mount—the cause and source of all delight.

§ 33. While, however, we find this greater honour paid to mountains, I think we may perceive a much greater dread and dislike of woods. We saw that Homer seemed to attach a pleasant idea, for the most part, to forests; regarding them as sources of wealth and places of shelter; and we find constantly an idea of sacredness attached to them, as being haunted especially by the gods; . . . and so the wood is sought as a kindly shelter by Ulysses, in spite of its wild beasts; and evidently regarded with great affection by Sophocles, for, in a passage

[1] "Three times the length of the human body."—*Purg.* x. 24.

[2] *Purg.* xii. 102.

which is always regarded by readers of Greek tragedy with peculiar pleasure, the aged and blind Œdipus, brought to rest in "the sweetest resting-place" in all the neighbourhood of Athens, has the spot described to him as haunted perpetually by nightingales, which sing "in the green glades and in the dark ivy, and in the thousand-fruited, sunless, and windless thickets of the god" (Bacchus); the idea of the complete shelter from wind and sun being here, as with Ulysses, the uppermost one. . . . To Dante the idea of a forest is exceedingly repulsive, so that, as just noticed, in the opening of his poem, he cannot express a general despair about life more strongly than by saying he was lost in a wood so savage and terrible, that "even to think or speak of it is distress,–it was so bitter,–it was something next door to death;" and one of the saddest scenes in all the Inferno is in a forest, of which the trees are haunted by lost souls: while (with only one exception), whenever the country is to be beautiful, we find ourselves coming out into open air and open meadows.

It is quite true that this is partly a characteristic, not merely of Dante, or of mediæval writers, but of *southern* writers; for the simple reason that the forest, being with them higher upon the hills, and more out of the way than in the north, was generally a type of lonely and savage places; while in England, the "greenwood," coming up to the very walls of the towns, it was possible to be "merry in the good greenwood," in a sense which an Italian could not have understood. Hence Chaucer, Spenser, and Shakspere send their favourites perpetually to the woods for pleasure or meditation; and trust their tender Canace, or Rosalind, or Helena, or Silvia, or Belphœbe, where Dante would have sent no one but a condemned spirit. Nevertheless, there is always traceable in the mediæval mind a dread of thick foliage, which was not present to that of a Greek; so that, even in the north, we have our sorrowful "children in the wood," and black huntsman of the Hartz forests, and such other wood terrors; the principal reason for the difference being that a Greek, being by no means given to travelling, regarded his woods as so much valuable property; and if he ever went into them for pleasure, expected to meet one or two gods in the course of his walk, but no banditti; while a mediæval, much more of a solitary traveller, and expecting to meet with no gods in the thickets, but only with thieves, or a hostile ambush, or a bear, besides a great deal of troublesome ground for his horse, and a very serious chance, next to a certainty, of losing his way, naturally kept in the open ground as long as he could, and regarded the forests, in general, with anything but an eye of favour.

§ 34. These, I think, are the principal points which must strike us, when we first broadly think of the poem as compared with classical work. Let us now go a little more into detail.

As Homer gave us an ideal landscape, which even a god might have been pleased to behold, so Dante gives us, fortunately, an ideal landscape, which is specially intended for the terrestrial paradise. And it will doubtless be with some surprise, after our reflections above on the general tone of Dante's feelings, that we find ourselves here first entering a *forest*, and that even a *thick* forest. But there is a peculiar meaning in this. With any other poet than Dante, it might have been regarded as a wanton inconsistency. Not so with him: by glancing back to the two lines which explain the nature of Paradise, we shall see what he means by it. Virgil tells him, as he enters it, "Henceforward, take thine own pleasure for guide; thou art beyond the steep ways, and beyond all Art;"[3]—meaning, that the perfectly purified and noble human creature, having no pleasure but in right, is past all effort, and past all *rule*. Art has no existence for such a being. Hence, the first aim of Dante, in his landscape imagery, is to show evidence of this perfect liberty, and of the purity and sinlessness of the new nature, converting pathless ways into happy ones. So that all those fences and formalisms which had been needed for him in imperfection, are removed in this paradise; and even the pathlessness of the wood, the most dreadful thing possible to him in his days of sin and shortcoming, is now a joy to him in his days of purity. And as the fencelessness and thicket of sin led to the fettered and fearful order of eternal punishment, so the fencelessness and thicket of the free virtue lead to the loving and constellated order of eternal happiness.

§ 35. This forest, then, is very like that of Colonos in several respects—in its peace and sweetness, and number of birds; it differs from it only in letting a light breeze through it, being therefore somewhat thinner than the Greek wood; the tender

3 [The last words of the line, "fuor sei dell'arte," mean "you are beyond the narrow [ways]." *Purg*. XXVII, 132.]

lines which tell of the voices of the birds mingling with the wind, and of the leaves all turning one way before it, have been more or less copied by every poet since Dante's time. They are, so far as I know, the sweetest passage of wood description which exists in literature.

Before, however, Dante has gone far in this wood,—that is to say, only so far as to have lost sight of the place where he entered it, or rather, I suppose, of the light under the boughs of the outside trees, and it must have been a very thin wood indeed if he did not do this in some quarter of a mile's walk,—he comes to a little river, three paces over, which bends the blades of grass to the left, with a meadow on the other side of it; and in this meadow

> A lady, graced with solitude, who went
>   Singing, and setting flower by flower apart,
> By which the path she walked on was besprent.
> "Ah, lady beautiful, that basking art
>   In beams of love, if I may trust thy face,
> Which useth to bear witness of the heart,
> Let liking come on thee," said I, "to trace
>   Thy path a little closer to the shore,
> Where I may reap the hearing of thy lays.
> Thou mindest me, how Proserpine of yore
>   Appeared in such a place, what time her mother
> Lost her, and she the spring, for evermore."
> As, pointing downwards and to one another
>   Her feet, a lady bendeth in the dance,
> And barely setteth one before the other,
> Thus, on the scarlet and the saffron glance
>   Of flowers, with motion maidenlike she bent
> (Her modest eyelids drooping and askance);
> And there she gave my wishes their content,
>   Approaching, so that her sweet melodies
> Arrived upon mine ear with what they meant.
> When first she came amongst the blades, that rise,
>   Already wetted, from the goodly river,
> She graced me by the lifting of her eyes.
>
> CAYLEY

§ 36. I have given this passage at length, because, for our purposes, it is by much the most important, not only in Dante, but in the whole circle of poetry. This lady, observe, stands on the opposite side of the little stream, which, presently, she explains to Dante is Lethe, having power to cause forgetfulness of all evil, and she stands just among the bent blades of grass at its edge. She is first seen gathering flower from flower, then "passing continually the multitudinous flowers through her hands," smiling at the same time so brightly, that her first address to Dante is to prevent him from wondering at her, saying, "if he will remember the verse of the ninety-second Psalm, beginning 'Delectasti', he will know why she is so happy."

And turning to the verse of this Psalm we find it written, "Thou, Lord, hast made me glad *through Thy works.* I will triumph *in the works of Thy hands*" . . .

§ 37. Now we could not for an instant have had any difficulty in understanding this, but that, some way farther on in the poem, the lady is called Matilda, and is with reason supposed by the commentators to be the great Countess Matilda of the eleventh century; notable equally for her ceaseless activity, her brilliant political genius, her perfect piety, and her deep reverence for the see of Rome. This Countess Matilda is therefore Dante's guide in the terrestrial paradise, as Beatrice is afterwards in the celestial; each of them having a spiritual and symbolic character in their glorified state, yet retaining their definite personality.

The question is, then, what is the symbolic character of the Countess Matilda, as the guiding spirit of the terrestrial paradise? Before Dante had entered this paradise he had rested on a step of shelving rock, and as he watched the stars he slept, and dreamed, and thus tells us what he saw:—

> A lady, young and beautiful, I dreamed,
> Was passing o'er a lea; and, as she came,
> Methought I saw her ever and anon
> Bending to cull the flowers; and thus she sang:
> "Know ye, whoever of my name would ask,
> That I am Leah; for my brow to weave
> A garland, these fair hands unwearied ply;
> To please me at the crystal mirror, here
> I decked me. But my sister Rachel, she
> Before her glass abides the livelong day,
> Her radiant eyes beholding, charmed no less
> Than I with this delightful task. Her joy
> In contemplation, as in labour mine."[4]

[4] [All translations are from Cary's version unless indicated otherwise.]

This vision of Rachel and Leah has been always, and with unquestionable truth, received as a type of the Active and Contemplative life, and as an introduction to the two divisions of the paradise which Dante is about to enter. Therefore the unwearied spirit of the Countess Matilda is understood to represent the Active life, which forms the felicity of Earth; and the spirit of Beatrice the Contemplative life, which forms the felicity of Heaven. This interpretation appears at first straightforward and certain; but it has missed count of exactly the most important fact in the two passages which we have to explain. Observe: Leah gathers the flowers to decorate *herself*, and delights in *Her Own* Labour. Rachel sits silent, contemplating herself, and delights in *Her Own* Image. These are the types of the Unglorified Active and Contemplative powers of Man. But Beatrice and Matilda are the same powers, Glorified. And how are they Glorified? Leah took delight in her own labour; but Matilda—"in operibus *manuum Tuarum*"—*in God's labour:* Rachel in the sight of her own face; Beatrice in the sight of *God's face.*

§ 38. And thus, when afterwards Dante sees Beatrice on her throne, and prays her that, when he himself shall die, she would receive him with kindness, Beatrice merely looks down for an instant, and answers with a single smile, then "towards the eternal fountain turns."

Therefore it is evident that Dante distinguishes in both cases, not between earth and heaven, but between perfect and imperfect happiness, whether in earth or heaven. The active life which has only the service of man for its end, and therefore gathers flowers, with Leah, for its own decoration, is indeed happy, but not perfectly so; it has only the happiness of the dream, belonging essentially to the dream of human life, and passing away with it. But the active life which labours for the more and more discovery of God's work, is perfectly happy, and is the life of the terrestrial paradise, being a true foretaste of heaven, and beginning in earth, as heaven's vestibule. So also the contemplative life which is concerned with human feeling and thought and beauty—the life which is in earthly poetry and imagery of noble earthly emotion—is happy, but it is the happiness of the dream; the contemplative life which has God's person and love in Christ for its object, has the happiness of eternity. But because this higher happiness is also begun here on earth, Beatrice descends to earth; and when revealed to Dante first, he sees the image of the twofold personality of Christ reflected in her *eyes;* as the flowers, which are, to the mediæval heart, the chief work of God, are for ever passing through Matilda's *hands.*

§ 39. Now, therefore, we see that Dante, as the great prophetic exponent of the heart of the Middle Ages, has, by the lips of the spirit of Matilda, declared the mediæval faith,—that all perfect active life was "the expression of man's delight *in God's work*"; and that all their political and warlike energy, as fully shown in the mortal life of Matilda, was yet inferior and impure,—the energy of the dream,—compared with that which on the opposite bank of Lethe stood "choosing flower from flower." And what joy and peace there were in this work is marked by Matilda's being the person who draws Dante through the stream of Lethe, so as to make him forget all sin, and all sorrow; throwing her arms around him, she plunges his head under the waves of it; then draws him through, crying to him, "*hold me, hold me,*" and so presents him, thus bathed, free from all painful memory, at the feet of the spirit of the more heavenly contemplation.

§ 40. The reader will, I think, now see, with sufficient distinctness, why I called this passage the most important, for our present purposes, in the whole circle of poetry. For it contains the first great confession of the discovery by the human race (I mean as a matter of experience, not of revelation), that their happiness was not in themselves, and that their labour was not to have their own service as its chief end. It embodies in a few syllables the *sealing* difference between the Greek and the mediæval, in that the former sought the flower and herb for his own uses, the latter for God's honour; the former, primarily and on principle, contemplated his own beauty and the workings of his own mind, and the latter, primarily and on principle, contemplated Christ's beauty and the workings of the mind of Christ. . . .

§ 42. Having thus received from Dante this great lesson, as to the spirit in which mediæval landscape is to be understood, what else we have to note respecting it, as seen in his poem, will be comparatively straightforward and easy. And first, we have to observe the place occupied in his mind by *colour.* It has already been shown, in the *Stones of Venice,* that colour is the most *sacred* element of all visible things. Hence, as the mediæval mind contemplated them first for their sacredness, we should, beforehand, expect that the first thing it would seize would be the colour; and that we should find its expressions and renderings of colour infinitely more loving and accurate than among the Greeks.

§ 43. Accordingly, the Greek sense of colour seems to have been so comparatively dim and uncertain, that it is almost impossible to ascertain what the real idea was which they attached to any word alluding to hue: and above all, colour, though pleasant to their eyes, as to those of all human beings, seems never to have been impressive to their feelings. They liked purple, on the whole, the best; but there was no sense of cheerfulness or pleasantness in one colour, and gloom in another, such as the mediævals had. . . .

§ 46. Now, without going out of the terrestrial paradise, in which Dante last left us, we shall be able at once to compare with this Greek incertitude the precision of the mediæval eye for colour. Some three arrowflights farther up into the wood we come to a tall tree, which is at first barren, but, after some little time, visibly opens into flowers, of a colour "less than that of roses, but more than that of violets."

It certainly would not be possible, in words, to come nearer to the *definition* of the exact hue which Dante meant—that of the apple-blossom. Had he employed any simple colour-phrase, as a "pale-pink," or "violet-pink," or any other such combined expression, he still could not have completely got at the delicacy of the hue; he might perhaps have indicated its kind, but not its tenderness; but by taking the rose-leaf as a type of the delicate red, and then enfeebling this with the violet grey, he gets, as closely as language can carry him, to the complete rendering of the vision, though it is evidently felt by him to be in its perfect beauty ineffable; and rightly so felt, for of all lovely things which grace the spring-time in our fair temperate zone, I am not sure but this blossoming of the apple-tree is the fairest. . . .

§ 47. Again: . . . if we remember carefully the general expressions, respecting grass, used in modern literature, I think nearly the commonest that occurs to us will be that of "enamelled" turf or sward. This phrase is usually employed by our pseudo-poets, like all their other phrases, without knowing what it means, because it has been used by other writers before them, and because they do not know what else to say of grass. If we were to ask them what enamel was, they could not tell us; and if we asked why grass was like enamel, they could not tell us. The expression *has* a meaning, however, and one peculiarly characteristic of mediæval and modern temper.

§ 48. The first instance I know of its right use, though very probably it had been so employed before, is in Dante. The righteous spirits of the pre-Christian ages are seen by him, though in the Inferno, yet in a place open, luminous, and high, walking upon the "green enamel."

I am very sure that Dante did not use this phrase as we use it. He knew well what enamel was; and his readers, in order to understand him thoroughly, must remember what it is,—a vitreous paste, dissolved in water, mixed with metallic oxides, to give it the opacity and the colour required, spread in a moist state on metal, and afterwards hardened by fire, so as never to change. And Dante means, in using this metaphor of the grass of the Inferno, to mark, that it is laid as a tempering and cooling substance over the dark, metallic, gloomy ground; but yet so hardened by the fire, that it is not any more fresh or living grass, but a smooth, silent, lifeless bed of eternal green. And we know how *hard* Dante's idea of it was; because afterwards, in what is perhaps the most awful passage of the whole Inferno, when the three furies rise at the top of the burning tower, and catching sight of Dante, and not being able to get at him, shriek wildly for the Gorgon to come up too, that they may turn him into stone,—the word *stone* is not hard enough for them. Stone might crumble away after it was made, or something with life might grow upon it; no, it shall not be stone; they will make enamel of him; nothing can grow out of that; it is dead for ever.

> Venga Medusa, sì lo farem di *Smalto.*
> [*Inf.* IX, 53]

§ 49. Now, almost in the opening of the Purgatory, as there at the entrance of the Inferno, we find a company of great ones resting in a grassy place. But the idea of the grass now is very different. The word now used is not "enamel," but "herb," and instead of being merely green, it is covered with flowers of many colours. With the usual mediæval accuracy, Dante insists on telling us precisely what these colours were, and how bright; which he does by naming the actual pigments used in illumination,—"Gold, and fine silver, and cochineal, and white lead, and

Indian wood, serene and lucid, and fresh emerald, just broken, would have been excelled, as less is by greater, by the flowers and grass of the place." It is evident that the "emerald" here means the emerald green of the illuminators; for a fresh emerald is no brighter than one which is not fresh, and Dante was not one to throw away his words thus. Observe then, we have here the idea of the growth, life, and variegation of the "green herb," as opposed to the "smalto" of the Inferno; but the colours of the variegation are illustrated and defined by the reference to actual pigments: and, observe, because the other colours are rather bright, the blue ground (Indian wood, indigo?) is sober; lucid, but serene: and presently two angels enter, who are dressed in green drapery, but of a paler green than the grass, which Dante marks, by telling us that it was "the green of leaves, just budded."

§ 50. In all this, I wish the reader to observe two things: first, the general carefulness of the poet in defining colour, distinguishing it precisely as a painter would (opposed to the Greek carelessness about it); and, secondly, his regarding the grass for its greenness and variegation, rather than, as a Greek would have done, for its depth and freshness. This greenness or brightness, and variegation, are taken up by later and modern poets, as the things intended to be chiefly expressed by the word "enamelled"; and, gradually, the term is taken to indicate any kind of bright and interchangeable colouring; there being always this much of propriety about it, when used of greensward, that such sward is indeed, like enamel, a coat of bright colour on a comparatively dark ground; and is thus a sort of natural jewellery and painter's work, different from loose and large vegetation. The word is often awkwardly and falsely used, by the later poets, of all kinds of growth and colour; as by Milton of the flowers of Paradise showing themselves over its wall; but it retains, nevertheless, through all its jaded inanity, some half-unconscious vestige of the old sense, even to the present day.

§ 51. There are, it seems to me, several important deductions to be made from these facts. The Greek, we have seen, delighted in the grass for its usefulness; the mediæval, as also we moderns, for its colour and beauty. But both dwell on it as the *first* element of the lovely landscape; we saw its use in Homer, we see also that Dante thinks the righteous spirits of the heathen enough comforted in Hades by having even the *image* of green grass put beneath their feet; the happy resting-place in Purgatory has no other delight than its grass and flowers; and, finally, in the terrestrial paradise, the feet of Matilda pause where the Lethe stream first bends the blades of grass. Consider a little what a depth there is in this great instinct of the human race. Gather a single blade of grass, and examine for a minute, quietly, its narrow sword-shaped strip of fluted green. Nothing, as it seems there, of notable goodness or beauty. A very little strength, and a very little tallness, and a few delicate long lines meeting in a point,—not a perfect point neither, but blunt and unfinished, by no means a creditable or apparently much cared-for example of Nature's workmanship; made, as it seems, only to be trodden on to-day, and to-morrow to be cast into the oven; and a little pale and hollow stalk, feeble and flaccid, leading down to the dull brown fibres of roots. And yet, think of it well, and judge whether of all the gorgeous flowers that beam in summer air, and of all strong and goodly trees, pleasant to the eyes or good for food,—stately palm and pine, strong ash and oak, scented citron, burdened vine,—there be any by man so deeply loved, by God so highly graced, as that narrow point of feeble green. . . .

§ 52. There are several lessons symbolically connected with this subject, which we must not allow to escape us. Observe, the peculiar characters of the grass, which adapt it especially for the service of man, are its apparent *humility*, and *cheerfulness*. Its humility, in that it seems created only for lowest service,—appointed to be trodden on, and fed upon. Its cheerfulness, in that it seems to exult under all kinds of violence and suffering. You roll it, and it is stronger the next day; you mow it, and it multiplies its shoots, as if it were grateful; you tread upon it, and it only sends up richer perfume. Spring comes, and it rejoices with all the earth,—glowing with variegated flame of flowers,—waving in soft depth of fruitful strength. Winter comes, and though it will not mock its fellow plants by growing then, it will not pine and mourn, and turn colourless and leafless as they. It is always green; and is only the brighter and gayer for the hoarfrost.

§ 53. Now, these two characters—of humility, and joy under trial—are exactly those which most definitely distinguish the Christian from the Pagan spirit. Whatever virtue the pagan possessed was rooted in pride, and fruited with sorrow. It began in the elevation of his own nature; it ended but in the "verde smalto"—the hopeless green—of the Elysian fields. But the Christian virtue is rooted in self-debasement, and strengthened under suffering by gladness of hope. And remembering this, it is curious to observe how utterly without gladness the Greek heart appears to be in watching the flowering grass, and what strange discords of expression arise sometimes in consequence. There is one, recurring once or twice in Homer, which has always pained me. He says, "The Greek army was on the fields, as thick as flowers in the spring." It might be so; but flowers in spring-time are not the image by which Dante would have numbered soldiers on their path of battle. Dante could not have thought of the flowering of the grass but as associated with happiness. There is a still deeper significance in the passage . . . from Homer, describing Ulysses casting himself down on the *rushes* and the corn-giving land at the river shore,—the rushes and corn being to him only good for rest and sustenance,—when we compare it with that in which Dante tells us he was ordered to descend to the shore of the lake as he entered Purgatory, to gather a *rush*, and gird himself with it, it being to him the emblem not only of rest, but of humility under chastisement, the rush (or reed) being the only plant which can grow there;—"no plant which bears leaves, or hardens its bark, can live on that shore, because it does not yield to the chastisement of its waves." It cannot but strike the reader singularly how deep and harmonious a significance runs through all these words of Dante—how every syllable of them, the more we penetrate it, becomes a seed of farther thought! . . .

Perhaps the best lesson which we can finally take to ourselves, in leaving these sweet fields of the mediæval landscape, is the memory that, in spite of all the fettered habits of thought of his age, this great Dante, this inspired exponent of what lay deepest at the heart of the early Church, placed his terrestrial paradise where there had ceased to be fence or division, and where the grass of the earth was bowed down, in unity of direction, only by the soft waves that bore with them the forgetfulness of evil.

CHAPTER XV

§ 2. It will be remembered that . . . we supposed it probable that there would be considerable inaccuracies, in the mediæval mode of regarding nature. Hitherto, however, we have found none but, on the contrary, intense accuracy, precision, and affection. The reason of this is, that all floral and foliaged beauty might be perfectly represented, as far as its form went, in the sculpture and ornamental painting of the period; hence the attention of men was thoroughly awakened to that beauty. But as mountains and clouds and large features of natural scenery could not be accurately represented, we must be prepared to find them not so carefully contemplated,—more carefully, indeed, than by the Greeks, but still in no wise as the things themselves deserve.

§ 3. It was besides noticed that mountains, though regarded with reverence by the mediæval, were also the subjects of a certain dislike and dread. . . . In fact the place of the soul's purification, though a mountain, is yet by Dante subdued, whenever there is any pleasantness to be found upon it, from all mountainous character into grassy recesses, or slopes to rushy shore; and, in his general conception of it, resembles much more a castle mound, surrounded by terraced walks,—in the manner, for instance, of one of Turner's favourite scenes, the bank under Richmond Castle (Yorkshire); or, still more, one of the hill slopes divided by terraces, above the Rhine, in which the picturesqueness of the ground had been reduced to the form best calculated for the growing of costly wine, than any scene to which we moderns should naturally attach the term "Mountainous." On the other hand, although the Inferno is just as accurately measured and divided as the Purgatory, it is nevertheless cleft into rocky chasms which possess something of true mountain nature—nature which we moderns of the north should most of us seek with delight, but which, to the great Florentine, appeared adapted only for the punishment of lost spirits, and which, on the mind of nearly all his countrymen, would to this day produce a very closely correspondent effect; so that their graceful language, dying away on the north side of the Alps, gives its departing accents to proclaim its detestation of hardness and ruggedness; and is heard for the last time, as it bestows on the noblest defile in all the Grisons, if not in all the Alpine chain, the name of the "*evil* way"—"la Via Mala."

§ 4. This "evil way," though much deeper and more sublime, corresponds closely in general character to Dante's "Evilpits," just as the banks of Richmond do to his mountain of Purgatory;

and it is notable that Turner has been led to illustrate, with his whole strength, the character of both; having founded, as it seems to me, his early dreams of mountain form altogether on the sweet banks of the Yorkshire streams, and rooted his hardier thoughts of it in the rugged clefts of the Via Mala. . . .

§ 6. It is with peculiar interest, as bearing on our own proper subject, that we must examine Dante's conception of the rocks of the eighth circle. And first, as to general tone of colour: from what we have seen of the love of the mediæval for bright and variegated colour, we might guess that his chief cause of dislike to rocks would be, in Italy, their comparative colourlessness. With hardly an exception, the range of the Apennines is composed of a . . . limestone so grey and toneless, that I know not any mountain districts so utterly melancholy as those which are composed of this rock, when unwooded. Now, as far as I can discover from the internal evidence in his poem, nearly all Dante's mountain wanderings had been upon this ground. He had journeyed once or twice among the Alps, indeed, but seems to have been impressed chiefly by the road from Garda to Trent, and that along the Cornice, both of which are either upon those limestones, or a dark serpentine, which shows hardly any colour till it is polished. It is not ascertainable that he had ever seen rock scenery of the finely coloured kind, aided by the Alpine mosses: I do not know the fall at Forlì (*Inferno*, xvi. 99), but every other scene to which he alludes is among these Apennine limestones; and when he wishes to give the idea of enormous mountain size, he names Tabernicch and Pietra-pana,—the one clearly chosen for the sake of the last syllable of its name, in order to make a sound as of cracking ice, with the two sequent rhymes of the stanza,—and the other is an Apennine near Lucca.

§ 7. His idea, therefore, of rock colour, founded on these experiences, is that of a dull or ashen grey, more or less stained by the brown of iron ochre, precisely as the Apennine limestones nearly always are; the grey being peculiarly cold and disagreeable. . . . The whole of Malebolge is made of this rock, "All wrought in stone or iron-coloured grain."[5]

Perhaps the iron colour may be meant to predominate in Evilpits; but the definite grey limestone colour is stated higher up, the river Styx flowing at the base of "malignant *grey* cliffs"[6]

[5] (Cayley.) "Tutto di pietra, e di color ferrigno."—*Inf.* xviii. 2.

[6] "Maligne piagge grige."—*Inf.* vii. 108.

(the word malignant being given to the iron-coloured Malebolge also); and the same whitish grey idea is given again definitely in describing the robe of the purgatorial or penance angel, which is "of the colour of ashes, or earth dug dry." Ashes necessarily mean *wood*-ashes in an Italian mind, so that we get the tone very pale; and there can be no doubt whatever about the hue meant, because it is constantly seen on the sunny sides of the Italian hills, produced by the scorching of the ground, a dusty and lifeless whitish grey, utterly painful and oppressive; and I have no doubt that this colour, assumed eminently also by limestone crags in the sun, is the quality which Homer means to express by a term he applies often to bare rocks, and which is usually translated "craggy," or "rocky." . . .

§ 9. But although this would cause a somewhat painful shock even to a modern mind, it would be as nothing when compared with the pain occasioned by absence of colour to a mediæval one. We have been trained, by our ingenious principles of Renaissance architecture, to think that meal-colour and ash-colour are the properest colours of all; and that the most aristocratic harmonies are to be deduced out of grey mortar and creamy stucco. Any of our modern classical architects would delightedly "face" a heathery hill with Roman cement; and any Italian sacristan would, but for the cost of it, at once whitewash the Cheviots. But the mediævals had not arrived at these abstract principles of taste. They liked fresco better than whitewash; and, on the whole, thought that Nature was in the right in painting her flowers yellow, pink, and blue;—not grey. Accordingly, this absence of colour from rocks, as compared with meadows and trees, was in their eyes an unredeemable defect; nor did it matter to them whether its place was supplied by the grey neutral tint, or the iron-coloured stain; for both colours, grey and brown, were, to them, hues of distress, despair, and mortification, hence adopted always for the dresses of monks; only the word "brown" bore, in their colour vocabulary, a still gloomier sense than with us. I was for some time embarrassed by Dante's use of it with respect to dark skies and water. Thus, in describing a simple twilight—not a Hades twilight, but an ordinarily fair evening—(*Inf*. ii. 1) he says, the "brown" air took the animals of earth away from their fatigues;—the waves under Charon's boat are "brown" (*Inf*. iii. 118); and Lethe, which is perfectly clear and yet dark, as with oblivion, is "bruna-bruna," "brown *exceeding* brown." Now, clearly in all these cases, no *warmth* is meant to be mingled in the colour. Dante had never seen one of our bog-streams, with its porter-coloured foam; and there can be no doubt that, in calling Lethe brown, he means it was dark slate grey, inclining to black; as, for instance, our clear Cumberland lakes, which, looked straight down upon where they are deep, seem to be lakes of ink. I am sure this is the colour he means; because no clear stream or lake on the Continent ever looks brown, but blue or green; and Dante, by merely taking away the pleasant colour, would get at once to this idea of grave clear grey. So, when he was talking of twilight, his eye for colour was far too good to let him call it *brown*, in our sense. Twilight is not brown, but purple, golden, or dark grey; and this last was what Dante meant. Farther, I find that this negation of colour is always the means by which Dante subdues his tones. Thus the fatal inscription on the Hades gate is written in "obscure colour," and the air which torments the passionate spirits is "aer nero," *black air*, called presently afterwards malignant air, just as the grey cliffs are called malignant cliffs. . . .

This being his idea of the colour of rocks, we have next to observe his conception of their substance. And I believe it will be found that the character on which he fixes first in them is *frangibility*—breakableness to bits, as opposed to wood, which can be sawn or rent, but not shattered with a hammer, and to metal, which is tough and malleable.

Thus, at the top of the abyss of the seventh circle, appointed for the "violent," or souls who had done evil by force, we are told, first, that the edge of it was composed of "great broken stones in a circle"; then, that the place was "Alpine"; and, becoming hereupon attentive, in order to hear what an Alpine place is like, we find that it was "like the place beyond Trent, where the rock, either by earthquake, or failure of support, has broken down to the plain, so that it gives any one at the top some means of getting down to the bottom." This is not a very elevated or enthusiastic description of an Alpine scene; and it is far from mended by the following verses, in which we are told that Dante "began to go down by this great *unloading* of stones," and that they moved often under his feet by reason of the new weight. The fact is that Dante, by many expressions throughout the poem, shows himself to have been a notably bad climber, and being fond of sitting in the sun, looking at his fair Baptistery, or walking in a dignified manner on flat pavement in a long robe, it puts him seriously out of his way when he has to take to his hands and knees, or look to his feet; so that the first strong impression made upon him by any Alpine scene whatever, is, clearly, that it is bad walking. When he is in a fright and hurry, and has a very steep place to go down, Virgil has to carry him altogether, and is obliged to encourage him, again and again, when they have a steep slope to go up,—the first ascent of the purgatorial mountain. . . .

But for Lucan's mention of Aruns at Luna [Dante] would seemingly not have spoken of the Carrara hills in the whole course of his poem: when he does allude to them, he speaks of their white marble, and their command of stars and sea, but has evidently no regard for the hills themselves. There is not a single phrase or syllable throughout the poem which indicates such a regard. Ugolino, in his dream, seemed to himself to be in the mountains, "by cause of which the Pisan cannot see Lucca"; and it is impossible to look up from Pisa to that hoary slope without remembering the awe that there is in the passage; nevertheless, it was as a hunting-ground only that he remembered those hills. Adam of Brescia, tormented with eternal thirst, remembers the hills of Romena, but only for tne sake of their sweet waters:

> The rills that glitter down the grassy slopes
> Of Casentino, making fresh and soft
> The banks whereby they glide to Arno's stream,
> Stand ever in my view.

And, whenever hills are spoken of as having any influence on character, the repugnance of them is still manifest; they are always causes of rudeness or cruelty:

> But that ungrateful and malignant race,
> Who in old times came down from Fesole,
> *Ay, and still smack of their rough mountain flint,*
> Will, for thy good deeds, show thee enmity.
> Take heed thou cleanse thee of their ways.

So again—

> As one *mountain-bred,*
> Rugged, and clownish, if some city's walls
> He chance to enter, round him stares agape.

§ 18. Finally, although the Carrara mountains are named as having command of the stars and sea, the *Alps* are never specially mentioned but in bad weather, or snow. On the sand of the circle of the blasphemers—

> Fell slowly wafting down
> Dilated flakes of fire, as flakes of snow
> On Alpine summit, when the wind is hushed.

So the Paduans have to defend their town and castles against inundation,

> Ere the genial warmth be felt,
> On Chiarentana's top.

The clouds of anger, in Purgatory, can only be figured to the reader who has

> On an Alpine height been ta'en by cloud,
> Through which thou sawest no better than the mole
> Doth through opacous membrane.

And in approaching the second branch of Lethe, the seven ladies pause,—

> Arriving at the verge
> Of a dim umbrage hoar, such as is seen
> Beneath green leaves and gloomy branches oft
> To overbrow a bleak and Alpine cliff.

§ 19. Truly, it is unfair of Dante, that when he is going to use snow for a lovely image, and speak of it as melting away under heavenly sunshine, he must needs put it on the Apennines, not on the Alps:

> As snow that lies
> Amidst the living rafters, on the back
> Of Italy, congealed, when drifted high
> And closely piled by rough Sclavonian blasts;
> Breathe but the land whereon no shadow falls.
> And straightway, melting, it distils away,
> Like a fire-wasted taper; thus was I,
> Without a sigh, or tear, consumed in heart.

The reader will thank me for reminding him, though out of its proper order, of the exquisite passage of Scott which we have to compare with this:

As wreath of snow on mountain-breast
Slides from the rock that gave it rest,
Poor Ellen glided from her stay,
And at the monarch's feet she lay.
[*Lady of the Lake*, VI, 27]

Examine the context of this last passage, and its beauty is quite beyond praise; but note the northern love of rocks in the very first words I have to quote from Scott, "The rock that gave it rest." Dante could not have thought of his "cut rocks" as giving rest even to snow. He must put it on the pine branches, if it is to be at peace.

§ 20. There is only one more point to be noticed in the Dantesque landscape; namely, the feeling entertained by the poet towards the sky. And the love of mountains is so closely connected with the love of clouds, the sublimity of both depending much on their association, that, having found Dante regardless of the Carrara mountains as seen from San Miniato, we may well expect to find him equally regardless of the clouds in which the sun sank behind them. Accordingly, we find that his only pleasure in the sky depends on its "white clearness,"—that turning into "bianco aspetto di cilestro" which is so peculiarly characteristic of fine days in Italy. His pieces of pure pale light are always exquisite. In the dawn on the purgatorial mountain, first, in its pale white, he sees the "tremolar della marina"—trembling of the sea; then it becomes vermilion; and at last, near sunrise, orange. These are precisely the changes of a calm and perfect dawn. The scenery of Paradise begins with "Day added to day," the light of the sun so flooding the heavens, that "never rain nor river made lake so wide"; and throughout the Paradise all the beauty depends on spheres of light, or stars, never on clouds. But the pit of the Inferno is at first sight obscure, deep, and so *cloudy* that at its bottom nothing could be seen. When Dante and Virgil reach the marsh in which the souls of those who have been angry and sad in their lives are for ever plunged, they find it covered with thick fog; and the condemned souls say to them,—

We once were sad,[7]
In the *sweet air made gladsome by the sun.*
Now in these murky settlings are we sad.

[7] [Cary wrote, "Sad once were we."]

Even the angel crossing the marsh to help them is annoyed by this bitter marsh smoke "fummo acerbo," and continually sweeps it with his hand from before his face.

Anger, on the purgatorial mountain, is in like manner imaged, because of its blindness and wildness, by the Alpine clouds. As they emerge from its mist they see the white light radiated through the fading folds of it; and, except this appointed cloud, no other can touch the mountain of purification.

> "Tempest none, shower, hail, or snow,
> Hoar-frost, or dewy moistness, higher falls,
> Than that brief scale of threefold steps. Thick clouds,
> Nor scudding rack, are ever seen, swift glance
> Ne'er lightens, nor Thaumantian iris gleams."

Dwell for a little while on this intense love of Dante for light, —taught, as he is at last by Beatrice, to gaze on the sun itself like an eagle,—and endeavour to enter into his equally intense detestation of all mist, rack of cloud, or dimness of rain; and then consider with what kind of temper he would have regarded a landscape of Copley Fielding's, or passed a day in the Highlands. He has, in fact, assigned to the souls of the gluttonous no other punishment in the Inferno than perpetuity of Highland weather:

> Showers
> Ceaseless, accursed, heavy and cold, unchanged
> For ever, both in kind and in degree,—
> Large hail, discoloured water, sleety flaw,
> Through the dim midnight air streamed down amain.

§ 21. However, in this immitigable dislike of clouds, Dante goes somewhat beyond the general temper of his age. For although the calm sky was alone loved, and storm and rain were dreaded by all men, yet the white horizontal clouds of serene summer were regarded with great affection by all early painters, and considered as one of the accompaniments of the manifestation of spiritual power; sometimes, for theological reasons which we shall soon have to examine, being received, even without any other sign, as the types of blessing or Divine acceptance; and in almost every representation of the heavenly paradise, these level clouds are set by the early painters for its floor, or for thrones of its angels; whereas Dante retains steadily, through circle after circle, his cloudless thought, and concludes his painting of heaven, as he began it, upon the purgatorial mountain, with the image of shadowless morning:

> I raised my eyes, and as at morn is seen
> The horizon's eastern quarter to excell, . . .
> So likewise, that pacific Oriflamb
> Glowed in the midmost, and toward every part,
> With like gradation paled away its flame.
>
> [Cayley]

But the best way of regarding this feeling of Dante's is as the ultimate and most intense expression of the love of light, colour, and clearness, which, as we saw above, distinguish the mediæval from the Greek on one side, and, as we shall presently see, distinguished him from the modern on the other. For it is evident that precisely in the degree in which the Greek was agriculturally inclined, in that degree the sight of clouds would become to him more acceptable than to the mediæval knight, who only looked for the fine afternoons in which he might gather the flowers in his garden, and in nowise shared or imagined the previous anxieties of his gardener. Thus, when we find Ulysses comforted about Ithaca, by being told it had "plenty of rain," and the maids of Colonos boasting of their country for the same reason, we may be sure that they had some regard for clouds; and accordingly, except Aristophanes, of whom more presently, all the Greek poets speak fondly of the clouds, and consider them the fitting resting-places of the gods; including in their idea of clouds not merely the thin clear cirrus, but the rolling and changing volume of the thunder-cloud; nor even these only, but also the dusty whirlwind cloud of the earth, as in that noble chapter of Herodotus which tells us of the cloud, full of mystic voices, that rose out of the dust of Eleusis, and went down to Salamis. Clouds and rain were of course regarded with a like gratitude by the eastern and southern nations—Jews and Egyptians; and it is only among the northern mediævals, with whom fine weather was rarely so prolonged as to occasion painful drought, or dangerous famine, and over whom the clouds broke coldly and fiercely when they came, that the love of serene light assumes its intense character, and the fear of tempest its gloomiest; so that the powers of the clouds which to the Greek foretold his conquest at Salamis, and with whom he fought in alliance, side by side with their lightnings, under the crest of Parnassus, seemed, in the heart of the Middle Ages, to be only under the dominion of the spirit of evil. I have reserved, for our last example of the landscape of Dante, the passage in which this conviction is expressed; a passage not less notable for its close description of what the writer feared and disliked, than for the ineffable tenderness, in which Dante is always raised as much above all other poets, as in softness the rose above all other flowers. It is the spirit of Buonconte da Montefeltro who speaks:

> Then said another: "Ah, so may thy wish,
> That takes thee o'er the mountain, be fulfilled,
> As thou shalt graciously give aid to mine!
> Of Montefeltro I; Buonconte I:
> Giovanna, nor none else, have care for me;
> Sorrowing with these I therefore go." I thus:
> "From Campaldino's field what force or chance
> Drew thee, that ne'er thy sepulture was known?"
> "Oh!" answered he, "at Casentino's foot
> A stream there courseth, named Archiano, sprung
> In Apennine, above the hermit's seat.
> E'en where its name is cancelled, there came I,
> Pierced in the throat, fleeing away on foot,
> And bloodying the plain. Here sight and speech
> Failed me; and finishing with Mary's name,
> I fell, and tenantless my flesh remained.
>
> . . . .
>
> *That evil will, which in his intellect*
> *Still follows evil, came;* . . .
> . . . the valley, soon
> As day was spent, *he covered o'er with cloud,*
> From Pratomagno to the mountain range,
> And stretched the sky above; so that the air,
> Impregnate, changed to water. Fell the rain;
> And to the fosses came all that the land
> Contained not; and, as mightiest streams are wont,
> To the great river, with such headlong sweep,
> Rushed, that nought stayed its course. My stiffened frame,
> Laid at its mouth, the fell Archiano found,
> And dashed it into Arno; from my breast
> Loosening the cross, that of myself I made
> When overcome with pain. He hurled me on,
> Along the banks and bottom of his course;
> Then in his muddy spoils encircling wrapt."

Observe, Buonconte, as he dies, crosses his arms over his breast, pressing them together, partly in his pain, partly in prayer. His body lies by the river shore, as on a sepulchral monument, the arms folded into a cross. The rage of the river, under the influence of the evil demon, *unlooses this cross*, dashing the body supinely away, and rolling it over and over by bank and bottom. Nothing can be truer to the action of a stream in fury than these lines. And how desolate is it all! The lonely flight,—the grisly wound, "pierced in the throat,"—the death, without help or pity,—only the name of Mary on the lips,—and the cross folded over the heart. Then the rage of the demon and the river,—the noteless grave,—and, at last, even she who had been most trusted forgetting him,—

Giovanna, nor none else, have care for me.

There is, I feel assured, nothing else like it in all the range of poetry; a faint and harsh echo of it, only exists in one Scottish ballad, "The Twa Corbies."

XIV

CHARLES ELIOT NORTON

From "*The New Life*" *of Dante*

I

"At that season," says Boccaccio, in his Life of Dante, "when the sweetness of heaven reclothes the earth with its adornments, and makes it all smiling with flowers among the green leaves, it was the custom in our city for the men and for the ladies to celebrate festivals in their own streets in separate companies. Wherefore it happened, that, among the rest, Folco Portinari, a man held in much honor in those times among the citizens, had collected his neighbors at a feast in his own house on the first of May. Among them was the before-named Alighieri,—and, as little boys are wont to follow their fathers, especially to festive places, Dante, whose ninth year was not yet finished, accompanied him. It happened, that here, with others of his age, of whom, both boys and girls, there were many at the house of the entertainer, he gave himself to merry-making, after a childish fashion. Among the crowd of children was a little daughter of Folco, whose name was Bice,—though this was derived from her original name, which was Beatrice. She was, perhaps, eight years old, a pretty little thing in a childish way, very gentle and pleasing in her actions, and much more sedate and modest in her manners and words than her youthful age required. Beside this, she had very delicate features, admirably proportioned, and full, in addition to their beauty, of such openness and charm, that she was looked upon by many as a little angel. She then, such as I depict her, or rather, far more beautiful, appeared at this feast before the eyes of our Dante, not, I believe for the first time, but first with power to enamor him. And although still a child, he received her image into his heart with such affec-

Reprinted from *The Atlantic Monthly*, 3 (January–March, 1859): 62–69; 202–12; 330–39.

tion, that, from that day forward, never, as long as he lived, did it leave him."[1]

It was partly from tradition, partly from the record which Dante himself had left of it, that Boccaccio drew his account of this scene. In the *Vita Nuova*, "The New Life," Dante has written the first part of the history of that love which began at this festival, and which, growing with his growth, became, not many years after, the controlling passion of his life. Nothing is better or more commonly known about Dante than his love for Beatrice; but the course of that love, its relation to his external and public life, its moulding effect upon his character, have not been clearly traced. The love which lasted from his boyhood to his death, keeping his heart fresh, spite of the scorchings of disappointment, with springs of perpetual solace,—the love which, purified and spiritualized by the bitterness of separation and trial, led him through the hard paths of Philosophy and up the steep ascents of Faith, bringing him out of Hell and through Purgatory to the glories of Paradise and the fulfilment of Hope, —such a love is not only a spiritual experience, but it is also a discipline of character whose results are exhibited in the continually renewed struggles of life.

The earthly story of this love, of its beginning, its irregular course, its hopes and doubts, its exaltations and despairs, its sudden interruption and transformation by death, is the story which the "Vita Nuova" tells. The narrative is quaint, embroidered with conceits, deficient in artistic completeness, but it has the *naïveté* and simplicity of youth, the charm of sincerity, the freedom of personal confidence; and so long as there are lovers in the world, so long as lovers are poets, so long will this first and tenderest love-story of modern literature be read with appreciation and responsive sympathy.

But "The New Life" has an interest of another sort and a claim, not yet sufficiently acknowledged, upon all who would read the "Divina Commedia" with fit appreciation, in that it contains the first hint of the great poem itself, and furnishes for it a special, interior, imaginative introduction, without the knowledge of which it is not thoroughly to be understood. The character of Beatrice, as she appears in the "Divina Commedia,"

[1] *Vita di Dante*. Milan, 1823, pp. 29, 30.

the relation in which the poet stands to her, the motive of the dedication of the poem to her honor and memory, and many minor allusions, are all explained or illustrated by the aid of the "Vita Nuova." Dante's works and life are interwoven as are those of no other of the poets who have written for all time. No other has so written his autobiography. With Dante, external impressions and internal experiences—sights, actions, thoughts, emotions, sufferings—were all fused into poetry as they passed into his soul. Practical life and imaginative life were with him one and indissoluble. Not only was the life of imagination as real to him as the life of fact, but the life of fact was clothed upon by that of imagination; so that, on the one hand, daily events and common circumstances became a part of his spiritual experience in a far more intimate sense than is the case with other men, while, on the other, his fancies and his visions assumed the absoluteness and the literal existence of positive external facts. The remotest flights of his imagination never carry him where his sight becomes dim. His journey through the spiritual world was no less real to him than his journeys between Florence and Rome, or his wanderings between Verona and Ravenna. So absolute was his imagination, that it often so far controls his reader as to make it difficult not to believe that the poet beheld with his mortal eyes the invisible scenes which he describes. . . .

From this close relation between his life and his works, the "Vita Nuova" has a peculiar interest, as the earliest of Dante's writings, and the most autobiographic of them in its form and intention. In it we are brought into intimate personal relations with the poet. He trusts himself to us with full and free confidence; but there is no derogation from becoming manliness in his confessions. He draws the picture of a portion of his youth, and lays bare its tenderest emotions; but he does so with no morbid self-consciousness, and no affectation. Part of this simplicity is due, undoubtedly, to the character of the times, part to his own youthfulness, part to downright faith in his own genius. It was the fashion for poets to tell of their loves; in following the fashion, he not only gave expression to real feeling, but claimed his rank among the poets, and set a new style, from which love-poetry was to take a fresh date.

This first essay of his poetic powers exhibits the foundation upon which his later life was built. The figure of Beatrice, which appears veiled under the allegory, and indistinct in the bright cloud of the mysticism of the "Divina Commedia," takes her place in life and on the earth through the "Vita Nuova," as definitely as Dante himself. She is no allegorized piece of humanity, no impersonation of attributes, but an actual woman,—beautiful, modest, gentle, with companions only less beautiful than herself,—the most delightful figure in the midst of the picturesque life of Florence. She is seen smiling and weeping, walking with stately maidenly decorum in the street, praying at the church, merry at festivals, mourning at funerals; and her smiles and tears, her gentleness, her reserve, all the sweet qualities of her life, and the peace of her death, are told of with such tenderness and refinement, such pathetic melancholy, such delicate purity, and such passionate vehemence, that she remains and will always remain the loveliest and most womanly woman of the Middle Ages,—at once absolutely real and truly ideal.

It was in the year 1292, about two years after the death of Beatrice, and when he himself was about twenty-seven years old, that Dante collected into this *libretto d' amore* the poems that he had written during Beatrice's life, adding to them others relating to her written after her death, and accompanying all with a narrative and commentary in prose. The meaning of the name which he gave to the book, "La Vita Nuova," has been the cause of elaborate discussion among the Italian commentators. Literally "The New Life," it has been questioned whether this phrase meant simply early life, or life made new by the first experience and lasting influence of love. The latter interpretation seems the most appropriate to Dante's turn of mind and to his condition of feeling at the time when the little book appeared. To him it was the record of that life which the presence of Beatrice had made new.[2]

But whatever be the true significance of the title, this "New Life" is full not only of the youthfulness of its author, but also

[2] For *vita nova* in the sense of *early life*, see *Purgatory*, xxx. 115, with the comments of Landino and Benvenuto da Imola; and for *età novella* in a similar sense, see Canzone xviii, st. 6. Fraticelli, who supports this interpretation, gives these with other examples, but none more to the point. Mr. Joseph Garrow, who had a translation into English of the *Vita Nuova*, printed at Florence in 1846, entitles his book "The Early Life of Dante Allighieri."

of the fresh and youthful spirit of the time. Italy, after going through a long period of childhood, was now becoming conscious of the powers of maturity. Society, (to borrow a fine figure from Lamennais,) like a river, which, long lost in marshes, had at length regained its channel, after stagnating for centuries, was now again rapidly advancing. Throughout Italy there was a morning freshness, and the thrill and exhilaration of conscious activity. Her imagination was roused by the revival of ancient and now new learning, by the stories of travellers, by the gains of commerce, by the excitements of religion and the alarms of superstition. She was boastful, jealous, quarrelsome, lavish, magnificent, full of fickleness,—exhibiting on all sides the exuberance, the magnanimity, the folly of youth. After the long winter of the Dark Ages, spring had come, and the earth was renewing its beauty. And above all other cities in these days Florence was full of the pride of life. Civil brawls had not yet reduced her to become an easy prey for foreign conquerors. She was famous for wealth, and her spirit had risen with prosperity. Many years before, one of the Provençal troubadours, writing to his friend in verse, had said,—"Friend Gaucelm, if you go to Tuscany, seek a shelter in the noble city of the Florentines, which is named Florence. There all true valor is found; there joy and song and love are perfect and adorned." And if this were true in the earlier years of the thirteenth century, it was still truer of its close; for much of early simplicity and purity of manners had disappeared before the increasing luxury (*le morbidezze d' Egitto,* as Boccaccio terms it) and the gathered wealth of the city,—so that gayety and song more than ever abounded. "It is to be noted," says Giovanni Villani, writing of this time, "it is to be noted that Florence and her citizens were never in a happier condition." The chroniclers tell of constant festivals and celebrations. "In the year 1283, in the month of June, at the feast of St. John, the city of Florence being in a happy and good state of repose,—a tranquil and peaceable state, excellent for merchants and artificers,—there was formed a company of a thousand men or more, all clothed in white dresses, with a leader called the Lord of Love, who devoted themselves to games and sports and dancing, going through the city with trumpets and other instruments of joy and gladness, and feasting often together. And this court lasted for two months, and was the most noble and famous that ever was in Florence or in all Tuscany, and many gentlemen came to it, and many rhymers,[3] and all were welcomed and honorably cared for." Every year, the summer was opened with May and June festivals. Florence was rejoicing in abundance and beauty.[4] Nor was it only in passing gayeties that the cheerful and liberal temper of the people was displayed.

The many great works of Art which were begun and carried on to completion at this time show with what large spirit the whole city was inspired, and under what strong influences of public feeling the early life of Dante was led. Civil liberty and strength were producing their legitimate results. Little republic as she was, Florence was great enough for great undertakings. Never was there such a noble activity within the narrow compass of her walls as from about 1265, when Dante was born, to the end of the century. In these thirty-five years, the stout walls and the tall tower of the Bargello were built, the grand foundations of the Palazzo Vecchio and of the unrivalled Duomo were laid, and both in one year; the Baptistery—*Il mio bel San Giovanni*—was adorned with a new covering of marble; the churches of Sta Maria Novella, of Or San Michele, (changed from its original object,) and Sta Croce,—the finest churches even now in Florence,—were all begun and carried far on to completion. Each new work was at once the fruit and the seed of glorious energy. The small city, of less than one hundred thousand inhabitants, the little republic, not so large as Rhode Island or Delaware, was setting an example which later and bigger and richer republics have not followed.[5] It might well, indeed, be called a "new life" for Florence, as well as for Dante. When it was determined to supply the place of the old church of Santa Reparata with a new cathedral, a decree was passed in words of memorable spirit: "Whereas it is the highest interest

[3] The word in the original (Villani, Book vii. c. 89) is *Giocolari*, the Italian form of the French *jongleur*,—the appellation of those whose profession was to sing or recite the verses of the troubadours or the romances of chivalry.

[4] See Boccaccio, *Decamerone*, Giorn. vi. Nov. 9, for an entertaining picture of Florentine festivities.

[5] The feeling which moved Florence thus to build herself into beauty was one shared by the other Italian republican cities at this time. Venice, Verona, Pisa, Siena, Orvieto, were building or adding to churches and palaces such as have never since been surpassed.

of a people of illustrious origin so to proceed in its affairs that men may perceive from its external works that its doings are at once wise and magnanimous, it is therefore ordered, that Arnolfo, architect of our commune, prepare the model or design for the rebuilding of Santa Reparata, with such supreme and lavish magnificence that neither the industry nor the capacity of man shall be able to devise anything more grand or more beautiful; inasmuch as the most judicious in this city have pronounced the opinion, in public and private conferences, that no work of the commune should be undertaken, unless the design be to make it correspondent with a heart which is of the greatest nature, because composed of the spirit of many citizens united together in one single will."[6] The records of few other cities contain a decree so magnificent as this.

It would be strange, indeed, if the youthful book of one so sensitive to external influences as Dante did not give evidence of sympathy with such pervading emotion. And so apparent is this, that one may say that only at such a period, when strength of sentiment was finding vent in all manner of free expression, was such a book possible. Confidence, frankness, directness in the rendering of personal feeling are rare, except in conditions of society when the emotional spirit is stronger than the critical. The secret of the active power of the arts at this time was the conscious or unconscious resort of those who practised them to the springs of Nature, from which the streams of all true Art proceed. Dante was the first of the moderns to seek Poetry at the same fountain, and to free her from the chains of conventionality which had long bound her. In this he shows his close relation to his times. It is his fidelity to Nature which has made him a leader for all successive generations. The "Vita Nuova" was the beginning of a new school of poetry and of prose as completely as Giotto's O was the beginning of a new school of painting.

The Italian poets, before Dante, may be broadly divided into two classes. The first was that of the troubadours, writing in the Provençal language, hardly to be distinguished from their contemporaries of the South of France, giving expression in their verses to the ideas of love, gallantry, and valor which formed the base of the complex and artificial system of chivalry, repeat-

[6] Cicognara, *Storia della Scultura,* II. 147.

ing constantly the same fancies and thoughts in similar formulas of words, without scope or truth of imagination, with rare exhibitions of individual feeling, with little regard for Nature. Ingenuity is more characteristic of their poetry than force, subtilty more obvious in it than beauty. The second and later class were poets who wrote in the Italian tongue, but still under the influence of the poetic code which had governed the compositions of their Provençal predecessors. Their poetry is, for the most part, a faded copy of an unsubstantial original,—an echo of sounds originally faint. Truth and poetry were effectually divided. In the latter half of the thirteenth century, however, a few poets appeared whose verses give evidence of some native life, and are enlivened by a freer play of fancy and a greater truthfulness of feeling. Guido Guinicelli, who died in 1276, when Dante was eleven years old, and, a little later, Guido Cavalcanti, and some few others, trusting more than had been done before to their own inspiration, show themselves as the forerunners of a better day.[7] But as, in painting, Margheritone and Cimabue, standing between the old and the new styles, exhibit rather a vague striving than a fulfilled attainment, so is it with these poets. There is little that is distinguishingly individual in them. Love is still treated mostly as an abstraction, and one poet might adopt the others' love-verses with few changes of words for any manifest difference in them of personal feeling.

Not so with Dante. The "Vita Nuova," although retaining many ideas, forms, and expressions derived from earlier poets, is his, and could be the work of no other. Nor was he unaware of this difference between himself and those that had gone before him, or ignorant of its nature. In describing himself to Buonagiunta da Lucca in Purgatory, he says, "I am one who, when Love breathes, mark, and according as he dictates within, I report;" to which the poet of Lucca replies, "O brother, now I

[7] Guido Guinicelli will always be less known by his own verses than by Dante's calling him

> father
> Of me and all those better others
> Who sweet chivalric lovelays formed.
> *Purg*. xxvi. 97–99.

And Guido Cavalcanti, "he who took from this other Guido the praise of speech," (*Purg*. xi. 97,) is more famous as Dante's friend than as a poet.

see the knot which kept the Notary and Guittone and me back from that sweet new style which now I hear. I see well how your pens have followed close on the dictator, which truly was not the case with ours."[8] As Love was the common theme of the verses from which Buonagiunta drew his contrast, the difference between them lay plainly in sincerity of feeling and truth of expression. The following close upon the dictates of his heart was the distinguishing merit of Dante's love-poetry over all that had preceded it and most of what has followed it. There are, however, some among his earlier poems in which the "sweet new style" is scarcely heard,—and others, of a later period, in which the accustomed metaphysical and fanciful subtilties of the elder poets are drawn out to an unwonted fineness. These were concessions to a ruling mode,—concessions the more readily made, owing to their being in complete harmony with the strong subtilizing and allegorizing tendencies of Dante's own mind. Still, so far as he adopts the modes of his predecessors in this first book of his, Dante surpasses them all in their own way. He leaves them far behind him, and goes forward to open new paths which he is to tread alone.

But there is yet another tendency of the times, to which Dante, in his later works, has given the fullest and most characteristic expression, and which exhibits itself curiously in the "Vita Nuova." Corresponding with the new ardor for the arts, and in sympathy with it, was a newly awakened and generally diffused ardor for learning, especially for the various branches of philosophy. Science was leaving the cloister, in which she had sat in dumb solitude, and coming out into the world. But the limits and divisions of knowledge were not firmly marked. The relations of learning to life were not clearly understood. The science of mathematics was not yet so advanced as to bind philosophy to exactness. The intellects of men were quickened by a new sense of freedom, and stimulated by ardor of imagination. New worlds of undiscovered knowledge loomed vaguely along the horizon. Philosophy invaded the sphere of poetry, while, on the other hand, poetry gave its form to much of the prevailing philosophy. To be a proper poet was not only to be a writer of verses, but to be a master of learning. Boccaccio describes Guido Cavalcanti as "one of the best logicians in the

[8] *Purg.* xxiv. 58–60.

world, and as a most excellent natural philosopher,"[9] but says nothing of his poetry. Dante, more than any other man of his time, resumed in himself the general zeal for knowledge. His genius had two distinct, and yet often intermingling parts,—the poetic and the scientific. No learning came amiss to him. He was born a scholar, as he was born a poet,—and had he written not a single poem, he would still be famous as the most profound student of his times. Far as he surpassed his contemporaries in poetry, he was no less their superior in the depth and the extent of his knowledge. And this double nature of his genius is plainly shown in many parts of "The New Life." A youthful incapacity to mark clearly the line between the work of the student and the work of the poet is manifest in it. The display of his acquisitions is curiously mingled with the narrative of his emotions. This is not to be charged against him as pedantry. His love of learning partook of the nature of passion; his judgment was not yet able, if indeed it ever became able, to establish the division between the abstractions of the intellect and the affections of the heart. And above all, his early claim of honor as a poet was to be justified by his possession of the fruits of study.

But there was also in Dante a quality of mind which led him to unite the results of knowledge with poetry in a manner almost peculiar to himself. He was essentially a mystic. The dark and hidden side of things was not less present to his imagination than the visible and plain. The range of human capacity in the comprehension of the spiritual world was not then marked by as numerous boundary-stones of failure as now limit the way. Impossibilities were sought for with the same confident hope as realities. The alchemists and the astrologers believed in the attainment of results as tangible and real as those which travellers brought back from the marvellous and still unachieved East. The mystical properties of numbers, the influence of the stars, the powers of cordials and elixirs, the virtues of precious stones, were received as established facts, and opened long vistas of discovery before the student's eyes. Curiosity and speculative inquiry were stimulated by wonder and fed by all the suggestions of heated fancies. Dante, partaking to the full in the eager

[9] *Decamerone*, Giorn. vi. Nov. 9. *Logician* is here to be understood in an extended sense, as the student of letters, or *arts*, as they were then called, in general.

spirit of the times, sharing all the ardor of the pursuit of knowledge, and with a spiritual insight which led him into regions of mystery where no others ventured, naturally connected the knowledge which opened the way for him with the poetic imagination which cast light upon it. To him science was but another name for poetry.

Much learning has been expended in the attempt to show that even the doctrine of Love, which is displayed in "The New Life," is derived, more or less directly, from the philosophy of Plato. It has been supposed that this little autobiographic story, full of the most intimate personal revelations, and glowing with a sincere passion, was written on a preconceived basis of theory. A certain Platonic form of expression, often covering ideas very far removed from those of Plato, was common to the earlier, colder and less truthful poets. Some strains of such Platonism, derived from the poems of his predecessors, are perhaps to be found in this first book of Dante's. But there is nothing to show that he had deliberately adopted the teachings of the ancient philosopher. It may well, indeed, be doubted if at the time of its composition he had read any of Plato's works. Such Platonism as exists in "The New Life" was of that unconscious kind which is shared by every youth of thoughtful nature and sensitive temperament, who makes of his beloved a type and image of divine beauty, and who by the loveliness of the creature is led up to the perfection of the Creator.

The essential qualities of the "Vita Nuova," those which afford direct illustration of Dante's character, as distinguished from those which may be called youthful, or merely literary, or biographical, correspond in striking measure with those of the "Divina Commedia." The earthly Beatrice is exalted to the heavenly in the later poem; but the same perfect purity and intensity of feeling with which she is reverently regarded in the "Divina Commedia" is visible in scarcely less degree in the earlier work. The imagination which makes the unseen seen, and the unreal real, belongs alike to the one and to the other. The "Vita Nuova" is chiefly occupied with a series of visions; the "Divina Commedia" is one long vision. The sympathy with the spirit and impulses of the time, which in the first reveals the youthful impressibility of the poet, in the last discloses itself in maturer forms, in more personal expressions. In the "Vita Nuova" it is a sympathy mastering the natural spirit; in the "Divina Commedia" the sympathy is controlled by the force of established character. The change is that from him who follows to him who commands. It is the privilege of men of genius, not only to give more than others to the world, but also to receive more from it. Sympathy, in its full comprehensiveness, is the proof of the strongest individuality. By as much as Dante or Shakspeare learnt of and entered into the hearts of men, by so much was his own nature strengthened and made peculiarly his own. The "Vita Nuova" shows the first stages of that genius, the first proofs of that wide sympathy, which at length resulted in the "Divine Comedy." It is like the first blade of spring grass, rich with the promise of the golden harvest.

II

Were the author of the "Vita Nuova" unknown, its story of youth and love would still possess a charm, as standing in the dawn of modern literature,—the first book in which modern sentiment finds free expression. It would be of interest, as contrasted with the later growth of the sentimental element in literature, which speedily exhibits the influence of factitious feeling, of self-conscious effort, and of ambitious display. The sentiment of the "Vita Nuova" is separated by the wide gulf that lies between simplicity and affectation from the sentimentality of Petrarch's sonnets. But connected as it is with Dante's life,—the first of that series of works in which truth, intensity, and tenderness of feeling are displayed as in the writings of no other man,—its interest no longer arises merely from itself and from its place in literature, but becomes indissolubly united with that which belongs by every claim to the "Divina Commedia" and to the life of Dante.

When the "Vita Nuova" was completed, Dante was somewhat less than twenty-eight years old. Beatrice had died between two and three years before, in 1290; and he seems to have pleased himself after her loss by recalling to his memory the sweet incidents of her life, and of her influence upon himself. He begins with the words:—

"In that part of the book of my memory before which little can be read is found a rubric which says: *Incipit Vita Nova* ['The New Life begins']. Under which rubric I find the words written which it is my intention to copy into this little book,— if not all of them, at least their meaning."

This introduction, short as it is, exhibits a characteristic trait of Dante's mind, in the declaration of his intention to copy from the book of his memory, or, in other words, to write the true records of experience. Truth was the chief quality of his intellect, and upon this, as upon an unshaken foundation, rest the marvellous power and consistency of his imaginations. His heart spoke clearly, and he interpreted its speech plainly in his words. His tendency to mysticism often, indeed, led him into strange fancies; but these, though sometimes obscure, are never vague. . . . It happened one day that he was taken, by a friend who thought to give him pleasure, to a feast at which many ladies were present. "They were assembled," he says, "to attend a lady who was married that day, and, according to the custom of the city, they bore her company at her first sitting at table in the dwelling of her new husband." Dante, believing thus to do pleasure to his friend, proposed to stand in waiting upon these ladies. But at the moment of this intention he felt a sudden tremor, which caused him to lean for support against a painting which ran round the wall,[10] and, raising his eyes, he beheld Beatrice. His confusion became apparent; and the ladies, not excepting Beatrice herself, laughed at his strange appearance. Then his friend took him from their presence, and having asked him what so ailed him, Dante replied, "I have set my feet on that edge of life beyond which no man can go with intent to return." Then leaving him, he went to the chamber of tears, weeping and ashamed; and in his trouble he wrote a sonnet to Beatrice, in which he says, that, if she had known the cause of his trouble, he believes that she would have felt pity for him.[11]

[10] This is, perhaps, the earliest reference in modern literature to the use of painting as a decoration for houses. It is probable that it was a recent application of the art, and resulted from the revival of interest in its works which accompanied the revival of the art. We shall have occasion again to note a reference to painting.

[11] To this period, apparently, belong Sonnets xxix. and xxx. of the general cellection. The last may not unlikely have been omitted in the *Vita Nuova* on account of the tenderness with which the death of Beatrice had invested every memory of her, preventing the insertion of a poem which might seem harsh in its expression:—

I curse the day on which I first beheld
The light of thy betraying eyes.

From "The New Life" of Dante

The foregoing passage, like many others in the "Vita Nuova," is full of the intense and exaggerated expressions of passionate feeling. But this feeling is recorded with a frank simplicity which carries conviction of the sincerity of emotion. It may be laughed at, but it cannot be doubted. It is possible, though hardly probable, that the scene took place at the wedding festival of Beatrice herself. She was married sometime previous to 1287, and unless a reference to this event be found here, no notice of it is taken by Dante in what he has written concerning her. That the fact of her marriage changed in no degree the feeling with which Dante regarded her is plain. His love was of no low quality, to be altered by earthly circumstance. It was a love of the soul. No change or separation that left the being untouched could part him from it. To the marriage of true souls there was no impediment, and he would admit none, in her being the wife of another. The qualities which she possessed as a maiden belonged to her no less as a wife.

It was in the same year, probably, as that in which the "Vita Nuova" was composed and published, that Dante himself was married to Gemma Donati. There are stories that their married life was unhappy. But these stories have not the weight of even contemporary gossip. Possibly they arose from the fact of the long separation between Dante and his wife during his exile. Boccaccio insinuates more than he asserts, and he concludes a vague declamation about the miseries of married life with the words, "Truly I do not affirm that these things happened to Dante, *for I do not know*." Dante keeps utter silence in his works,—certainly giving no reason to suppose that domestic trials were added to his other burdens. One thing is known which deserves remembrance,—that, when, after some years, a daughter was born to him, the name which she received was Beatrice. . . .

With the incomparable sonnet, "so gentle and so modest does appear," [Dante closes] that part of the "Vita Nuova" which relates to the life of Beatrice. It fitly completes the golden record of youth. Its tender lines are the epitaph of happy days, and in them is found that mingled sweetness and sadness which in this world are always the final expression of love. Its tone is that of the wind of autumn sighing among the leaves of spring. Beneath its outward meaning lies a prophecy of joy,—but that joy is to be reached only through the gates of death.

III

The year 1289 was one marked in the annals of Florence and of Italy by events which are still famous, scored by the genius of Dante upon the memory of the world. It was in this year that Count Ugolino and his sons and grandsons were starved by the Pisans in their tower prison. A few months later, Francesca da Rimini was murdered by her husband. Between the dates of these two terrible events the Florentines had won the great victory of Campaldino; and thus, in this short space, the materials had been given to the poet for the two best-known and most powerful stories and for one of the most striking episodes of the "Divina Commedia."

In the great and hard-fought battle of Campaldino Dante himself took part. "I was at first greatly afraid," he says, in a letter of which but a few sentences have been preserved,[12]—"but at the end I felt the greatest joy,—according to the various chances of the battle." When the victorious army returned to Florence, a splendid procession, with the clergy at its head, with the arts of the city each under its banner, and with all manner of pomp, went out to meet it. There were long-continued feasts and rejoicings. The battle had been fought on the 11th of June, the day of St. Barnabas, and the Republic, though already engaged in magnificent works of church-building, decreed that a new church should be erected in honor of the Saint on whose day the victory had been won.

A little later in that summer, Dante was one of a troop of Florentines who joined the forces of Lucca in levying war upon the Pisan territory. The stronghold of Caprona was taken, and Dante was present at its capture; for he says, (*Inferno*, xxi. 94–96,) "I saw the foot-soldiers, who, having made terms, came out from Caprona, afraid when they beheld themselves among so many enemies."[13]

Thus, during a great part of the summer of 1289, Dante was in active service as a soldier. He was no lovesick idler, no mere

[12] See Lionardo Aretino's *Vita di Dante.*

[13] Landino, and most of the commentators after him, state that Dante refers in this passage to the fear of the garrison taken in the place when it was recaptured the next year by the Pisans. But as Florence and Pisa continued at desperate enmity, Dante could hardly have witnessed this latter scene.

home-keeping writer of verses, but was already taking his part in the affairs of the state which he was afterwards to be called on for a time to assist in governing, and he was laying up those stores of experience which were to serve as the material out of which his vivifying imagination was to form the great national poem of Italy. But of this active life, of these personal engagements, of these terrible events which took such strong possession of his soul, there is no word, no suggestion even, in the book of his "New Life." In it there is no echo, however faint, of those storms of public violence and private passion which broke dark over Italy. In the midst of the tumults which sprang from the jealousies of rival states, from the internal discords of cities, from the divisions of parties, from the bitterness of domestic quarrels, —this little book is full of tenderness and peace, and tells its story of love as if the world were the abode of tranquillity. No external excitements could break into the inner chambers of Dante's heart to displace the love that dwelt within them. The contrast between the purity and the serenity of the "Vita Nuova" and the coarseness and cruelty of the deeds that were going on while it was being written is complete. Every man in some sort leads a double life,—one real and his own, the other seeming and the world's,—but with few is the separation so entire as it was with Dante.

But in these troubled times the "New Life" was drawing to its close. The spring of 1290 had come, and the poet, now twenty-five years old, sixteen years having passed since he first beheld Beatrice, was engaged in writing a poem to tell what effect the virtue of his lady wrought upon him. He had written but a portion when it was broken off, never to be resumed . . .

> I was yet engaged upon this Canzone [he writes], and had finished the above stanza, when the Lord of justice called this most gentle one unto glory under the banner of that holy Queen Mary whose name was ever spoken with greatest reverence by this blessed Beatrice.
>
> And although it might give pleasure, were I now to tell somewhat of her departure from us, it is not my intention to treat of it here for three reasons. The first is, that it is no part of the present design, as may be seen in the proem of this little book. The second is, that, supposing it were so, my pen would not be sufficient to treat of it in a fitting manner. The third is, that, supposing both the one and the other, it would not be becoming in me to treat of it, since, in doing so, I should be obliged to praise myself,—a thing altogether blameworthy in whosoever

does it,—and therefore I leave this subject to some other narrator.

Nevertheless, since in what precedes there has been occasion to make frequent mention of the number nine,[14] and apparently not without reason, and since in her departure this number appeared to have a large place, it is fitting to say something on this point, seeing that it seems to belong to our design. . . . I say, that, according to the mode of reckoning in Italy, her most noble soul departed in the first hour of the ninth day of the month; and according to the reckoning, in Syria, she departed in the ninth month of the year, since the first month there is Tismim, which with us is October; and according to our reckoning she departed in that year of our indiction, that is, of the years of the Lord, in which the perfect number[15] was completed for the ninth time in that century in which she had been set in the world; and she was of the Christians of the thirteenth century[16] . . .

A certain passage in the "Vita Nuova" is of peculiar interest, as illustrating the personal tastes of Dante, and the common modes of his life. "I was drawing," he says, "the figure of an Angel;" and this statement is the more noticeable, because Giotto, the man who set painting on its modern course, was not yet old enough to have exercised any influence upon Dante.[17]

[14] In the earlier part of the *Vita Nuova* there are many references to this number. We translate in full the passage given above, as one of the most striking illustrations of Dante's youthful fondness for seeking for the mystical relations and inner meanings of things. The attributing such importance to the properties of the number nine, though it might at first view seem puerile and an indication of poverty of feeling, was a portion of the superstitious belief of the age, in which Dante naturally shared. The mysterious properties of numbers were a subject of serious study, and were connected with various branches of science and of life.

[15] The perfect number is ten.

[16] Thus it appears that Beatrice died on the 9th of June, 1290. She was a little more than twenty-four years old.

[17] In this year, 1291, Giotto was but fifteen years old, and probably a student with Cimabue. Benvenuto da Imola, who lectured publicly at Bologna on the *Divina Commedia* in the year 1378, reports, that, while Giotto, still a young man, was painting at Padua, Dante visited him. And Vasari says, that it was a tradition, that Giotto had painted, in a chapel at Naples, scenes out of the *Apocalypse*, from designs furnished him by the poet. If we may believe another tradition, which there seems indeed little reason to doubt, Giotto went to Ravenna during the last years of Dante's life, that he might spend there some time in company with his exiled friend.

From "The New Life" of Dante

The friendship which afterwards existed between them had its beginning at a later period. At this time Cimabue still held the field. He often painted angels around the figures of the Virgin and her Child; and in his most famous picture, in the Church of Sta. Maria Novella, there are certain angels of which Vasari says, with truth, that, though painted in the Greek manner, they show an approach toward the modern style of drawing. These angels may well have seemed beautiful to eyes accustomed to the hard unnaturalness of earlier works. The love of Art pervaded Florence, and a nature so sensitive and so sympathetic as Dante's could not but partake of it in the fullest measure. Art was then no adjunct of sentimentalism, no encourager of idleness. It was connected with all that was most serious and all that was most delightful in life. It is difficult, indeed, to realize the delight which it gave, and the earnestness with which it was followed at this period, when it seemed, as by a miracle, to fling off the winding-sheet which had long wrapped its stiffened limbs, and to come forth with new and unexampled life.

The strength and the intelligence of Dante's love of Art are shown in many beautiful passages and allusions in the "Divina Commedia." There was something of universality, not only in his imagination, but also in his acquisitions. Of the sources of learning which were then open, there was not one which he had not visited; of the fountains of inspiration, not one out of which he had not drunk. All the arts—poetry, painting, sculpture, and music—were alike dear to him. His Canzoni were written to be sung; and one of the most charming scenes in the great poem is that in which is described his meeting with his friend Casella, the musician, who sang to him one of his own Canzoni so sweetly, that "the sweetness still within me sounds."

"Dante took great delight in music, and was an excellent draughtsman," says Aretino, his second biographer; and Boccaccio reports, that in his youth he took great pleasure in music, and was the friend of all the best musicians and singers of his time. There is, perhaps, in the whole range of literature, no nobler homage to Art than that which is contained in the tenth and twelfth cantos of the "Purgatory," in which Dante represents the Creator himself as using its means to impress the lessons of truth upon those whose souls were being purified for the final attainment of heaven. . . . The sonnet, "Beyond the sphere that widest orbit hath," was the last of the poems which Dante composed in immediate honor and memory of Beatrice, and is the last of those which he inserted in the "Vita Nuova." It was not that his love grew cold, or that her image became faint in his remembrance; but, as he tells us in a few concluding and memorable words, from this time forward he devoted himself to preparation for a work in which the earthly Beatrice should have less part, while the heavenly and blessed spirit of her whom he had loved should receive more becoming honors. The lover's grief was to find no more expression; the lamentations for the loss which could never be made good to him were to cease; the exhibition of a personal sorrow was at an end. Love and grief, in their double ministry, had refined, enlarged, and exalted his spirit to the conception of a design unparalleled in its nature, and of which no intellectual genius, unpurged by suffering, and unpenetrated in its deepest recesses by the spiritualizing heats of emotion, would have been capable of conceiving. Moreover, as time wore on, its natural result was gradually to withdraw the poet from the influence of temporary excitements of feeling, resulting from his experience of love and death, and to bring him to the contemplation of life as affected by the presence and the memory of Beatrice in its eternal and universal relations. He tells us in the "Convito," that,

> after some time, my mind, which neither such consolation as I could give it, nor that offered to it by others, availed to comfort, determined to turn to that method by which others in grief had consoled themselves. And I set myself to read that book, but little known, of Boethius, in which in prison and exile he had consoled himself. And hearing, likewise, that Tully had written a book, in which, treating of friendship, he had offered some words of comfort to Lælius, a most excellent man, on the death of Scipio, his friend, I read this also. And although at first it was hard for me to enter into their meaning, I at length entered into it so far as my knowledge of language, and such little capacity as I had, enabled me; by means of which capacity, I had already, like one dreaming, seen many things, as may be seen in the "New Life." And as it might happen that a man seeking silver should, beyond his expectation, find gold, which a hidden chance presents to him, not, perhaps, without Divine direction, so I, who sought for consolation, found not only a remedy for my tears, but also acquaintance with authors, with knowledge, and with books.

From "The New Life" of Dante

Nor did these serious and solitary studies withdraw him from the pursuit of wisdom among men and in the active world. Year by year, he entered more fully into the affairs of state, and took a larger portion of their conduct upon himself.

His heart kept fresh by abiding recollections of love, his faith quickened by and intermingled with the tenderest hopes, his imagination uplifted by the affection which overleaped the boundaries of the invisible world, and his intellect disciplined by study of books and of men, his experience enlarged by constant occupation in affairs, his judgment matured by the quick succession of important events in which he was involved,—every part of his nature was thus prepared for the successful accomplishment of that great and sacred design which he set before himself now in his youth. Heaven had called and selected him for a work which even in his own eyes partook somewhat of the nature of a prophetic charge. His strength was to be tested and his capacity to be approved. Life was ordered for the fulfilment of his commission. The men to whom God intrusts a message for the world find the service to which they are appointed one in which they must be ready to sacrifice everything. Dante looked forward, even at the beginning, to the end, and saw what lay between.

The pages of the "New Life" fitly close with words of that life in which all things shall be made new, "and there shall be no more death, neither sorrow, nor crying, neither shall there be any more pain; for the former things are passed away." The little book ends thus:—

> Soon after this, a wonderful vision appeared to me, in which I saw things which made me purpose to speak no more of this blessed one until I could more worthily treat of her. And to attain to this, I study to the utmost of my power, as she truly knoweth. So that, if it shall please Him through whom all things live, that my life be prolonged for some years, I hope to speak of her as never was spoken of any woman. And then may it please Him who is the Lord of Grace, that my soul may go to behold the glory of its lady, the blessed Beatrice, who in glory looks upon the face of Him, *qui est per omnia sæcula benedictus* [who is Blessed forever]!

In 1320, or perhaps not till 1321, the "Paradiso" was finished; in 1321, Dante died.

XV

ALDO S. BERNARDO

Dante, Petrarch, and Boccaccio

Introduction

The period encompassed by the essays in this volume was historically as earth-shaking as our own mid-twentieth century. Political, social, and intellectual upheaval was such as to signal not only the rise of the democratic institutions that have since sought to assert themselves in a variety of forms, but the birth of a nationalism whose momentum has only recently begun to show signs of arrest. It is strange, therefore, to see the European nations that were in the vanguard of these developments seeking their cultural roots in the Middle Ages, that period when Europe had last known any form of unity. And yet, it is also generally recognized that the Romantic "discovery" of the Middle Ages sprang from a desire to unearth a past anchored in independence and individuality of spirit. That Dante, Petrarch, and Boccaccio should all three have seriously attracted the attention of English writers and men of letters of the time attests to their universal appeal regardless of national boundaries. This universality, as we shall see, resulted from the breadth and depth that each gave to a particular literary perspective.

With the end of the nineteenth century, when the study of these three writers moved from the cultured audience of polite society and men of letters to the "thorny groves of Academe," their general significance and importance spread beyond European shores and invaded America. The deeper insights into their life and times provided further evidence of their unparalleled greatness as representatives of a crucial cultural epoch. To show how the stature of all three has evolved in the last three centuries is the purpose of this concluding essay.

Dante

I

If there is one point on which Dante scholars agree, it is that confusion still reigns over what constitutes the "greatness" or "beauty" of the *Divine Comedy*. This is as true among Italian scholars as it is among English and American ones. Despite the obvious danger of oversimplification, one can safely generalize the history of this confusion by asserting that it started in that early period of the Italian Renaissance when, in reaction against the tendency of the Humanists to frown upon the use of the vernacular, Bembo led the movement to restore dignity to Italian as a literary language. To Bembo's contention that the primary merits of the *Divine Comedy* lay in its doctrinal values, a relatively obscure Florentine man of letters, Vincenzo Borghini, responded that he considered such values "as servants of that poem, and not as overseers, and I admire the poet as a poet, and not as a philosopher or theologian."[1] What makes Dante a great poet, Borghini concludes, are certain inventive qualities which he outlines, and not "the sciences, which should be learned by turning to such sources as Aristotle or learned theologians, and not to Dante who is not read for this purpose."[2]

The next milestone in the development of this antithesis or dichotomy in Dante criticism comes with Vico, who, in an attempt to make Dante fit neatly into his theory of the three ages, maintained that Dante would have been a great poet indeed, "if he had known nothing either of scholasticism nor of Latin." Indeed, Dante's learning had a negative effect on his poetry, whose foundations consist exclusively of "imagination."[3]

The subsequent evolution of the dichotomy through the Romantic and Positivistic eras that in turn reacted against the elimination of those elements in the *Comedy* indicative of the poet's life, learning, and times, since they possessed so much in common with the political and cultural situation of the early nineteenth century, is too well known to require elaboration here.[4] It might be well to recall, however, that as a result of the excesses into which some of the mid-nineteenth-century critics fell (some maintaining, indeed, that the poetic qualities of the *Comedy* re-

[1] Carlo Grabner, "Tre grandi tappe della critica sulla 'Divina Comedia': Borghini, Vico, De Sanctis," in *Dante nella critica d'oggi*, ed. Umberto Bosco, (Firenze, 1965), p. 315.

[2] *Ibid.*, p. 316.

[3] *Ibid.*, p. 317.

[4] See Aldo Vallone, "Studi sulla fortuna e sulla storia dell'esegesi di Dante," with complete bibliography, in *Dante nella critica*, pp. 227–37.

sided exclusively in the solution of problems relating to the fundamental allegory of the poem), there arose a De Sanctis whose views on Dante represent not only a return to the distinction between what is and what is not poetry in the *Comedy* but the original seeds that gave birth to Croce's position, which, moving beyond Vico's antithesis between imagination and reason, poetry and culture, defined the distinction as between "poetry" and "structure." In actuality, De Sanctis held a moderate position by maintaining that the *Comedy* is great poetry because Dante paradoxically achieved something contrary to what he set about doing. While he meant to write a didactic work based on medieval doctrine and poetics, his natural artistry enabled him to admit "air and light" into the dull and lifeless world of abstractions. For De Sanctis, therefore, those portions of the *Comedy* reflecting moral, political, or religious concerns or having allegorical implications often, though not always, become poetry as a result of Dante's natural genius. "While he pursues a syllogism, the light of the image shines forth. And while he theologizes, the flame of feeling bursts out." On the contrary, for Croce and his followers, who continue to exert a strong influence on Dante criticism, these very elements constitute the "structure" and non-poetic portion of the *Comedy*.[5]

Croce's theories formally dominated Dante criticism between the first appearance of his book, *La poesia di Dante*, on the occasion of the seven hundredth anniversary of Dante's death in 1921 and, roughly, 1945. But by 1965, on the occasion of the seven hundredth anniversary of Dante's birth, an Italian critic could write: "In other words, we have understood that such criticism led, of necessity, to too many reservations and limitations, or rather, to a consideration and fragmentary (and antihistorical) evaluation of the poem. This results in the negation of or forgetting the inherent structural, doctrinal and exhortatory values of the *Comedy*. . . . On the basis of these ideas we have emphasized the great importance of the doctrinal, ethical, political and religious world of the *Comedy;* and we have asserted that the very poetry of the poem springs from that world, by virtue of

[5] See Grabner, pp. 318–31. Mario Fubini has recently shown how unfair it is to restrict Croce's views to the thesis appearing in his 1921 study. There is ample evidence that Croce modified his view extensively during his last years. See Fubini's study "Rileggendo 'La Poesia di Dante' di Benedetto Croce," in *Dante nella critica,* pp. 17–19.

and because of the world, and not in opposition or despite it."[6]

Of perhaps even greater interest is Natalino Sapegno's assertion on a similar occasion in 1965: "One will probably be forced to abandon not merely certain of Croce's critical opinions but his entire system if one is to adopt the kind of critical position we have outlined–in which poetry is no longer conceived as existing in timeless categories, and in which it is recognized that the form and essence of each work of poetry are always determined in strict relation to the history and culture of the period in which it was born."[7]

Most significant, however, is Sapegno's admission that what is really about to happen is a return to the work of Dante's earliest commentators, now that we can "approach the evaluation of the medieval heritage without bias." Having "repudiated all polemical attitudes derived from Humanism, the Renaissance, the Enlightenment or even from Romanticism," and having developed "a thoroughly mature historical sense," we are now in a position to take up and continue the work of the early commentators. "We have found our way back to the path which they were following and which their immediate successors lost. For, despite a certain ingenuousness, those early commentators were essentially on the right lines: they had no axe to grind and they interpreted Dante's poetry by methods that were in harmony with its spirit." Thus, in the forty-four years that marked the distance between the seven hundredth anniversaries of Dante's death and birth, Dante criticism has moved from a position that was about as alien to Dante and his times as could be imagined, to a position which calls for a reading of the poem "of which Dante's first commentators in the fourteenth century offer a permanent example."[8]

II

As the essays in this volume indicate, the fortune of Dante and his *Comedy* fared somewhat differently in England and

[6] Bruno Maier, "Le principali 'Cruces' della 'Divina Commedia' nella critica contemporanea," in *Dante nella critica*, p. 274.

[7] "Genesis and Structure: Two Approaches to the Poetry of the 'Comedy,'" in *The Mind of Dante*, ed. U. Limentani (Cambridge, 1965), pp. 15–16.

[8] See also Francesco Mazzoni, "La critica dantesca del secolo XIV," in *Dante nella critica*, pp. 285–91.

America. Unlike the case in Italy where a Boccaccio could give formal public lectures on the *Comedy* a very few years after Dante's death, Dante was not truly discovered in England until the eighteenth century and in America not until the nineteenth. In both countries, furthermore, the interest remained strictly amateurish until the latter part of the nineteenth century. In both countries the Protestant heritage caused readers to shy away from the role played by the doctrinal elements in the *Comedy* in creating the "power" and "intensity" that everyone readily acknowledged as being present in the poem. While the Romantic concern for moral meaning in judging a work of art did prompt a Coleridge to speak of a "combination of poetry with doctrine," in general other explanations were sought to account for the effectiveness of the *Comedy*, and the problem never became an actual issue.

It is interesting to note that it was with an art historian, Charles Eliot Norton, that the study of Dante passed into the universities. This lingering interest in Dante's artistry was in part responsible for saving Dante studies from the fate that befell so many past masters during the heyday of positivistic scholarship when the scrutiny of biographical, historical, and philological facts was the primary concern of both scholar and critic. Thus in England we find, between the last decades of the nineteenth century and 1921, the painstaking and erudite scholarship of Edward Moore and of Paget Toynbee counterbalanced by such critical studies as Edmund Gardner's *Dante and the Mystics* and P. H. Wicksteed's *Dante and Aquinas* (both 1913).

The period between the two world wars proved lean ones for Dante studies in England. Except for the continuing work of Moore, Toynbee, Gardner and Wicksteed, the only bright light on the horizon of British Dante studies during this period was Cesare Foligno, whose long tenure of the chair of Italian at Oxford kept Italian studies very much alive among English scholars.[9]

Following World War II, interest in Dante studies in England underwent a steady increase. The new focus was on interpretation, meaning, and value of Dante's work as a whole, but particularly of the *Comedy*. This renewed interest was stimulated

[9] Perhaps the names of T. S. Eliot, for his brief excursion of 1929, and of W. H. V. Reade also deserve mention here.

in part by the many studies appearing in Italy, France, and the United States that posed old problems in new terms. As Kenelm Foster has pointed out, the common denominator of all these studies was the new attempt to see in the *Comedy* the fullest expression of Dante's personality.[10] The primary areas of investigation thus became the general structure and meaning of the poem and revolved about three themes: (1) Dante's philosophy and theology; (2) his use of symbol and allegory; (3) the relation of the poem to Dante's minor works, particularly whether its doctrinal and moral position was consistent with the positions taken in the *Convivio* and the *Monarchia*. "So," Foster concludes, "the stress tends to fall on doctrine—not, of course, as mere theory but as involved in the poet's life and emotions—and this in turn leads to a stress on biography." Strictly critical or linguistic considerations in turn tended to recede until the 1960's.

The principal issue on which English critics and scholars concentrated was whether the dualism that was clearly present in the *Convivio* and the *Monarchia* in connection with the independence of philosophy from theology, of civil power from the Church, and of man's two final ends was also present in the *Comedy*. The effect of the presence, or absence, of this dualism on the "humanism" of the poem and on the interpretation of such figures as Virgil and Beatrice thus became the primary preoccupations of such English writers as J. H. Whitfield, D. Sayers, C. Hardie, and K. Foster between 1947 and 1960. Of these four critics, C. Hardie, a classicist by training, takes the most extreme position on the discontinuity theme. For Hardie, Dante's poem represents a return to a truly integral Christianity following a period of near-paganism in the *Convivium* and *Monarchia*. Dante's return to Christianity is closely allied to his return to poetry. In short, Dante's religious calling is identical with his inescapable calling as a poet. According to Hardie, the fusion of these two moments was so compelling that such difficult allegories of the *Comedy* as the puzzling procession at the end of the Purgatory or the enigmatic DXV, can be seen to refer respectively to Dante's personal spiritual drama and to his conviction that he had been divinely ordained to lead the world

[10] The bulk of this section is based on Foster's "Dante Studies in England, 1921–1964," *Italian Studies*, 20 (1965): 1–16.

back to the straight path. Hardie's conviction that the deeper sense of the *Comedy* lies in its being viewed as a vehicle for Dante's individual salvation and divine mission is so strong that it eventually led him to question the authenticity of the letter to Can Grande.

Between 1961 and 1964, again according to Foster, the only discernible shift of emphasis in British Dante Studies was in the direction of Dante's literary and linguistic development prior to the *Comedy*. The "continuity" thesis, however, still holds the attention of some scholars who, like Cecil Grayson, question Hardie's position. Similarly, Hardie and others continue examining the wider aspects of doctrine and symbolic expression in Dante's works. Still other younger critics openly reject the distinction between "poetry" and "structure" in the *Inferno*.[11]

In England, then, the De Sanctis-Croce poetics had little or no influence on Dante studies. In fact, textual and philological work held sway in England during the period of De Sanctis' popularity in Italy. Similarly, a distinct lull occurred at a time when Croce's position was being hotly debated among Dante scholars in Italy. It appears almost as though English Dante studies marked time as they awaited the outcome of the Crocean debate. A new spark appeared following World War II when the inevitable pendulum swing began to move away from Croce's world. The "message" or "structure" of the *Divine Comedy* would simply not be overlooked, and English critics who had generally always felt most at home with these aspects of the *Comedy* once again began turning to the poem.

III

While Dante's fortune in America followed a course not too unlike the case in England, a number of signs point to a more abiding concern for and interest in the various dimensions of meaning in the *Divine Comedy*.[12] As early as 1817, however, Francis Gray, a diplomat and political figure, carefully distin-

[11] A. C. Charity, "Dante and the Aesthetes," *Blackfriars*, 44 (1963): 452–63.

[12] For more detailed information the reader is referred to the indispensable study of Angelina la Piana, *Dante in America* (New Haven, 1948) as supplemented by Howard R. Marraro, "Dante negli Stati Uniti," in *Dante nel mondo* (Firenze, 1965), pp. 433–559.

guished between the narrative structure and poetic greatness of the *Comedy* on the one hand and its mystical and doctrinal character on the other. For Gray, no one well acquainted with the Italian language should experience difficulty in grasping the former. On the other hand, many early American lovers of Dante did find the universal moral lesson of his poem as it related to the drama of sin, expiation, and retribution appealing and important for a proper appreciation of the poem. There were even those who, like Margaret Fuller, a disciple of Emerson, viewed the *Comedy* as a work of high philosophical speculation and profound spiritual experience. Nor were there lacking hostile critics such as Samuel Gilman Brown, who in 1846 expressed his dismay at Dante's "grossness" and "vindictiveness" while at the same time conceding that the power of his poetry lay in the Hegelian concept of pure imagination.

A similar disparity of views existed among the famed "Cantabrigian triad," to cull an expression from Miss La Piana, who seems to have some doubt whether the Harvard days of Longfellow, Lowell, and Norton (1836–1908) did indeed mark the classical age of Dante in America. For Longfellow the allegory of the *Comedy* constituted a blemish rather than a beauty. In fact, he could never be persuaded that the poem from start to finish was an allegory that served as a kind of scaffold on which Dante's poetry hung as an ornamental feature.

James Russell Lowell, on the other hand, credited the *Comedy* with what love of learning he possessed. While he displayed little patience with the commentators of minutiae, he realized that "in the allegory lies the profound meaning and the permanent force of the *Divine Comedy*."

Unlike his two predecessors, Charles Eliot Norton came to the *Comedy* following a thorough immersion in the beauties and mysteries of the *Vita Nuova*. Progressing from a literal interpretation of Dante's youthful work to an acceptance of a studied allegory underlying the narrative, Norton could not avoid grasping the important role played by allegory in the *Divine Comedy*. The Introduction to his famous translation affords ample evidence of this.

Nor was Norton alone in moving from a strictly literal interpretation of Dante to one in which allegorical meaning played a central role. There were others, like William Torrey Harris, famed American Hegelian, whose change of position represented a still more radical shift. As a young man, Harris considered the *Comedy* highly childish. Later he became so taken with the infinite possibilities of inner meaning in the poem that, to cite Miss La Piana, he "made Dante express himself in the vaporous language of a nineteenth-century German professor of philosophy." In fact, in his book *The Spiritual Sense of the "Divina Commedia"* (New York, 1889) Harris considers Dante's doctrine of Hell "the first appearance in a conceptive form of the deepest of all comprehensions of Personality." As a result, Dante was able to conceive of a citizen as "completely universal by the laws of the state as in modern times."

With the turn of the century, as Dante's general popularity in America declined, scholarly research on the poet and his works began appearing with greater frequency in new learned periodicals, editions, and studies. The "Dante furore" that had marked the turn of the century was superseded by a critical appreciation of Dante's artistry and thought. It is at this point that the symbolic and allegorical dimensions of the *Comedy* came under ever increasing scrutiny. Thus, in his famous edition which began appearing in 1909 Grandgent states: "I have tried to give the 'allegorical and true meaning', as Dante calls it, the place it deserves, but seldom receives, beside the literal." In trying to explain Dante's enduring power across the centuries Grandgent concedes that it does not lie primarily in his theological and philosophical learning, nor in his symbolism and allegory. Yet, while not in sympathy with those who would apply to the *Comedy* the medieval method of Biblical exegesis with its multiple symbolism, Grandgent does not overlook the importance of respecting the poet's desire to be understood allegorically.

In 1910 George Santayana expounded his view whereby Lucretius, Dante, and Goethe sum up the chief phases of European philosophy, naturalism, supernaturalism, and romanticism. For Dante, the soul is but a pilgrim on earth, the world is fallen, pain and suffering are normal, and happiness is impossible in this life. Santayana indeed prophetically held that "the science and philosophy of Dante did not have to be put in verse in order to become poetry; they were poetry fundamentally and in their essence. . . . Dante's vision of the universe, where all is love, magic and symbolism, may charm mankind exclusively as poetry," but only in some future time. Then "no one will think of reproaching Dante with his bad science, and bad history, and minute theology. These will not seem blemishes in his poetry, but an integral part of it."

The *Vita Nuova* also had scholarly adherents who regarded its symbolic and allegorical significance as indispensable elements for a proper grasp of its meaning. Thus, in the notes to his edition of Dante's youthful work which first appeared in 1922, Kenneth McKenzie reminds the reader that Dante also subscribed to the medieval view which considered allegory as containing a higher truth than reality. In his method of allegorizing, however, Dante did not intend to make the allegory correspond perfectly to the original reality. "The method of Dante is to start with a literal meaning and proceed thence to the allegorical; the latter being more 'true' because in accord with permanent underlying principles."

The end of the first World War, unlike the case in England, marked the start of the ascendency of the symbolist school of Dante scholars in America. Jefferson Butler Fletcher first showed the way with his *Dante* (New York, 1916). Perhaps the most important contribution of this study lies in its calling attention to the fact that to understand the *Comedy* a reader must be acquainted with all of Dante's works. Unlike St. Augustine's, Dante's confessions are not to be found in one book. They are scattered through several works, especially the *Vita Nuova*, the *Convivium* and the *Divine Comedy*. Like St. Augustine, however, Dante too tried to trace "his own progress from bad to good, and from good to better, and from better to best." He also undertakes to describe his spiritual evolution, not for purposes of self-glorification, but for the greater glory of God. In fact, "Dante is not his own hero in his writings . . . his true hero, his real protagonist is God. The action of his drama is how God drew him to himself by the agency of Beatrice."

According to Fletcher, for Dante "all reality is symbolic . . . the higher allegory is only the inner truth of reality." The *Vita Nuova* shows how love captured the poet's heart first in a transitory way and finally through grace of God became permanent. "In other words, the inner truth of which his experience was but a running symbol or allegory written by God's hand, reached his sense-darkened mind at first only confusedly, then as veil after veil is lifted, with perfect clarity." In a second book, *The Symbolism of the Divine Comedy* (New York, 1921),

Fletcher tries to show how the many threads of Dante's tapestry become fused in the *Paradiso*, where Dante depicts himself spiritually uplifted to the level of a revealer and a prophet. Dante's letter to Cangrande provides clear proof of this, in Fletcher's opinion. Most importantly, a reader of Dante must understand that the poet wanted him to believe in the unbroken continuity and unity of his symbolism.

As was to be expected, there were also symbolists who interpreted Dante in a highly esoteric fashion. In her book, *Symbolism in Medieval Thought and its Consummation in the Divine Comedy* (1929), Helen Flanders Dunbar, like Fletcher before her, also considered Dante's letter to Cangrande basic evidence of Dante's conscious use of symbolism. Dante's statement that writings may be taken and should be understood chiefly in four senses has led to chaotic confusion among his commentators and interpreters. This, in turn, has led some critics to view the *Comedy* primarily as an aesthetic and imaginative masterpiece in which the symbolism plays no role whatsoever. Others have disagreed and have emphasized the confessional nature of the poem or its patriotic and social intent. Still others have concentrated on the ethical, philosophical, or mystical values contained in the poem. According to Miss Dunbar, these critics are all right and all wrong. She then proceeds to give an exaggerated esoteric interpretation of the *Comedy* based on primitive religions and rites. She is convinced that the core of Dante's symbolism comes from esoteric sources that had been integrated into Christianity by Dante's time but that also persisted as an essential part of the medieval interest in magic. Despite the questionableness of her interpretation, Miss Dunbar displays real acumen when she writes that "the only salvation for the student of the *Divine Comedy* lies in the visualization of Dante in his setting amid the thought currents of his time, and against the background that produced them." As we saw at the beginning of this essay, this is essentially the position which such contemporary critics as Sapegno are presently espousing.

By 1927 Croce's views had infiltrated American Dante scholarship, producing both adherents and antagonists. In that year John J. Chapman saw Dante as a great poet, not because the *Comedy* was a great poem as a whole, but for its moments of poetic genius, all of which are essentially lyrical. Within ten years, however, Giuseppe Borgese could take serious issue with

Croce. In his opinion "pure poetry" is but a figment of the mind. "The *Comedy*," he wrote, "is a unity, Dante's structure and poetry, Dante's personality and work are a unity, and his personality and work are organically united to his society and his age." While there are moments of higher lyricism scattered throughout the poem, they are but the "beauties" that serve as "beams" to support the undeniable beauty of the entire structure.

T. S. Eliot also disagreed with the Croceans, but felt that the exclusively allegorical approach to the poem had its own serious pitfalls. The poetry of the *Comedy* can be enjoyed without excessive concern for its general framework and philosophy, but full enjoyment and understanding of its poetic power can be achieved only by means of the study of the poem as a whole. "In good allegory, like Dante's, it is not necessary to understand the meaning first to enjoy the poetry, but our enjoyment of the poetry makes us want to understand the meaning." Not only do we have in the *Comedy* a complete scale of the depths and heights of human emotions, but "every degree of the feeling of humanity, from lowest to highest, has moreover, an intimate relation to the next above and below, and all fit together according to the logic or sensibility. . . . The vital matter is that Dante's poem is a whole; that you must in the end come to understand every part in order to understand any part."

Other critics and scholars, meanwhile, felt that even the rational and dialectical qualities of the *Comedy* could not be overlooked in a true assessment of its poetry. As early as 1921, Henry E. Conklin, while conceding that the beauty of Dante's poem is realized intuitively, forcefully maintained that final aesthetic judgment can result only from a synthesis of an emotional analysis with an intellectual analysis. Similarly, in 1941, Charles G. Osgood not only extolled Dante's spirituality but felt that in judging his poem "the briar of dialectic is indispensable to the rose of poetry."

IV

We have seen that what might be called the Crocean period in Italy was marked by a lull in Dante studies in England. The same period saw the rise of the symbolist school of Dante scholars in the United States with Fletcher's *Dante* and particularly his *The Symbolism of the Divine Comedy*, which appeared in the same year as Croce's famous study. The realist school that descended from Norton included such scholars as Grandgent, K. McKenzie, J. E. Shaw, and E. H. Wilkins. Being genuine *italianisti*, all four of these scholars produced studies that were "learnedly philological," to borrow a phrase from K. Foster. In general, the concern of these scholars was primarily historical and biographical rather than critical. Their assessment of Dante's works was based on "verifiable" facts about the works and the manner in which they evolved within the context of the poet's life and historical period.

Following World War II, numerous writers and critics representing new trends also tried their hand at interpreting Dante. In 1952, F. Fergusson edited a special issue of the *Kenyon Review* entitled *Dante Alighieri, a Symposium of Modern Critics.* Eliot, Tate, Auerbach, Blackmur, and Maritain were among the contributors to the issue. Other journals enjoying the favor of the new critics, such as the *Hudson Review* and the *Sewanee Review*, likewise began publishing studies on Dante with some regularity. By the early 1960's, followers of every type of "school" or "theory" of criticism from the aesthetic impressionists through the psychological analysts to the Chicago Critics and philosophical analysts similarly had had something to say about Dante's art. Among these the most penetrating and intriguing were F. Fergusson's *Dante's Drama of the Mind: A Modern Reading of the Purgatorio* which appeared in 1953 and which tried to interpret Dante's religious experience in the language of psychology; J. Mazzeo's *Structure and Thought in the Paradiso* (1958), with its strong Platonic focus, and Bernard Stambler's *Dante's Other World: The "Purgatorio" as Guide to the "Divine Comedy"* (1957), perhaps the best introductory work for the general reader because of its straightforward handling of the spiritual and religious implications of Dante's poem. There were still others, such as Auerbach and Montano, whose training had been European but whose careers had evolved in part in America, whose basic approach consisted in struggling with those structural, historical, or spiritual elements that Croce had tended to discard. Unfortunately, lack of space makes possible only the briefest mention of such critics. Similarly, the great number of studies and books appearing in England and in the United States in commemoration of Dante's birth in 1965 will require many years to be judged properly. Two works by American scholars do, however, deserve passing mention for their intrinsic value. The first is Thomas G. Bergin's *Dante*, published in New York, Boston, and London and offering a comprehensive introduction to Dante's life and works. The second is the monumental *A Concordance to the Divine Comedy of Dante Alighieri*, edited for the Dante Society of America by E. H. Wilkins, T. G. Bergin, and A. J. De Vito.

But in 1949, a rather "unorthodox" Dantista had begun to bring focus to a view of the *Comedy* that in many ways has proven as controversial as Croce's. This was Charles S. Singleton, whose *Essay on the Vita Nuova*, published in 1949, marked the birth of an approach to Dante that was so eclectic and yet so consistent and unified that almost any latter-day "school" of criticism could claim some influence on it.

The two primary criticisms levelled at Singleton's approach are, first, that it is too heavily theological and allegorical and, second, that it tends to be mystical. Both are clearly the result of a superficial reading of Singleton's studies. Indeed, the charge of mysticism often approaches the absurd. To have a scholar such as E. R. Vincent seriously maintain in a study entitled "The Crisis in the *Vita Nuova*" (*Centenary Essays on Dante* [Oxford, 1965], pp. 132–42) that Singleton's view—that one of the authors of the *Vita nuova* is God—shows how highly exalted he is by his own mysticism would appear almost offensive were it not for the naiveté of the paper's basic thesis. Critics, according to Vincent, waste their time when they try to explain crises of love such as that found in the *Vita nuova*. According to the last sentence of the essay, "The revelations of love are personal and they are private." Even more incredible is Vincent's second main point which urges us not to refer any longer to the beloveds of courtly poetry as *ladies* or *maidens*. What we must bear in mind is that "these charming creatures of the late thirteenth century, now so faint with the passing of the years and only alive by the grace of art . . . Beatrice herself, who is to end in splendid pre-eminence by the side of God in Paradise, were all just girls." Therefore, Vincent concludes rather shockingly, let us call them so!

Singleton's position on mysticism may be seen in his review of Dorothy Sayers' *Introductory Papers on Dante*.[13] After remarking "that the special language of mysticism in which

[13] *Kenyon Review*, 17 (1955): 656–61.

(Charles) Williams had written his *Figure of Beatrice* was to be hers (Sayers') when she wrote of Dante," he refers to Sayers' belief that Williams' book "initiated what is likely to prove the next great movement in Dantism." He then adds, "One may have some rather serious doubts about that likelihood or at least take hope from the fact that there is so far no sign of the movement getting under way." If there is any mysticism connected with Singleton's approach, it is the "mysticism" of a modern literary critic who has implicit faith in the powers of criticism to penetrate into and define the chief ingredients of Dante's incomparable artistry. Unfortunately, the failure to recognize this has prompted most English and American critics to regard Singleton's approach respectfully but skeptically, and most other foreign critics who are still awaiting reliable translations of Singleton's major studies to observe extreme caution in assessing their value.[14]

The time has clearly come for a reassessment of Singleton's substantive contributions to Dante criticism. Limitations of space make it possible to advance only the barest outline of such a reassessment here.

First of all, it is essential to recall that Singleton's career started with a special interest in Lorenzo's Florence and in the art of the *Decameron*. His Ph.D. dissertation led to a critical edition of the *Canti carnascialeschi del Rinascimento* which became part of the reputable *Scrittori d'Italia* series in 1936. This was followed by an edition of additional carnival songs published by the University of Rome in 1941 but already identified in part in an article appearing in 1938 in *Italica*, 15: 175–78. It was not until 1941 that he published a short study on " 'Dante' in the Divine Comedy."[15] Meanwhile, he had begun a fifteen-year project on a critical edition of the *Decameron*, and in 1944 pub-

[14] Perhaps the most interesting example of this is to be found in the review of the special Dante issue of the *Kenyon Review*, cited previously, which appeared in *Studi danteschi*, 33, pt. 1: 208–17, and was signed simply C. F. According to the reviewer, while Singleton's complicated analysis of Dante's journey metaphor might be interesting, it must be assumed wrong for the simple reason that Dante would have made some reference to it in one of his other works had he meant his journey to signify the kinds of meanings advanced by Singleton. In fact, in the opinion of C. F., the entire issue is filled with nothing but excessive *sottilizzare* by a group of almost amateurish modern American critics.

[15] *Italica*, 18: 109–16.

lished a provocative article in the manner of the New Critics entitled "On Meaning in the Decameron."[16] The first visible sign of a movement toward an original approach to Dante appeared in an article significantly entitled "*Vita Nuova* XII: Love's Obscure Words," which appeared in the *Romanic Review* in 1945.[17]

This much should suffice to show that Singleton's interests are neither narrow nor one-sided. By his own admission, it was in the teaching of graduate courses in Dante at Johns Hopkins and at Harvard that he acquired the insights that have led to his approach. Direct confrontation, getting involved, coming to grips with a text, and getting inside of it are Singleton's favorite expressions for describing both his classroom and scholarly approach to Dante. This accounts not only for the flowing style of his studies but for the disturbing absence of scholarly acknowledgment of certain details or ideas that were consciously or unconsciously borrowed from others.

Singleton's basic concern is with the poetry of the *Comedy* and not with its ideas, allegories, or spiritual meanings for their own sake. Time after time we find him repeating that to treat properly the artistic dimensions of the poem, we must learn and use the medieval idiom. He believes that too often critics and scholars have been led astray by the beautiful trees that compose the forest that is the *Comedy*. If Dante's poetic inspiration rested on religious and spiritual convictions, these cannot be overlooked in analyzing the artistic power and intensity of the poem. They are indeed at its core, and the critic's responsibility is to discover the magic with which Dante's genius transformed such convictions into a poem whose structure was modeled on God's creation with all its complex and unfathomable beauty.

The concept of a poet undertaking an imitation of God's creation is a key factor in the misunderstandings that have arisen concerning Singleton's approach. Had Dante tried to imitate the painting techniques of a Cimabue or a Giotto, modern critics would have applauded the scholar who sought to analyze the elements involved in such imitation. But because Singleton has abundant evidence to prove his hypothesis that Dante consciously wrote his *Comedy* in a manner which he believed re-

16 *Ibid.*, 21: 117–24.

17 *Ibid.*, 36: 89–102.

flected the "style" of the Master Craftsman, such applause is withheld in the name of modern theories of aesthetics.[18]

Actually, Singleton's method is quite simple. Starting with the premise that the educated medieval reader would have little difficulty in detecting the similarity between Dante's way of writing and the Christian God's two "books," the book of the Universe and Holy Scripture, he proceeds to a close analysis of the main ingredients of such similarity.[19] First, however, he posits two points to be kept constantly in mind for a proper understanding of the *Comedy*. The first is that the medieval mind viewed the two "books" of God as primary sources of the mysterious ways and means offered by God to man for his salvation. The second is the essentiality of remaining at all times in touch with the entire structure of the *Comedy* and its medieval foundations. As he states in the previously mentioned review of Dorothy Sayers' *Introductory Papers on Dante*, "Since in our attempts today to understand Dante's poem there is nothing we so much need as a grasp of the whole form in its broader outlines and several dimensions of meaning, these papers . . . deserve special notice. For whatever their failure in particular focus on some aspect may seem to be, it is their merit in general to remain constantly in touch with the entire structure of Dante's poem and its foundations in the medieval imagination." He also applauds Miss Sayers for having realized that "in our reflective understanding of the poem, the end comes first, that Hell gets its proper meaning from Heaven, that all depends on that fixed point of dazzling light at the end."

The feasibility of Dante's conscious imitation of God's two "books," a firm grasp and appreciation of how the doctrine of salvation through Christ permeated medieval life and thought, the need for understanding the poem as a whole—these are the basic principles underlying Singleton's approach to the *Comedy*. These principles could already be seen operating in the early *Essay on the Vita Nuova*, whose main thesis is that Dante meant Beatrice to be seen within the framework of an analogy with Christ. Furthermore, the entire form of Dante's youthful book depends on the opening metaphor of the Book of Memory, some

[18] See particularly his "The Poet's Number at the Center," *MLN*, 80: 1–10.

[19] *Dante Studies*, I (Cambridge, 1954), pp. 26–29.

pages of which the poet-scribe wants the reader to believe are extracted from God's Book of the Universe. What so many critics have failed to realize is that Singleton is here speaking of artistic strategy, of Dante as poet. Thus, when at the very end of the *Essay* he asks whether there is perhaps "a way by which we may see a necessary connection between that image of a Book of Memory which controls the outward form of the *Vita Nuova* and that analogy with Christ which is the principle of its inner form," he is not asking whether Dante's beliefs were doctrinally sound. And when he finds in a popular hymn attributed to St. Bernard, whose opening words are *Jesu dulcis memoria*, the answer to his question, the honest reader can only marvel at the potentialities of modern scholarship to bring back dimensions of meaning whose total effect is as aesthetic as it is intellectual, despite Singleton's later assertion that "aesthetics as the science of the beautiful can never deal with Plato's myth or Genesis or Dante's poem. For they aim neither at beauty (not first of all) nor illusion. Theirs is a vision of an objective order of things in its goodness and its rightness. And for them anything short of this were ugliness."[20]

Singleton's analysis of Dante's artistry is even more impressive in his first comprehensive, though brief, study of the *Comedy* entitled *Dante Studies I, Commedia, Elements of Structure* which appeared five years later, in 1954. Here he first examines in detail three dimensions of the poem's structure: its allegory, its symbolism, and the pattern of analogy which it displays at its center. He then proceeds to show how the entire structure is firmly anchored in a faith leading to profound insights into the substance of things seen. As a result, "A human poem is thus by analogy participating in a divine poem, can be seen to be made in its image. In so doing, a poem does what all created things do in a Christian universe, a poem participates in true existence, in Being."

In an Appendix to this volume we find Singleton's famous and highly controversial discussion of the kind of allegory used by Dante in the *Comedy*. In distinguishing between what Dante meant by "allegory of poets" and "allegory of theologians" as defined in the *Convivio* and by maintaining that it was the latter type that Dante used in his poem, Singleton started a debate

20 *Ibid.*, p. 82.

that has perhaps done more harm to his approach than by avoiding the issue altogether. The fact remains that if Dante did indeed succeed in writing his poem in imitation of Scripture and of Creation, the literal meaning simply cannot be a fiction as viewed from within the poem. As Singleton's basic formula would have it, "The fiction is that it is not a fiction." What name tag to use in describing Dante's method matters little, except, of course, insofar as it affords deeper insights into the nature of the poem. This Singleton meant to do, but somehow was generally misunderstood. He therefore undertook a second book to show precisely how Dante's mode of allegory produces almost infinite patterns or dimensions of meaning by providing the reader with a double focus that unquestionably results in a richer reading of the poem.

In *Dante Studies 2, Journey to Beatrice* (Cambridge, 1958), Singleton concentrates on the basic element of the *Commedia's* structure, its allegory. He examines in considerable detail features of Dante's allegory that most scholars and critics had failed to see. Ultimately he tries to have the reader see what in his previously cited review he maintains Dorothy Sayers had failed to see, "that the character Dante in his journey to God is allegorically fulfilling broader patterns of salvation, such as the descent to humility before true ascent can begin, which is the way through Hell to the girding on of the rush at the foot of Purgatory; and such as the pattern of *justificatio impii* which is his way up the mountain of Purgatory to the summit where Beatrice comes" (p. 660). And indeed the reader does come away from this difficult book with new insights into the infinite layers of meaning that are to be found almost anywhere and everywhere in the *Comedy*, and especially in those portions which seemed most familiar and yet somehow seemed to be veiled in mystery. But perhaps the most impressive thing the book does is to convince us of the following statement that appears in its Preface: "Dante's allegory is explicit in the theology of his day. We have only to learn to recognize it there when we meet it. And when we become able to do this, then at once we find ourselves confronted with an embarrassment of riches. Instead of one good text to cite in evidence of a given point or pattern, there are at least twenty."

The texts cited are sufficiently persuasive to make a reader feel that there is still a wealth of undiscovered treasure lying beneath the surface of the *Comedy*, treasure which recalls Matthew's "pearls" rather than the stone-filled husks that Augustine warns us against in what might be called his theory of medieval poetics.[21] The fact that one reviewer of the volume can lament that "In all this there is more theology than Dantology, . . ." and can wonder "if even in the Middle Ages Dante could have expected many to follow him in such a subtle theological design,"[22] and that another reviewer can marvel that "an agnostic tells the modern Dante readers . . . that they cannot understand the *Commedia* because they do not read it with Catholic eyes, . . ."[23] serves to dramatize the distance that Dante criticism has travelled since Croce's essay of 1921. It is furthermore perhaps significant that among the younger Dante scholars in the United States, the ones who have shown signs of continuing productivity (Freccero, Bernardo, Pellegrini, Musa, Locke) are all former students of Singleton. But perhaps even more significant is the fact that in recent years Singleton has not only been involved in such projects as editing Toynbee's *Dante Alighieri, His Life and Works* for Harper Torchbooks and Toynbee's *Dante Dictionary* for the Clarendon Press but is on the verge of completing a monumental multivolume edition of the *Comedy* for the Bollingen Foundation including both a translation and a meticulous commentary on words, verses, cantos, cantiche, and the structure in detail. Scheduled also for early publication by the Bollingen Foundation is a two-volume work entitled *The Early Illustrations of the Divine Comedy*, done in collaboration with two art historians and containing a long essay by Singleton. There is, in short, little question that Singleton will leave an indelible mark on all aspects of Dante studies.

With Singleton, Dante scholarship returns full circle to its earliest beginnings. In fact, at the very end of his study of Dante's allegory as an element of structure, Singleton has occasion to point out how certain words written by Benvenuto da Imola regarding the meaning of Beatrice have a strange way of smiling back at Edward Moore's criticism of Benvenuto's

[21] B. F. Huppé, *Doctrine and Poetry* (New York, 1959), p. 15.

[22] T. G. Bergin, "Dante Shelf, 1958," *Italian Quarterly*, 3, no. 9 (Spring, 1959): 66–67.

[23] H. Hatzfeld in *Italica*, 32 (1955): 195.

interpretation. He then proceeds to show how in effect Benvenuto's words reflect his own approach to the *Comedy*. Now that Natalino Sapegno has suggested a return to and a continuation of the work of the earliest commentators, let us not overlook the fact that an American Dante scholar who considers himself an autodidact has already begun to show the way.

Petrarch

Petrarch's fortune did not fare too differently from Dante's. The appeal of the love story, the haunting presence of Laura, the technical perfection of the verses all contributed to an almost exclusive focus on Petrarch's craftsmanship or on his sensitivity to the nuances of human sentiment. Any attempt to see in his *Canzoniere* something beyond "fragments" of intimate experience was and continues to be viewed with skepticism. Whatever "super-structure" there may be in the collection is generally viewed as contributing minimally to its poetic merits. It is hardly surprising, therefore, to find Croce asserting that when the poet maintains that his love raises him to the Eternal Good and teaches him the straight path to heaven, it is a mere manner of speaking, for the poet himself does not really believe it. This is not where the power of Petrarch's poetry lies.[24]

Foscolo's admiration for Petrarch's purity and depth of inspiration was of course in keeping with the Romantic attitude. However, his observation that the overwhelming nature of Petrarch's feelings and reflections compelled him to communicate them first in prose forms in his correspondence with his intimate friends and later to rework them progressively in Latin verse and finally in the vernacular in a kind of distilled form is in keeping with recent trends that insist that Petrarch's works must be viewed as a whole. Foscolo's compassion for Petrarch for having had to use word plays and conceits (such as the Daphne myth) in order to satisfy the taste of his contemporaries remains at the level of a negative criticism and does not induce him to assert the need to penetrate the stylistic glitter in an attempt to grasp what Petrarch's contemporaries found poetic in such a style. Other significant observations of Foscolo's include the reference to the fact that Petrarch's finest imitations are

[24] "La poesia del Petrarca," in *Poesia popolare e poesia d'arte* (Bari, 1946), pp. 65–80.

drawn from sacred writings: the allusion to Petrarch's mastery of the lute as an explanation of the musicality of his verse, the calling attention to Petrarch's assertion in the second Triumph that an overpowering passion may well cause a lover actually to be transformed into the beloved, and the indication of the importance of Laura's backward glance in Sonnet 346 to see if her lover is following. We shall see that all these points reflect an amazingly modern sensitivity to Petrarch's poetry.

As the Introduction to this volume points out, the rise of Victorian taste and the biographical approach to literature dimmed Petrarch's poetic reputation in England in the last half of the nineteenth century. By the third quarter of the nineteenth century Petrarch the Latin scholar and humanist began to eclipse the Italian lyric poet in both England and America. This general tendency culminated in the two well-known milestone studies that were to appear on either side of the Atlantic between the turn of the century and 1930. The first, published in New York and London in 1898, was *Petrarch, The First Modern Scholar and Man of Letters*, by J. H. Robinson, a professor of history at Columbia, and H. W. Rolfe, a professor of Latin at Swarthmore. The second, never completed and entitled *Francesco Petrarca, The First Modern Man of Letters,* was by E. H. R. Tatham and appeared in two sizable volumes in London in 1925–26. The trend of translating Petrarch's Latin works set by Robinson and Rolfe continued with the translation of Petrarch's *Letters to Classical Authors* by M. E. Cosenza in Chicago in 1910 and the translation of the *Secret* by W. H. Draper in London in 1911. In 1924 the University of Illinois published a translation of Petrarch's *The Life of Solitude* by J. Zeitlin.

Meanwhile, as we saw with Dante, an American scholar who had published regularly since 1905 on various aspects of Italian literature was slowly beginning to focus his attention on Petrarch. By 1925 a student of his at Chicago, Ruth Phelps, had her Ph.D. dissertation on *The Earlier and Later Forms of Petrarch's Canzoniere* published by the University Press. The following year Ernest Hatch Wilkins published the first in a series of studies that was to lead eventually to one of the greatest achievements in Petrarch scholarship, an almost day-by-day reconstruction of the making of the *Canzoniere*. The first article was entitled "The Pre-Chigi Form of the *Canzoniere* of Petrarch." There followed in rapid succession a series of studies on Petrarch's life and works culminating in *The Making of the "Canzoniere" and Other Petrarch Studies* published in Italy in 1951. The following ten years were highly productive ones, including a half dozen books dealing with a variety of carefully researched studies on the poet and his works. The last two of these are perhaps among the finest of all, one on the *Life of Petrarch*, the other a translation of the *Triumphs*, both published by the University of Chicago Press in 1962. Each book, however, represents a gem of philological research, being the result of a highly meticulous and scientific collection and presentation of data. So complete and masterful are Wilkins' studies that henceforth a Petrarchan scholar can easily dispose of most problems involving factual information by checking through his works.

For Professor Wilkins also, therefore, it was Petrarch the man of letters and the man of his times that had to be disinterred from the encrustations of haphazard investigation. As a result, he does succeed in giving readers for the first time a highly reliable portrait of Petrarch whom he considers " the most remarkable man of his time; and . . . one of the most remarkable men of all time." Unlike Professor Singleton's work on Dante, Professor Wilkins generally tends to avoid a critical evaluation of Petrarch's poetry. His principal concern is to provide the reader with as complete a picture as possible of the historical-biographical background against which each of the works must be read. Even in his *History of Italian Poetry* published in 1954, where one would expect to find some attempt at an assessment of Petrarch's lyrics, we find, rather, a description of what the poetry tells us about the poet. "Yet Petrarch, even in his lyrics, is inevitably a man of letters. His poetry comes from his heart, but it comes through a mind that is steeped in older verse, made newly personal through their absorption into his own consciousness. There are poems, also, in which the gift of the heart is but slight, while the artist spends himself in the elaboration of concepts that are mainly formal . . ."

The inestimable value of Professor Wilkins' work is perhaps best attested by the international array of scholars and institutions subscribing to the edition of his *Petrarch's Correspondence* on the occasion of his eightieth birthday in 1960 and by the bestowal of a honorary citizenship upon him by Arquà, the little Italian town where Petrarch spent the very last years of his life.

Dante, Petrarch, and Boccaccio

During the 1930's and 40's in the United States, such European-trained scholars as Ullman, Spitzer, Kristeller, Baron, and Mommsen contributed new and significant dimensions to Petrarch's role as a humanist and thinker. In England, J. H. Whitfield alone made a similar comparable contribution with his *Petrarch and the Renaissance*, published in 1943.

In 1962, the present writer, a former student of Wilkins, published a study of Petrarch's *Africa* that tried to define the basic nature and quality of Petrarch's poetic inspiration. Entitled *Petrarch, Scipio and the "Africa,"* the study represented a kind of milestone in the numerous studies that I had devoted to Petrarch over a number of years. These had started with a study on "The Importance of the Non-Love Poems in Petrarch's *Canzoniere*,"[25] had continued through several others dealing with stylistic techniques in Petrarch's prose letters[26] and through a study on Petrarch's poetics entitled "Petrarch's Attitude Toward Dante,"[27] and had culminated in a comprehensive article on Petrarch in Collier's *Encyclopedia* of 1962. In the central chapter of my book on the *Africa*, I try to show that while Scipio had represented the ideal inspiration for the youthful Petrarch, who saw in Scipio's dream the secret of amalgamating the basic humanistic studies of History, Philosophy and Poetry, Laura remained a life-long inspiration to Petrarch, the man of his century, who felt in his love the key to a Christian salvation through human aspiration. If combining History and Philosophy under the alluring mantle of Poetry could lead to human wisdom at its best, it follows that by singing of an earthly Glory solidly anchored in Virtue and Beauty (Poetry) a poet could point the way to a superior wisdom that might be called divine. This attempt to arrive at a synthesis of "tutto il Petrarca" was in keeping with the latest trends in Petrarchan criticism, but horrified the more puristic critics.[28]

In 1963 Morris Bishop published his popularizing biographical

25 *Italica*, 24 (1950): 302–12.

26 "Dialogue in the Prose Letters of Petrarch," *Symposium*, 5 (1951): 302–16; "Dramatic Dialogue and Monologue in Petrarch's Works II," *Symposium*, 7 (1953): 92–119; "Letter-Splitting in Petrarch's *Familiares*," *Speculum*, 33 (1958): 236–41; "The Selection of Letters in Petrarch's *Familiares*," *Speculum*, 35 (1960): 280–88.

27 *PMLA*, 70 (1955): 488–517.

28 See R. Montano in his strangely crusading periodical *Umanesimo*, 2 (1966): 69–71.

Petrarch and His World and in 1966 his *Letters from Petrarch* containing some 110 letters in whole or in part.

It is obvious from what has been said that English and American scholarship has contributed minimally to the critical study of Petrarch's *Canzoniere*. It is perhaps just as obvious that the principal reason is the lack of good or dependable translations of Petrarch's poetry. While the continuing vogue of Latin studies has equipped English-speaking scholars with the necessary tool to come to grips with the humanistic Petrarch, the corresponding decline of Italian studies has caused these same scholars to shy away from Petrarch's Italian poetry. One must, therefore, turn to Italian sources in order to grasp the latest trends in the critical evaluation of Petrarch's *Canzoniere*, which is our primary concern. Among the most important of these are De Sanctis, Croce, Calcaterra, Contini, and Bosco. For the sake of brevity, this discussion will be confined to those views of these critics that attempt to define Petrarch's chief source of inspiration for his Italian poetry, namely, Laura.

In his *Saggio critico sul Petrarca* which first appeared in 1868, De Sanctis notes that while Petrarch's accomplishments as a man of letters won him great fame, his true glory as a great man resides in his Italian poetry. "He comes to us, accompanied by Laura." In attempting to define this wondrous beloved who seemed to constitute Petrarch's entire world, De Sanctis can only conclude that "Laura is a Goddess, she is not yet a woman . . . she is the female species." She has not yet assumed human form nor entered the stream of human events. She is, rather, Man's ideal in life's journey, his star, the beacon that marks his ultimate destination. From her come virtue and holiness; she is a ladder to the Creator. While the poet always seems to start with her physical beauties, he makes Laura undergo a "glorious transfiguration" in which she assumes the characteristics of an actress before the play starts. She is not yet mother, bride, nor mistress; nor is she any particular woman in any particular situation. She is like a closed book, and almost like inert, spiritless nature. She is in the middle of events and yet remains outside of them; she is in contact with passions and yet keeps herself above them; she is on earth and yet no human misery touches her. One almost feels that she is beyond death.

For Croce also, Petrarch's love penetrated all his being completely and forever and became its center and its fulcrum.[29] However, since this love caused the poet to "bargain with death," it was essentially a passion and not a religious, moral, political, or other ideal. When the poet asserts that his love raises him to the Eternal Good and teaches him the straight path to heaven, it is a mere manner of speaking, for he himself does not believe it. His happiness resides not in heaven but in Laura, who is no ladder to something else but is, herself, the beginning and end of all things.

In his attempt to define what Laura means to Petrarch, Contini uses a particularly happy phrase.[30] His analysis of the structure and movement of poem No. 188 of Petrarch's *Canzoniere* in which the reader beholds the mysterious transformation of the laurel tree into a Laura who in turn is completely fused in an Apollo-sun image leads to the observation that in the poem we actually witness a "system of universal interpenetration of nature." There are times, indeed, when such interpenetration is so complete that the poet actually sees himself assuming the same forms assumed by Laura, such as the phoenix in No. 135 or the laurel in No. 23.

In 1946 Umberto Bosco set the tone of the most recent direction of Petrarch criticism in his perceptive *Francesco Petrarca.* The premise of the book is that there is no true evolution of Petrarch's thought or works, for practically all his works underwent life-long revisions that ceased only with the poet's death. Consequently every page of the poet that has come down to us reflects "all of Petrarch: immobile, in his perplexity, from beginning to end." As for Laura, she does indeed constitute but a single episode in the life of Petrarch, but an episode which the lyric poet wants us to consider truly central and crucial, not unlike a poetic myth. Whether Laura actually existed or not is basically unimportant. What is important is to try to define "the essence of that vaster hope and despair which the poet chose to sing under the species of the hope and despair he experienced in his love." The poet's love of Laura is so all-embracing that time after time we confuse it with other images and ideals being sung by him. This is why her figure seems so often to evaporate

[29] *Poesia popolare e poesia d'arte*, pp. 65–80.

[30] *Saggio d'un commento alle correzioni del Petrarca volgare* (Firenze, 1943), p. 22.

into a symbol while the symbol in turn assumes her physical qualities. The love of Laura is therefore but a means used by the poet to give body to his lyrical treatment in a wide spectrum of complex and sentimental experiences. This explains the lack of truly realistic or sensualistic details in his representations. Ultimately, what we are made to behold is the struggle of a highly sensitive and learned poet revealing his secret conflict between his earthly and spiritual aspirations, which he tries desperately to reconcile in an attempt to avoid confessing the vanity of earthly striving.

It was Carlo Calcaterra, however, who in his series of studies collected under the title of *Nella Selva del Petrarca* appearing in 1942 gave the most intriguing analysis of what Laura meant to Petrarch. Starting with Petrarch's youth when Laura appeared as the very beauty of life itself, and poetry and glory as the ultimate goals of his activities, Calcaterra recalls Petrarch's own admission that he was seized by a kind of "pagan and apollonean intoxication" that made him view these images as the very apex of happiness. This had led the poet into a "splendid abyss" from which he had never quite extricated himself. He was lured into the "abyss" by the myth of *Parnasia laurus* in which he felt the correspondence between his love for the fleeing Laura and the myth of Apollo and Daphne. He had come to conceive Daphne as the immortal image of earthly love, which, fleeing the senses, becomes pure beauty in art. This is why Petrarch focused his earliest poems on the name of Laura and on the green laurel.

In time, Petrarch's poetic horizons widened beyond the daphnean. The irreproachable conduct of Laura inspired him to superimpose a Christian sense over his love poetry, and he began endowing his image of Laura with the characteristics of a lady-guide to the Christian heaven. Later, indeed, he anchored the entire architecture of the *Canzoniere* in the spiritual contrast between the two configurations of Laura-Daphne and Laura-guide-to-heaven, and even referred to the region where his love had evolved as ". . . my Parnassus." The overall structure of the *Canzoniere* is consequently not only aesthetic but moral and religious in its attempt to reflect an "internal redemption." For Calcaterra, the true beauty of the collection emerges when the two themes of *Parnasia laurus* and the "dì sesto d'aprile" (recalling Christ's passion) are complemented by an imaginative handling of the poet's inner restlessness and uncertainty which he defines in the *Secretum* as an *inexpletum quoddam* that is always present in his heart.

The prevalence of the Daphne theme diminishes in the early 1340's following Petrarch's coronation and the writing of the *Secretum.* A new theme seems to emerge in the *Canzoniere* as a result of the poet's assimilation of the Ciceronean-Senecan concept that virtue possesses a loftier moral value than glory. Something of this may already be seen in No. 142, the *sestina* that closed the first form of the collection. In the poem the two themes are clearly juxtaposed and lead to the poet's desire to turn to a "new love" and a "new tree." Yet the perennial wavering recurs shortly thereafter, in No. 148, where the traditional laurel and its inescapable appeal appear once again. Indeed, in the final form of the *Canzoniere*, the very last poem of the first part, No. 263, is a hymn to the laurel.

Following Laura's death, according to Calcaterra, a fusion of the two themes seems to take place in the tercets of No. 269, which express the conviction that the poet had procured a justifiable glory for his beloved inasmuch as she had "operato virtute" in him. In fact, as he asserts in No. 318, that "live laurel," though now in heaven, had left deep roots in his heart. The extent to which Petrarch was obsessed with the implications of the laurel and its tie-in with the name of his beloved may perhaps best be seen in his coronation oration, whose central theme is the laurel and the extensive network of meanings that Petrarch ascribed to it. It represents one of those moments indicated by Calcaterra when "the poet really immersed himself, ecstatic, in a forest of laurel. . . ."

As for the Christian superstructure that Petrarch obviously tried to inject not only in his *Canzoniere* but in most of his other works, here too Calcaterra provides new and exciting insights. He devotes Chapter VII of his book to Petrarch's concern to place his two most important works, the *Africa* and the *Canzoniere*, within the framework of the Christian ethic by emphasizing the role played by the drama of Holy Week in both the biographical and artistic textures of the works. In a masterfully thorough way Calcaterra shows how for Petrarch the date April 6 represented the true day of Christ's Passion without regard to the movable recurrence of Good Friday. This explains the puzzling problem of how Petrarch was able to set his first meeting with Laura as well as her death on the day of

Christ's death despite the fact that neither in 1327 nor in 1348 did Good Friday fall on April 6. In fact, April 6 was also traditionally considered the day on which Man was created and Adam sinned, which tied in with Petrarch's acceptance of the Augustinian position that "omnis homo Adam et omnis homo Christus." By connecting his love of Laura to all these divine events, Petrarch was consciously implying a connection with the Christian drama of the redemption.

In summarizing how Petrarch had organized his personal life around the date of April 6, Calcaterra outlines and analyzes the chronology of events as spotlighted by the poet. Love had first smitten him on April 6, 1327, as he observed the rites of Holy Week. Eleven years later, in 1338, while again meditating during his observance of Holy Week, he was inspired to write his *Africa.* Three years later, having arrived in Rome on April 6, he was crowned poet laureate on Easter Sunday. Seven years later, in 1348, Laura died on Easter Sunday. Laura had thus captured him on the day of Christ's Passion and had freed him on the day of the Resurrection. There is little doubt that the numbers three, seven, and twenty-one were intended to provide further symbolic meaning. In short, as with the *Divine Comedy*, the poet naturally expected his readers to feel the additional dimensions of meaning afforded by this superstructure both in the *Africa* and in the two parts of the *Canzoniere.* For Calcaterra the full force of these various dimensions can be felt even in such individual verses as "Era de l'anno e di mia etate aprile" ("It was April of the year and of my life").

Thus, as we move from De Sanctis' mysterious and deathless goddess, to Croce's "center and fulcrum," to Contini's "universal interpenetration of nature," to Bosco's "vaster hope and despair," and finally to Calcaterra's Parnassus and Calvary, Laura's image in Petrarch's poetry certainly assumes complex proportions. For all these critics, Laura's image emerges from the final form of the *Canzoniere* as we know it today—a form that required the better part of Petrarch's lifetime to assume its present physiognomy; a form, furthermore, that contains not only 366 poems (implying year-round involvement) but one which opens with a recantation, proceeds to a roughly chronological history of the poet's overwhelming passion within the framework of other distracting tensions, is neatly divided into the life and death of the hauntingly beautiful beloved, and ends with a hymn to the Virgin Mary.

We know, however, that the present form is the last of a long series of earlier forms undergone by the collection. Because Petrarch stands almost alone among writers of his day in having had not only autographs but actual worksheets come down to present times in relatively large quantities, it has been possible to reconstruct in an amazingly complete manner the processes whereby the collection evolved from its earliest to its last form. It should, therefore, be possible to follow the evolution of the poetic image of Laura as it progressed from one form of the collection to the next. This should provide us with a truer measure of the various dimensions that constitute the final image.

The full story of the development of each form, as was indicated earlier, has been remarkably told by the late Ernest H. Wilkins.[31] To try to summarize the evolution of the thirteen forms identified by Wilkins would require far more space than is available to us here. We can, however, by arriving at certain general conclusions regarding the first five forms, shed further light on the complexity of Laura's image.

The first cluster of poems selected by Petrarch to create the earliest form of the collection does indeed reflect "the pagan and apollonean intoxication" that Calcaterra associated with Petrarch's early youth. The full mythic power of the poet's love emerges as he continuously depicts scenes in which the mysterious forces of nature seem to participate directly in his love drama, which in turn seems to be inextricably bound to the Apollo-Daphne myth.

The second form, put together just one year before Laura's death, clearly reflects the start of the conflict that was to plague Petrarch throughout the remainder of his life, namely, whether his love of Laura, with all it implied, could only lead to ultimate damnation. It was this conflict, rather than the death of Laura, that apparently determined the basic form of the collection at this stage since the two parts are clearly delineated here for the first time with the introduction of poem No. 1, providing a distinct recantation of the poet's love, and No. 264, defining the

[31] *The Making of the "Canzoniere" and Other Petrarchan Studies* (Rome, 1951), chaps. 4–9, 22.

inescapable pull of that love despite the poet's strong awareness of its negative implications for ultimate salvation.

Some ten years later we find the poet adding a block of poems that focus on what Calcaterra refers to as the theme of the "dì sesto d'aprile." In this third form, the time that had elapsed since the death of Laura had led the poet to conceive of his beloved as a lady-guide to heaven. But perhaps the most important new movement to be seen in this form is the poet's attempt to avoid a complete recantation by introducing the subtle distinction between the laurel tree and the new leaves and branches of another tree—the cross—to which he wants to turn.

About twenty years after Laura's death we find the poet starting a fourth form by adding blocks of poems to Part I that seem to restore a distinctly classical aura to the poet's love. On the other hand, the poems added to Part II concentrate on the extension of the theme of the lady-guide to a Christian heaven. One might almost say that Calcaterra's two themes reach a kind of stalemate in this fourth form.

It is with the fifth form that Calcaterra's formula seems no longer to suffice. As a result of the poems added by the poet to create this form, which, according to Wilkins, represents the first moments of the final set to be given by the poet to the collection, a new theme emerges that later proved somewhat too daring for the poet not to tone down. We see a kind of catalytic reaction emerging from the poet's discovery that, once age and time had mellowed the excessive passion involved in his pursuit of the laurel, the serenity that comes with maturity enabled him to view such pursuit as not necessarily detrimental to salvation. In Nos. 310–14 the poet has not only turned away from this earth but can now view Laura in heaven "Ornata de l'alloro / che meritò la sua invicta honestate" ("adorned with the laurel / that her invincible uprightness deserved"). The old "live" laurel overthrown by death is now replaced by a new internal one that is fostered both by love and by the Muses. It grows from the roots left in the poet's heart by the old laurel. Some twenty-five years earlier he had defined these roots as "Fama, Honor et Vertute et Leggiadria / casta bellezza in habito celeste" ("Fame, Honor, and Virtue and Charm / chaste beauty in celestial garb"). This he had done in No. 228, which interestingly is one of the very last poems that he was to add later to Part I. From these roots now emerges a new Laura who is internal rather than external. Like the transformed Daphne, this new Laura incites a new kind of passion—the pursuit of excellence and beauty. She is now symbolized variously as a broken laurel, a dry fountain, a phoenix, and a lovely lady clad in white and having her upper half hidden by a mysterious mist while a serpent bites her heel. She is not only a "cosa nova" but an "angel novo." Before Petrarch, poets had dared compare a beloved to an "angioletto," but never to an "angelo." In No. 326 where this comparison occurs, there is even a shift in the form of address, from the intimate *Tu* to the formal *Voi*. We are also told that while death had indeed transformed the former Laurel by depriving her of her body, the new Laura possesses something that death itself cannot touch, "fama e valor."

Henceforth this is the Laura that the poet tries to sing. There even are moments in such poems as Nos. 333 and 334 when the poet's song approaches the proportions of worshipping a saint, but as De Sanctis has pointed out, it is an incomplete saint.

Throughout the remaining forms of the *Canzoniere* Petrarch's song tries to become that of a Christian Apollo for a Christian Daphne, but the very terms were too contradictory. The Christian heaven could never admit of the purely humanistic dimensions of the pagan myth. Consequently, the poet's vain and endless attempts to reconcile the two in the figure of Laura is what endows his book of songs with dimensions of poetic power that go far beyond the mere singing of a passionate love for a beautiful lady. What confronts us are veritable convolutions of a humanistic mind intent on showing that Mt. Parnassus and Calvary are not *necessarily* contradictory. At the summit of each is something too beautifully human and too beautifully divine to be mutually exclusive. And this something is the power of creativity for which Man is crowned with a crown of laurel and God with a crown of thorns. This explains Petrarch's near-obsession with Good Friday and Christ's Passion, which remains constantly in the background of all his accomplishments but so nebulously that a reader hardly takes notice. In point of fact, this is what has led astray so many readers of the concluding poem of the collection, which is a prayer to the Virgin. This very last poem of the *Canzoniere* is far from being a recantation of the poet's love of Laura. It is a desperate turning to a substitute image that complements rather than replaces the image of

Laura. The poet turns to Mary for those very qualities she shares with Laura. It was her perfect humanity that made her the Chosen Vessel, and imperfect humanity that made her role necessary. It is the poet's potential divinity that will surely move her to pity. He should, indeed, love her even more than Laura. If she would but bring this about, he would devote his thought and pen to her. He is confident that if she would but intercede with her Son in his behalf, He would favor him with at least a peaceful death, for He is as human as he (the poet) is divine. But the implication remains that meanwhile the image of Laura will continue haunting him until his last breath, for she is the very essence of human striving.

The general movement of this last poem sheds considerable light on Petrarch's basic dilemma. As he has St. Augustine point out in the *Secretum*, his fundamental error lay in placing the creature before the Creator. Love of Laura is unquestionably an obstacle to the poet's love of God. To love God because of Laura is clearly a perversion and an indication of a confused perspective. The laurel crown and the crown of thorns must remain irreconcilable as long as the poet's angle of vision is from the bottom up rather than from the top down. Unlike Dante, Petrarch's feet were too firmly implanted on this earth. As he openly confesses at the very end of the *Secretum*, he suffered from a "limp" that, like Dante's limp at the opening of the Inferno, reflected a malady of the will rather than of the intellect, a malady that presumably never left him.[32] He certainly *knew* what was needed but did not truly *want* to change his ways. This is why he wrote poetry that was as incomparably human as Dante's was divine.

Laura's poetic image remains essentially an intellectual construct inextricably bound by the "shackles" of an overpowering earthly beauty and attraction whose sinfulness the poet simply cannot accept fully. This is why the love romance continues to attract the attention of readers. And this is why Petrarch, while calling his love poems in the vernacular *mere trifles*, never tired of trying to redefine Laura in poem after poem until the very end of his life. Humanism, the conviction that learning and culture, beauty and glory, poetry and art are essentially good

[32] See Nancy H. Rosenberg, "Petrarch's Limping; The Foot Unequal to the Eye," *MLN*, 77, no. 1 (1962): 99–105.

and therefore not impediments to ultimate salvation, had indeed dawned with Petrarch.

BOCCACCIO

Boccaccio's fortune, at the hands of critics generally, was subject to strange vicissitudes, compared with Dante's or Petrarch's. Although the *Comedy* and the *Canzoniere* were from the beginning taken seriously by learned and intellectual circles, the *Decameron* was not. Instead, it enjoyed popularity primarily among the new middle class of merchants whose wealth enabled them to multiply manuscripts of the work almost at will. Furthermore, the passage of time has inexorably yielded fresh evidence to support the position that since it first appeared the *Decameron* was viewed as straight storytelling, in the fashion of the minstrels, with no other motive than to afford delight and enjoyment. As a consequence, it was Boccaccio's Latin works that were first taken seriously by literary circles. Indeed, as H. G. Wright has pointed out, in the fifteenth century "Boccaccio had the approval of the Church everywhere. In Spain friars vied with canons and bishops in their eulogies, and *De casibus* and *De claris mulieribus* were quoted side by side with the book of Genesis and the works of Saint Augustine."[33]

When these same circles began to turn to the *Decameron* by the middle of the fifteenth century, they concentrated primarily on its linguistic merits; and by Bembo's time in the early sixteenth century it had come to be considered a model for Italian prose. On the other hand, just as with the Latin works, royal personages also took an interest in the *Decameron*. The Duke of Berry, brother of Charles V, owned a copy as did Queen Margaret of Navarre, sister of Francis I, who actually commissioned a French translation. Even the Royal Library of Scotland contained a copy in 1578. The fact nevertheless remained that throughout the sixteenth century the *Decameron* still enjoyed a certain diffusion among the humbler ranks of society.[34]

Factors such as the nearly complete absence of classical influences and particularly the presence of licentious and ribald tales doubtless played a central role in the critic's reluctance to

[33] *Boccaccio in England from Chaucer to Tennyson* (London, 1957), p. 4.

[34] *Ibid.*, pp. 113–14.

pass judgment on the contents of the *Decameron*. The further fact that the first complete edition published in 1559 was almost at once placed in the *Index* also contributed to such reticence. With the onset of the Reformation, however, the tradition arose of considering the tales dealing with the highly questionable activities of clerics as "exposures" and indictments in the spirit of the Reformation. This view was shortly brought to a logical conclusion by those who now began to see in the *Decameron* the Renaissance spirit of enlightenment and secularism, a human comedy of the senses and of the flesh as opposed to the *Divine Comedy* of transcendent reality and mystical contemplation. And yet, as we shall presently see, the latest criticism makes of the *Decameron* an exemplary medieval work that completes rather than opposes the world of the *Divine Comedy*.

Considering Chaucer's debt to Boccaccio, it is surprising that the *Decameron* was not translated into English very early. Instead, it was Boccaccio's Latin works that were translated first, the *De casibus virorum illustrium* being translated by John Lydgate in 1494 and the *De claribus mulieribus* by Lord Morley in mid-sixteenth century. Even the *Fiammetta* saw a translation by Bartholomew Young in 1587, while the first translation of the *Decameron* did not appear until 1620. It is interesting to note that a translation appeared in 1625 bearing the title *The Modell of Wit, Mirth, Eloquence, and Conversation*. Only in the eighteenth century did the number of translations see a significant increase and the *Decameron* itself come under the scrutiny of recognized men of letters.

As Professor Corrigan has indicated in the Introduction, Boccaccio's subsequent fate was not a particularly happy one. The *Decameron* was slowly degraded to the level of a book to be read furtively, despite its continuing to serve as a source of inspiration to poets such as Tennyson and Longfellow. Nevertheless, English translations continued to appear with regularity, a good dozen appearing between 1890 and 1930. As for book-length studies, the great bulk of these concentrated primarily on Boccaccio's life.[35] The short scholarly articles in English have

[35] J. A. Symonds, *Giovanni Boccaccio as Man and Author* (London, 1895); J. P. Ker, *Boccaccio* (London, 1900); E. Hutton, *Giovanni Boccaccio* (London, 1910); T. C. Chubb, *The Life of Giovanni Boccaccio* (London, 1930); Catherine Carswell, *The Tranquil Heart* (London, 1937). On the other hand, A. C. Lee in 1909 undertook to trace the sources of

dealt primarily with Boccaccio's influence on English literature. A few have examined particular aspects of the Latin works or individual tales or the framework of the *Decameron.*

Following World War II, a flurry of activity on both sides of the Atlantic led to the publication of new editions of the *Decameron* based on the careful examination and collation of the manuscript tradition. In 1951, V. Branca published an annotated edition based on a limited tradition that indicated a Paris manuscript as possibly archetypal. Three years later, as we have already seen, Charles Singleton concluded fifteen years of labor diligently collating almost sixty manuscripts that indicated a Berlin manuscript as most likely the copy of an original. Since this first critical edition of 1954, further investigation has adduced evidence that the Berlin Hamilton manuscript on which Singleton based his edition may well be an autograph.[36]

The fortune of the *Decameron* throughout Europe and in Italy is much too complex to relate here. Suffice it to state that few were the countries in which the short story flourished whose writers did not owe some debt of gratitude to Boccaccio. Indeed, few were the great playwrights who were not similarly indebted. Names such as Lope de Rueda, Shakespeare, Molière, La Fontaine, Dryden, and Cervantes come to mind most readily.

In Italy, aside from the artistic influences of the *Decameron* that abound everywhere and in writers of all periods down to the present time, critical polemics on its merits and value continued the tradition started by Bembo. However, while linguistic disputes over the contribution of the *Decameron* to the national language received constant attention through the centuries,[37] in the eighteenth century a number of attempts were made on the one hand to exonerate Boccaccio from the charges of immorality under which his reputation labored and on the other to establish

---

each tale of the *Decameron* in his curious work, *The Decameron: Its Sources and Analogues,* which was republished by Haskel House (New York) in 1966.

36 Vittore Branca and Pier Giorgio Ricci, *Un autografo del Decamerone* (Padova: CEDAM, 1962).

37 In the 17th century the trend started by Galileo, Tassoni, Boccalini, and Aretino, who had reacted against the despotic hold of the *Decameron* on Italian prose style, is brought to a climax by Beni, who found Boccaccio bombastic, forced, ungrammatical, and excessively plebeian.

the historical veracity of the individual tales. This renewal of critical and historical research on the *Decameron* throughout the eighteenth century led to a sharp increase in the influence of the tales on the writers of the time.

In the nineteenth century, on the other hand, Boccaccio scholarship began to take the direction that continues to characterize it, an involvement with "the whole Boccaccio" as he appears to emerge from all his works, be they early or late, Latin or Italian. The *Decameron* was thus viewed, not so much as an isolated masterpiece, but as the culmination of an artistic experience and the junction of complex popular and cultural currents. The various directions taken by the new scholarship may be classified under four general headings. First there was the purely historical research into the life and works of Boccaccio. This was undertaken by such scholars, both inside and outside of Italy, as Baldelli, Landau, Koerting, Crescini, and Hauvette. Other scholars such as Moutier, Fanfani, Wiese, Massera, and Barbi concentrated their efforts on philological problems dealing with textual criticism. A third group, including names such as Manni, Bartoli, Landau, Gröber, and Di Francia, fascinated by current literary theories that sought sources and influences in the mysterious flow of literary and popular themes from the fabulous Orient to the West, tried to establish the *Decameron* as the last link of a long chain of such themes.

Beside these three tendencies of Boccaccio criticism there existed also the more purely literary type stretching from Foscolo and the Romantics to De Sanctis and Carducci, and finally to Croce and his followers. The period from Foscolo to Carducci is characterized primarily by the conviction that the *Decameron* marks the birth of a new age that negates and ridicules medieval values and is the opposite of Dante's *Comedy* in spurning the transcendental and placing upon the altar instead man with all his senses. The subsequent period, dominated by Croce, sought rather the poetic unity of Boccaccio's work by focusing on the sentimental or impressionistic analysis of the individual stories and by attempting to apply the Crocean distinction between poetry and nonpoetry. The most recent tendencies have been toward very precise philological and linguistic-stylistic investigation of texts and toward the study in depth of those aspects of medieval culture and poetics that seem clearly to characterize

Boccaccio's art. This has in turn led to a more rigorous reconstruction of his life and thought.[38]

To complete this necessarily sketchy outline of the evolution of Boccaccio criticism, it might be best, even at the risk of oversimplification, to attempt a definition of the extremes within which such criticism has developed, and then to see in which direction the very latest research seems to tend. Since the principal concern of the essays contained in this volume is to arrive at an evaluation of the three great Italian writers by means of interpretive analyses in English of the recognized masterpiece of each, we shall limit ourselves to two relatively recent studies in English that seem briefly and succinctly to summarize the extremes of interpretation toward which Boccaccio criticism has tended through the centuries; and we shall then try to indicate the relative position taken by Branca in his monumental study of 1956 entitled *Boccaccio medievale*.

In 1943 Angelo Lipari, in a collection dedicated to Albert Feuillerat, published an essay entitled "The Structure and Real Significance of the Decameron" (New Haven, pages 43–83). His main thesis was that in view of Boccaccio's theory of poetic art as expounded particularly in the concluding books of his *Genealogia deorum gentilium libri*, the *Decameron* was meant to be allegorical in character in accordance with the author's definition of allegory. It follows, therefore, that in dedicating his stories to "ladies" Boccaccio was speaking allegorically.

According to Lipari the term *donna* was highly symbolic in early Italian literature. "Whenever it designated the special object of the poet's usually unrequited love, it implied the personification of a humanistic poetic ideal and an artistic perfection rarely achieved, in his own opinion, by the poet. The virtues, or qualities and ornaments, of this 'lady' described the character and excellence of the poet's conception of the ideal of human

[38] Scholars most closely associated with these latest tendencies include Billanovich, Russo, Sapegno, Chiari, Bosco, Momigliano, Getto, Grabher, and most particularly Vittore Branca. For fuller discussions of Boccaccio's fortune inside and outside of Italy see V. Branca, "Giovanni Boccaccio," in *Letteratura Italiana*, vol. 1 of *I Maggiori*, in the series *Orientamenti Culturali*, edited by C. Marzorati (Milano, 1956), pp. 185–244. See also A. Chiari, "La fortuna del Boccaccio," in *Problemi e orientamenti critici di lingua e letteratura italiana* (Milano: 1949), 3: 275–348.

perfection and at the same time the qualities and effectiveness of his humanistic poetic art. Finally, by metonymy, the term stood for the poet himself, or for his principles and achievements in life." This is why Boccaccio asserts that they were *like muses* to him, representing as they did the source of his poetic inspiration and the object of his humanistic art. Such a view, Lipari asserts, leads to a "wonderful real significance of the *Decameron.*"

Having reviewed Bocaccio's position as expressed in the *Geneologia,* Lipari concluded that in addressing "ladies" Bocaccio was addressing "humanist poets like himself, or at least . . . the cultured class." As for the ladies being in love, this refers to the true nobility of the poet and his propensity for Supreme Beauty. This was indeed intended in Dante's immortal line, "Amore e 'l cor gentil sono una cosa" ("Love and the noble heart are but one"). The tales, therefore, do conceal a meaning below the surface that demands what Boccaccio calls "strong intellectual effort and various interpretation" in order to extract it. Furthermore, Boccaccio's attack on licentious poets and his contention that "in various licentious or grotesque incidents and names are implied many wise and pure thoughts" would appear to afford further evidence that the tales did contain hidden meanings. This position is further supported by the conclusion that "no Don Juan was ever a true poet, nor was great art ever produced by a base mind."

Ultimately, according to Lipari, Boccaccio's purpose in the *Decameron* was to set forth his experience of the "life of love" and his concept of the poetic art. First, however, he finds it necessary to repeat still once again Boccaccio's use of the word *donne* and his defense of the tales as found in the Proem, the Introduction to the Fourth Day, and in the Conclusion of the *Decameron.* He then proceeds to show that the writer's love for these *donne* was the ardent love of an artist for his art, and concludes that they personified the "poetic-artistic ideal which the poet-humanist pursued and sought to incarnate in his works of art." This might be conceived as extending all the way from using the term *donne* to address the poets of his day, to defining particular aspects of his art. If, therefore, they personified the various aspects of his own poetics, Boccaccio "was actually engaged in the composition of a treatise on modern poetics." Thus a masculine "donna" like Panfilo is the personification of the poet's enthusiasm for his noble art; while a feminine "donna" like Pampinea personifies the classical derivation of Boccaccio's art; and so forth with each of the other "donne" of the frame story.

Lipari's intentions should by now be clear. Starting with the assumption that Boccaccio's poetics simply did not admit of a merely literal reading of the *Decameron*, he undertakes an interpretation that ascribes to the collection of tales a hidden meaning which was not the traditional "allegorical" one having spiritual or religious implications, but a more "modern" one intended to conceal an entire treatise on poetics under the cloak of 100 short stories carefully placed within a specially devised frame.

Lipari's "allegorical" interpretation was, surprisingly, attacked by the formalistic interpretation of Charles Singleton, who disagreed with Lipari's approach in a study appearing in 1944.[39] For Singleton, the framework of the *Decameron* was intended to give unity to the whole and to establish a mood that he characterizes as "escape from menace" and that is part of the artistic strategy of the author. If there is a *sovrasenso* in the framework, it was Boccaccio's attempt to justify his new art of escape in which he firmly believed. Fully aware that his was "an art completely bare and defenseless, for it could not claim to teach," Boccaccio tried to indicate in the framework of the *Decameron* the manner in which he intended his work to be read. Unlike the typical medieval work of art whose sole reason for being was to teach a moral, philosophical, or religious lesson, the *Decameron* was intended simply as enjoyment and delight for their own sake. It resembled the moment in Dante's *Purgatory* when all the souls of the second canto are completely absorbed in the beauty of Casella's song after emerging from the "menace" of Hell. Boccaccio knew that, just as in that scene of Purgatory, a voice of Cato could come and scatter his art and condemn it. So he constructed a framework that is an effort to justify and protect a new art, "an art which simply in order to be, to exist, required a moment free of all other cares, the willingness to stop *going anywhere* (either toward God or toward philosophical truth)." In the *Decameron*'s Introduction Boc-

[39] *Italica*, 21: 117–24.

caccio creates the perfect moment for his art and provides the setting it needed as cover and protection. It occurs when the stories are just about to begin, and the author writes: "As you see, the sun is high and the heat is great, and all we can hear is the cricket on the olive tree. It would, therefore, surely be foolhardy to try to go anywhere right now."

Later in life the voice of Cato did catch up with Boccaccio both in the form of a threatening friar and of the scholarly humanist. Both condemned the kind of art contained in the *Decameron*. But though Boccaccio was momentarily terror-stricken, he could not destroy "the perfect and calm moment of art which had been built into his *Decameron*." Lipari is, therefore, wrong in trying to carry back into the *Decameron* views expressed by Boccaccio in later life and in insisting that such views must obtain retroactively. For Singleton, therefore, Boccaccio is to be viewed as of an age other than Dante's. His art was not intended to instruct or lead the way to God. It was indeed very close to pure art and in that sense very modern. In short, the same Singleton who insists on an allegorical reading of the *Divine Comedy* minimizes and almost denies such a reading of the *Decameron*.

Perhaps the most recent general study of the *Decameron* in English is that of Aldo Scaglione, *Nature and Love in the Late Middle Ages* (Berkeley, 1963). Unfortunately the study is a victim of that most dangerous of scholarly pitfalls, an overriding thesis that leads to sketchy and tendentious conclusions whose irrelevance and superficiality are often shocking. Intended both as "an essay on the cultural context of the *Decameron*," and a case study "of Boccaccio's *Decameron* . . . treated in the context of literary works which I consider relevant to the understanding of the place and 'function' of this most significant masterpiece within the framework of the concept of 'naturalistic love' . . . ," the relatively short book disintegrates under the weight of such an ambitious undertaking. The main thrust of the study is to show that Boccaccio's masterpiece is truly a "Naturalist Manifesto," a battle cry against the restraint and supernaturalism of the Middle Ages. Indeed, ". . . the novelty of Boccaccio's position lay in his bold and unequivocal proclamation of the 'law of nature' as a new creed for everybody. . . ." (P. 126.) This curious use of the *Decameron* as a historical document leaves the reader confused as to what the author is implying about its artistic merits. But other critics have written on these same shortcomings.[40] The study does contain on pages 48–56 a valuable summary in English of Italian criticism on the *Decameron.*

Vittore Branca, who is generally recognized as the most recent authority on Boccaccio, in 1956 published the results of many years of research on Boccaccio and his works that clearly indicated that perhaps the true interpretation of the *Decameron* lies somewhere between the positions of Lipari and Singleton.[41] He summarized his findings in a shorter study appearing that same year.[42]

Having shown that the composition of the *Decameron* extended over a considerable number of Boccaccio's early years and that the plague of 1348 afforded the author a kind of catalyst with which to give the stories a distinct form, Branca proceeds to an analysis of how the collection was quickly distributed throughout the Italian peninsula. In his examination of over eighty manuscripts of the work, Branca establishes the interesting and significant fact that, though the great majority of those manuscripts whose ownership could be identified belonged to wealthy merchant families, none belonged to illustrious libraries or were produced by famous scribes. He also offers epistolary evidence to show that the work evoked most enthusiasm among the merchant classes. This "bourgeois enthusiasm" similarly found no counterpart among literary or learned circles. Even Petrarch's famous reaction to the work reflects a certain reservation. On the other hand, the enthusiasm of the middle classes does not diminish in the face of the obvious diffidence on the part of the world of letters. Instead it spills over into the lower classes, and we find much evidence of the influence of many stories on such daily and personal events as the songs of minstrels and the motifs on bridal chests.

The *Decameron* thus did not descend from the rich classical tradition that was already becoming so venerable in Tuscan prehumanism, but from the bawdy and brash narrative that had arisen quite spontaneously among the middle and lower classes

40 See R. H. Green's review in *MLN*, 79 (1964): 58–70; also Singleton's in the same issue, pp. 71–76.

41 *Boccaccio medievale*, Firenze.

42 *Letteratura Italiana*, pp. 120–55.

of the preceding centuries for whom storytelling, both oral and written, had become a popular daily pastime without literary pretentions. Consequently the manuscript tradition does not reveal signs of respect and admiration as in the case of literary masterpieces, but instead freeplaying insertions, deletions, and supressions according to the taste or whim of the owner. This general view of the *Decameron* as a work lying outside the parameters of literature is reflected in its being dedicated to lovely ladies.

Among the many traits that characterize the art of the *Decameron* as essentially medieval, the most obvious are the nearly total absence of the classical world; the casual mixture of great varieties of sources; the tone and diction reminiscent of the *fabliaux*, the *lamenti*, the *romans*, and the *chansons;* and, finally, the masterful use of the medieval stylistic techniques of the *cursus* and of rhymed prose. All these traits contribute to the general gothic architecture of the work as a whole.

The coherence that Boccaccio sought in organizing his stories was rhetorical and moral rather than strictly literary. A similar precision of design and comprehensiveness of meaning had already appeared in his *Filocolo* and *Ameto*, which anticipated the *Decameron.* In this last work we have, in the movement from the first to the last day, an ideal itinerary, proceeding from the sharp censure of the vices of the great (Day I) to the elaborately constructed eulogy of magnanimity and courtesy in the tenth day. In between are carefully placed huge frescoes depicting the "comedy of man," who reveals his humanity in full by staking his claim to the realm of virtue on his contest with those mysterious forces that seem to rule the world: Fortune, Love, and Wit. We thus behold the orderly sequence of scenes depicting man as a toy of Fortune (Day II) or victorious over Fortune through his industry (Day III); or undergoing trials of joy or of grief at the hands of that merciless despot, Love (Days IV and V). Then there are the merry episodes of men trying to outdo one another either through wit or through practical jokes or trickery, with major emphasis on affairs of the heart (Days VII and VIII). Day IX represents a kind of pause in which all the motifs are interlaced at random since each story-teller is free to choose his own theme. But in Day X we have what Branca calls a "splendid crescendo" that seems to fix on an almost metaphysical plane the basic motifs and driving forces that had characterized the human comedy up to this point. This last day affords a new view of Fortune (stories 1–3), Love (4–7), and Wit (8–9) as measures of man's nobility by subordinating these mysterious forces to that virtue that sublimates purely natural feeling and traits. In the very last story, indeed, the three forces receive their loftiest expression in the tale of Griselda, whom Fortune transformed into a lady of the court, Love made heroic while at the same time changing Gualtieri, and Wit or Ingenuity subjects to the difficult trials of fidelity conceived by her future husband.

The itinerary thus proceeds "a principio horribilis et fetidus, in fine prosperus desiderabilis et gratus," while the design "inchoat asperitatem alicuius rei sed eius materia prospere terminatur." This was, of course, the architectural formula prescribed for "Comedy" by the highest medieval authorities and applied by Boccaccio in other works.

The frame-story, for Branca, serves to underline the more salient features of this architecture. It, too, echoes the themes of the various days as we witness the narrators themselves moving from the "horrible beginning" of the plague to their use of wit and ingenuity in order to escape Fortune's frightening blow, and finally to their competition in narrating examples of outstanding virtue in the last day. The frame, furthermore, also partakes of the symmetry required by the rhetorical ideals of the time. In its very center (end of Day V) occurs the charming episode of the Vale of Lovely Ladies. The series of days presided over by the ladies is symmetrically interrupted by the turns of the young men. The first day is politely assigned to the eldest of the ladies, Pampinea, while the last day is reserved for the most mature of the men, Panfilo. The ballads that crown each day follow the popular paradigm 3:3:3, with the first group having an allegorical development, the second group containing lofty love plaints, and the third group echoing a diffused song of exultation and rejoicing.

The nature of the landscape and of the participants in the frame similarly reflects the refined, elegant, and aristocratic circles so dear to the readers of the time and leads to the creation of a human world that is not psychologically real but consists rather of those ideal and aristocratic moments of life furthest removed from the humdrum preoccupations of daily existence.

It is even possible to discern in the frame-story a close analysis of the leading themes and ideas that compose the medieval architecture of the *Decameron*. Both Fortune and Love undergo theoretical expositions in the frame-story that are clearly scholastic and medieval. It is Pampinea, the "wise one," who, in the prologue to the third story of the second day and to the second story of the sixth day, develops briefly and elegantly the Thomistic and Dantean concept of Fortune as the handmaiden of Divine Providence and Justice. In the same way, practically every portion of the frame gives evidence of the author's medieval alarm and dismay at the frightening power of Love. This is true not only in the Proem, the Introduction to Day IV, and the Conclusion, but even in the bodies of the stories themselves and in prologues such as that of the seventh story of Day IV where Emilia presents a theoretical distinction between the love of noble and common people much as had Andreas Capellanus; or the introduction of the sixth story of Day III and the conclusion of the sixth story of Day X in which Fiammetta speaks of the gradations of love in the fashion of the same Capellanus. In the same manner echoes of Richard of St. Victor, of Guittone d'Arezzo, of St. Thomas, and of Dante are discernible in such moments as the crescendo of themes of the last day, the subtle connections between the first three ballads, and the relationships between love and reason expounded in Days V and VII.[43]

Boccaccio's immersion in the thought and "exemplars" of the time led to his tendency to present his stories as actual historical occurrences. This also explains the chronological limits of the actions narrated, which, except for three instances, all took place just before Boccaccio's time. As a result, what we really have in the *Decameron* is the epic of the twilight of the Middle Ages in Italy when there occurred an almost miraculous evolution of the age of knights of the sword into an age of the knights of ingenuity or intelligence and of human industry. It was the spirit and drama of this evolution that Boccaccio succeeded in capturing and projecting most artistically in his masterpiece. This is why the *Decameron* must be viewed as complementary to the *Divine Comedy* rather than antithetical. The true medieval world consisted in a combination of the two visions of life, one transcendental and spiritual, the other worldly and pragmatic.

[43] For a formal aesthetic analysis of the frame-story and its relation to the whole, see Giovanni Getto, *Vita di forme e forme di vita nel Decameron* (Torino, 1958), pp. 1–33.

Therefore, Branca's position would seem to imply that the views of both Lipari and Singleton represent extremes requiring revision and refocusing.

Conclusion

If, as Branca would have it, the *Decameron* is but an extension of the world of the *Comedy*, there is little question that the axis of the two worlds must be represented vertically rather than horizontally. The world of the *Comedy* continues Boccaccio's world upward, and indeed at a certain point seems to abandon it entirely. And yet, as Boccaccio tells us in his own Conclusion, his world also offers important lessons for those people who are deeply involved in life and are not simply theorists or detached observers. In fact, he does not hesitate to compare his stories to the sermons of preachers, who must likewise embellish their homilies to bring home a lesson. To imagine Boccaccio's literary world completely apart from Dante's would also mean doing violence to historical fact since Boccaccio's devotion to Dante and his *Comedy* is well documented.[44]

If, then, there is no clash between the world of Dante and of Boccaccio, what can be said about the world of Petrarch? Had Petrarch written only his *Canzoniere* in Italian, one could speak of the waning of courtly love in a world of pure form and technique. But there is the strange world of the *Triumphs* to cope with. Then there are the many Latin works, and particularly the *Secretum* and the *Africa*, that add still other dimensions. In fact there is the entire classical world and Petrarch's almost obsessive desire to resuscitate it as though nothing had inter-

44 Indeed, there is some reason for wondering whether in a work like the *Decameron*, possessing such a clearly medieval structure, it is not permissible to attempt an allegorical reading (a technique certainly subscribed to by Boccaccio) that simply calls for a kind of double vision capable of recognizing and righting perversion. This would seem to be the key offered by the very first story, in which Ciappelletto appears to make a fool of God but instead obviously wallows in the depths of hell. I hope some day to develop this idea fully. Meanwhile, the reader is referred to the concluding words of the narrator of the first tale, Panfilo, who, having deduced that it would be more logical to assume Ciappelletto in Hell, renders thanks to God's mercy "la quale, non al nostro errore ma alla purità della fe riguardando," was able to convert the sinful acts of an evil intermediary into good works. One cannot help recalling that the *Decameron* itself is also a *mezzano*, not unlike Ciappelletto, since its subtitle is *Prencipe Galeotto*.

vened since its downfall. There is also his strange attitude toward Dante that Boccaccio tried so hard to change. It is perhaps here that one must seek for clues that might give the simplest and most direct answer.

My analysis of Petrarch's attitude toward Dante, which appeared in 1955,[45] contains at least a partial answer to what is distinctive about Petrarch's world. It is essentially a matter of literary perspective that demands of poetry an almost perfect balance between Classical (read: secular and learned) and Christian elements. Unlike David, whose poetry "makes frequent reference to the citizens and walls of the Little Jerusalem and never wanders from there (and who) is always ready with tears and breathes hoarsely in his breast," his preferred poets "sing of Rome, Troy, the battle of kings; the power of grief and love and wrath; the spirit that rules the waves and the winds and the stars." The true poets of the future will be

> Lofty intellects and noble spirits
> who will combine within their minds
> the ancient love of the Muses and Christian doctrine.
> [*Africa,* IX, 459–61]

We have already seen the implications of Boccaccio's substituting "ladies in love" for the Muses. It would appear, therefore, that were we to plot Petrarch's world on the same chart as Dante's and Boccaccio's we would find it intersecting horizontally the point at which the other two worlds met on a vertical axis. There is very little of the metaphysical at the end of either the *Canzoniere* or the *Triumphs.* The former ends with a muffled cry to a very human Virgin Mary, petitioning that the poet's days end in peace; while the latter ends with a vision of the earthly Laura, cloaked in a sublime beauty, leading a procession of great men of the past toward a "new world" of timelessness and glory that is but a projection of humanity's most noble aspirations as expressed especially by the great classics. Both these endings are as different from the ending of the *Comedy*, where the protagonist achieves a kind of mystical union with the "Love that moves the sun and the other stars," as they are from the opening of the *Decameron*, whose very first words are "Umana cosa è l'avere compassione degli afflitti . . ." ("A human thing it is to have compassion for the afflicted . . .").

[45] "Petrarch's Attitude Toward Dante."

For Petrarch, the poetic world of neither of his two compatriots was sufficiently aristocratic. Both seemed excessively involved with ordinary people and with ordinary concerns. What he sought was a veritable republic of letters where the great writers, thinkers, and heroes of all time could enjoy to the fullest whatever reward awaited them in the afterlife for their prominent roles in the unfurling of Creation.

Perhaps the simplest way to distinguish between the worlds of our three writers is in terms of the angle of vision through which each seems to view the universe or Creation as a whole. In his *Comedy* Dante attempts to view a clearly Christian Creation through the eyes of the Christian God. In his Italian poetry Petrarch depicts an apparently Christian Creation as seen through the eyes of a highly learned man. In his *Decameron* Boccaccio projects a distinctly man-made creation as seen by a worldly man of wide experience. Notwithstanding the dangers inherent in such oversimplified formulas, they do help to clarify the extent to which the three masterpieces of Dante, Petrarch, and Boccaccio together reflect dimensions of literary perspective that can be truthfully called total vision, beyond which literature has yet to venture.

SELECTIVE BIBLIOGRAPHY

I. Bibliographical Studies

Recent Italian bibliographical surveys of critical studies on the three authors.

Mazzamuto, Pietro. *Rassegna bibliografico-critica della letteratura italiana.* 3d ed., rev. Florence: Le Monnier, 1956. This is an outline of the history of criticism, and includes sections on Dante (pp. 15–82); Petrarca (pp. 83–119); and Boccaccio (pp. 120–55), with special reference to the *Decameron*).

Orientamenti culturali: Letteratura italiana. Milan: Carlo Marzorati, 1956. Vol. I *(I maggiori):* "Dante," by Siro A. Chimez, pp. 1–109; "Petrarca," by Umberto Bosco, pp. 111–83; "Boccaccio," by Vittore Branca, pp. 185–244.

II. Works on Individual Authors

Works on the individual authors. As the material on Dante is so vast it has been divided into two parts: (a) surveys of criticism in Italian and English; (b) monographs in English on Dante and the *Divine Comedy*, recently published or reprinted. For Petrarch and Boccaccio there is no such division, and the bibliography is not restricted to works in print.

For articles and other studies, the reader is referred to the annual bibliographies in *PMLA* and *Italian Studies*, and to the quarterly bibliographies in *Italica*. Three specialized journals should also be consulted: the *Annual Report of the Dante Society of America* (called as of 1966, *Dante Studies*); *Studi Danteschi; Studi Petrarcheschi;* and *Studi sul Boccaccio.*

A. Dante

(i) *Surveys of Criticism*

Bosco, Umberto, ed. *Dante nella critica d'oggi: risultati e prospettive.* Florence: Le Monnier, 1965.

Cicciò, Domenico. "Bibliografia Dantesca." *Narrativa* 10 (1965): 62–77, 110–26, 168–93. Continued in *Biologia Culturale* 1 (1966): 14–42, 101–18, 152–65. [Dante studies in Italy in 1965.]

Cunningham, Gilbert F. *The Divine Comedy in English: A Critical Bibliography.* Vol. I, 1782–1900, II, 1901–1966. Edinburgh and London: Oliver and Boyd, 1965, 1967.

Dédéyan, Charles. "Dante en Angleterre." *Revue des Études Italiennes* 8 (1961): 185–268; 10 (1964): 56–80, 203–19; 12 (1965): 7–18, 136–64.

De Sua, William J. *Dante into English: A Study of the Translation of "The Divine Comedy" in Britain and America.* Chapel Hill: University of North Carolina Press, 1964.

Donno, Daniel J. "Recent Scholarship on Dante." *Renaissance Quarterly* 20 (Summer, 1967): 273–78.

Foster, Kenelm. "Dante Studies in England, 1921–1964." *Italian Studies* 20 (1965): 1–16.

La Piana, Angelina. *Dante's American Pilgrimage.* New Haven: Yale University Press, 1948.

Marraro, Howard R. "Bibliografia dantesca americana dal Settecento al 1921." *Atti del R. Istituto Veneto di Scienze, Lettere ed Arti, Venezia, Classe di scienze morali e lettere* 122 (1964–65): 189–277.

Toynbee, Paget, ed. *Britain's Tribute to Dante in Literature and Art: A Chronological Record of 540 Years (c. 1380–1920).* London: Milford, 1921.

Toynbee, Paget. *Dante in English Literature from Chaucer to Cary.* London: Methuen, 1909.

Toynbee, Paget, comp., and Singleton, C. S., ed. and rev. *Dictionary of Proper Names and Notable Matters in the Works of Dante.* Oxford and New York: Oxford University Press, 1965.

Werner, P. Friederich. *Dante's Fame Abroad, 1350–1850.* Chapel Hill: University of North Carolina Press, 1966.

Wilson, F. P. "A Supplement to Toynbee's *Dante in English Literature.*" *Italian Studies* 3 (1964): 50–64.

(ii) *Monographs in English*

Auerbach, Erich. *Dante, Poet of the Secular World.* Chicago: University of Chicago Press, 1961.

Bergin, Thomas G. *Dante.* New York: Orion Press, 1965.

———. *Perspectives on the "Divine Comedy."* New Brunswick, N.J.: Rutgers University Press, 1967.

Bernardo, Aldo S., and Pellegrini, Anthony I. *Key-Indexed Study Guide to Dante's "Divine Comedy".* Philadelphia: Educational Research Associates (in association with Bantam Books), 1967.

Croce, Benedetto. *The Poetry of Dante.* New York: Holt, 1921.

Eliot, T. S. *Dante.* London: Faber & Faber, 1929.

Fletcher, Jefferson Butler. *Dante.* With an introduction by Mark Musa. Notre Dame, Ind.: University of Notre Dame Press, 1965.

Gilson, Étienne. *Dante and Philosophy.* New York: Harper & Row, 1963.

Grandgent, Charles. *Dante Alighieri.* New York: Ungar, 1966.

SAYERS, DOROTHY L. *Introductory Papers on Dante*. London: Methuen, 1954.

———. *Further Papers on Dante*. London: Methuen, 1957.

SINGLETON, CHARLES S. *Dante Studies*. Vol. 1, *Commedia: Elements of Structure*. Vol. 2, *Journey to Beatrice*. Cambridge: Harvard University Press, 1954, 1958.

TOYNBEE, PAGET. *Dante Alighieri: His Life and Works*. Edited and with an introduction and bibliography by CHARLES S. SINGLETON. New York: Harper Torchbooks, 1965.

VOSSLER, KARL. *Mediaeval Culture: An Introduction to Dante and His Times*. New York: Ungar, 1966.

WILLIAMS, CHARLES. *The Figure of Beatrice*. London: Faber, 1943.

B. PETRARCH

BERNARDO, ALDO S. *Petrarch, Scipio and the "Africa": The Birth of Humanism's Dream*. Baltimore: Johns Hopkins Press, 1962.

BISHOP, MORRIS. *Petrarch and His World*. Bloomington: Indiana University Press, 1963.

BORGHESI, PIETRO. *Petrarch and His Influence on English Literature*. Bologna: Zanichelli, 1906.

HOLLOWAY-CALTHROP, HENRY. *Petrarch, His Life and Times*. London: Methuen, [1907].

JERROLD, MAUD F. *Francesco Petrarca, Poet and Humanist*. London: Dent, 1909.

TATHAM, E. H. R. *Francesco Petrarca: The First Modern Man of Letters*. London: Sheldon Press, 1925.

WATSON, G. *The English Petrarchans: A Critical Bibliography of the "Canzoniere."* London: Warburg Institute, 1967.

WEINBERG, BERNARD. "Recent Studies on Petrarch." *Renaissance News* 17 (1964): 61–65.

WHITFIELD, JOHN H. *Petrarch and the Renascence*. New York: Russell, 1966.

WILKINS, E. H. "An Introductory Petrarch Bibliography." *Philological Quarterly* 27 (1948): 27–36.

———. *Life of Petrarch*. Chicago: University of Chicago Press, 1961.

———. *The Making of the "Canzoniere" and Other Petrarch Studies*. Rome: Edizioni di Storia e Letteratura, 1951.

———. *Petrarch's Eight Years in Milan*. Combridge, Mass.: Mediaeval Academy of America, 1958.

———. *Petrarch's Later Years*. Cambridge, Mass.: Mediaeval Academy of America, 1959.

C. BOCCACCIO

BRANCA, VITTORE. *Linee di una storia della critica sul* Decameron. Milan: S.A.E. Dante Alighieri, 1939.

CARSWELL, CATHERINE. *The Tranquil Heart: A Portrait of Giovanni Boccaccio.* London: Lawrence & Wishart, [1937].

CHUBB, THOMAS CALDECOTT. *The Life of Giovanni Boccaccio.* London: Cassell, [1930].

LEE, A. C. *The* Decameron, *Its Source and Analogues.* New York: Haskell, 1967.

MCMANUS, FRANCIS. *Boccaccio.* London: Sheed & Ward, 1947.

QUAGLIO, ANTONIO ENZO. "Rassegna boccacciana." *GSLI* 142 (1965): 581–613.

SCAGLIONE, ALDO D. *Nature and Love in the Late Middle Ages.* Berkeley and Los Angeles: University of California Press, 1963.

WRIGHT, HERBERT G. *Boccaccio in England from Chaucer to Tennyson.* London: Athlone, 1957.

INDEX